NOVANTIQUA
Rhetorics as a Contemporary Theory

Advances in Semiotics

General Editor, Thomas A. Sebeok

NOVANTIQUA

Rhetorics as a Contemporary Theory

PAOLO VALESIO

INDIANA UNIVERSITY PRESS

Bloomington

Library of Congress Cataloging in Publication Data
Valesio, Paolo, 1939–
Novantiqua.

(Advances in semiotics)
Bibliography: p.
Includes index.
1. Rhetoric—Philosophy. 2. Discourse analysis.
I. Title. II. Series.
P301.V34   808'.00141   79–9632
ISBN 0–253–11055–6   1   2   3   4   5   84   83   82   81   80

P
301
V 34

per Assunta

على مجاز اللفظ ومجرى الكتابة

'By way of figure of speech and the flow of writing'

*(from an epistle addressed to Abū al-ʿAlāʾ al-Maʿarrī,
a renowned 11th-century Arab scholar and writer)*

CONTENTS

Preface

Rereading one's own book for the last time before consigning it to print is always, of course, a difficult process: it is then that the author sees with the most painful clarity the gap between the book he wanted to write and what he actually produced.

The most useful service, then, that a preface can perform is perhaps that of indicating what—beyond his regrets and second thoughts on the one hand, and the ideas about his next and different book on the other—the author still would *not* change in the work at hand.

What I feel least dissatisfied with here is the general dimension, the sketch of a theory of rhetoric: not a history of rhetoric or a taxonomy of its figures—but a theory. Efforts of this sort, after Aristotle, are very few. While this fact alone does not, of course, put the present attempt beyond criticism, it can at least justify its presence.

All this is not to deny the essential role of concrete empirical analyses: indeed some of the investigations in this book have opened the way to my present research. But at this point in the development of rhetorical studies, it is essential to insist on the crucial role of philosophical reflection, of general views and syntheses.

A book written between two continents and two cultures acquires along the way such a large quantity of debts that it is impossible to acknowledge them all. The following, then, is a summary list.

In the course of my work I have been assisted by a John Simon Guggenheim fellowship (1975); the hospitality of the Center for the Humanities and its director, Hayden White, at Wesleyan University; and an A. Whitney Griswold Award from Yale University, which helped me in preparing the final draft of the text.

I am grateful to Umberto Eco for his encouragement and his advice on how to organize the book, and to Allen Mandelbaum and Thomas A. Sebeok for introducing me to Indiana University Press. I am also grateful to many colleagues and students (at New York University, Wesleyan University, Yale University) for their patience, their responses, their questioning.

Carolyn Springer and Leslie Morgan helped me in revising the bibliography; and especially helpful—going over the whole text with intelligence while still preserving their sense of humor—were Ann Mullaney and Barbara Spackman. Mary Christoforo skillfully typed the manuscript. The Arabic calligraphy was provided by Sana'a Azmi. Needless to say, any remaining errors or infelicities are my responsibility.

I dedicate this book to my wife, Assunta, for a host of reasons which cry out with the strongest voice—that of silence.

Paolo Valesio
New Haven, Connecticut

NOVANTIQUA
Rhetorics as a Contemporary Theory

Chapter I

WHAT AND WHY
The Ontology

I I THE PROBLEM

When does a reflection become a philosophy? Not when it takes up the technical tools that we usually label as philosophy today. For, before picking up these tools (and in order that the handling of them be not devoid of sense) something else must take place: the theme on which reflection has concentrated must appear so often and with such insistence as to become obsessive—a word that I make bold to use here in a positive sense. (My subject calls, like any other significant theme, for responsibility: it does not, because of this, bind the writer to any genteel obligation of verbal restraint.) So obsessive, indeed, must the theme become as to present itself, not in the form of a problem to be solved, but as the solution to the problem evoked by it.

It is only when we have gone beyond this threshold that theoretical constructs (whether stricto sensu philosophical or not) can be used fruitfully; on the other hand, if this beneficent obsession is absent, the ensuing discourse might very well have the form of philosophy; it will not have the force of philosophical thought. The author of these pages thought for a time that rhetoric was a problem—that is, a prescientific object to which one needed to apply a scientific metalanguage, preferably that of linguistics, since this is clearly the science closest to rhetoric. There was nothing particularly new either in this attitude or in the ambiguity that it implies. It is the long-recognized

1

ambiguity existing in the case of other human sciences and their names: "grammar," for instance, or "history."

In these cases, the same term is used in order to designate both a complex of objective structures (figures of speech, other linguistic units at their various levels, events in the "real" world—especially past events), and the subjective, often conflicting, accounts of these clusters of phenomena (description and interpretation of figures and other linguistic structures, mention and explanation of events).

Once this ambiguity is recognized, what matters is to clarify, in each concrete case, which of the two dimensions evoked by the term is relevant; as for the purely terminological discussion, it should not be carried too far. This, however, does not mean that the terminological problem is a frivolous one (it never is, at least in the human sciences— for it is always the symbol of a conflict in ideologies and mental styles).

The problem is made intricate by the differences among natural languages. English, for instance, here gives me an edge over Italian; for in the former language I can take advantage of certain suffixes widely used in the field of technical terminology in order to distinguish *rhetoric* (the complex of objective phenomena to be described) from *rhetorics* (the systematic description and analysis of these phenomena), and correspondingly to differentiate between *rhetor* and *rhetorician*. (The only recent text I know that makes, however sketchily, a distinction analogous to that established through the former pair is Steinmann 1966; the theory proposed by me corresponds to what that author calls "basic rhetorical research," but the present exposition also contains elements of what is there called "metatheoretical research").

The rhetor is the speaker/writer insofar as he is engaged in constructing discourses (which, as we will see, is the same as doing rhetoric), and the listener/reader insofar as he decodes, informally and for his immediate usage, these structures. The rhetorician's role, on the other hand, is that of those speakers/writers and listeners/readers (belonging to a restricted group) who are systematically engaged in the elaboration and decodification of discourses. In this sense, it is not only linguists, professors of rhetoric, stylisticians, who can be called rhetoricians—all writers as such are applied rhetoricians.

At any rate, I will try in what follows, if not always to use only these two terms (this monotony would simply be yet another instance of that useless and prim imitation of scientific jargon that plagues linguistics and criticism today), at least never to employ them in such a way as to confuse the distinction that I have just presented.[1] But, one could object, why bother so much about terminological niceties? After all, if the family of words clustered around the root of *rhetoric* is too restricted, one can always find synonyms with different roots, whether constituted by one word or by a whole phrase, that could reflect the distinction described above. Is not such a discussion, then, a waste of time—especially in a study like this, which started with a call to broad thinking?

The answer must be a flat "no." These are not niceties; on the contrary, such debates about words embody a part of the theory of rhetoric presented here. For one of the basic points of this theory is that in rhetoric more than in any other of the language sciences the metalanguage is closely interwoven with the ambiguities and conflicting connotations of the object language. Consequently, the distinction between rhetorics and rhetoric, which is indispensable if conducted with the proper critical attitude, would become simplistic if it were conceived of as an absolute opposition: it is not possible for an ambiguous and confused rhetoric to be explained by a luminous and neutral rhetorics. Every effort must be made to make of rhetorical analysis a precise and scientifically sober tool, but such efforts must be accompanied by the critical awareness that rhetorics will never be able to escape completely from the circle of rhetoric: that is, every rhetorical criticism embodies one or the other form of rhetoric.

This, as noted, is a problem common to all language sciences; but it is particularly acute for rhetorics, because this discipline deals with the structure of discourse as a whole, not with the smallest parts of this structure. The relationship between, say, phonology as a metalanguage and its phonetic content is not such as to cause large ambiguities (although one would be naive to assume innocence even in this apparently most neutral of metalanguages); but since there is no critical statement that is not embodied in a discourse—and, on the other hand, there is no discourse so simple as not to realize a critical act—it is clear that no form of rhetorical criticism can be completely "pure" with respect to the discourse it analyzes. Every form of rhetorics, then, is the critical metalanguage of a certain rhetoric that constitutes its object, and at the same time it is, in itself, the embodiment of a certain rhetoric.[2] The difference, then, is one of relative adequacy: there is a big difference between a form of rhetorics that is blind to its own rhetoric (this image of blindness has a particular halo, after de Man 1971), and a variety of rhetorics that is critically aware of this, and that tries to choose the most lucid and precise form of rhetoric in order to express itself. Most of the terms used in current textual analysis are duplications of terms already present in the rhetorical tradition; but it is not only in order to avoid this duplication that the terminology of rhetoric should be used. One of the most fascinating phenomena in the history of ideas occurs when certain concepts seem to snap together as a constructive system, emerging from a welter of sardonic critiques and negative assertations; when, I mean, the tables are turned, and epithets that had been thrown as insults to the practitioners of some form of thought or action are hurled back to the adversaries like grenades—just before they go off; and in the process their connotations are completely changed, from negative to positive.

For instance: the epithet *Junggrammatiker* (coined about a century ago as an ironical hint that the novelty of approach they were asserting was only apparent) is now a respectably bland designation, and the chapter devoted to the *Neo-Grammarians* is one of the most important in every history of historical linguistics. Or, at an earlier date and in a different domain (literary history): the proud reaction in France to the epithets *décadent, décadence* (both of which still retain, in the more dour folklore of English intellectual history, an almost completely negative, and strongly moralistic, meaning); a reaction that culminated in the institutionalization of the first as the name of a literary journal (*Le Décadent*, edited by the enterprising Anatole Baju in the 1886–89 period). Or, in a slightly later period (circa 1898–1908), and in a still different domain, that of art history: the ironically named *Fauves* who, undaunted by this imagery of wild beasts, proceeded to solemnize it in *fauvisme*. And one could continue, of course, adding such examples as the bucolic irony originally implicit in the disparaging *Lakers* (or *Lake poets*, or poets of the *Lake school*), and so on and so forth.

I intend to try and turn the tables in this way with respect to rhetoric. Not that this is the first time that such need has been felt. The pendulum has been swinging back and forth for a long time now:

without mentioning for the moment the debates in Ancient Greece and in Rome, one might recall (remaining in the area of ambiguous epithets) the label [*grands*] *rhétoriqueurs* (for there were also, it seems, the *petits rhétoriqueurs*) as applied, centuries after their flourishing, to a group of fifteenth-century French poets, whose checkered history is still remembered today, when we assist in a revival of respect and scholarly interest in these *rhétoriqueurs*.[3] At the risk of oversimplification, the basic outline of this development can be summed up as follows—leaving aside the period of the seminal ambiguities, between Gorgias and Plato: from late Classical times, through the Renaissance triumph, to the Enlightenment, rhetoric designates a "neutral" or a "good" discipline—a *tékhnē* or *ars* in the well-known sense of methodology, more precisely (let us not be timid) of science. From the late Enlightenment/early Romantic period to some decades ago *rhetoric* loses its innocently positive meaning and acquires a pejorative one. Of course, I am referring here to the mainstream; in certain milieus rhetoric always maintained its respectability. However, this position is not the same as that of creative leadership: staid survival, although better than complete disappearance, is not the best possible condition. There is no need to describe the latter meaning, since it still survives in the vulgate of everyday speech. And certain recent attempts at reevaluation show, *a contrario*, the persistence of this negative meaning, when, with a defensive move that is at least clumsy (and in later repetitions becomes slightly demagogic) the practitioners feel the need to append the adjective "new" to it. (It was Perelman and Tyteca who introduced the term, although, as explained in Perelman 1970, the term "nouvelle rhétorique" had already taken shape by the fifties.)[4] In any case, the term "new" as applied in this book is rather a misnomer, since the work does not embody a new theory of rhetoric (this is not to diminish its value as a precious organization of data and stimulus for research). Aside from the work of these Belgian pioneers, I do not know of any case in which the call to rhetoric, in recent years, was uttered with the same vigor—a clarion sound, so to speak, rather than an erudite flute timidly playing in the background. I will have occasion to quote many of these flutes (and with the gratitude due to all serious workers in this field); but as for the clarion, Kenneth Burke (who will be often quoted later) is almost the only exception.[5] But I do not intend to pursue this line of discourse because, for all the need for a *critical* history of rhetoric, my approach here is (as suggested at the beginning) ontological rather than historical; it is, indeed, a clear exhortation to free ourselves from what can be called the archaeological approach to rhetoric, that gives to a term like rhetorician (to make a last terminological remark) the old-fashioned and slightly condescending (or antisystematic) connotation of so many -*ian* words: *grammarian* (before the recent reevaluation), *linguistician*, *stylistician*, and so forth; and—why not?—*politician*. (What follows will show that the rhetorician and the politician share much more than a suffix: the moralistic reaction to both roles is a deformed reflection of the large part that they have in common).

In this archaeological approach, it is not rhetoric that helps us to describe and understand certain phenomena; rather, rhetoric is one of the phenomena that are themselves in need of analysis by means of a scientific metalanguage (that of linguistics or of philosophy or even—*incredibile dictu*—that of literary criticism). This explains why discussions of rhetorical systems usually turn out to be (as noted) *histories* of rhetoric. The situation of rhetoric today is, unfortunately, not remote from that of alchemy—in fact, worse in some respects. For rhetoric is still too often treated with the same naively condescending tone, that presumes to speak out of a higher scientific plane, with which alchemy used to be treated before being "rediscovered" as a cognitive system in its own right (within limits, of course)—suffice it to cite Jung 1970*a*.

One of the main themes of this book is that such a view is false. Rhetoric has been, and (if properly implemented) still is, an autonomous theory, and whatever important things disciplines like stylistics and literary criticism have to say about verbal art in particular and human language in general, they are able to say them insofar as these disciplines have been born out of rhetoric. What does the recognition of linguistics and history as sciences imply? Among other things, the avoidance, in their respective fields of inquiry, of the "Confusion between a description of how things are, or are supposed to be, and the historical process that has brought man to the point of being able to describe them" (Rossi-Landi 1974). Thus, for instance, one does not consider that linguistics provides an adequate description only of "dead" languages, or of the old stages of living languages, nor does one grant scientific status to linguistics only insofar as the analysis is restricted to, say, the spoken dimension of modern languages. Rather, we all assume that the linguist and the historian speak about things as they actually are (or were)—that is, they speak of things as, to the best of their knowledge, they think they are—not about things as they were thought, in a prescientific past, to be. This amounts to saying that to recognize linguistics and other disciplines as sciences means to recognize that they have an ontological *approach* (this is different from the ontological *basis* of the data for each discipline—a separate problem that will be taken up below). Now, rhetoric amply deserves to be granted the same ontological approach: rhetoric speaks about the ways in which human discourse works and has worked, and it speaks about these things as one of the fundamental branches of the human sciences, in terms relevant to all our contemporary concerns.[6] What I have just said essentially answers the question that naturally occurs at this point—the one about the ontological basis of rhetorics: if rhetorics is a theory, what is it a theory of? I have already noted that rhetorics is the theory of rhetoric; I specify now that rhetoric is the functional organization of discourse, within its social and cultural context, in all its aspects, exception made for its realization as a strictly formal metalanguage—in formal logic, mathematics, and in the sciences whose metalanguages share the same features. In other words: rhetoric is *all* of language, in its realization as discourse. For, to exclude strictly formalized metalanguages from the domain of rhetoric (and even this tentatively—until one investigates the possible rhetorical elements in those metalanguages) is to discard something that is not, properly speaking, language; the catholicity of rhetoric, that ranges over the whole of linguistic structure, is thus confirmed rather than weakened.

1.2 *THE FIELD OF RHETORIC*

Is all this clear? Yes, I dare say—to the extent that it shows how the definition of the field of rhetoric that serves as a background to this research is much broader than the classic definition. However, what is probably still unclear is the implication of this broader vista. Indeed, this could give the impression of mere legerdemain, a terminological manipulation: with a sweeping gesture the field of rhetoric is made to cover the whole of language—rearranging various commonly used labels, but without actually reshaping the landscape. What follows shows that much more is at stake here. First of all, it is necessary to clarify the notions of "function" and "discourse." I will briefly review some of the basic usages; such a review, undertaken with a modicum of historical perspective (although, let me insist, the purpose here is to orient actual research), is all the more necessary since linguistic research in these areas usually exhibits an exasperating parochialism. In reading certain analyses, one has the impression that certain notions have just been invented, or alternatively, that they are taken out of a repertory of clear terms with univocal meaning. But neither of these two simplifications is realistic: the notions used in any linguistic description have, first of all, a long and complex history; second (and this ought to convince even the strictest partisans of purely synchronic descriptions that the problem is an important one), essentially the same notions are often used in different lines of study—so the scholar must become aware that the differences in terminologies and contexts mask the underlying similarities.

The novelty of what follows is, of course, not absolute but relative: distinctions of this sort have been already presented, but not (*salvo errore*) on such a broad typological scale. A consequence of this relative novelty is that many of my decisions, with regard to assigning this or that work to this or that category, will appear objectionable; but I prefer this risk, that implies the effort to actually reorder substantive entities in this field, to that of merely juggling with the terms.

The *légende des origines*, as far as the modern usage of the term "function" in literary and linguistic descriptions is concerned, brings us back to the period between the end of the last century and the first decades of ours, and to intellectual circles in Eastern Europe (especially Russia and Czechoslovakia). On this background, Propp's usage of the term is best known. For him, at a certain point in his evolution, function was "an act of a character, defined from the point of view of its significance for the course of the action" (Propp 1958:21; originally 1928).

This usage of the term lies at the root of that discipline—more semiotic in the broad sense than linguistic—that is now more and more frequently called narratology. Now, a theory experiencing a rebirth, like rhetoric, needs all the friends it can get—and narratology is certainly a significant one among the sources of suggestions and comparisons to which I will try to remain open throughout this research. Yet distinctions are necessary, for a theory must know its limits as well as its potentialities: narratology is at the same time too broad and too restricted as a descriptive technique to be directly useful for the elaboration of a theory of rhetoric. Too broad, because (as the definition of function quoted above shows) its units are vaguer than those with which linguistic analysis usually operates; and too restricted, since it confines itself to the study of narrative, while we are interested in the structure of any type of discourse.

By speaking of *légende* I did not mean to cast doubts on the primary role of the Eastern European experience (although, of course, further historiographical explorations may refine this picture and modify several details—but, to repeat, this is not my concern here); rather, I wanted to draw attention, indirectly, to the dangers implicit in repetition and excessively narrow concentration on one line of work. Our present concern is a good illustration: the halo of renewed excitement that has surrounded the idea of function in the narratological sense since it was rediscovered, some decades after its initial formulation has perhaps partially obscured a less exciting idea of function, one that is more concretely relevant to the structure of discourse: what has come to be called Functional Sentence Perspective—born, interestingly enough, at about the same period and (broadly speaking) in the same cultural and geographical area where the other notion was elaborated.

This technique combines semantic and syntactic analysis in an attempt to establish the perspective of each given sentence from the point of view of the relations, established within it, between the part of the sentence taking up old information (often called the theme, but terminology varies—cf. Valesio 1976a) and the part conveying new information; the old information is what can be taken for granted, on the basis of the logic and pragmatic presuppositions valid for the proposition underlying the sentence, or what is already known thanks to the preceding context, while the new information is what substantially enriches the knowledge gained by the listener or reader of the given sentence.[7] The reference in the statement above to the preceding context must be emphasized, because it is this kind of functionality that is central for the present analysis. When saying that a sentence is functional one thinks (and here I probably go beyond the tradition) of three different phenomena; a sentence is functional insofar as it (1) links itself, through certain of its constituents and features, to the preceding and the following sentence, thus constituting a connected discourse; (2) builds up relationships between some of its constituents and features and elements of its semiotic framework (its "context of situation," as it has been called); and (3) uses the grammatical resources available at several levels in the language by implementing special configurations ("figures of speech").

This latter aspect is not usually brought to the fore in functional analysis of sentences (hence the reference to going beyond the tradition). But this aspect is essential, since it shows most clearly that this functionality, which enables us to see the sentence in its reality, without artificially isolating it, had been identified, although roughly, by classical rhetoric. The functional structure of discourse, then, is seen in its entirety only when the whole equipment of the rhetorical tradition is applied to it; on the other hand, rhetoric is appreciated in its seriousness and relevance only when it is viewed as the locus where syntactic and semantic structures are concretely linked—as the locus, in short, of solid and detailed analysis, rather than of frilly digressions. The first aspect of sentence functionality is the one on which the tradition just sketched insisted, and also the one on which the tradition of American structuralism has contributed a, by now, long series of studies that can be put under the category of "discourse analysis." The central aspect of this analysis is the study of the cohesion (and also *the lack* of cohesion, but more on this later) between successive sentences in discourse; but this syntagmatic aspect is integrated by various paradigmatic relationships hinted at above.[8] The results of these analyses of discourse are still not definitive, their assumptions often too simplistic. But, for all this, we have in them a scientific literature whose procedures are explicit and clearly formulated, and that is respectful toward the collection of data and the patient development of empirical research. Does all this sound like something we should take for granted? A look at the diverse array of works on text and discourse, and especially at some of the most talked-about experiments, will show that this is far from being the case: we cannot take these virtues as a matter of course.[9] We should, by now, be able to see the flimsiness of two clichés still current in linguistic expositions and discussions: that the structuralist tradition has been superseded, and that linguistic concern with units larger than the sentence is still a desideratum. Information like that presented above may dispel the latter cliché, but the former involves a deeper misunderstanding. In effect it could be argued that, at least in the field of discourse analysis, structuralism has never been so promising and suggestive as it is now.

All this had to be pointed out, because otherwise one can experience a needless difficulty in making what should be a smooth transition from discourse analysis to the kind of study now often called in English "text grammar," but whose more widespread designation (in homage to the language in which most of the literature has been written) is *Textlinguistik*. This technique is essentially a type of discourse analysis that is more formalized and more strictly bound, in most cases, to one grammatical model—the transformational-generative one. The main limitation of this kind of study is that its statements are in large part programmatic; indeed, the complacent tone with which theoretical projects are announced rather than tested verges, at times, on unconscious irony. But this line of research must not be underestimated; it is indispensable to the elaboration of the contemporary linguistic analysis of discourse.[10] In these works, *Pragmatik* has become as important a term as "text" (see Stalnaker 1970, Abraham and Braunmüller 1971, Mey 1975); this links this research to the other sense of function—the one that, so to speak, opens up to the outside rather than concentrating on the inside of the discourse. The study of the various functions of language in society is the concern of psycholinguists and sociolinguists. But, as we saw above, it would be a mistake to assume that such a concern is a new development: these investigations have always taken place, if only sketchily, under the category of rhetoric. We should not be deceived by the apparent prissiness of the rhetoric of classical rhetorical analyses into thinking that these studies are not relevant. Also (and this caution will, I hope, justify the aridity of the present enumeration) we should not rush headlong down any one of these paths without realizing that the parallel paths are so numerous that the scholar has the duty—no matter how impatient (and rightly so) he is to try and set things straight in his own way—to link them together. Thus, *Pragmatik* and *Textlinguistik* are connected to the study of speech acts (see Searle 1969, Ohmann

1971, the bibliography in Verschueren 1976, etc.), and they both must, as shown above, be related to the tradition of discourse analysis, and all this in turn is relevant to the psycholinguistic (sociolinguistic and ethnolinguistic) study of what we may call the external functions of language.[11] But the story does not end here, for all this has to do with the American (and not only American) tradition of content analysis—a technique that combines thematic and close verbal examination of discourses. The label is not felicitous, for any systematic study of the structure of discourse is as much an investigation of "style" as it is of "content"—indeed, a systematic analysis of linguistic structures must leave such crude dichotomies behind.[12] If the preceding review has given the impression that by now the problems of text and discourse have been cultivated to exhaustion, let me note that the reality is quite different (unless the exhaustion at issue is that of the reader, wearied by this array of bibliographical data). Indeed, this typology would be incomplete (and thus would lose the originality that, within the modesty of its limits, it claims with respect to shorter efforts) if it did not sketch the two extreme poles at which analyses of discourse are developed. All the fields of research that have been presented make up a sort of middle ground; I am now going to sketch the more "radical" wings.

The better known of the two—the one, indeed, that appears nothing less than glamorous today—is the analysis of tests in a semiotic perspective that goes from broad to vague. For instance, the framework of the brilliant experiments by the Russian formalists is rather vague (there is no need, at any rate, to rehearse here the well-known data), while works such as that by Mukařovský in the already-evoked period of the *origines* (and see now Mukařovský 1970), and by Lotman 1972 (see also Lotman and Pjatigorskij 1969) are more systematic. Vagueness is still the main danger today, whether we consider the hermeneutic tradition or works where notions like "discourse" and "text" float around without contact either with an ontological commitment or with communicable and repeatable specifications— with a technique, in short, as a form of responsible consistency.

The danger is as urgent as it is clear: the analysis of discourse may end up being considered an irresponsible exercise even before it has deployed all its brilliant possibilities—a fate that befell structuralism, now often snubbed as an old-fashioned enterprise although its resources still have not been systematically tapped.[13] The danger of the ideologism of obfuscation cannot be checked by evading the confrontation with textual structures and by taking refuge in a commentary on its subjective side—the act of reading. This concentration seems to be one of the distinctive features of what is called poetics, or at least of a variety of it (see Culler 1975). The choice here lies, clearly, in a different direction: facing up to the challenge of discourse and dealing with it in a scientific and objective manner—risking all the accusations of aridity, prosaicness, and pedantry often leveled at empirical studies.

It is in this light that the other pole of analysis appears preferable. This is the pole of realistic, close study of configurations within the text—especially (until now) but not exclusively the texts of poems. Since analyses of figures will often recur in the following pages, I will not present here a bibliographical review of these studies, and will confine myself to remarking that such investigations are fruitful only when they are extremely detailed—and thus only when they really go beyond stylistic criticism as traditionally known (this masqueraded stylistic criticism is frequent today). But, as we shall see, the limit of even the very detailed analyses is that they concentrate only on the top of a more complex rhetorical object.[14] But figural analysis does not exhaust what I presented as the pole of concreteness; for its hardest core—the one that until yesterday appeared hopelessly out of fashion—is actually of crucial importance for a general theory of rhetoric. Here the specter of terminology reappears: how many ambiguities and distinctions will we have to deal with, if we use—in order to designate this concrete analysis of texts—the term *textual criticism* (cf. Italian *critica testuale*, and so forth)? Better to avoid this overlapping by using the expression *textual editing* (as in the subtitle of Gottesman and Bennett 1970); better still to have recourse to the term *textology*, where the danger of excessive solemnity is more than offset by the advantage of giving the correct idea of the importance of what is involved here: not the humble skill of dry-as-dust practitioners whose minute work is merely subservient to "higher" criticism, but an approach that has its own theoretical justification.

Textology is a calque on Russian *tekstologija*, and not by chance: for it was in that cultural area, in the thirties, that textual editing seems to have begun a new life as a systematic study.[15] It would be fruitful (and not merely of terminological interest) to establish whether textology is better viewed as a branch of rhetoric, or of linguistics in general, or—even more generally—of semiotics. What is clear in any case is that this kind of analysis is essential for the full description of any text, and that—in this sense—textology is of crucial importance for rhetorics, although rhetorical analysis can be performed without having to be supplemented by textological study.

Let me try to make clearer what is involved. Textology is viewed here as the systematic study of *all* semiotic aspects (including all the physical details, whether or not they have linguistic implications) of the written representations of linguistic structures. The core of textology is its concern with variants: collecting them (in as full a way as possible), presenting them explicitly, and analyzing in detail their linguistic (and cultural) implications. But textology is also concerned—as noted—with all details of the manuscripts and printed books containing the texts under consideration, even beyond the analysis of the relationships among the different versions that is essential in order to establish an apparatus of variants. Textology, in other words, opens up a new vista on the ontology of the text by establishing a full homology (not just a casual metaphorical connection) between the concept of text and that of language.

A "text" does not have a unitary mode of existence, any more than a "language" does; that is, a text is not a monolith but a family composed of several main varieties: those can be called (textual) dialects. Each textual dialect, in turn, is made up by a large number of textual idiolects: the various manuscripts or copies of printed volumes embodying (each one in its unique way, no matter how standardized the procedure) the text. This is, to a certain extent, a new interpretation of the task of textology; as such, it requires a full-fledged, autonomous discussion. This is why the theory of rhetoric presented here will not contain a detailed textological account, although textology will be kept constantly in mind.

For instance, some of the data here are taken from sixteenth-century texts that have been transmitted to us through several manuscripts and ancient printings. Each one of these "texts," therefore, confronts us with a series of specific, local, problems that affect the shape and variety of each one of the words I am going to quote. We must be aware, then, both of the legitimacy of leaving the textological conditions aside (for the purposes of this research)—thus reducing our perception of a complex semiotic object to the terms of the linguistic discourse it transmits—and of the reduction that it implies; a scientifically functional convention is acceptable as long as it is critically perceived as a convention.

The preceding remarks already explain the way in which the concept of "text" and that of "discourse" will be systematically differentiated throughout this book. The often-used distinction between "text" as referring to the written aspect and "discourse" as referring to the oral aspect is, in the light of the preceding observations, too crude to be of much use. In fact, once textology is recognized in its proper role, it is difficult not to feel that the way the notion of text is used today—even in the apparently most sophisticated descriptions—is too loose. But the description above allows us to be more precise: the text is the complete semiotic object (the linguistic structure plus the graphemic structure plus all other signs connected to it as a physical object), while the discourse is only the linguistic structure—moreover, the linguistic structure in a relatively narrow sense, that is, the language analyzed with only occasional and partial references, if any, to the linguistic implications of its graphemic form and to its constellation of variant readings.

Let us now step back for a moment, after this review of modern research, in order to gain a sense of perspective. Rhetoric, in a sense, has always been there, as a linguistic discipline, at least from the times of the Sophists (as far as the "European" tradition is concerned). Much of what linguistics (including stylistics), literary criticism, and even the social sciences are saying is simply a rephrasing, at times enlightening, at times clumsy, of what rhetoric has already said. What is needed, to quote from a book from which several leaves will be borrowed, *The Philosophy of Literary Form*, in a partially different perspective, here—Burke 1973:114 (1941b), is "a development from first approximation to closer approximation as against the tendency, particularly in impressionistic criticism and its many scientific variants that do not go by this name, to be forever 'starting from scratch.'"[16] But if the illusion of inventing rhetoric is naive, the pretense of presenting it as a venerable system of thought untainted by modern developments (this is, partly at least, the rhetoric of Howell 1975, among others) tends to obscurantism. If we look closely, these two attitudes are not too distant, for they share one defect: a demagogical streak. The former is the tendency to the stridently demagogical rhetoric of the *modernes*, the latter the rhetoric of the *anciens*—no less demagogical for its being more pompous. We need to reexamine classical rhetoric in all its components, and to fashion a consistent theory out of it; for, notwithstanding its geniality, it is doubtful whether classical rhetorics has given us a unified theory of rhetoric. Perhaps the very fact of thinking in terms of a unified theory is sufficient to characterize as modern the present approach to rhetoric. But there is more to it than that, and we have already seen a part. The definition of rhetoric whose framework has been delineated above goes beyond the classical definition especially in this: that it is not confined to that ambiguous psychological category, persuasion.

Persuasion can be (and actually has been) interpreted in such a shallow and intellectualistic way as to make rhetoric appear irrelevant. In dealing with the classics and their statements—with words, for instance, like Aristotle's *tò pithanón*—we often must be more imaginative than their terminology would at first sight seem to allow. It is not a matter of philological irresponsibility. On the contrary, when we dare to move more freely we usually end up discovering that the term in question is richer and more ambiguous than its canonical translation, and especially that the actual analyses in the classic texts already go beyond these canonical formulations.

This is, for instance, the case with Aristotle, as we are going to see in detail below. His rhetorical analyses, especially as enlarged in the third book of his standard treatise, in fact go beyond the narrow frame of persuasion, and are relevant to the broad framework developed here. This framework, to repeat, is that of rhetoric as the functional organization of discourse, both in its internal aspect of syntactico-semantic structuring and in its external aspect of dialectic relationship with the surrounding semiotic frame—for, as will be made clear, discourse is not directly linked to anything like "real" things and events.

This functional organization is, by its nature, pertinent not only to efforts aiming at persuasive communication, but to all forms of linguistic expression, including the most egocentric and narcissistic monologues. Rhetoric is not even confined to consciously intended discourse: anything that is structured as a discourse that is grammatically acceptable, at least in part (something that, as is well known, does not guarantee that the discourse makes sense), is rhetoric. Thus any automatic, not-consciously-controlled discourse that still is at least partly intelligible within the code of a given natural language is a proper object of rhetorical analysis; and this includes the discourses of persons talking in their sleep, or while under the influence of alcohol or other drugs, or in states of temporary or permanent mental unbalance (insofar as these do not preclude the utterance of partially grammatical sentences). But the rhetorical theory for our times must be other things as well. It must be post-"Marxian," post-"Freudian," and post-"structuralist." If this sounds obvious and banal to some readers, a perusal of the literature on rhetoric in this century will convince them that we cannot afford to take these points for granted. These "posts-," on the other hand, should not be interpreted as a *post mortem*, a dissection of intellectual corpses (on the contrary, it is the "pre-" Marxian, etc., contemporary literature on rhetoric that too often gives the impression of deadly rigidity and ossification). What I am talking about is a critical relationship with the shaping forces of modern thought in the sciences of man and society—those disciplines still catalogued under the ambiguous label of "humanities."

My trinity, then, should not be viewed as a set of scholastic allegiances (hence the quotes around those names); every one of them is, in fact, a metonym. When I say "Marx," for instance, I mean here the various moments of radical reorientations in philosophy as well as in the social sciences from the second half of the nineteenth century on, especially but not exclusively in the Hegelian tradition ("right" as well as "left"). It should not come as a shock, at this point, that my "Marx" is a metonym for, among others, Bentham and Nietzsche; or that my "Freud" is a metonym (or rather, a slightly perverse antithesis?) for Jung.[17] Finally, here "structuralism" covers modern linguistics in its various trends (no proper name, Saussurean mythology notwithstanding, could adequately symbolize it: for better or for worse, there are no giants towering in the history of modern linguistics). This label, then, not only covers what is commonly called structural linguistics, the story of which (in Europe and in the United States) has been often told, but also reaches back to its distant predecessors in the late nineteenth century, and simultaneously takes in its successors: tagmemics, transformational-generative grammar, stratificational grammar, and the other European and American variants (the suggestion is that, for all the claims to radical innovation, what counts more in a general view of these trends is their continuity with respect to the early structuralist tradition). In short, and to put it very simply: today a theory of rhetoric can be built only on a critical contemporary view of human society, human psyche, and human language.

On the other hand, this necessary critical awareness should not become a way of colonizing rhetoric. As already observed, rhetoric (more precisely, rhetorics) is not an object, it is not a collection of raw data and folkloristic notions, but a scientific discipline; that is, a subject that creates its own mode of reflection. So much so that, just as we need linguistics, sociology, psychology in order to understand rhetorics, this latter in its turn is indispensable in order to have a critical and analytic view of these sciences.

The tone here is necessarily ambitious, for it is not a matter of personal whim, but rather of the objective importance of this science. Rhetorics will lead us to understand (and therefore, to a certain extent, to demystify) all systems of ideas, including those that have just been evoked. If rhetoric is coextensive with human discourse, nothing can be safe from rhetorics—not even (as noted) its own proceedings. Rhetorics, like any other theory, will stand or fall on its ability to coordinate and analyze empirical data. This is why, in the pages that follow, examples will not be occasional touches of bright color, but the essential supports of the whole enterprise. As such, they will be analyzed in detail, and often the same piece of linguistic material will be taken up at different points in the exposition, so as to analyze the coexistence of different figures and the structure of different levels. The structure, then, of this book can be described by the now-fashionable imagery of the rhizome (see Deleuze and Guattari 1976): a rootlike stem growing in a profusion of secondary forms, rather than a simple root. But a more appropriate image here is the musical one of theme and variations: the same text will appear again and again, each time with a more developed analysis. But, before describing this phenomenology, it is necessary to try and delineate the basic traits of an ontology of rhetoric.

Chapter II

THE COMMONPLACE
AS THE COMMON PLACE

2.1 THE ARISTOTELIAN DILEMMA

In any effort at building a theory, ontological claims are inextricably bound together with demonstrations and descriptions of a detailed and empirical nature. In the face of this, a frequent reaction of the too-cautious reader (that is, of each one of us, at one moment or another) will be perplexity or irritation because he feels that too much is being asked of him. He partially adhered to a certain descriptive technique—one that gave him, if not full conviction, at least the reassurance of rational procedure—and now he discovers that by doing this he has been dragged into accepting certain general claims about the structure of the world that—if they had been presented alone, without the prestigious halo of science—he would have rejected with an ironic smile. On the other hand, the other type of reader, who had been attracted by those same broad claims, starts squirming in his chair with increasing impatience when he discovers that they hinge on a host of minute technicalities. There is no escape, it seems: the philosophical discourse leans toward the arbitrary and the vacuous, while the scientific discourse slides into aridity. There is enough, we have to admit, to exasperate the intelligent observer and make him escape into the harmless collecting of historical lore on his subject (this is indeed—as I have repeatedly noted—what has happened to rhetorical studies).

It is better to face the risks, however, dealing (albeit summarily)

19

with ontology rather than pretending not to see it. The philosopher, by the necessity of his discourse, is usually blunt about his ontology; the scientist or scholar, on the other hand, does not directly point to certain realities as the ultimate ones (thus he can always delude himself into saying that he is not doing any metaphysics); but actually he does indicate these realities indirectly, by the very fact of isolating certain facts rather than certain others from the heap of raw data, the *húlē*, with which everyday reality confronts us. No dedicated and continuous observation is free from ultimate beliefs.

Any systematic inquiry, then, on any aspect of what we (in our slap-dash metaphysics) call reality, will assume certain entities as crucial, as its *raison d'être* as an inquiry—no matter how many divergent interpretations of such entities can be entertained within its framework. Therefore, my basic question is more narrow than the deceptively simple one, "What is there?" asked today by some logicians as *the* ontological question (see the essay by this title in Quine 1964). What I am asking is: "What is there in rhetoric?" That is: What should one look for, when one wants to think in rhetorical terms? And in what occasions, faced with what problems, does he need to think in those terms?[1] What I will try to define, then, can be called a regional ontology, although this similarity with phenomenological language should not mislead anybody.[2] It is true that (as noted at the very beginning) any systematic reflection on rhetoric inevitably becomes a philosophy, and as such it needs a unified framework, not an action of "cutting out, as it were, with the critical scissors here and there a fragment of philosophical doctrine" (thus in "Philosophy as a rigorous science" from Husserl 1965:75). But phenomenology cannot be the background of this research: the present approach could in fact be characterized as in some respects the opposite of a phenomenological approach in the Husserlian tradition.

The ontology of rhetoric as developed here is not an ontology of ultimate essences: in fact, the horizons of this region are those of skepticism and dialectic (two attitudes that seem alien, not to say contrary, to the basic slant of phenomenology). However simple my sketch (or perhaps just because of its simplicity), this effort will probably be greeted with much criticism. Faced with this inevitable problem, the rhetorician has, in a sense, an advantage over many of his fellow scholars (even if this advantage is soon translated into a further burden of work): critical responses to rhetorical analysis are in themselves an appropriate object of scholarly study for the rhetorician, since they constitute rhetorical strategies (recall what has already been noted about the rhetoric of rhetorical analysis).

The task of the rhetorician, in this respect, is that of establishing a dialectic relationship between divergent attitudes that would otherwise remain simply extraneous to one another—as we can read in Burke 1973:68 quoted in chapter 1: "the charge that the critic is 'too intuitive' or 'idiosyncratic' in his methods could be happily revised into a charge that he is too 'derivative' and is following an 'overly mechanical routine.' Our critical vocabulary is rich in such resourcefulness." The rhetorician can, then, even less than other scholars, afford the luxury of an ironical attitude toward "critics-who-write-critiques-of-critical-criticism" (strange how this cliché—a weak echo of Marxian rhetoric—comes, with an error of judgment, from the pen of the critic just quoted, Burke [1968:5]).

I hope that this does not evoke the image of a game, or of a safe and "impartial" contemplation, a chronicle of events. On the contrary, any ontological hypothesis requires a complete intellectual commitment (it is in its leaving historicism aside that the present approach comes close to phenomenology; cf. several statements in Huserl 1965). The regional ontology of rhetoric is, to put it concisely, the following: *every discourse in its functional aspect is based on a relatively limited set of mechanisms—whose structure remains essentially the same from text to text, from language to language, from historical period to historical period—that reduce every referential choice to a formal choice.*

Thus, in any form of behavior involving human language (not only, as I said, those where the communicative aspect predominates or seems to predominate, but also those where the main element is that of self-expression) it is never a question—or at least, never primarily and directly a question—of pointing to referents in the "real" world, of distinguishing true from false, right from wrong, beautiful from ugly, and so forth. The choice is only between what mechanisms to employ, and these mechanisms already condition every discourse since they are simplified representations of reality, inevitably and intrinsically slanted in a partisan direction. These mechanisms always appear (so much more convincingly if the discourse is more polished and well organized) to be gnoseological, but in reality they are *eris-*

tic: they give a positive or a negative connotation to the image of the entity they describe in the very moment in which they start describing it.

We begin to see, at this point, in what sense rhetoric is an integral component of language—in what sense, indeed, rhetorics is essential for a renewal of general linguistic theory. Linguistics—even in the directions sketched above, which provide basic tools for the present analysis—still shows what could be defined as an illuministic bent. For linguistics keeps telling us that straightforward, well-integrated, informative communication is the norm, while devious, metaphoric, ambiguous linguistic communication (or expression/communication, in an inextricable and potentially misleading blend) is something secondary, a parasitic growth on the robust and healthy tree of language.

But doesn't literature, all of literature (and if not literature, history; if not history, our own private life), if we gaze at it without blinking, tell us that the real hierarchy is the inverse one, that this optimistic image of life and language to which linguistics still seems to adhere is actually an image standing on its head, which (to revive, beyond its original intent, the well-known polemic suggestion) must be turned right side up again?

"In general," we are told,

> one expects the various components of meaning of a large unit to be integrated so that each supports the other. Occasionally this is not true, in the sense that a combination of small components may produce a higher-level component sharply diverse from the components themselves. A double negative, for example, may result in a positive. A conversation which concerns the weather may in fact not be concerned with items about the weather at all, but may rather have as its basic purpose or meaning the putting at ease of people or the getting acquainted with people. Similarly, there may be mixed motives in an event. Internal meanings may contradict one another, or may contradict the over-all meaning or purpose of the larger utterance. An address may be given without an overt purpose, but have concealed within it a quite different purpose, and a quite different reaction on the part of the audience from that which the audience assumes is desired by the speaker: *For Brutus is an honorable man.* (Pike 1967:610)

This is a very convincing description of the way in which human language works, except for its opening: for it is not only "occasionally" that integration in larger units is not true; it is almost never true.

The only conversations about the weather that really concern the weather are those among meteorologists, and even then only when they take place in a technical environment. Steiner (1975:221–28) eloquently treats of the ambiguity of human speech, and his quote from Adorno's *Minima moralia* ("The only true thoughts are those which do not grasp their own meaning") acquires particular resonance if put side by side with my quote from Peirce in chapter 1, note 5 concerning "somewhat dark" reasonings.

But isn't there a contradiction between my previous insistence on functions and this problematic view? Not really, since one should not confuse the descriptive and critical analysis of functions with an apology for the functional—of what in Italian is called *funzionalità*, as the quality of what is practical, easy of access and handling, immediately useful. A dissertation on the various meanings of "function" is not indispensable here; but let me recall that both what I have called *internal* function and what I have termed *external* function fall under the nonmathematical, intuitive meaning of this concept: in this sense, the function of a linguistic entity is its fulfilling a certain role, its occupying a certain structural position with certain consequences as far as other entities in other positions are concerned (see the remarks on function in Parret 1971:146–58 and passim). This notion, I repeat, is descriptive, and it does not imply a simplistic view of language as a mechanism that ticks peacefully away like an old clock in a living room.

Thus, the internal function of discourse is not basically one of straightforward cohesion—in fact, it is almost the opposite: it is that of managing a continuous battle among its components. Human discourse is the result of the delicate, uneasy, never-to-be-taken-for-granted tension between two opposite forces—one that pushes it into a compact mass (so that the discourse holds together, holds tight), the other that pulls it apart, tries to tear it to pieces, freeing its different and conflicting components. The internal battle has a parallel (not fully symmetrical, point by point) in the external one: the external functions of discourse cannot simply be reduced to rules of correct and acceptable performance (rules, let us say, of good behavior). They, too, are born out of the conflict between conformity and violation of the social patterns. But (and this is essential) this struggle is not to be interpreted in a realistic—or, better, naturalistic—sense. It is basically a struggle among ghosts: the images of actions, things, and events—for this is the peculiar reality of language. This is what was implied in the previous insistence on the *semiotic* framework of discourse—an expression that (for all its appearance of technicality) is actually clearer than an expression like *social* framework.

The latter phrase, in fact, is ambiguous: does "social" refer to patterned signs of things related (directly or indirectly, consciously or unconsciously) to the participants in that speech event that is the discourse—including signs existing only in their private thoughts, and including the participants themselves as signs, rather than as "real" persons? Or does it simply refer to things "out there" in the world? Or does it designate a mixture of these two aspects? The last (with all its confusion) seems to be the most usual meaning of the adjective "social" as it is casually employed in many linguistic descriptions. In the face of this confusion, the insistence on semiotics is revealed as much more than a touch of pedantry: it points to the specific mode of existence of language.[3] The ontology of rhetoric has begun to take shape. The filtering of reality through the sieves of the common places, the conflicts among the functions of discourse (both internally and externally), and the eristic slant present in any discourse, at any level, on any topic—these are its main distinctive features. Linguistic analysis, as noted, has not clearly recognized these traits of language; hence the strategic role of rhetorics as a component of any linguistic theory.

Let us try to be more precise about what I called the sieves of the common places. Here, it seems that the best path to follow is the one that leads us straight to the basic classic analysis *that has survived* (the importance of this qualification will soon be apparent).

There is a point, in Aristotle's *Rhetoric*, where the peculiar ontology underlying it begins to pierce through: it is no longer the tip, but the whole bulk of the iceberg that starts floating into the light, although it will soon disappear again; and the hesitating way in which it emerges is at least as interesting as the fact of its appearance. For this seminal book is a reticent masterpiece, one whose brilliant insights are hidden in a maze of oscillations and ambiguities, not so much because the book in its present form does not have its definitive shape, but above all because (as I hope to show) the whole treatise is

born out of a laborious and delicate compromise. We still need a serious but, so to speak, irreverent commentary on this classic, one that
will set the text free from the mists of archaeology, and will dare to
confront it on terms of equality. (Standard commentaries like Cope
1867, although still useful, do not satisfy this exigence.) This is not a
Philosopher, towering alone, but a skillful synthesizer who weaves together preceding and contemporary treatises of rhetoric (some of
which he refers to, with subtle qualifications and caution). Who will
ever know exactly where Aristotle systematizes and where he glosses
over, where he sharpens and where he blunts?

Some more precise suggestions will be advanced below; for the moment, I want simply to note that the result of all this is a groping
attitude (no "classical" limpidity here), an ever-present hint at dissat-
isfaction, a tendency to strike out into many different paths, trying
them out for a brief time. Thus, the ontological identification mentioned above occurs after what could be called a series of false starts.
The book, we recall, is opened by a tactical, or sectorial, systematization: "Rhetoric is the counterpart of dialectics . . . " (1.1.1354^a 1); this
is followed by the brilliant general definition: "Let us agree that
rhetoric is the faculty of observing what are, in every situation, the
available means of persuasion" (1.2.1355^b 25–26).[4]

This is followed by a series of homages to archetype—that is, tripartite divisions (cf. the description of the alternation between trinitarian and quaternarian structures in Jung 1959 and Jung 1970b,
passim, and the application to certain linguistic-rhetorical problems
in Valesio 1974a). No less than five trinities are brought together in
breathless succession.

> The species of rhetoric are three in number: and as many are the
> categories of persons who listen to speeches. For speech is composed
> of three elements: who speaks, the topic about which he speaks, and
> who he speaks to; and the fulfillment of speech has to do with this
> last, I mean the listener. Also the listener is necessarily either an ob-
> server or a judge, and in the latter role he judges either past or future
> events. He who judges about future events is the assembly member,
> and the judge of the past is the juror, and the one who judges the
> value of the speech is the critical observer; so that, of necessity, there
> are three categories of rhetorically organized speeches: the political,
> the forensic, and the epideictic. (1. 3. 1358^a–1358^b 36–39, 1–8)

Furthermore:

> Each one of these categories of speech has its ends, and since they are three, three are the different ends. For the political orator the end is what is an advantage and what on the contrary is noxious . . . and for those who praise or blame, the concern is for what is noble versus what is base. (1. 3. 1358^b 20–28)

Nor do the tripartite schemata stop here:

> From what has been said it emerges clearly that the orator must have propositions ready primarily for those issues [i.e.: advantage, justice, and nobility]. In fact: complete proofs, probabilities, and signs constitute the rhetorical propositions. In general, syllogism is based on propositions, and the enthymeme is a species of syllogism constituted by the three kinds of propositions mentioned above. (1. 3. 1359^a 9–10)

But these taxonomies, important as they are, still do not strike at the heart of the matter. The author seems to perceive this, for he pauses to adopt a somewhat broader perspective:

> Firstly, now, one must grasp the entities, presented as good or bad, about which the political orator offers recommendations; for his concern is not with things in general, but with those for which it is possible that they either take place or do not take place. . . . (1. 4. 1358^a 30–32)

Some other binary oppositions follow, and then:

> One might say that the most important issues about which all men deliberate and the political orators debate in the assembly are five in number, namely, they concern: revenues, war and peace, and besides, the defence of the territory, imports and exports, and legislation. (1. 4. 1359^b 19–23)

These categories are expanded and analyzed; yet the author is still dissatisfied, and he changes his path once again, with a transition that does not succeed in masking the abruptness of the shift:

> These, then, are the most important matters with regard to which the person who wants to make political speeches must have propositions ready. But now, let us go back and speak about the arguments—con-

cerning both these and different matters—with which the orator must either exhort to certain actions or dissuade from certain others. (1. 4. 1360ᵇ 38–41)

Only now has the author found himself, because only now has he made up his mind to plunge into substantial claims, committing himself to a specific ontology for his field of study:

> Probably one can identify, for every individual person and for all men together, something at which they aim, and which determines the distinction between what they prefer and what they avoid; and this something is, to put it briefly, happiness and its components; thus let us consider, as a model illustration, what is—speaking simply—happiness and of what elements its components are made up. . . . Let us say that happiness is: good fortune accompanied by virtue; or self-sufficiency in the means of living; or the most pleasant kind of life compatible with security; or prosperity of possessions and body, together with the capacity of protecting them and making good use of them. Nearly everybody agrees that happiness is one or more of these things.
>
> If such, then, is happiness, it necessarily follows that its components are: good birth, abundance of friends, having good friends, wealth, having fine children, having many children, a happy old age; furthermore, the good qualities of the body—such as health, beauty, strength, large stature, athletic ability—and also fame, honor, prosperity, virtue. (1. 5. 1360ᵇ 4–23)

But, what is this? Is this string of summary labels—or, to utter the dreaded judgment—clichés, an adequate way of discussing the concept of happiness? When confronted with these paragraphs we may—if we do not approach the field of rhetoric with a sense of its peculiarity—feel disappointed, or at least uneasy. Solmsen's remarks in his 1954 edition of the *Rhetoric* are as good an illustration as any of this kind of response. Having (in his "Introduction") reassured the reader that book I of the *Nicomachean Ethics* contains a more philosophic discussion of happiness, he notes that the lists in the quoted section:

> hold a middle position between a philosophical ethics and popular valuations; while consideration is shown for the man in the street (these sections often teach us more about the average Greek's 'view of life' than the corresponding ones in the *Ethics*) it is nonetheless ob-

vious that these are not the 'goods' the knowledge of which would
come in handy for a speaker in the political assembly. Clearly it is the
philosopher who speaks here, descending a little, it is true, from the
height of his sovereign position, yet still intent on enlightening us
about the true goods.

This comment expresses a significant intuition, but if we leave it as it
stands we still miss the basic point. Indeed, it is because we usually
remain at this level in our comments on rhetorical discussions, and
do not grant the field its ontological autonomy, it is because of this
(more than for any lack of technical linguistic equipment) that we still
do not have an adequately articulated theory of rhetoric. And all this
aside from the fact that the quoted comment is objectionable in the
terms of the *Rhetoric* itself. That is, it perpetuates the old reductionist
attitude (already adopted by the Roman rhetoricians) that sees in
rhetoric only the dimension of performance (to use a current term in
linguistic descriptions), neglecting that of competence. For the objection concerning the kind of knowledge "coming in handy for the
speaker in a political assembly" is appropriate only if rhetorical
theory is identified with performance, and thus defined as the technique of persuading through speech (as, in effect, it has been too
often defined).

But the reason why Aristotle's definition of rhetoric is brilliant is
just that it does not fall into the reductionist trap, and it appropriately
concentrates on competence; rhetoric studies the objective structures
in human language that are susceptible of being used with a certain
function. Rhetoric is not a manner of performing, but of "observing"
what are, in every situation, the "available means of persuasion." As
has already become apparent, my definition is much broader than
the Aristotelian one, but it owes much to the theoretical advance of
Aristotle and his rejection of a superficial (and ultimately simplistic)
approach based on immediately utilitarian criteria.

What we must recognize is that, while analyses like the beginning
of the *Nicomachean Ethics* on the one side and this section of the *Rhetoric* on the other are on the same level of commitment, they identify
different ontological fields. The former is the ontology of traditional
philosophical speculation, where the abstraction from the data of the
"real" world is systematic and critical. It is the ontology in which we
are *not* content to state, with tranquil informality, that "nearly every-

body agrees" that happiness is "one or more" elements in a list such as the one quoted above. Rather, in this more strictly philosophical perspective, we may note that, while "As far as the name is concerned, most people seem to agree" on happiness, "the many do not give the same definition as the wise" (*Nicomachean Ethics* 1. 2. 1095ᵃ 17–18, 21–22). In this ontology, the progression is toward greater and greater abstraction:

> Happiness is an activity of the soul according to perfect virtue. . . . We call human virtue not that of the body but that of the soul; and happiness also we call an activity of the soul. But if this is the case, it is clear that the student of politics must know the facts about the soul, just as the man who cures the eyes [must know] the whole body; and all the more so, since politics is more valuable and of higher quality than medicine. (ibid. 1. 13. 1102ᵃ 5–6, 16–21)

And what about the other ontology, the one pertinent to rhetoric? First of all we must note that, in the Aristotelian system, this field is hierarchically ordered with respect to the one just described. The hierarchy is implicit, but just because of this it is important to bring it to the light. In fact, we are told, in the text cited above, that politics appears to be the "master art," because

> Which of the sciences are necessary in the various political communities, and which of them each individual must learn, and up to what degree, it [politics] disposes all this; and we see even the most highly valued faculties falling under it; for instance, strategy, economics, rhetoric. (ibid. 1. 1. 1094ᵇ 1–3; for all these passages, see the text in Bekker 1960–61: 2. 1094–1181)

This makes for a neat hierarchical schema: just as rhetoric is the science subordinated to the master science of politics, so the ontology of rhetoric, one of whose basic principles is the complex of ideas clustered around happiness, is subordinated to the ontology of politics (or, better, of the peculiar Aristotelian combination of ethics and politics) whose basic principle is that of virtue; that is, the essential validation of happiness.

This subordination of rhetoric to politics is significant, for it reveals a realistic attitude, an awareness of the serious links between rhetoric and social life—something that we must treasure all the more since later rhetorical tradition has become progressively more detached from them and, to this degree, more shallow. However, I will not adhere to the ontology implicit in this hierarchy; indeed, from now on I must leave the protecting shadow of Aristotle and strike out on my path, shouldering the responsibility of the remarks that follow.

Let me first of all repeat the conviction that in both cases sketched above the ontological commitments are equally serious, so that, in this sense, there is no hierarchy between them. Indeed, the apparently naive concepts of popular notions of happiness expressed in the passage above from the *Rhetoric* and in all similar passages from the same work came to us through the centuries unimpaired, while the formidable conceptualizations in the *Nicomachean Ethics* and all similar treatments have much more deeply felt the assaults of time, and have today, for us, a prevalently historical interest, rather than a direct ontological relevance.

This is not to deny that there are features distinguishing the "European" and "American" view of life from the ancient Greek one (and see the comment by Solmsen quoted above). For instance, in a modern list of such sources of happiness written in an English (or Italian, or French, etc.) text, a good spouse—or a good marriage— would be put down as an entity distinct from that of good progeny. It is typologically significant that this does not happen here. And, apropos of progeny, does the separation and sequence of "fine children" and "many children" reflect a hierarchy? And so on and so forth, in the perspective of a cultural anthropological description as the semiotic background of every fully developed rhetorical analysis. The quotation marks around the words European and American are meant to point critically (as is necessary in an analysis that pays attention to the rhetoric of rhetorics) to their limitations and their conventional nature. For instance, "American" culture is not a monolith, unless one interprets this word metonymically as designating only the United States. And as for Europe, it is high time to put an end to the appropriation of Greek thought (a move still executed, for instance, at the beginning of Barthes 1966) by a "Western" history of rhetoric. The fact is, of course, that ancient Greece is as Eastern as it is Western (and later, Byzantium and the experience of the Arab translators will confirm this East-West unity); so that no history of rhetoric that harks back to the Greeks can be considered purely Western.

At any rate, Aristotle's notions about happiness belong to a *philoso-phia perennis*—the one that is implicit in the ontology of rhetoric, which is essentially the ontology of human discourse insofar as it has become second nature to every speaker. A concrete, contemporary example of what I mean? Consider:

> There is . . . a revealing contrast between the mathematician's insis-tence on the precise definition of terms and the pollster's use of vague ones. Since 1947 the Gallup organization has been regularly asking, "In general, how happy would you say you are?" While the mathe-matician defines carefully in order to delimit meaning, the pollster prefers to leave a notion like "happiness" undefined, not because he presumes his respondent to be a philosopher who has spent a lifetime puzzling over this most elusive moral notion, but because he knows that the respondent represents a "sample" of opinion shaped by the social milieu and its media. The respondent, who is being asked to submit an appraisal of his life to a stranger, and who probably looks upon the latter as a scientific representative of society, can be expected to think of happiness in socially approved terms. (Wolin 1975)

This is not, however, a novel consideration; this political theorist of the seventies should have noted the pioneering intuition of the "lit-erary" critic of the thirties, who, observing that "All questions are leading questions," proposed the example of somebody who, wanting to weaken a statesman's reputation in the most "scientific" manner, would send forth investigators from some bureau for the polling of public opinion, with the task of posing a series of questions making an issue, or "problem," of the man's integrity. After a move like this, he notes, even the defenders of the statesman would by their very defense increase the element of "doubtfulness" about the statesman's integrity which had been created by the initial questions.

But, one might ask, what has this to do with the problem of hap-piness? The answer is that this illustration and its development clearly show the general picture of which the definition of happiness is only a part: namely, the inevitable *stylization* (simplification, "biased" structure, eristic use, or any other term of this kind that one would care to employ) that is the ontological basis of rhetoric. The questions referred to above, notes Burke,

> would automatically select the field of controversy—hence, they would automatically deflect the attention from other possible fields of

controversy. Questions might have been asked, for instance, that bore wholly on the *measures* which the statesman advocated. And the whole tenor of the discussion would have changed accordingly. It is in this sense that an institute for the polling of public opinion could not avoid "leading questions" no matter how hard it tried (and I doubt whether such enterprises usually try very hard). Every question selects a field of battle, and in this selection it forms the nature of the answer. In this sense, also, we could say that Marxist criticism in recent years "triumphed" over its most emphatic opponents. Even those critics who had previously been answering questions about "pure form" now began answering questions about "the relation between art and society," i.e., Marxist questions. (Burke 1973:67–68; italics in original)

Actually, questions about the relationship between art and society can be called "Marxist" (rather than, say, "Platonic") only if they are made much more precise than that. But this is not the basic point here—the intuition at the basis of the quoted statement is a crucial one, and it should be enlarged. For it is not only a question that selects a field of battle, but *any* statement, in *any* shape, on *any* topic. We can express reality only through selection or stylization. This is the root of rhetoric, this is what explains its essential importance for all the sciences of man and society.

A great part of the opposition to rhetoric (especially as it takes place in the ideology of Romanticism) stems from an obscure intuition of this peculiar ontology, which is felt as something deadening and threatening rather than as what I propose it is: namely, a profoundly reassuring element, since it brings us into contact with our common human nature (in both senses of the word *common*: 'shared' and 'ordinary'). Rhetoric was (and often still is) felt as deadening because it shows us in a glaring light that what is creative in the use of language is a superstructure; exciting, yes, important, certainly—indeed, indispensable to human life—but still a superstructure. (It is to shield us from this glaring light that much of literary criticism today is cultivated—to elaborate an ideology of vague exaltation of the creativity of language.)

Rhetoric forces us to realize that, insofar as the basic structure of human discourse is concerned, all had already been said before the first speaker made the first speech. We will never know, of course, at what stage in human prehistoric (more precisely—for us here—preliterary) culture the first speech was made; nor will we ever know the specific linguistic structure of that speech. But, all the evidence we can muster from the study of speech in different languages and the study of their functional, communicative context assures us of one thing: that, seen as a functional act of communication/expression, even that first speech did not say anything new. That is: it could be identified, and made sense of, as a speech only insofar as it drew, not only on a preestablished frame of linguistic expression, but on a set of *koinoì tópoi* or *loci communes*. These topoi had already seen to it, so to speak, that speech would not approach reality—the referential world—directly, but only through them; so that they frustrated the conception of referential content as the bedrock of speech and thought. Already then (and always afterward) no appeal to the referents in order to solve any basic dilemma (true or false, ethically right or wrong, beautiful or base) was possible.

The content of man's vision has always been expressible only through a set of ready-made simplifying forms (very different from the Forms in the Platonic sense). And, I claim, this is a hard empirical reality; it does not call for a metaphysical act of faith, nor for an abstract process of deduction; it merely requires a long, cold look at the underlying similarity of all acts of human communication, where it is always the same mechanisms, always the same frames that keep reappearing. "Merely requires," I said; but I did not mean to imply that this is a quick and easy task. Although I suggest that the intuition of this ontological basis of rhetoric should be made explicit by us here and now, as the general orientation preliminary to significant research, nevertheless this intuition would remain sterile if it were not followed by a systematic work of empirical exploration: we must describe the structure of this mechanism as precisely as we can, and in order to do this we must collect—and abstract, and compare, and discard, and reexamine, and correct. In short, this is the beginning of rhetorical research as a contemporary scientific venture.

It was not out of a desire to be picturesque that I spoke of a long, cold look: the implicit critical reference was to the "hot" Romantic rhetoric of individualism, which leaps into the exaltation of the original value of a given text before having systematically examined the common background against which the alleged originality should be evaluated. Who has established that evaluations of originality are something "humanistic" and exciting, while the insistence on the common underlying structure is somehow unworthy of literary criticism and the related disciplines?

It is time to call into question this absurdly antiscientific attitude, and to revive those hints of well-aimed criticism (too soon, it seems, forgotten)—like the remark on "the nominalist line of thought that treats a *group as an aggregate of individuals*, in contrast with the realistic position . . . that treats *individuals as members of a group*" (Burke 1973:194; italics in original), or the awareness that such a broad (and seriously humane, as opposed to academically "humanistic") procedure

> might occasionally lead us to outrage good taste, as we sometimes found exemplified in some great sermon or tragedy or abstruse work of philosophy the same strategy as we found exemplified in a dirty joke. . . . You can't properly put Marie Corelli and Shakespeare apart until you have first put them together. First genus, then differentia. The strategy is common in the genus. The *range* or *scale* or *spectrum* of particularizations is the differentia. (ibid:302)

The distance between this program and what I called academic humanism may be measured by the neglect with which the former is still surrounded in academia. (On humanism, see also: "Principled humanist ideology is spontaneously and deeply reactionary, in theory as well as in practice . . . " [Macherey 1966:83–84], where I object only to the choice of words—the clumsiness of "spontaneously" and of the division between theory and practice with reference to an ideology.)

But it is not only in academia, unfortunately, that this broad and realistic perspective is faced by the narrow cliché of the anti-cliché. In order to appreciate the persistence on our contemporary scene of this Romantic prejudice, let us look at a preface that (to my mind) is more interesting than the prefaced novel. Commonplace, notes the author, is a word of many meanings: "It designates, of course, our most hackneyed thoughts, inasmuch as these thoughts have become the meeting place of the community. It is here that each of us finds himself as well as the others."

When appropriating a commonplace, "I shed my particularity in order to adhere to the general, in order to become generality. Not at all *like* everybody but, to be exact, the *incarnation* of everybody." This analysis is thin as a razor's edge: if these statements are connected to their specific intellectual context, we have to recognize that the picture sketched here is meant as a dark one. We can feel indignation mounting behind this analysis, ready to burst out in the refusal of a state of things that could be defined as inauthentic. But what if we free ourselves from this ideology, what if we reconsider these statements, seeing in them descriptions rather than critiques, so that what we have under our eyes is not a perversion of discourse but its basic way of functioning? Let us read on:

> I have the right, on this level, to chatter away, to grow excited, indignant even, to display my own personality, and even to be an "eccentric," that is to say, to bring commonplaces together in a hitherto unknown way, for there is even such a thing as the "hackneyed paradox" . . . the more subjective I am within these narrow frontiers, the more pleased people will be; because in this way I shall demonstrate that the subjective is nothing and that there is no reason to be afraid of it. . . .

The connection between this analysis and the philosophical tradition will by now have become clear. In fact, the author himself points to Heidegger, and his concept of the "babble," from which point the path is easy to the conflict of authenticity and inauthenticity—but we are now in a position where we can feel the hollow ring of this exhortation. Authenticity is defined in this text as "the real connection with others, with oneself and with death." Through the commonplaces, it is "suggested at every turn, although remaining invisible." But then the analysis veers off, and we are left with a fascinating but ultimately inconclusive description: "the sacred conversation, the ritualistic exchange of commonplaces, hides a 'half-voiced conversation,' in which the valves touch, lick and inhale each other. There is first a sense of *uneasiness*; if I suspect that you are *not*, quite simply, quite entirely, the commonplaces that you are *saying*, all my flabby monsters are aroused; I am afraid . . . " (italics in original).

This picture sticks in the mind, but we should not allow it to hide the fact that, since no alternative has been explicitly presented, we are authorized to ask the question: Does this description apply only to one aspect of human language—a corrupted, debased usage that evokes, by contrast, an authentic use of language—or does it in fact cover the whole of human language, at its basic level? The text quoted (Sartre 1958) suggests that the former alternative is the pertinent one, but it is not by chance—it seems to me—that no immediate alternative is presented. In fact, it is the thesis of this chapter that this is the ontological basis of human language, and that it is misleading to suggest that the "real connection" (with others, the self, death) can be expressed by going against the commonplaces: as if they were not really *common*, as if there were—somewhere—a more edifying, more "beautiful" language.

Let me note, at this point, that my attitude here is constructive—indeed, enthusiastic. The understanding of commonplaces leads us to a sober, but at the same deep and broad, comprehension of the nature of man. I must insist on this connection in order to dispel the possible secondary connotations that accompany (because of the exaggerated role played by the Romantic rhetoric criticized above) an insistence on repetition and equality (always the same mechanisms, always the same frames . . .). Indeed, I consider the achievement of this equality of structure (in the objective structure of *rhetoric*, whatever divergent subjective accounts of it can be given in *rhetorics*) as one of the great achievements of mankind.

A dramatic one, too; for, from the fact that discourse is based on ready-made, stylized topoi it does *not* (*pace* the current critical rhetoric) follow that the discourse we handle is bland and conformistic. Stylization also means heightening the contrasts. Thus, the intrinsic realism of rhetoric is not what goes by this name in the nineteenth-century literary rhetoric (still surviving) about realism: on the contrary, what rhetoric shows is that the basis on which people "really" think is a dialectic of heightened contrast, and not that ghost which is still bandied around, the life of people "as they really are"—a shapeless, unverifiable entity that cannot be expressed in speech.

The importance of this role of rhetoric emerges—as often happens—through the persistence of the attacks led against it, and it becomes even clearer when the contradictory nature of these attacks is examined. In a classic instance of the "damned-if-you-do-and-damned-if-you-don't" principle, rhetoric ends up being attacked on the one side for its rigidity of stereotypes that allegedly constrain and imprison linguistic expression, and on the other side for its supposed frivolity, its skimming the surface of language.

Rousseau quotes the admonition that it is vain to hope the dramatic

writer can show "les véritables rapports des choses" ['the true relationships among things'], because "en général, le poète ne peut
qu'altérer ces rapports, pour les accomoder au goût du peuple" ['generally speaking, the poet cannot but tamper with these relationships,
in order to adapt them to popular taste']. Then Rousseau continues
on his own:

> Dans le comique il les diminue et les met au-dessous de l'homme; dans
> le tragique, il les étend pour les rendre héroiques, et les met au-dessus
> de l'humanité. Ainsi jamais ils ne sont à sa mesure, et toujours nous
> voyons au théâtre d'autres êtres que nos semblables. J'ajouterai que
> cette différence est si vraie et si reconnue qu'Aristote en fait une règle
> dans sa *Poétique*: *Comoedia enim deteriores, Tragoedia meliores quam nunc
> sunt imitari conantur*. Ne voilà-t-il pas une imitation bien entendue, qui
> se propose pour objet ce qui n'est point, et laisse, entre le défaut et
> l'excès, ce qui est, comme une chose inutile?[25]

This attitude still persists; but in the face of it our task at this point is
clear: to defend the realistic ontology of rhetoric (that touches human
nature at the only level at which it can be reached—*on the surface*)
against the false ontology. Its falsity derives from its adialectic nature:
it is based on the topos of Size and Division and thus it exploits an
abstract, geometric imagery, aiming at an imaginary middle point between allegedly "too high" and supposedly "too low."

How much wiser (although darkly so), against this timid middle-of-
the-road humanism, is the insight that Plutarch attributes to Demo-
critus, and Montaigne takes up when he notes that the philosopher
"disoit que les dieux et les bestes avoient les sentiments plus aiguz que
les hommes, qui sont au moyen estage" ['(he) said that gods and animals have sharper feelings than men, who occupy a middle level']
(*Essais* 1. 54, in Rat 1962:345).

Of course, what counts is the reinterpretation of this statement that
we are ready to give today. I suggest that we cannot declare our dis-
dain for the gray clichés through which our everyday conversation is
filtered and at the same time express a nostalgia for "middle" human
dimensions. In fact, it is only when we fully realize that this middle-
level man is an ideological figment, that man at any given moment
oscillates between god and beast; it is only when we realize this that
we are ready to see the topoi for what they really are: not the domain

of mediocrity, but the places of dramatic tension between opposite extremes; places where to simplify does not necessarily mean to water down—rather, it often means to heighten the contrasts.

Topoi, then, are not uncontroversial places of bland conformity. Once the misleading appearances of frivolity and complacency have been discarded, rhetoric appears in its true light, as something that requires a commitment; and it could not have been otherwise, for this is the price that every significant cultural system exacts of the person who considers it steadily and seriously.

The engagement in rhetorics leads to battle, because the system it studies—rhetoric—essentially questions every ideology as such, and in particular some of the ideologies dominant in the human sciences today. A systematic list of these ideological trends requires a book in itself—and such a book, when it is written, will mark the beginning of the *critical* history of rhetorics.[6] Am I too severe in thus implying that rhetorical historiography until now still has not reached this critical awareness? I do not think so—*if* what is meant by criticism is something more than philological attention to who said what when. Such attention is obviously necessary, but it is not sufficient, whatever impression to the contrary one might gain by perusing current discussions of the history of rhetoric. What is called for is what is now often called an "epistemological break" (*coupure épistémologique*); that is, "the break which marks the transformation of a prescientific set of problems into a scientific set of problems."[7] Such a break between ideology and science has taken place already as far as general linguistics *below the level of discourse* is concerned (the qualification, as will be clear by now, is important; also, let me note that it is still an open problem in the history of linguistics when exactly to place the decisive *coupure*); it is this, in fact, that explains the prestigious position that linguistics still manages to occupy within the human sciences. But, as far as rhetoric is concerned, the break has not yet been made. At any rate, the challenge of rhetorics goes beyond the confrontation with this or that intellectual trend—it aims at the whole of the philosophical tradition. "Since the rhetorician offers to speak and write about everything, and the philosopher tries to think about everything, they have always been rivals in their claim to provide a universal training of the mind." Thus, pithily, Kristeller (1961:12). Unfortunately, he does not develop this intuition, and falls back on the usual, precritical review; for instance, almost immediately after the quoted lines: "The relation between the two traditions has been complicated by the fact that the rhetoricians ever since Isocrates have been concerned with morals and have liked to call themselves philosophers, whereas the philosophers ever since Aristotle have tended to offer their own version of rhetoric as a part of philosophy." An interesting conflict is thus evoked—and one on which the concerned intellectual of today must take a position. But this glimpse is immediately obscured by the flight into historicism: "The historical significance of rhetoric cannot be fully understood unless we take into consideration not only the rhetorical theories of philosophers such as Aristotle and his scholastic successors, or of rhetoricians who tried to combine rhetoric and philosophy such as Cicero, but also the rhetoric of the rhetoricians, that is, of the authors professionally concerned with the practice of speaking and writing."

In the wake of these and similar recommendations, rhetoric has been loved not wisely but too well. The result is a proliferation of information (as documented in note 6), with the already described disadvantages. The trees are growing with such profusion that it is necessary, at this point, to step back a little and survey the forest. The present book is such an attempt: to identify the foundations and the general plan of the forest of rhetoric, thereby creating an adequate rhetorics. As we have already seen, modern statements about the importance of rhetoric are not lacking—but they do not, generally speaking, take this recognition as the point of departure for a general, theoretical redefinition of rhetoric and rhetorics. And they do not do this because they do not move from a sufficiently radical redefinition of the nature of rhetoric.

This redefinition (which amounts to the called-for and long-prepared new rhetorics) has already been sketched here. Let me emphasize its three most important distinctive features: rhetoric as the whole functional dimension of human discourse (not restricted to this or that function, nor constrained within the boundaries of successful—or even of conscious—communication); rhetoric as an integrated structure (embracing the topoi, the arguments, and the figures—without being confined to any of these three components alone); and finally, rhetorics as not merely a technical linguistic description, but a philosophic alternative.

These traits of the theory will be developed and explicated in what
follows. But they are recalled here in order to show in what sense this
rhetorics may be seen as the response (originally not planned as such)
to some of the programmatic hints that Peirce gave in this direction
of study. There is, in his corpus, a succession and alternation not only
of labels (terminology again!) but also of perspectives. At first, even
while recognizing "the advantage of an old association of terms" he
shies away from the label thus implied (*rhetorica speculativa*), prefer-
ring that of *objective logic*, although it is less than precise, "because it
conveys the correct idea that it is like Hegel's logic." At this point,
what is designated are "the laws of the evolution of thought," that
coincide "with the study of the necessary transmission of meaning by
signs from mind to mind, and from one state of mind to another."
The same discipline, it seems, is that which should deal with those
symbols that, in a tripartite classification, "independently determine
their *interpretants*, and thus the minds to which they appeal, by prem-
issing a proposition or propositions that such a mind is to admit.
These are arguments." (Isn't this very close to the Aristotelian definition, quoted above, of the *pithanón*?) In another passage, *speculative
rhetoric* (or *methodeutic*) is the term proposed for this kind of study.

By now, the terminological diffidence has shifted to its contrary,
and Kant is indicated as a model for preserving "old associations of
words" in "the nomenclature for new conceptions." The object of this
terminological attention is pure rhetoric, whose task "is to ascertain
the laws by which in every scientific intelligence one sign gives birth
to another, and especially one thought brings forth the other." Another aspect is that evoked by the term *formal rhetoric*, which would
"treat of the formal conditions of the force of symbols, or their power
of appealing to a mind." The ultimate distinctions and connections
among these statements, given the development of a rich literature
on this subject, are perhaps best left to Peirce specialists. Indeed, the
technique followed above—that of roughly following in the quotations the order in which the statements appear in Peirce's *Collected
Papers* (henceforth *CP*) 1958—could appear as a "copout." Actually,
however, I have not avoided the risk of interpretation, because the
very decision of considering all these as variations on the same basic
theme—a general unified program for rhetoric—could conceivably
be open to objections. At any rate, it must be noted once again that

the interest here, in taking up this and similar threads, is ontological rather than historical or philological.[8] One could go on, quoting other statements and indications by other authors. But, as noted, we would not find (*salvo errore*) any systematic perspective for a theory of rhetoric. Indeed one is struck, in surveying contemporary literature on rhetoric, by its derivative tone and by its tendency to water down earlier insights, more bold and open in their attempts to connect rhetorical structures to the whole range of human activities, and consequently more systematic in not shying away from the realization that there is a political dimension intrinsically and inevitably present in every rhetorical structure.[9]

2.2 THE RHETORIC OF ANTIRHETORIC

Let us turn back again to confront the ontology of rhetoric, and the ways of escaping from its recognition into ideology. One of the most important ideological moves is the one that can be called the rhetoric of antirhetoric. In essence, what happens is that a sophisticated rhetorical mechanism is employed to convey a message that attacks "rhetoric." Illustrative examples of this are legion (indeed, one could devote a whole monograph to a "local history"—as part of the future, general, critical history of rhetoric—of this rhetorical strategy in different periods and languages, or within one and the same literary-linguistic tradition). The following is as impressive as any:

> La verità vuole essere nuda, e quanto è più nuda, tanto più inclina. E però avemo veduto che più hanno inclinato e più hanno possuto gli apostoli con la nuda e semplice verità, che gli oratori con le loro ornate parole e le loro orazioni piene di eloquenzia. La nuda verità tira gli uomini a quello che lo intellecto loro repugna, il che non arebbe mai potuto tirare oratore alcuno con sua arte e sua eloquenzia.[10]

Gerolamo Savonarola (from one of whose sermons, harking back to 1495, this passage is taken—see Savonarola 1969:102–103) was a great political and literary figure, and there is no intention here to adopt a debunking approach. But the rhetorician's criticism should never be confused with gleeful debunking, anyway; his task is that of showing that things are not what they seem—that literary texts are even more deceitful than texts in other genres or everyday discourses in pretending to refuse rhetoric, or to handle it as they please; whereas in reality they are the reflex of an underlying rhetorical mechanism that speaks through the speaker-writer, often against his intention, and almost always with a depth and complexity of which he, the "author," can see only a limited part.

What is necessary here, in order not to fall into the trap of this strategy of innocence, is to realize how pervasive the rhetorical structure in this antirhetorical statement is. This rhetorical structure manifests itself both at the semantic level (in the ideological contrast that is set up) and at the level of the syntactico-semantic (or syntactico-lexical) form of the message: that is, respectively, both at the level of the topoi and at the figurative level. At the former level, Savonarola offers us the topos of the antithesis between the corrupt sophistication of the pagan intellectuals and the straightforwardness and simplicity of the Christians—a topos that has little to do with actual history, of course, since it is by now clear that there is a continuity of rhetorical tradition from the pagan to the Christian discourse even in theology, not to mention literature at large.

Interestingly, the latter level—the one of figures—constitutes here an indirect disavowal of the topical level; for this praise of plain speech is couched in a rhetorically sophisticated language. We find here the figure of Epanaphora (realized by the fourfold repetition of the adjective *nuda* 'naked') and Synonymic Dittology—that is, the expression of a given semantic nucleus through two (less frequently, three or more) synonymous words or phrases; this is one of the most extensively cultivated rhetorical devices (perhaps a universal rhetorical feature? It is certainly a good candidate for a set of universals of rhetoric—another needed task for the completion of a full-fledged theory of rhetoric). Synonymic dittology is well known in Classical Latin, and in the European literary languages from their earliest stages (see Elwert 1954) to at least the end of the Renaissance.[11]

The realizations of dittology are, in this passage: *più hanno inclinato e più hanno possuto; nuda e semplice; sua arte e sua eloquenzia.* Nor should the personification be forgotten: the "cliché" of *nuda veritas* is enlivened here by, first of all, the quantifying expression ("quanto è più nuda, tanto più inclina"), and also by the sheer strength of Repetitio in the Epanaphora. We have thus seen that contrast between the topical and the figurative level of discourse that is the dominant distinctive feature in the rhetoric of antirhetoric. Such a contrast creates an ambiguous situation, an objective irony. It tells something about different rhythms of development in different literary languages that such an example is almost one century older than the examples of objective irony scattered throughout a more famous French text. Consider just one instance from it:

> On alloit, dict-on, aux autres Villes de Grece chercher des Rhetoriciens, des peintres et des Musiciens; mais en Lacedemone, des legislateurs, des magistrats et empereurs d'armée. A Athenes on aprenoit à bien dire, et icy à bien faire; là, à se desmeler d'un argument sophistique, et a rabattre l'imposture des mots captieusement entrelassez; icy, à se desmeler des appats de la volupté, et à rabattre d'un grand courage les menasses de la fortune et de la mort; ceux là s'embesongnoient après les parolles; ceux cy, apres les choses; là, c'estoit une continuelle exercitation de la langue; icy, une continuelle exercitation de l'ame. (Montaigne 1. 25; Rat 1962, 1:153)[12]

Doesn't this realization of the figure Amplificatio definitely clarify what is meant here by objective irony? Consider what happens: the master-essayist—perhaps the writer of his age in France who is most punctiliously concerned with the form and the minute detail and the eloquent impact of what he writes—this essayist composes a paean to Laconic speech, and this in a copious (the term Amplificatio is realistic) and sophisticated style! (The rhetorical maneuver of the praise of Spartan simplicity, a praise developed with Athenian sophistication, will enjoy a long life: it will last at least until Rousseau, in a text that will be quoted below to illustrate a different point.)

This Amplificatio is built through a series of Antitheses, with careful syntactico-semantic symmetry (*là . . . icy*—twice, with a *ceux là . . . ceux cy* contrast interspersed—and the key words are repeated in each member of the antithesis: *bien, desmeler et rabattre, après, continuelle exercitation*). Let us round out this analysis of specific passages with another, still later, Renaissance text, one that is, to my mind, one of the most striking illustrations of the rhetoric of antirhetoric, both from a general point of view (the one that most interests us here), and for the whole economy of the literary text where it appears. It does not seem an exaggeration to claim that Cordelia's speeches in the first scene of *King Lear*, the speeches in which she attacks "that glib and

oylie Art,/To speak and purpose not" (and what else is this Art, if not
rhetoric?) will be found upon close investigation to contain the whole
nexus of psychological ambiguity between father and daughter that
unfolds through the rest of the play.*

But to start analyzing the "psychologies" and stances of the various
characters as if they were solid, independent entities would be to fall
into the trap of ideology (here, an ideology of modern bourgeois mo-
rality), that dominates even the apparently most technical statements,
like those of stylistic criticism. What is it that is ideological in these
endeavours? Briefly put (for this is only a sketch): the *appearance* of a
close contact with the text, whereas actually it is not the structure of
the text as such that is scrutinized, but a series of abstractions. The
"break" is realized only by rhetorical analysis (as distinct from stylistic
criticism): in this analysis, the text is seen as the locus of a dialectic
tension and conflict among different blocks of rhetorical structure, or
rhemes (which will be analyzed in chapter 4). The rhemes contain, so
to speak, the skeleton of the literary language, or, put another way,
they constitute its biology (yes, biology: it is time to confront the coy-
ness and complacency with which most contemporary literary criticism has chosen to regard empirical, detailed analyses as "merely" a
form of [neo]positivism, and therefore as something bad—an attitude that is in itself a conservative ideological move).

The partitions among rhemes are not in a one-to-one relationship
with the divisions among characters, which occupy a more superficial
level. Actually, they often do not even coincide with the "text" (that
is, the complex of textual dialects), for a specific chain of rhemes—
that, as such, should be studied in its entirety—can go beyond the
frontiers of a given textual complex.

Now, to study (beyond the conventional divisions *within* a text and
among this and other texts) the structures of the different rhemes and
their dialectic relationships is to study the rhetoric of those "texts."
Rhetoric so conceived (and see what has already been noted on the
pulling together and the pulling apart of the text) is *the politics* of
discourse. To see rhetoric in this light is especially important in the
case of the literary discourse, where the ideological mystification

* A slightly altered version of the following analysis has been published separately:
"'That glib and oylie art': Cordelia and the rhetoric of antirhetoric," *Versus: Quaderni di
Studi Semiotici*, 16:5 (1977), 91–117.

(from the "left" as well as from the "right") of the political structure has been, and still is, the dominant trend.

To be sure, the politics of literature has some peculiar features—to be emphasized later—that distinguish it from the politics of other types of discourse. But is it necessary to warn that I am *not* speaking here of politics in the traditional sense—that is, politics as a crude admixture of behavioral descriptions and ideological statements indirectly connected to squabbles among parties?

To study rhetoric as the politics of discourse means to implement rhetorics as a scientific discipline; whereas generally (and, of course, with remarkable exceptions) the rhetorical structure of the text has not even been reached yet. In its place, its ideological superstructure (that can *indifferently* be labeled "style" or "content") is discussed; with rhetoric thus overwhelmed by ideology, the kind of rhetorics that is performed can only function at an ideological, prescientific, stage.

But what is the place of the fair Cordelia in all this intellectual turmoil? Actually, it is an important one, right in the midst of things, for she is not too frail to shoulder the burden of a political fight— especially since (as noted) the fight transcends her, as it transcends her sisters, and any other character in the tragedy; she is "spoken by" a certain rhetorical strategy.

In fact the whole scene is, as a discourse, built upon the contrast between two divergent rhetorical strategies: one established by the king, with such an explicit gesture that the rhetoric of the play gives way for a moment to the metalanguage of rhetorics, the other embodied in Cordelia's speeches.

Things are not what they seem: this homely formulation of dialectic is particularly apt here, since a close examination of the actual rhetorical struggle reverses the roles that the piety of moralistic criticism has traditionally assigned. The "bad" sisters embody, in fact, a frank and straightforward rhetorical approach. They follow instructions, and they are sincere; yes, sincere, in the only serious sense that this word can have applied to any discourse—namely, their rhetorical performance conforms to the explicitly established pattern, so that the resulting discourse fits consistently in the larger frame. But—the objection is perhaps inevitable—they lie. Deep down, they do not mean what they say! To which one must reply: who is to establish this, what can (at this time and age) such a complacent confirmation of a black-and-white metaphysics still tell us that really helps us in deciphering the discourse?

The relevant conflict is not one between surface and depth (and—for all its correct disclaimers as to the technical nature of this imagery—transformational-generative grammar has contributed to a revival of this simplistic opposition, in the language of literary criticism); everything takes place on the surface, insofar as we as human speakers are concerned, because everything that is expressed in language is—by the very nature of language—brought to the surface. What, if anything, lies behind this surface can be reached only by nondiscursive means. The ancient parallelism between "discursive" and "rational" as equivalent attributes is preserved, but with a significant qualification, in the context of this research. What is proposed here, in fact, is nothing so sunny and optimistic as the idea that human discourse, insofar as it is intrinsically and fully rational, reflects Truth. Rather, the concept is proposed that the only rationality that can be attained is the "superficial," stylized, modestly topical ("commonplace") rationality implemented by human discourse. As for a merely possible fuller rationality, it can be reached only by those who are bold enough to forsake the frail rationality of discourse, and plunge into silence.

Back to Cordelia, now, back to the "good" sister, who is insincere, if we look at the real politics of the discourse (over and against its ideology). For she embodies (I am, to repeat, speaking here not of a "character" but of a point through which a certain strategy pierces, in the texture of this particular discourse)—she embodies a different rhetorical strategy, one that implies a violation of the framework established by the king. This violation, however, is a local one; but she presents this local, and after all modest, change in strategy as if it were a bold gesture of total purification—a cleansing of speech from all hypocrisy, a flight beyond rhetoric. Thus Cordelia exploits the nostalgia of all of us, the hypocritical readers, for a utopic world of complete sincerity; and why shouldn't the common reader believe this rosy lie when the professional reader (the critic) misleads him into thinking that such a utopia is a real possibility?[13]

It is high time to present an analysis, however sketchy, of this discourse, that will anticipate the structure of the rheme. In accordance with what was indicated above—the text as a unitary structure does not exist; it is merely a family of (more or less strictly) related dialects—I will quote this discourse as it has come down to us in the textual dialect of the "First Folio" of 1623.

At the level of Inventio the dominant rhematic structure is established by the kind (no senility, or madness, or primitive, childlike naiveté, or some other such psychological figment, here!):

> Lear   . . . Tell me my daughters
> (Since now we will diuest vs both of Rule,
> Interest of Territory, Care of State)
> Which of you shall we say doth loue vs most,
> That we, our largest bountie may extend
> Where Nature doth with merit challenge, *Gonerill*,
> Our eldest borne, speake first. (1. 1. 46–52 [= p. 773])

One of the cells in any rheme is constituted by the semiotic context. In the present case, this context is structured as one of the three basic genres of speech identified in the Aristotelian classification quoted above: namely, the epideictic one (*epideiktikón*), i.e. (in the translation I suggest), speech of *display*; and this very gesture casts the king in the role of critical observer, whose task is to judge the value of the various performances of this type (he is *tēs dunámeos ho theōrós*). Moreover, Lear as *theōrós* also thematizes this general epideictic content, by specifying for it the topos of Size and Division. Goneril adheres to this framework. What item will she choose now, out of the class generally indicated by this topos?

> Gon.   Sir, I loue you more then word can weild ŷ matter,
> Deerer then eye-sight, Space, and libertie,
> Beyond what can be valewed, rich or rare,
> No lesse then life, with grace, health, beauty, honor:
> As much as Childe ere lou'd, or Father found.
> A loue that makes breath poore, and Speech vnable,
> Beyond all manner of so much I loue you.
> Cor.   What shall *Cordelia* speake? Loue, and be silent. (ibid.,
> 53–61)

As we see, Goneril chooses that dialectic component of the topos of Size and Division that exploits a positive comparison of sizes; and, at the level of Elocutio, this component is implemented as a Hyperbole

(see Lausberg, *Handbuch der literarischen Rhetorik*, 1960 [henceforth
HR]: pars. 579, 909–10); moreover, she puts this Hyperbole in the
frame of the figure of Adynaton (beginning: "I loue you more then
word can weild ŷ matter," and ending: "A loue that makes breath
poore, and Speech vnable,"—a rhetorical confession of rhetorical im-
potence). The phenomenology and definition of this figure are still
problematic (cf. some indications in Canter 1930, Fucilla 1936, and
Dutoit 1936), but I will provisionally accept this syncretistic definition: "A stringing together of impossibilities. Sometimes, a confession
that words fail us" (Lanham 1968:2). Of course, what is relevant here
is the second aspect of the definition.

As any other figure, this does not mark an invention for the nonce,
an individual *écart* (for we must not confuse the type with the token—
the figure with its specific realization), but a deeply rooted structure,
both (so to speak) phylogenetically and ontogenetically—that is, endowed with a long chain of historical antecedents and with deep roots
in the unconscious performance of everyday, nonliterary (often also
nonliterate) speech.[14]

I did not cut my quote at the end of Goneril's speech, but included
also Cordelia's first utterance in the play, in order to show concretely
what I mean when I speak of rhetoric talking through the single
speakers, and of discourse as overriding the characters. In fact, at
this point in the development of the dramatic discourse (a point that
is crucial, as all opening moves are), and at this basic level of rhetoric,
there is no difference between Goneril and Cordelia: they are speaking, in every sense of the word, the same language. So much so, that
Cordelia takes up the figure Adynaton that Goneril has just introduced (thus, the systematic class in the rheme remains the same), although she inflects it differently—as an item within the class—by expressing it in the form of the figure Dubitatio; that is, instead of
addressing the king directly, Cordelia addresses the public, in an "a
parte," pretending incertitude—for Dubitatio takes place "cum si-
mulamus quaerere nos, unde incipiendum, ubi desindendum, quid
potissime dicendum" ['when we pretend to ask whence to begin,
where to end, what preferably to say'] (thus Quintilian; see *HR*: pars.
776–78). The discourse now speaks through the other sister:

> *Reg.*   I am made of that selfe-mettle as my Sister,
>   And prize me at her worth. In my true heart,

> I finde she names my very deede of loue:
> Onely she comes too short, that I professe
> My selfe an enemy to all other ioyes,
> which the most precious square of sense professes,
> And find I am alone felicitate
> In your deere Highnesse loue.
>
> Cor.   Then poore *Cordelia*,
> And yet not so, since I am sure my loue's
> More ponderous then my tongue. (68–77)

The basic ways of realizing a Hyperbole syntactically are (and I re-phrase here some of the definitions recorded in the quoted *IIR* 909–10, modifying Lausberg's distinction, which does not seem per-suasive): Metaphor, Similitudo, and Comparatio. Goneril has used (within the frame of the Adynaton) a mixture of Similitudo and Com-paratio; Regan decides to remain within the same thematic perspec-tive—that is, to implement the same aspect of the same topos, and, through the same figure, Hyperbole. But her problem, then, is that of achieving a realization of the rheme that is distinct enough from the preceding one; what she does is to leave Adynaton aside, discard Similitudo, and concentrate on Comparatio, in the form that Italian grammar calls *comparativo di maggioranza*; and this she does on two successive comparative constructions—with respect to her sister's dis-course, and with respect to the affections and joys of the world in general. In both these cases, she specifies that her feelings for her father are stronger: stronger than any other feelings, for anything or anybody else (" . . . I professe/My selfe an enemy to all other ioyes . . . ").

Once again, Cordelia's utterance does not stand by itself, but con-stitutes an integral part of the preceding discourse. Apparently it is simply a repetition of her preceding statement: an Adynaton couched in the form of a Dubitatio. But in reality, something has happened in between—Regan's move—that has changed the situation. I do not know whether it has even been remarked that, even if Cordelia were ready to go along with her sisters' rhetorical strategy, it would be very difficult, not to say impossible, for her to do so, for their accumula-tion of Hyperboles leaves her practically no room to move. Hyper-bole, let us remember, is one of the figures that are most exposed to grotesque—as the ancient rhetoricians with their masterful insights into the actual functioning of language, did not fail to note (e.g.,

Quintilian recorded in *HR loc. cit.*: "pervenit haec res frequentissime ad risum" ['this thing very frequently leads to laughter']). Thus, even if, for the sake of discussion we accept the category of "evil," summarily applied by critical ideology to this contrast, we see that the evil here is subtler than in the usual interpretation, which blames the sisters for their flattery: actually, their rhetorical strategy is at the same time an indirect attack on Cordelia's own—an attempt to crowd her out of the discourse. But, if this maneuver is lost on a criticism that has substituted vague psychological notions for rhetorical analysis, it is not lost on Cordelia, as we are going to see.

Cordelia (or rather, the mature Renaissance rhetoric of which she is a mouthpiece) realizes that the matter is much more complex than going a step beyond Regan, who is already a step beyond Goneril—for there do not seem to be any more steps left, if one does not want to slip into clumsiness. Indeed, it would be useful and cognitively pertinent (if space did not forbid it) to try and delineate the general rhetorical shape of the speech that Cordelia might have produced had she accepted her father's and her sisters' rhetorical strategy. It would *not* be an otiose game (and, at any rate, I am not speaking of an imitation of Elizabethan English, but of the general—semiotic-semantic—shape of the rhetorical structure); rather, it would be a scholarly contribution to *experimental rhetoric* as the counterpart of experimental syntax; that is, to the experimenting with optional deformations of syntactic units—especially, syntactic units larger than the sentence—in order to establish which ones are acceptable, which ones lead to obligatory reformulations, and which ones are agrammatical (or have a very low degree of grammaticalness), in various languages and literary periods (for experimental syntax, cf. proposals and references in Pike and Pike 1972*a* and 1975, a specific experiment in Valesio 1976*b*). Experimental rhetoric, then, would de-form and re-form various rhetorical strategies, stretching to the limit the resources of a given linguistic code.

But since this cannot be done here, let us consider the linguistic material that we actually have at our disposal—and that turns out to be quite interesting in its own right. Cordelia's utterance, in its apparent simplicity, is ambiguous: on one dimension, she is reiterating her previous statement; but on the other dimension, she is hinting at what will be her own rhetorical strategy. In other words, the message she is really giving us (if we strain our ears to listen, over the moral-istic rhetoric of innocence that critical tradition has dinned into our ears) is, essentially, this: Regan's bringing the Hyperbole to its ex-treme development does not leave me any choice but to violate the constraints they have been accepting tacitly; actually, I want to do the reverse of what they have been doing, since it seems I cannot steal the limelight by stepping higher on their "ladder" (the etymology of Climax is, for once, useful and revealing and—exceptionally—the current meaning in English directly reflects its technical meaning in rhetorics). In this case (let us imagine Cordelia still speaking—with a critical device well used by Burke 1951 and 1964), I will draw dra-matic attention to myself by abruptly breaking this particular thread, and making the Climax crumble into an Anticlimax, and I will turn my sisters' verbal weapons against them.

In order to accomplish this, Cordelia—i.e., Cordelia's strategy ("Then *Hamlet* does it not, *Hamlet* denies it:/Who does it then? His Madnesse?")—exploits a component of the figure of Hyperbole that is present in the tradition, but is rarely (indeed, it seems, almost never) recognized and exploited: that the movement of hyperbole does not have to take place always upwards, but may also point low down. In other terms, hyperbole can manifest itself as an intensifica-tion of the "negative" semantic features of the linguistic unit (in this case, the complex of sentences designating the women's affection to-ward their father) involved.[15]

Thus a downward hyperbole is suddenly opposed to the upward one—the best strategy, it appears, to recreate drama and excitement; *now* the limelight is on Cordelia!

Lear	. . . What can you say, to draw
	A third, more opilent then your Sisters? Speake.
Cor.	Nothing my Lord.
Lear	Nothing?
Cor.	Nothing.
Lear	Nothing will come of nothing, speake againe.
Cor.	Vnhappie that I am, I cannot heaue
	My heart into my mouth: I loue your Maiesty
	According to my bond, no more nor lesse. (84–92)

The importance of this case for the general theory of rhetoric devel-oped here is that it shows the close interrelationship among the vari-

ous constituents of the rheme. Apparently Cordelia introduces a
variation only at the level of Elocutio, and then only by changing the
realization of the figure as a specific item (or, token), leaving the gen- .
eral type of the figure and—a fortiori, it would seem—all the rest,
intact. But the continuing fascination of the scene (its shocking force,
which continues to work on us) shows that the actual situation is more
complex: this modification in the elocutional realization of a single
item has consequences deeper down (or up, according to the imagery
one prefers)—that is, at the level of Inventio, changing the aspect of
the Topos of Size and Division that is relevant here, and consequently
changing the relevant semiotic context.

Indeed, what is chosen is the dialectic opposite of the element in
the topos required by the king and dutifully performed by the elder
sisters—and this destroys the encomiastic context. But Cordelia is not
satisfied: now she moves in for the kill. She has already managed, as
we have just seen, to become the center of attention, outshining her
rivals; now, she proceeds to hold forth longer than they did (how
many critics have pointed out that Goneril's and Regan's speeches—
these allegedly corrupt exhibitions—are in fact quite short statements?).

In doing this, Cordelia shows her hand, to a point; that is, she begins to develop her political strategy—the all-or-none move that is
enough to strike ("the Order, the Secret, and the Kill" quoted above),
and that the poet has described elsewhere with brilliant concision
when Brutus—advising against making Cicero a party to the con-
spiracy against Caesar—explains: "For he will neuer follow any thing/
That other men begin" (2. 1 [= p. 705 of the fascimile]).

Cordelia does not accept the semiotic, *and political*, context of her
sisters; and here we are at the delicate junction between the inner
politics of the text as such—that is, rhetoric—and the traditional,
"real-world" politics to which the general semiotic context of the play
points. She will not, then, share with them: rather, she sets herself up
as a total alternative. First, she explicitly attacks her competitors (note
that her sisters do not attack Cordelia in their speeches to the king,
now or later):

    Cor.   Good my Lord,
           You haue begot me, bred me, lou'd me.
           I returne those duties backe as are right fit,

Obey you, Loue, and most Honour you.
Why haue my Sisters Husbands, if they say
They loue you all? Happily when I shall wed,
That Lord, whose hand must take my plight, shall carry
Halfe my loue with him, half my Care, and Dutie,
Sure I shall neuer marry like my Sisters. (94–102)

We do not need the addition from another textual dialect (that of the Quartos) to the last quoted line, "To love my father all," in order to understand (to use the Dantesque cliché) the poison in her argument (indeed, it is difficult to credit the quoted gloss to Shakespeare, because it gives away the rhetorical move, whose efficacy lies in its indirectness, in favor of an oversimple symmetry with line 100, "They love you all").

That is: the hyperbole implies a semiotic framework where the participants in the speech act (listeners as well as speakers) accept the tension between a level of 'actual truth (alétheia)' (a conventional, stylized, not-ontologically-based-as-absolute truth; a truth, in short, not a Truth), and a 'lifting up' of it. And for this kind of alétheia, consider the ancient skeptic Anaesidemus, as quoted in Sextus Empiricus, who once said that the true (aléthés) is called thus "as a carry-over from the name" (pheronúmōs), that is, it is what "is not hidden from common opinion" (tò mè léthon tèn koinèn gnómen, cf. Stough 1969:94).[16]

Now, by discarding the upward-moving hyperbole, Cordelia kills the proverbial two birds with one stone: she shifts the attention away from her own device, the downward-moving hyperbole described above, and at the same time she manages to suggest that her sisters are lying about their feelings, either to their father or to their husbands. Next, she turns to her suitors and—assuming the dominant role of the king (isn't this an impressive proof of her political aggressiveness?)—she puts them to the test, by deploying her rhetorical strategy in all its ambition; nothing less will do than a rhetoric to end all rhetoric.

Cor. I yet beseech your Maiesty.
      If for I want that glib and oylie Art,
      To speake and purpose not, since what I will intend,
      Ile do't before I speake, that you make knowne,
      It is no vicious blot, murther, or foulenesse,
      No vnchaste action or dishonoured step
      That hath depriu'd me of your Grace and fauour,

But euen for want of that, for which I am richer,
A still soliciting eye, and such a tongue,
That I am glad I haue not, though not to haue it,
Hath lost me in your liking. (222–32[= p. 775])

By now, Cordelia has succeeded in expounding on her feelings much
longer than her sisters, *and* with a more elaborate rhetorical structure: for not only did she take up again, with a vengeance (*glib and
oylie; vicious blot, murther, or foulenesse; vnchaste action or dishonoured step;
your Grace and fauour*) the figure of synonymic dittology (completing
it, as we just saw, in one case to a "triptology," in another to a dittology
connecting two symmetrically constructed noun phrases—adjective
+ head in each case—rather than simply two words), that Goneril
had used more sparingly (two occurrences, although one of them is
long, and both are more than *di*ttologies: *eye-sight, space, and libertie;
life, with grace, health, beauty, honor*—cf., by the way, the list of the elements of happiness in the Aristotelian passage discussed above), and
soberly avoided by Regan (is any illusion still possible about the innocence of Cordelia's way of speaking?); but she is more perversely
"oylie" in her verbal performance, since—unlike her sisters in their
(by now) tame discourses—she has, twice, recourse to one of the most
ornate of figures, Oxymoron (from the Greek term *oksúmōron*).

This class—which may provisionally be defined as the "tightly-knit
syntactic linking of conflicting concepts in one unit, that therefore
comes to support a stretch of strongly contrasting elements" (see *HR*:
par. 807, with examples like *un cruel secours*, 'a cruel help') is specifically realized, in the passage just quoted, first by the syntactic connection between the noun *want* and the adjective *richer*, respectively in
the adverbial relater-axis phrase *for want of that* and the relative clause
(*for which I am richer*) embedded into it (the lexical contrast is heightened by the background of syntactico-semantic similarity—both
strings contain the preposition *for*, and with the same causal function—and even phonological similarity: the two forms immediately
following *for*, *want* and *which*, alliterate); then, by linking sentences
describing two indirectly conflicting concepts (her gladness on the
one side, her loss of her father's affection on the other) to two synonymic sentences describing one and the same entity—the fact that
she does not have the kind of "eye" and "tongue" that go together
with the apparently scorned "Art."[17] These two items realizing the

class of oxymoron follow each other immediately; not only this, but they are further linked together because both clusters are extended qualifications of one and the same phrase: *A still soliciting eye, and such a tongue.* Finally, it should not be passed under silence that, while until now the rhetoric had been confined to a description of *thoughts* and *feelings* with no mention of physical attributes, here Cordelia introduces the *visual* element ("Still soliciting eye"); and she does this as a devious stab, presenting a caricature—with a faintly whorish connotation—of her sisters' physical attitude during their speeches.

Simplicity, plain speech—where are they now? Where, indeed, have they ever been? But this rhetorical move of Cordelia is not only an attack on her sisters-rivals, it is also a test of the political acumen of her suitors. The King of France immediately understands what is at stake, while at the same time perceiving that his competitor does not grasp the importance of what is quickly developing—so he allows himself the luxury of offering Cordelia to the Duke of Burgundy:

> My Lord of *Burgundy*
> What say you to the Lady? Loue's not loue
> When it is mingled with regards, that stands
> Aloofe from th'intire point, will you haue her?
> She is herself a Dowrie. (236–40)

This is a taunt, a play on the ambiguity of the last-quoted statement. The easier interpretation (on which the rhetoric of antirhetoric relies in order to attain its effect) is the metaphoric one: the virtues of Cordelia, her spiritual advantages, constitute her dowry, offsetting the need for a dowry of money and land. But at another level, this utterance is actually a metonymy: that is, what this statement really means—in the politics of this discourse (that we reach, as always, only when we have rent the veil of ideology)—is that Cordelia, by virtue of her all-or-nothing strategy (that makes her, as of this moment, the most serious candidate to the inheritance of Lear's power) has a weight analogous to that of her sisters, who bring an already sanctioned chunk of power to their respective husbands. But the Duke does not understand the suggestion—thereby giving the reader the vicarious pleasure of feeling morally superior, and thus making this reader (who is not sufficiently a "hypocrite") forget that *he*, too, is missing the real point.

The Duke wants to play it safe, to stick to what is sure; thus he stations himself in the middle of the road (he will marry Cordelia with "that portion" that was originally planned)—and thus he loses his chance, and offers Cordelia an excellent opportunity of echoing the statement of the French King, thus aligning herself with him and furthering her political strategy:

> *Cor.*   Peace be with *Burgundie*,
> Since that respect and Fortunes are his loue,
> I shall not be his wife. (246–48)

Here again, we notice how the discourse envelops and transcends the single characters, who influence each other's speech: Cordelia's *respect* is the response to the cue offered by "France" with his *regards* (the point is not essentially changed if we accept the reading *respects of fortune* of the Quartos—cf. Furness 1965:35–36). Her maneuver is rewarded by the king in the immediately following lines:

> *Fra.*   Fairest Cordelia, that are most rich being poore,
> Most choice forsaken, and most lou'd despis'd,
> Thee and thy vertues here I seize vpon,
> Be it lawfull I take vp what's cast away.
> ....(249–52)

It is now France that "seizes upon" Cordelia's cue; and he does more than respond to Cordelia's two complicated oxymoronic items with three simple ones. What he does is to establish a *general* oxymoron, a conglomerate that will become one of the dominant images of late-Romantic and Victorian narrative and will survive, in the literature of the Feuilleton, until today (it is still one of the basic strategies in the rhetoric of the Italian *fotoromanzi*). Suffice it to think of apparently naive charm, actually powerful in its almost morbid erotic implication, that the "Most choice forsaken, and most lou'd despis'd" figure will give to many of Dickens' unassuming heroines (the coy narrator in *Bleak House*, for instance).

But I digress; for Cordelia is still not finished—she now turns directly to her sisters, and makes clear that the political contrast between her and them is not a new development, made on the spur of the moment:

Cor.   The Iewels of our Father, with wash'd eies
      Cordelia leaues you, I know you what you are,
      And like a Sister am most loth to call
      Your faults as they are named. Loue well our Father:
      To your professed bosomes I commit him,
      But yet alas, stood I within his Grace,
      I would prefer him to a better place,
      So farewell to you both. (267–74)

Finally, in her last utterance in this scene, she intimates that this is but the beginning of her strategy:

Cor.   Time shall vnfold what plighted cunning hides,
      Who couers fault, at last with shame derides:
      Well may you prosper. (279–81)

It is time to sum up. This illustration has served two main purposes: to make clear—in a definitive way, I hope, and completing the insights gained in the analysis of the Savonarola and Montaigne passages—how discourses that affect a plain and candid opposition to rhetoric ornament are in themselves a subtle and deceitful form of rhetoric; and how—once the veil of ideology is pierced (in this case, what is at issue is the moralistic ideology of the allegedly simple speech straightforwardly translating the movements of the heart—the able mystification, in short, that will triumph in the following century with Rousseau)—the rhetorical structure is seen to constitute the bones and sinews, or rather the biological structure, of the text. In other words, the rhetorical structure constitutes the real politics of the text—the only kind of politics that is really relevant to its interpretation; the other kind—the politics of external relationships between the text as message and its social background, the "reality of the times" that historicism in its various shapes is so fond of evoking—being only a thin disguise for ideology, and as such the province of those master-ideologues, the traditional literary critics.

Let me be more precise on this latter point with reference to the chosen example. The politics of this scene—that sets the tone for the whole political background of the play—is the politics of the conflict between two rhetorics, both aiming at a transition of power that cannot be anything less than the dispossession of a ruler who has become too old and weak to keep his kingdom together. Both rhetorical

strategies (that embodied in Cordelia as well as that realized through
the two elder sisters) agree not only in this ultimate aim, but also in
their general outline: that is, both are implemented as rhetoric
through their discarding the immediacy of a direct, crude assertion
(but is anything like this at all possible?) and through their conveying
their message in an oblique way: so oblique, indeed, that while one of
the strategies has been revealed and understood the other has re-
mained, by and large, hidden. The similarity here between the
dramatist's strategy and the strategy of a military leader is impressive:
the "enemy" (the audience as potential enemy, the reader as a judge
to be feared and coaxed) is led to a partial success that deludes him
into thinking that he has won (we think that we are wise and moral
because we blame Goneril and Regan, because we "see through" their
scheming)—while the bulk of the army has been lying in ambush
(thus, we go home or close the book satisfied, not realizing that Cordelia's scheming has escaped us).

However, the similarities between the two strategies stop at the general level that has just been described, and beyond that one must (as
I tried to do above) distinguish as clearly as possible two different
strategies—or, perhaps more exactly, two divergent tactics. The Gon-
eril/Regan tactic is one of simple opportunism (a term used here in a
technical sense, not as a simplistic ethical label): they accept the semiotic framework established by the king, conforming to it with their
discourse; and their political behavior at large is the consequence of
this textual politics: each in turn borrows her slice of power and then
proceeds, working from within, to transform these borrowings into
permanent acquisitions. All the while their rhetoric is one of encom-
ium, of idyllic assertion.

Cordelia's strategy, on the other hand, is one of open confrontation: she rejects the semiotic system that the king tries to force on her
as on the other sisters, and she develops (as we saw) a rhetoric of
moralism, of pretended disgust for those very weapons that she is
handling with consummate skill. Here, too, the politics in the "world"
parallels the politics in the text. For this is a clear instance of *reculer
pour mieux sauter*: by setting herself up against her father, Cordelia is
saying that she does not want a slice of the kingdom—she is getting
ready to take it all; at the end, she will disembark at Dover with the
French army. The tragedy in this play, then, is a clearly—I dare say,

a brutally—political one. The tragedy is that none of the three factions (the king, Goneril and Regan, Cordelia) succeeds in its intent, and the scepter falls from their grip after *all* of them have scrambled in blood and desperation to conquer it.

We have seen the link between the politics of the text and the politics of society that the former evokes; is there no other dimension of life evoked by this discourse? Of course there is another dimension: the politics of the text (any text) cannot help entailing a politics of eros, in addition to the politics of society. To say "eros" is not a genteel way of escaping the necessity to call a spade a spade—it is not simply a more learned way of saying: the politics of sex. For, as I have tried to show, characters in a dramatic discourse are essentially ideological constructs. And if, in reality, there are no characters, we cannot speak simplistically of sex—a word that inevitably carries the connotation of material relationship between consenting (here, perhaps, reluctant) adults.

The virulent ambiguity of the erotic politics at work here has emerged already at two different points in the quoted discourse—and both are utterances by Cordelia. "Why haue my Sisters Husbands, if they say/They loue you all?" and she has hinted at the "still soliciting eye" that they show. There is, in these utterances, more than the gusto for scoring points in a debate (and in any case rhetoric is, of course, always more than this): an almost uxorial jealousy speaks here (or whispers, fighting the temptation to shriek shamelessly), that is the dark, obstinate core of the erotic politics throughout the discourse. "Through every wail or gust of this awful symphony of madness, ingratitude, and irony, we feel a woman's breath" writes a critic quoted in Furness 1965:97; I agree, while being aware that behind this agreement lies a complete disagreement as to the nature of that "woman's breath." Thus the social politics and the erotic politics make up the rhetorical network holding together the strategy of this discourse.[18]

So much for the second point in my summing up; now for the first. A study of the rhetoric of antirhetoric such as the one just presented has a strategic importance for the theory of rhetoric. In fact, if I have (as I hope) succeeded in showing that even the type of discourse that is explicitly contrary to rhetoric and tries to detach itself from its mechanism is completely under the sway of rhetoric, that it is actually more sophisticated and devious than the rhetoric from which it pretends to shy away, I have considerably strengthened my contention that rhetoric is coextensive with human discourse and it is no more possible to speak without being rhetorical than it is to live without breathing.

But there is another, more technical, aspect for which this study of (apparent) antirhetoric is important—and this has to do with the notion of iconicity, that will be treated in chapter 4 as a specific topos. Here, I confine myself to noting that the main flaw in the debate about the iconic element in language has (except for Valesio 1969*b*) been its black-and-white quality, with some scholars strongly asserting and others flatly denying the presence of this element in language.

What is needed is a comprehensive view of the dialectic tension between the iconic and the anti-iconic tendency in the functioning of human discourse. The passages that I have just examined offer us an excellent illustration of the latter force at work. They are anti-iconic because, as we saw, their linguistic structure (including the lexical component) is finely wrought, while their basic semantic content is a strong assertion in favor of plain, unadorned speech. It is an assertion that either tacitly presupposes the idea that the very discourse embodying it is an example of such plain speech (as with the Savonarola and the Montaigne passages), or explicitly presents itself as a model of chastely unadorned communication (as is the case with Cordelia's speech—hence its special importance).

In short, the form of these speeches contradicts their substance. I do not think it an excessive claim to say that this very fact is a good proof, *a contrario*, that a strong iconic tendency exists in language. In fact, we are struck by this contrast, and feel that (whatever the intentions of the author) there is something objectively ironic about it, because in general *we expect iconicity*; in this case, we expect a congruence between the ideas advocated and the form in which they are advocated. But these speeches are an embodiment of what they are warning us against; they "speake and purpose not." To put it more precisely, in terms of the rheme as the basic structure: iconicity means congruence, collaboration between the given topos or cluster of topoi (at the level of Inventio) and the syntactico-lexical structure at the level of Elocutio; anti-iconicity, on the other hand, points to a tension between these two levels.

Chapter III

RHETORIC, IDEOLOGY, AND DIALECTIC

3.1 THE ROCK BOTTOM

Identifying the regional ontology of rhetoric means, then, abandoning the too-simple position according to which all that is not logical is rhetorical, and all that is not rhetorical is logical. But even if it were true (as, in a sense, it is) that "it is quite possible to analyze almost anything in Western culture (and perhaps in all cultures) in terms of its relationship to the logical and rhetorical poles" (Ong 1971:7), it seems too easy a way out to acquiesce in the same author's next observation that "Needless to say, there is no total theoretical statement of the nature of either rhetoric or logic, much less of their interrelation."

In fact, it is high time to provide such a statement if we want to put some order in the linguistic analyses that proliferate today, and to illuminate their various implications; and, though it would be presumptuous to claim that what is being offered here is anything like a "total" statement, yet it is toward completeness that we must strive.

The preceding characterization of the ontology of rhetoric, sketchy as it was, should have been sufficient to show what the real "enemy" of rhetoric is: not logic but ideology. If the struggle had been between rhetoric and logic, it would not have raged with such a continuity and force; but it did, and still continues to do so, because rhetoric is more or less clearly perceived as a threat to the assurance that any ideological system requires and confirms—and this perception is quite correct.

61

Any ideology assumes that, while truth and the other basic values (goodness, beauty, etc.) are nonlinguistic in nature, they can be faithfully expressed by language *provided it is used correctly*. Disputes arise, as can easily be predicted, on the criteria of correctness, for every different ideological system claims its own; but their basic agreement—which is what is crucial here—lies in their view of language as something whose structure is constituted only by what is technically required to transmit messages. Thus, the basic flaw of all ideologies consists in their pretending to use language as their neutral vehicle, as if language (at this level) were not already "ideologized"; ideologized, to be sure, not in the sense of being in itself the expression of certain ideas or ideals, but in the more prosaic (and, to the empirical student, more exciting) sense of being at every point shaped and slanted according to specific argumentative structures.

The ontology of rhetoric is at the rock bottom where all ontologies dissolve. Since language cannot be used except in a rhetorical framework, and since this framework reduces all choices to formal choices, there is never a real *adaequatio* between referents and linguistic forms. This explains the crudeness of any ideology and, on the other hand, the (so to speak) ascetic nature of any rhetorical analysis when it is pursued radically and consistently—no matter if the misleading appearances are those of frivolity. For we cannot completely divest ourselves of ideological assumptions, and thus the first victims of a rhetorical analysis are often our own beliefs.

I read, for instance, in a context for which I feel a technical solidarity (it is the discourse of a linguist) and an ideological sympathy (it is a critique, in a progressive perspective, of political and social jargon in the United States today):

> I have tailored my definition of truth to fit what speakers mean to have understood. Within a social setting, any other definition is a game. . . . I'll go a step farther and say that when two parties are in communication, anything that may be used which clogs the channel, and is not the result of accident, is a lie. (Bolinger 1973)

Honest, straightforward, but inadequate to the complexity of human discourse. For, unfortunately, this tailoring will not do: such a definition (aside from the difficulty of distinguishing what is accidental from what is not) would do little more than to reduce all linguistic usage to the status of a lie; not a bad formulation, perhaps, especially in order to puncture the unrealistic solemnity of pronouncements about Truth, but still not a real step forward. How much more realistic at any rate is the following, written (and this should make us pause) a century earlier:

> What, then, is truth? A mobile army of metaphors, metonyms, and anthropomorphisms—in short, a sum of human relations, which have been enhanced, transposed, and embellished poetically, and which after long use seem firm, canonical, and obligatory to a people: truths are illusions about which one has forgotten that this is what they are; metaphors which are worn out and without sensuous power; coins which have lost their pictures and now matter only as metal, no longer as coins.

To be sure, we should not (in a hasty homage to cultural fads) misuse this glittering Nietzschean sliver (from a posthumously published fragment of 1973 which has experienced a revival of sorts and whose title is significant: "On truth and lie in an extra-moral sense"—see Kaufmann 1975:46–47). Appreciations like this are really fruitful only if they are soberly and systematically developed; that is the task attempted here, in the humble awareness that we still have to respond to the challenge implicitly posited by Aristotle—the challenge, that is, to develop a contemporary theory of rhetoric as fully articulated as the one he put together. (For the full references to this fragment by Nietzsche, and to another one strictly related to it, cf. p. 76 of the faintly scholastic review by Keane 1975; see also Wilcox 1974).

I. A. Richards, at a chronological point almost halfway between the allusive, curt intelligence of Nietzsche's statement and the illuministic oversimplifications of contemporary linguistics, had already recognized that it is not a question of clear-cut contrast between truthful, plain speech and so-called deceitful, sophisticated, artful discourse: "For in the topics with which all generally interesting discussion is concerned, words must shift their meanings." And his exhortation is toward a full-fledged analysis of these shifts, which "recur in the same forms with different words; they have similar plans and common patterns. . . .We may reasonably hope that systematic study will in time permit us to compare, describe and explain the systematic ambiguity or transference patterns on a scale much surpassing our best present-day Dictionary Technique" (1936:72–73). And yet, *plus ça change. . . .*It is amazing to see how persistent the rhetorical complaints about rhetoric are (but it is not really so amazing, after the analyses above, which showed the strategic functions served by these apparent flights out of rhetoric). For instance, Booth 1965 repeats, without making the link with Richards, some of the criticisms more cogently expressed in the above-quoted text, and goes on in a tone of moralistic deprecation that, as shown, had already been objectively transcended in the thirties. Much graver, to my mind, as an example of an acritical acceptance of a rather crude rhetoric of antirhetoric is the undeserved consideration that surrounds the superficial statement in Orwell 1950, which has continued to appear in anthologies.

A different problem is posited by those statements where what is at issue is not the rhetoric of antirhetoric but another aspect discussed above (and indirectly connected to the former), namely the idea that there is, so to speak, something like a plain rhetoric; that is, rhetoric is taken seriously and no longer blamed as a travesty of straightforward linguistic communication. But the price paid for this is too high: rhetoric is treated in the same simplistic way that we found inadequate for linguistic communications at large. Rhetoric, we are told, has to do with truth (a step forward then, with respect to the negative view of rhetoric as exalting untruth); but this nexus is defined in the acritical way that has been already critized, as if, in this time and age, we could really speak simply of "a correspondence between the realities of the objective world and the equivalent verbal statement. The scientist and orator work to achieve this correspondence, their audience to accept or perchance to reject it" (Howell 1975:230–31)— where the final qualification ("perchance to reject it") essentially contradicts the initially stated "correspondence," because the problem would not arise if there were such a clear-cut correspondence.

The attempt to patch up this picture, nuancing it, is even worse than the original tableau, because it suggests that the only problem here is one of tinkering with details. Thus, we are told that "businessmen, lawyers, politicians, historians, and scientific writers" can sometimes confuse rather than clarify "the realities with which they deal." They "sometimes speak before they have understood the facts, or they sometimes speak after they have misunderstood or ignored or distorted them, and in any of these instances they fail to achieve what

rhetoric exists to foster—the transfer of accurate evaluations of reality to an audience in such a way that, without needing to construe
them by analogy, the audience accepts them as direct guides to conduct and life" (Howell 1975:246). First of all (since the quoted book
claims historical orthodoxy and the continuity of tradition), it is necessary to note that this is *not* what rhetoric was supposed to be in the
Aristotelian tradition: what we are offered here is a heavily modified
version of the tradition, where Aristotle's message has been very
much watered down with heavy splashes of Platonic and Romantic
rhetoric (ibid., p. 245, Pater's declamations on truth as the essential
criterion of style are presented as the key modern contribution, and
linked to Plato's *Phaedrus*). In this connection, it is bizarre to find
(ibid., p. 42) the defensively ironic statement that "Burke gelded
rhetoric," where exactly the opposite is true: the gelding of rhetoric
is what is performed in these idyllic treatments, in which rhetoric
becomes simply another way to take the sting (and the interest) out
of any discussion of the relationships among language, literature, and
society. In the second place and finally, I hope that all the preceding
discussion has shown that, aside from the historical realism of this
picture, this definition of rhetoric is ontologically inadequate.

In order to have a full picture of the regional ontology of rhetoric
we need to be on our guard against what I propose to call the rationalistic fallacy. I hasten to note that every such fallacy is, to a certain
point, functional, that is, every fallacious approach to rhetorics is
functional as a *rhetoric*—where it fails is as rhetorics, because its view
of the rhetorical region is too partial and narrow, and it does not
maintain the appropriate critical distance from its object.

This approach—to put it very simply and briefly—reflects the idea
that rhetoric is merely the "counterpart" (*antístrophos*, as in the very
first sentence of Aristotle's treatise) of logical argumentation (the *dialektikē* of that same sentence). This is understandable within an irenic view of the world; a view, that is, that contemplates the full agreement of the various components within a unified hierarchical system.
It is, in short, a philosophy devoid of dialectic (in one of the versions
of this concept that follow in the wake of Hegel). The intellectualistic
ontology of Aristotle, which is adialectic (in this modern sense of the
word), cannot but represent rhetoric as the counterpart of its own
rigid "dialectic." The contemporary theory of rhetoric, on the other

hand, must recognize that rhetoric is dialectical—more precisely (and we are going to see later the full extent of the identification) that rhetoric *is* dialectic. Rhetoric is the dimension of language where all cultural contrasts are revealed as conflicts that, however grave and serious, never hinge on absolute distinctions; they always, at a certain level, interchange and merge some of their elements.

What I have just given is, of course, a preliminary and informal characterization of one possible concept of dialectic. A discussion of dialectic once again?! I am afraid so; and (to give all the bad news right away), the following will be—more than a review of some accepted usages of this notion (although there will be some discussion to this effect), or the practical implementation of one of such usages—a basically new approach to the problem of dialectic. I will, however, move gradually; for the moment I will stick to this informal characterization, and I will not question the accepted meanings.

All that I am asking now is that the patient reader think of dialectic as the awareness of human culture viewed as contrast, where what is essential is the compenetration of opposite trends, views, statements; in such a way that each of these elements is, to a certain extent, imbued with the structure of its rival. What is particularly important here and must be salvaged is the implicit (but, in the context of this book, firm) refusal to take a stand: for dialectic is perhaps the most powerful weapon we can use against the continuous, subtle, pervasive assaults of ideology—while at the same time focusing our attention on the products of ideology, describing and analyzing them in detail. This, in fact, is the working definition of ideology that is at the horizon of my research: *ideology is decayed rhetoric—rhetoric that is no longer the detailed expression of strategies at work in specific discourses.* In other words, when rhetoric becomes detached from specific practices, it becomes ideology. When this happens, rhetoric loses its fluidity and becomes rigid, petrified in hypostases. For instance, what was a complex of discourse strategies comes to be ideologized into a text; what was a rhetorical procedure or complex of procedures is ideologized into a literary genre; and so on and so forth.

And as for dialectic, one of its basic ideological deformations is the obsessive search for conciliating the opposite elements (whatever they are in each particular case) in a higher synthesis; in the effort of devising tidy constructions of this sort, dialectic, ceasing to be a weapon

against ideology, becomes the victim of ideology. But we shall see below how deep this danger really is (so deep that it requires a radically
new definition of the scope of dialectic). For the moment, I confine
myself to referring to a text that seems to me to sum up beautifully
this concept of dialectic, both in its general import and in its particular relevance to rhetorical and literary structures: Diderot's *Le neveu
de Rameau*.[1]

Why is this dialogue of Diderot a brilliant realization of dialectic?
Because there a cultural contrast is explored at the same time as an
opposition and as an interpenetration of the opposite alternatives,
without any attempt to impose an external "solution," or "synthesis"
(ethical or cognitive) on this antinomy. Let us listen to Engels for a
moment, especially when he speaks about the "metaphysician," who

> thinks in absolutely irreconcilable antitheses. "His communication is
> 'yea, yea; nay, nay'; for whatsoever is more than these cometh of evil."
> For him a thing either exists or does not exist; a thing cannot at the
> same time be itself and something else. Positive and negative abso-
> lutely exclude one another; cause and effect stand in a rigid antithesis
> one to the other.
>   At first sight this mode of thinking seems to us very luminous, be-
> cause it is that of so-called sound common sense. Only sound common
> sense, respectable fellow that he is, in the homely realm of his own
> four walls, has very wonderful adventures directly he ventures into
> the wide world of research. (Engels 1935[1882]:46–47)

One of these adventures is the discovery that

> the two poles of an antithesis, positive and negative, *e.g.*, are as insep-
> arable as they are opposed, and that despite all their opposition, they
> mutually interpenetrate. And we find, in like manner, that cause and
> effect are conceptions that only hold good in their application to in-
> dividual cases; but as soon as we consider the individual cases in their
> general connection with the universe as a whole, they run into each
> other, and they become confounded when we contemplate that uni-
> versal action and reaction in which causes and effects are eternally
> changing places, so that what is effect here and now will be cause
> there and then, and *vice versa*. (ibid. 47–48)

The caustic style exemplified in these passages is still, today, a refreshing change from run-of-the-mill academic jargon, with its
phlegmatic rhetoric and its aping the manner of an imaginary gentle-

man. Yet the author is well aware that such a concept must be used with responsibility and caution; and he notes, about dialectic, that "to acknowledge this fundamental thought in words and to apply it in reality in detail to each domain of investigation are two different things" (ibid.). We will see presently the real extent of the difficulty, going much beyond what Engels seems to believe here. For the moment, we must be constantly on our guard for the innumerable avatars of that boring "respectable fellow," common sense, in literary criticism today—a survival that, of course, does not bespeak innocence or clumsiness, but rather the struggle against the attempt to clarify the real connections between analysis and ideology in criticism (a clarification without which no real progress is possible, no matter how fancy the jargon of linguistics, or of any other discipline, superficially applied to the critical work).

Even Diderot's dialogue, which I quote as one of the master realizations of this struggle against the delusions of common sense, does not escape this deadening manipulation. For instance, in the preface of a recent edition (Adam 1967:17) a hint at the difficulties of establishing who is *Moi* and who *Lui* in the dialogue is followed by this anticlimax: "Ce sont-là, malheureusement, purs jeux de dialecticiens, et la vérité est plus simple. Nous connaissons suffisamment, aujourd'hui, la vie du véritable Jean-François Rameau, et nous sommes assurés que Diderot n'a pas eu à regarder en lui-même pour imaginer le personnage de son dialogue. Il lui a suffi d'ouvrir les yeux." A strange way indeed of opening one's eyes at the complexity of the text! And the reference to dialectic as a "game" is one of the manifestations of the already-criticized moralistic rhetoric of antirhetoric.

On the other hand (and looking, now, in the opposite direction along the course of history), we should not overestimate the originality of Marx and Engels in the formulation of dialectical principles; and I do not mean their (acknowledged) dependence on Hegel—although here, too, revisions are necessary, for critics often follow the too nice and tidy version elaborated by Marx and Engels themselves— rather, I think of the pioneering formulations in the field of empirical literary analysis. I mention only one example, but there is ample field here for a critical history of ideas, and of literary criticism in particular.

The example on which I would like to dwell for a moment comes under the aegis of irony—a misleading term that, as we are going to see, still tends to obfuscate a proper understanding of dialectic. Thirlwall 1833 is a long and urbane essay on Sophocles that, as far as its full development is concerned, does not seem a memorable statement today. Yet its general framework (sketched at the beginning) is very remarkable, especially for such an early work: we find already, applied to the concrete analysis of literary texts, an essentially clear notion of dialectic—about thirty years before the "Anti-Dühring" elaborations of Engels and his "Introduction" to Socialism (1882). I must present a relatively lengthy quote to prove this point; starting with Thirlwall's statement of

> an universal law, which manifests itself, no less in the moral world than in the physical, according to which the period of inward languor, corruption, and decay, which follows that of maturity, presents an aspect more dazzling and commanding, and to those who look only at the surface inspires greater confidence and respect, than the season of youthful health, of growing but unripened strength. (1833:487)

More specifically:

> we observe, that, as all things human are subject to dissolution, so and for the same reason it is the moment of their destruction that to the best and noblest of them is the beginning of a higher being, the dawn of a brighter period of action. When we reflect on the colossal monarchies that have succeeded one another on the face of the earth, we readily acknowledge that they fulfilled the best purpose of their proud existence, when they were broken up in order that their fragments might serve as materials for new structures. (ibid.:489)

Isn't this, essentially, the vision of history that will become known as historical and dialectical materialism—the main difference residing in the style; here stately and phlegmatic, in the pioneers of Marxism, caustic and agitated (for important functional reasons)?

Consider this description, which closes in on the specific problems of a phenomenology of literary descriptions: "There is always a slight cast of irony in the grave, calm, respectful attention impartially bestowed by an intelligent judge on two contending parties, who are pleading their causes before him with all the earnestness of deep conviction, and of excited feelings." What follows is, objectively, an an-

ticipated critique of the sentimentality that still plagues literary criticism, especially the varieties written in English:

> What makes the contrast interesting is, that the right and the truth lie
> on neither side exclusively: that there is no fraudulent purpose, no
> gross imbecility of intellect, on either: but both have plausible claims
> and specious reasons to alledge, though each is too much blinded by
> prejudice or passion to do justice to the views of his adversary. For
> here the irony lies not in the demeanor of the judge, but is deeply
> seated in the case itself, which seems to favour each of the litigants,
> but really eludes them both. And this too it is that lends the highest
> degree of interest to the conflicts of religious and political parties.

Note the specification on the objective nature of this "irony"—against
any hurried imputations of simplistic psychological movements; "the
liveliest interest," he notes,

> arises when by inevitable circumstances, characters, motives, and
> principles are brought into hostile collision, in which good and evil
> are so inextricably blended on each side, that we are compelled to give
> an equal share of our sympathy to each, while we perceive that no
> earthly power can reconcile them.

Back to history, a review of its phenomena affords us

> a glimpse of the balance held by an invisible hand, which so nicely
> adjusts the claims of the antagonists, that neither is wholly trium-
> phant, nor absolutely defeated; each perhaps loses the object he
> aimed at, but in exchange gains something far beyond his hopes.
> (ibid.:489–90)

In a casuistic mood, we could be tempted to differentiate between a
"spiritualistic" or "idealistic" version and a "materialist" version, emphasizing that "invisible hand"; but I do not think it realistic to attribute such importance to this metaphor (and at any rate, the label of
"materialism" is every bit as ideological as the others).

   To be sure, in the following quote from *Ludwig Feuerbach and the
Outcome of Classical German Philosophy* by Engels the emphasis is on
men insofar as they "make their own history, whatever its outcome
may be, in that each person follows his own consciously desired end,
and it is precisely the resultant of these many wills operating in dif-

ferent directions and of their manifold effects upon the outer world that constitutes history" (1941:49). But what follows makes clear that we are far from the simplistic picture of an intellectualistic account; I quote it because I am not thinking here merely of history at large, but specifically of the application of this general picture to the particular case of *linguistic* history—the changes in linguistic structures, especially at the level of discourse:

> Thus it is also a question of what the many individuals desire. The will is determined by passion or deliberation. But the levers which immediately determine passion or deliberation are of very different kinds. Partly they may be external objects, partly ideal motives, ambition, "enthusiasm for truth and justice," personal hatred or even purely individual whims of all kinds. But . . . many individual wills active in history for the most part produce results quite other than those intended—often quite the opposite; . . . their motives, therefore, in relation to the total result are likewise of only secondary importance. . . . When . . . it is a question of investigating the driving powers which—consciously or unconsciously, and indeed very often unconsciously—lie behind the motives of men who act in history and which constitute the real ultimate driving forces in history, then it is not a question so much of the motives of single individuals, however eminent, as of those motives which set in motion great masses, whole peoples, and again whole classes of the people in each people; and this, too, not momentarily, for the transient flaring up of a straw-fire which quickly dies down, but for a lasting action resulting in a great historical transformation. (ibid:49–50)

What must be emphasized here is Engels' recognition of unconscious factors (the direction being that of Jung, as the context makes clear, rather than that of Freud; a whole field of research is to be explored here, which should take into account the psychology of the archetype, what is known as psychohistory, etc.). This program should excite linguists, it should give a broad view—beyond the quibbling over technicalities—of the task of historical linguistics:

> To ascertain the driving causes which here in the minds of acting masses and their leaders—the so-called great men—are reflected as conscious motives, clearly or unclearly, directly or in ideological, even glorified, form—that is the only path which can put us on the track of the laws holding sway both in history as a whole, and at particular periods and in particular lands. (ibid:50)

Why such a long quote, which may sound obvious to the philo-
sophically-minded reader and irrelevant to the person more interested in linguistic and literary analysis? Because these statements not
only seem to me as good an illustration of dialectic as one can find (in
that they show the vagueness of the concept, side by side with its
fruitfulness, and thus prepare us for a new critique of the notion);
but also because this description has still to be applied, in its full
force, to literary criticism (that, aware of the critical power of such an
approach, keeps trying to—so to speak—wiggle away from precise
applications) and to linguistics (which, for its part, seems not even to
be aware of the possibilities, rather than to be trying to avoid them—
a tactic that would at least show awareness).

In order to appreciate how statements like Engels' are probably the
strongest and broadest introduction to the real tasks of literary criticism, consider how pale—with respect to them—seem the indications
of even that critic who is among the closest to this tradition:

> People are neither animals nor machines (to be analyzed by the mi-
> gration of metaphors from biology or mechanics), but actors and ac-
> tees. They establish identity by relation to groups (with the result that,
> when tested by *individualistic* concepts of identity, they are felt to be
> moved by "deceptions" or "illusions," the "irrational"—for one's iden-
> tification as a member of a group is a role, yet it is the only active
> mode of identification possible, as you will note by observing how all
> *individualistic* concepts of identity dissolve into the nothingness of
> mysticism and the absolute). (Burke [1973:311])

I said that even these statements seem a little more flat than those
previously quoted; yet, what a difference between this identification
of the problems and the supercilious evasions of later literary criticism! Clearly, we must reestablish this link if we want to get out of the
ideological impasse of the criticism of literature today.

The view of language that rhetorics implies is the exact parallel to
the broad historical vision presented above: here, too, the basic question is not that of single individuals, but of general linguistic structures, and what is said there about the secondary question of motives—and the large role played by unconscious elements—is directly
pertinent to linguistic and "stylistic" research. When we come to this
realization—where the subtlety and majesty of linguistic structures *in
general*, of the literary language *as such*, finally makes its inroad—we

experience the same exhilarating feeling (a broadening of vistas, the view from the top of the mountain) that many historians and economists must have felt when the historical and dialectical criticism of the Hegelian tradition was making its presence felt.

But then the question arises: why do there not seem to have been any important consequences of this movement of ideas, as far as linguistics is concerned? The solemn accounts of the birth of structural linguistics (almost a century after this historical turmoil) should be reconsidered with more sobriety and coolness, for those ideas look rather tame and generic against this background. Such a large problem in the history of linguistics should be studied in detail, but only some broad lines can be presented here.

The general approach to language in its stylistic and rhetorical structuring never passed through that healthy period of scathing criticism to which historical, political, economic trends were exposed in the second half of the past century, between the "Economic and philosophic manuscripts" (Marx 1844), and the immediately following years: those of *The Holy Family* (see Marx–Engels 1845), *German Ideology* (see Marx–Engels 1845–46), *The Poverty of Philosophy* (cf. Marx 1847), etc. Linguistics never had this critique of idealism (even today, a pamphlet like Hall 1963—a superficial contribution by an otherwise meritorious scholar—is far from answering this need); and the result is that, several generations and one World War later, linguistics was caught (and to a large extent, is still caught) between the adialectic dichotomies of Saussure and the purely hortatory dialecticism that for a long time was represented (in Italy but not only in Italy) by the linguistic theorizing of Croce and Gentile.[2]

Rhetoric is crucial for a renovation of linguistic theory—which is the basic reason for this discussion of dialectic. Interestingly, in a recent review of some concepts of dialectic (the rather tame Prestipino 1972) rhetoric is used for one of the illustrations of the difference between "antagonistic contradictions" (where one of the two opposite directions of the process at issue tends to suppress the other) and "nonantagonistic contradictions" (where one of the two directions simply tends to separate from the other). Usually the nonantagonistic contradictions (or oppositions) are those that take place between elements in the superstructure. Yet it is possible to find antagonistic oppositions within the superstructure: "for instance, between rhetorical 'figures' and rationalized language (or 'natural' language—that tends to suppress rhetoric, although it does not succeed completely)" (ibid.).

This interesting example should, however, be discarded for at least two reasons. First of all, it is not clear why such an opposition should be defined as antagonistic rather than nonantagonistic (nor is the issue clarified by the author's qualification that what is involved here is an "antagonismo riflesso"). Secondly, and above all, we have already begun to see that there is no such thing as a nonrhetorical level of language (whatever we would like to call it: "razionalizzato," "neutral," "degré zéro," etc.). This last point, crucial as it is for the theory of rhetoric, does not constitute a refutation of dialectics as such; however, it is another indication of the vagueness that still plagues this concept, and it points out that one must be very cautious about establishing the specific content of any dialectic opposition: empirical research may always modify, often radically, the content and structure of the opposition. In fact, the whole distinction of antagonistic and nonantagonistic oppositions is one of the indications of the still ideological nature of what should be a weapon against ideology. We begin to see the verbal game involved, as in the following pretended distinction: "In the realm of the practical, a trend is 'opposed to' its counter-trend; but in the realm of ideality, this trend is merely 'balanced by' its counter-trend" (Burke 1973:226); clearly, what we have here is not a distinction between two dimensions of reality, the practical versus the ideal(ist) one, but simply a distinction between two ways of rhetorically structuring the same "facts." There are at least three main areas in which linguistics directly meets the concerns of rhetoric and shapes its theory. I will list and briefly discuss them, without any implication in my order as to their relative importance, but moving from the more broadly ontological to the more technical.

Rhetoric is not "clean"—and the awareness of this is essential (as we saw) in order to perceive its peculiar ontological basis. Now, linguistics in its aspect of rigorous descriptivism is the best expression for this aspect of the ontology. For a descriptive attitude, by its very nature, does not require that functional arguments, each resting on a well-tested topos, be fully "cleared" in advance by logic, or ethics, or both. In choosing not to choose with regard to these matters linguistics expresses the basic feature of the rhetorical enterprise: the mechanisms of rhetoric are recognizable as such because of their functionality; they do not need to be sanctioned by any superior authority—they merely have to possess a solid link with the *koinoì tópoi* on the one hand, and with their figural expression on the other.

What I am proposing can be also expressed by saying that it is high time to do away with that ceremonious, prim aspect of Aristotelian rhetoric (not, this time, the rhetoric analyzed, but the rhetoric performed, by Aristotle) that presumes to erect a solid barrier between the *Topics* (allegedly right) and the *Sophistici elenchi* (supposedly wrong); for the arguments in the latter work are in most cases as functional as those in the former. And I am encouraged in doing this when I see that the awareness of the basic logical and moral indifference of rhetoric often breaks through in the analyses by classical authors.

Rhetoric is made by busy human beings—busy in dead (and sometimes deadly) earnest. If one listens closely enough, these voices of busyness (in the market place as well as in secluded rooms and hallways, in the forum and also in places of worship) can be heard even from the impressive marble façade behind which we too often tend to relegate the discourse of the ancients.

3.2 STRATEGIES AND TACTICS

Let us come closer to this marble façade. A concrete case is the one where Aristotle is concerned with the technique of how to lead the adversary in a debate to utter a paradoxical statement, thereby disqualifying his line of argument. "The men of old," notes the philosopher, said that

> one must indeed confront the man who discourses according to the standard of nature with the standards of social convention [*nómos*], and on the other hand hold forth on the basis of nature against the man who speaks the language of social convention; because in both directions lies the possibility of uttering paradoxes. For them the statements made on the basis of nature constituted the truth, while those made according to social convention were the opinion of the majority. Thus it is clear that those men too, like the ones of today, endeavored to refute the respondent or to make him utter paradoxes.

Some of the questions are such that in both cases the response goes
against common opinion, as for instance, whether "one should obey
the men of wisdom or one's own father," and whether "it is preferable
to do harm or to tolerate an injustice." One should, then, lead [one's
adversaries] into statements opposite to the majority and to the philosophers: if any one speaks as the intellectuals (*hoi perì toùs lógous*) do,
[then lead him] against the view of the majority, and if he speaks as
the majority [lead him] against the views of the intellectuals. In fact,
some assert that the happy man is of necessity just; but to the majority
it goes against the common opinion that a king should not be happy.
To lead [a respondent] into statements thus contrary to common opinion is the same thing as to lead him into opposition to the views based
on nature and on social convention; for social convention represents
the common opinion [*dóksa*] of the majority, while on the other hand
philosophers speak according to nature and truth. (*De sophisticis elenchis* 13. 173ᵃ; cf. Bekker 1960–61, vol. 1)

Now, Aristotle cannot but be aware here that what he is presenting
is a completely "indifferent" rhetorical structure, where neither of
the two alternatives is logically or ethically superior, but rather, both
are considered only in their amoral functionality. The index of Aristotle's awareness that there is a basic contrast between rhetoric in its
real, full scope and the irenic view that he presents elsewhere is his
vague reference to "the men of old." It might be that this is simply a
way of evoking rhetorical argumentation in some indefinite ancient
period before the beginning of philosophy as a systematic enterprise;
but it is much more probable that this is a specific reference to the
Sophists, and that this veiled language is a way of protecting himself
from the scandal that can be attached to such a radical, "disrespect-
ful" way of handling human discourse (we will find several other such
maneuvers in the pages that follow).

On the other hand, this cover is rather flimsy since, having evoked
the *anciens*, Aristotle describes the procedure of the *modernes* with the
implication that he is one of them, and that the difference between
the former and the latter does not effect the basic nature of their
enterprise; that is, it does not touch rhetoric as such but merely
hinges on an intellectualistic qualification: while the men of old ap-
pealed to nature directly, the contemporaries do so through the me-
diation of philosophers.

I hope that I am not insultingly obvious if I try to explicate the
logical structure that, with ironic concision (and perhaps with political

prudence as well) Aristotle leaves implicit when he notes that "some assert that the happy man is of necessity just; but to the majority it goes against the common opinion that a king should not be happy." One way of making clear what the philosopher is actually telling us here is to express what is presented to the scrutiny of public opinion in the form of a categorical syllogism:

> Every happy man is just
> Every king is a happy man
> ∴ Every king is just

The syllogism works, formally; but what Aristotle suggests is that the conclusion of it conflicts with common opinion about kings; he leaves unsaid whether this popular view should be expressed as a *contradictory* proposition (with respect to the conclusive proposition above)—thus, 'Some king is not just'—or, more radically, as a *contrary* proposition: 'No king is just.' I do not know whether it has been noted before that almost certainly Aristotle here refers, indirectly but precisely, to an argument by Plato. In the latter's dialogue *Gorgias* (395–390 B.C.?) the sophist Polos—cast in the role of the villain, i.e., the rhetorician—is opposed to Socrates who, of course, represents the true wisdom. Polos has a certain idea of what can be called happiness; an idea that, with Polos' approval, "Socrates"—i.e., Plato—at a certain point summarizes as follows: "if, when doing what one likes, advantages follow, this is considered by you to be good, and such a thing, it appears, is what 'to have a great power' (*méga dúnasthai*) means; if this is not the case, it is a bad thing and a case of having little power (*smikròn dúnasthai*)." Now, faced with Socrates' refusal to attribute happiness to certain important leaders, Polos exclaims ironically: "It is indeed clear, O Socrates, that even of the Great King you are going to tell me that you do not know whether or not he is happy (*eudaímōn*)." This exchange follows: "*Socrates.* —And in saying this I will be telling the truth; for I do not know how he stands with regard to cultivation of the self (*paideía*) and justice. *Polos.* —What? Is it in this that the whole of happiness consists? *So.* —So I believe, Polos; I assert that a morally beautiful and good (*kalòs kagathós*) man or woman is happy, and on the other hand, the wicked and unjust is wretched" (Plato, *Gorgias* 470ᵇ and 470ᵉ, see Dodds 1959).

Aristotle's implication (hidden in the texture of the passage) is, then, that the popular view is the one represented by, and pandered to, the Sophists, while behind the generic "philosophers" looms the shadow of Plato. But, where does Aristotle stand? The answer is at the same time the explanation of his ambiguity, here and in all similar cases: for Aristotle is straddling the fence—he uses the technique of the Sophists while at the same time paying generic homage to his master. Here, for instance, in agreement with the procedure of "Socrates'" adversaries in *Gorgias*, he does not try to clarify the semantic ambiguity of the word "happiness" (as "Socrates" will be doing, by pushing his ontological-moralistic meaning to victory against the utilitarian and materialist meaning that the word has for Polos and the others); on the contrary, he teaches us (perfectly in line with the Sophistic tradition) how to exploit this ambiguity. But there is much more, and this is apparent even in the short passages quoted: Aristotle's definition of happiness (quoted in chapter 2) in his *Rhetoric* is now shown to be essentially the Sophistic definition, against the ontological moralism of Plato's quoted approach (that, as indicated, Aristotle does not hesitate to adopt and develop in his ethical treatises). This is a crucial divergence, significant both for the history and for the theory of rhetoric. For, as Plato says (through his mouthpiece) in the quoted dialogue: "These are the problems about which, perhaps, to know the truth is the most beautiful, and to ignore it the most shameful, thing; and their basic point is, to know or to ignore who is happy and who is not" (Dodds 1959):472^b).

As for the correlation between philosophers and the standards based on nature on the one side, the majority and its adherence to social convention (or 'law') on the other side, this becomes a traditional opposition, an effective theme in rhetorical performance. I would like to recall the form it assumes in Montaigne's famous "Apologie de Raymond Sebond" because that text, insofar as it is one of the basic Renaissance statements of skepticism, is one of the components of the philosophical background of this theory of rhetoric—a theory that, in fact, recognizes a modern version of skepticism as its philosophy. Writes Montaigne (whom I quote here in the only English version that is not anachronistic and therefore is least ideological, the almost-contemporary one by John Florio):

> *Lawes take their authoritie from possession and custome:* It is dangerous to reduce them to their beginning: In rowling on, they swell, and grow

greater and greater, as doe our rivers: follow them upward, unto their source, and you shall find them but a bubble of water, scarse to be discerned, which in gliding-on swelleth so proud, and gathers so much strength. Behold the ancient considerations, which have given the first motion to this famous torrent, so full of dignitie, of honour and reverence, you shall find them so light and weake, that these men which will weigh all, and complaine of reason, and who receive nothing upon trust and authoritie, it is no wonder if their judgements are often far-distant from common judgement. Men that take Natures first image for a patterne, it is no marvaile, if in most of their opinions, they misse the common-beaten path. As for example; few amongst them would have approved the forced conditions of our marriages and most of them would have had women in community, and without any private respect. They refused our ceremonies. . . .[3]

Going back, now, to the long Aristotelian passage quoted above: terms like this show us the true face of rhetoric—its real ontology, free from the veils of moralism and complacent intellectualism. It is this line of investigation that a critical history of rhetoric, and of course a contemporary theory of it, must follow. Let me be contemporary to the core, discussing everyday experiences in this light (for, *toute proportion gardée*, under the gaze of rhetorics Aristotle and Montaigne are neither closer nor more distant than this writer and his readers). One of the basic strategies in what it is no exaggeration to call the battle of the sexes is a latter-day variation on the theme of the nature/culture conflict. Whenever a conversation tends to get too heavily involved with subjects conventionally called "abstract," some friends will counter with statements reflecting a rhetoric of "nature": statements, I mean, of the "Oh, you men are so pompous and boring" variety. But if, by contrast, one tends to become light and skirt certain topics, one is often met by polemics: "Why, we women have a brain too, don't you know?"

Why did I polarize this conversational exchange as one of man versus woman, when it is clear that men/men and women/women conversations can also reveal the same conflicts? Because this strategy is a dramatically important component in the rhetoric of feminism; and it would be hypocritical to subscribe to liberal piety on these matters, refusing to see that (in the context, here described, of informal conversations) it is the debate across sexual lines that gives urgency and seriousness to this move and countermove.

Of course, I am aware that this description is subjectively colored—

as is every description of a given rhetoric, no matter how systematic and scholarly the system of rhetorics employed strives to be; and indeed, the subjective margin is larger here, since a man is describing the rhetoric of a woman. But wringing our hands about this situation would mean simply to acquiesce in the routine, gross exploitation of rhetorical moves, unenlightened by criticism. To analyze his own margin of subjectivity as an integral part of his analysis—this is the way in which the rhetorician can proceed scientifically. Now, how can subjectivity de-form the strategy which has just been described? Let us note that in such situations victory (more precisely, the limited and temporary advantage in the never-ending flow of conversation) is connected to a chronological phenomenon, which can be subsumed under one of the key concepts of the Sophists, the *kairós* (or, in a Latinate synonym, the *opportunitas*). *Kairós*, I propose, designates the "fit" between the rhetorical structure of a discourse and its general context of situation: in terms of the theory of rhetoric presented here, this "fit" has to be reconstructed for each given situation, on the basis of a comparison between a semiotic reconstruction of the sociocultural context of situation and the structural analysis at the "emic" level. This theory aims, then, at satisfying an ancient need: "No rhetorician or philosopher until now defined a theory (*tékhnē*) of *kairós*" (see fr. 13 in Untersteiner 1949–1962 [henceforth U]: vol. 2. 134–36).

In the particular case described above, the *kairós* is attained by the speaker who manages to utter his most important statement after a considerable stretch of statements pronounced by his interlocutor/opponent, and utters it as close as possible to what, for independent reasons, turns out to be the end of the conversation. Now, in the report I just made, I attributed the *kairós* to the woman; I seem, then, to pay homage to her—for, after all, by the very act of doing this I imply that she is the winner. But this is neither the first nor the last of such homages to turn out to be oriented in quite a different direction. Given certain moralistic connotations of rhetorical strategies (that, to be sure, the present theory tries to eliminate), my account can also be interpreted as a way of opposing an "innocent" linguistic behavior (mine) to a more captious strategy (hers)—which appears to take advantage, for eristic purposes, of words that I uttered in casual spontaneity. But, I tried to correct this slant: and the way I did it was to introduce some criticism of *my* verbal behavior in the very process of recounting it ("*too* heavily involved," "*skirt* certain topics"); by this self-criticism I deprive my verbal behavior—my strategy of symbolic action—of the illusory mask of innocence; and this is not a way of being nice, but a technique necessary in order to restore balance and thus to give a scientific, or scholarly, character to these analyses.

What is the position of the Aristotelian rhetoric vis-à-vis the earthy aggressiveness of these exchanges, which are the way of being of men in society, within the real and pervasive drama of their mutual relations, both at the level of institutionalized politics and at the level of the everyday politics of sex, money, power, rest, play, dreaming, and so on? It seems that the success of Aristotle's line—the moderate and hypocritical line of the respectable cultural establishment—is the prize that goes to an astute (and conformistic) compromise: the compromise between the radical insights of the Sophists, who had the political and intellectual courage to unveil the ontology of rhetoric, and the virulent rhetoric of the moralistic reaction by Plato, which, through Aristotle and the rest of the philosophers, Pagan and Christian, in the mainstream of "respectable" thought, continued until the present day.

We have seen, reflected in a specific example, the ontology of rhetoric: we have seen, that is, that its nature is essentially dialectic. For what other perspective is there (beside the one, quite inadequate, of the archaeological anecdote) from which to view the appeal to the majority against the experts, and vice versa, the recourse to the expert versus the majority? I am aware that this is almost certainly not the way in which Aristotle and the classical tradition would present this contrast, and actually this was pointed out already: their language is too often that of "yea, yea; nay, nay." But the post-Hegelian and post-structuralist scholar cannot afford this stark simplicity of vision.

In particular, it is the linguist's responsibility to indicate the discourse, or text, as the locus where the *coincidentia oppositorum* takes place: entities that—if presented in a purely ideological form—appear as incompatible and fully polarized, are instead revealed as sharing the same psycholinguistic structure, and as being completely interchangeable within the same structure of discourse. This lesson may seem obvious, but it is not, as many contemporary treatments show; on the contrary, this is the dialectic contribution of rhetorics to the understanding of human language. All the ideological polarizations of linguistic concepts are there to show us how easily forgotten that lesson is and, consequently, how much we need to restate it and to articulate it.

Also, it must be noted that within Aristotle's corpus there are various degrees of compromise between dialectical intuitions and linguistic codifications. For instance, in the quoted passage the dialectical relationship does emerge, whereas in the following one, on the same problem, it is emasculated and masked: "a dialectical proposition consists in asking something that is held by all men or by most men or by the philosophers, i.e., either by all, or by most, or by the most notable of these, provided it be not contrary to the general opinion; for a man would probably assent to the views of the philosophers if it be not contrary to the opinions of most men" (*Topics* 104ᵃ; Brunschwig 1967).

I have spoken, above, of compromise; and there is a passage in particular (from Aristotle's *Rhetoric*) which shows clearly that this is not an anachronistic invention of mine. The passage has a cautious, almost embarassed tone—showing both the awareness that accompanies the discovery of a whole ontological field, and the fear that the contrast between this new ontology and the traditionally accepted ideologies may turn out to be too strong, and dangerous for the intellectual who points it out:

> Moreover we must be able to apply persuasion in opposite directions, just like in syllogistic reasonings; not so that we may put both possibilities into practice since we must not persuade to what is worthless (*tà phaûla*), but in order that it be not hidden from us how things really stand; and in order that, if another person uses discourse in an unjust way, we ourselves may be able to put him down.
>
> No other of the disciplines (*tékhnai*) applies reasoning to opposite conclusions—dialectic and rhetoric are alone in doing this; for both maintain themselves at an equal distance from the opposite conclusions. However, the underlying matters do not stand in the same way; but the true facts and the more valuable ones are always, to put it plainly, easier to argue (*eusullogistótera*) and more convincing. (*Rh.*, 1. 1355ᵃ. 29–38)

What is taking place here is nothing less than this: a mercilessly sharp critical discovery is being masked—in a rather lame way—under a protective veil of moralism. This is something more than an intellectually fascinating performance—it is a turning point in the history of ideas. For the discovery which serves as background to this passage is that the house of human discourse cannot be built on solid rock, that (*pace* Descartes) its only possible foundation is ever-shifting sand.

What has been discovered, then, is the radical relativism of human discourse. But this was already an achievement of the Sophists, and what Aristotle adds of his own is probably the confusion into which he falls, trying to blunt the edge of the Sophists' statements. For rhetorics, as was pointed out, first of all and above all studies competence, and is not directly responsible for performance; but then, how can one prohibit the speaker from practically employing the opposite arguments with equal skill? And—as far as the "worthless" things are concerned—*quis custodiet custodes ipsos*? Moreover, what strength can the appeal to the "underlying matters" have in this context, where it is clear that we are not dealing with metaphysical speculations but with received opinions?

Yet Aristotle's retreat is an inevitable one, in the framework of a theory like his, which has not established clearly that the ontological bases of rhetoric are stylized *topoi*, not the referents themselves; and that the connection between the opposite arguments is dialectic, rather than moralistic and absolute. There is, indeed, a passage in the *Rhetoric* where the reference to Gorgias is like a shaft of light cutting through the moralistic fog and the academic intellectualism. If taken at face value it is, like many other passages in this work, deceptively simple; but we have already seen (in discussing the definition of happiness) how important these apparently simple statements are for identifying the ontological base of rhetoric.

"Jests," writes the philosopher, "seem to be of some utility in oratorical controversies, and Gorgias said that one should destroy the opponents' earnestness with joking, and their joking with earnestness—and he was right about it" (ibid. 3. 18. 1419^b 3–6). It is only now that we can appreciate the importance of this brief tribute to Gorgias. This statement—which contains in a nutshell the technique discussed in the quoted passage from *De sophisticis elenchis*—is essentially a recognition of the crucial importance of the Sophists for the establishment of the dialectical method in rhetoric.

"But," somebody could object, "this view of the dramatic, tense relationship between the systematizer of rhetorics (Aristotle) and the creators of rhetorics (the hated Sophists) is built on a passing reference to Gorgias; how can one accept this as sufficient evidence?" I have already sketched the context where even this passing reference can be seen in all its significance; but there is more. Let me quote just one example (slightly longer, but indispensable). This is the last (the ninth, or tenth, according to the division one establishes earlier in the list) of the "apparent syllogisms" that conclude Aristotle's review of the topoi.

> Again, just as in the eristic debates with what is absolute and what is not absolute, but rather something particular (tò haplôs kaì mè haplôs, allà tí), an apparent syllogism is generated . . . so in rhetoric there is an apparent enthymeme with regard to what in reality is not absolutely probable (eikós), but simply something in particular that is probable. . . for what is beyond probability happens [i.e., it may happen], so that also what is beyond probability is probable. However, this is not true in an absolute sense, but—just as in eristic the: "in relation to what" and "in comparison with what" and "how" not being applied produce the false contention (sukophantía)—there [i.e., in rhetoric] too [the same thing happens] because what is probable is not such in an absolute sense, but as something specific.
>
> And the treatment of rhetoric by Corax is composed on the basis of this topos; "for if he is not open to the charge, as for instance a weak man accused of assault—'why, it is not probable,' and if he is open to the charge, as when the accused is a strong man—'why, it is not probable [that he did it], since he was certain to appear as a likely candidate for this crime (eikòs émelle dóksein.)'"
>
> And similarly for the other cases: for necessarily, either he is open to the charge or he is not; and indeed, both alternatives appear to be probable, but the former is probable [absolutely], while the latter is not probable absolutely but [only] in the way in which it is verbally presented; and this is a case of that well-known tactic of "making the weaker argument the better." Hence people were right in being dissatisfied with what Protagoras professed; in fact it is a lie, and it is not a true but an apparent probability, and it is appropriate in no discipline but in rhetoric and in eristic. (Rh. 2. 24. 1402^a 3–28)[4]

This important passage confirms my analysis of the Aristotelian position as one of compromise. What are particularly intriguing are editorial attempts to obfuscate even the indirect glimpse of light that Aristotle sheds on rhetoric as a real strategy; for instance, this difficult-to-believe ideological tag, which Solmsen attaches at the end of the passage just quoted: "This remark entails no approval on the part of Aristotle." And who, pray, can assure us of this? Indeed, this is begging the question that should be studied, and it is yet another instance of the centuries-old tendency to be more Aristotelian than Aristotle. In this particular case, such clumsy help only succeeds in highlighting the obstacle which Aristotle had tried, with more elegance, to sidestep.

For—once again—under the guise of an attack against the Sophists, in the Platonic tradition, Aristotle is in reality cautiously recognizing the Sophists' expertise, and their mastery in the field that they first brought to the light of scientific analysis. He is, I dare say, saying: true, this kind of reasoning does not lead to metaphysical truth: it is *only* good for rhetoric! In other words, Aristotle is timidly and indirectly restating the bold, genial claim of the Sophists (under the guise of opposing this claim): that rhetoric is autonomous, and should not be colonized through forays from the domains of ethics and metaphysics.

Another example of the vitality of these strategies in the contemporary world (and one, this time, to which I was not an eye-witness). A man accused, by policemen who state they have followed him for nearly a mile, of exceeding the speed limit defends himself by noting that the police car, with its flashing blue light, was highly visible, and that he would never have been such a fool as to drive over the speed limit with a police car following him. (From a newspaper article quoted in Guthrie 1969:178–79.)

Have I succeeded in showing the dialectic nature of rhetorical structures in their concreteness? This is a question that will recur again and again in these pages. For the moment, I note that the Sophists are still waiting for an analysis that really does justice to their position in the history of rhetoric. For it is not enough to rehabilitate them if the motivations of this move are not clear, and their work is celebrated in the ideological mode of vague humanistic claims.[5]

What, then, is called for? In the first place, to take seriously and realistically the political aspect of the Sophists' activity (see for instance, Loenen 1941, Corbato 1958), comparing it with the same aspect in the activity of other kinds of rhetors and rhetoricians, like Isocrates (Mathieu 1925), and Aristotle (Kelsen 1969). Then, and above all, to be clear on the general philosophical implication of their work, there still seems to be some reluctance to view the Sophists as some of the main figures in the development of skepticism, especially in its linguistic aspect—which is of course the main interest here. Shall we consider it only a chance, or an instance of illegitimate appropriation, that the preserver of one of the basic versions of a fragment of Gorgias' seminal treatise, *On not Being and on Nature*, is Sextus Empiricus, in a work (*Adversus mathematicos*) which is capital for ancient skepticism? Shall we regard it as a mere coincidence that the anti-Sophistic rhetoric in philology and literary criticism and cultural history—and the related faith in the accessibility of the referents—are exactly parallel to the philosophical rhetoric of antiskepticism?[6] But I would like to conclude this section on the Sophists with some concrete points, rather than with generic suggestions. This is necessary given the importance of these thinkers as pioneers in systematic linguistic analysis, and especially in the structural analysis of discourse. In this perspective, it is an apt symbol of the nexus of theory and empirical research practiced by the Sophists that Protagoras is presented to us both as the one who "first said that for every event (*prâgma*) there are available two verbal interpretations (*lógos*) opposite the one to the other" (fr. 1 of U 1:14ff.), and that he "first divided the discourse (lógos) into four categories: wish, question, answer, command."[7] It is not essential, at this stage, to take a stand as to the choice between the division just reported and the one which immediately follows it in the quoted passage: "others instead [divide discourse into] seven [categories]: narrative (*diēgēsis*), question, answer, command, recital (*apaggelía*), appellation; these [the previous four divisions] he [Protagoras] called foundations (*puthmēn*) of discourses. Alcidamas speaks, on the other hand, of four kinds of discourses: assertion, negation, question, address" (ibid.:20). Nor does it much matter that what seems to be the only surviving instance of the application of these analytical categories in the case of Protagoras does not do full justice to their possibilities, since it misuses them in a scholastically rigid way; I refer to what Aristotle tells us is one critique levelled by Protagoras at Homer, because of the poet "thinking that he offers a prayer while he gives an order instead, when he says: 'Sing, o goddess, the wrath'; for, he [Protagoras] says, urging to do or not to do something is a command" (fr. 28 in U 1:70—most probably this quote reflects a late misunderstanding of what must have been a more sophisticated analysis by Protagoras; the attempt, at any rate—quoted by the editor in his footnote—to justify Protagoras' criticism seems even more absurd than that criticism).

What, then, matters? It matters that we have here one of the first (perhaps the first) explicit identifications of the fundamental functions of discourse—functions that, integrated into the structure of the rheme (which is shown in chapter 4) constitute one of the main components in this theory of rhetoric. These "foundations of discourse" should not be translated as *partes orationis*—either in the sense of basic grammatical categories (like noun, verb, etc.) or in the sense of elements which, in their succession, constitute the skeleton of a discourse. They are—to repeat—functions at the discourse level, which should be integrated but not confused with the other categories just mentioned.

This is not to deny the contributions of the Sophists as far as these other categories are concerned, for instance, the structural partition of texts of speeches. If (as Untersteiner notes in U 2:112 13) it is true that Gorgias probably was not the creator of a systematic structuring of speeches into several (especially, six) parts—for traces of this structure are already to be found in Euripides—the well-structured texture of Gorgias' texts cannot be disputed. Take for example the *Apologia of Palamedes* (Untersteiner), which clearly lends itself to a division into: 1.) proem, 2.) demonstration, 3.) direct address to the adversary, 4.) counteraccusations, 5.) direct address to the judges, 6.) final reminder. Can one state flatly (as Untersteiner does) that such a rich partition is not to be found in the speeches by Lysias, Isaeus, and Demosthenes? Whatever may turn out to be the case, this is a concrete starting point for a structural typology of discourse; one, moreover, that will not simply constitute a mechanical taxonomy, but that will reveal deep strategic conflicts—of cultures, forms and places of power, contrasting personalities—and that will lead us, beyond the appearances, through intriguing twists and turns, to a realistic view of how men work and struggle in society.

For instance: the Platonic "Socrates" in *Phaedrus* evokes these structural partitions (Robin 1933 266^d and ff.) with apparent irony; and yet, what he has just done (262^c–266^d) has been to submit the Lysias' speech which is the pre-text for this dialogue to a technical and structural analysis (which he had anticipated in 236ª, with his distinction between *heúresis*, i.e., *inventio*, and *diáthesis*, that is, *dispositio*), and he has found it defective in terms of its structure; in other words, he has applied the technique founded by the Sophists. The point is worth emphasizing in view of the persistent, coy rhetoric of antirhetoric: the speech by Lysias is found wanting not because it is too full of meretricious rhetorical ornaments but, on the contrary, because it is too unstructured! As a matter of fact, Lysias' speech (231ª–241ᶜ) seems, to me, striking just because of its skillful imitation of a hurried private note: beginning *in medias res*, with a reference to a past context which is left unexplained—"About my situation, you know; and you have heard how doing this constitutes an advantage for us"—and rather rigid, oft-repeated, transitions, of the type which one generally finds in private letters: 'furthermore' (*éti dé*), 'and also' (*kaì mèn dé*). (For *Phaedrus* cf. also Jowett 1964.)

This particular point should be discussed against the vast critical bibliography on this dialogue; but this is not indispensable here, just as it is not crucial for my purpose whether the speech be really by Lysias or not. What is important is to emphasize the inevitable contradictions in which every blanket critique of rhetoric falls—inevitable, and predictable: for rhetoric is the intrinsic structure of discourse, not a coolly calculated and more or less dispensable addition to it. In this specific case, the would-be negator of rhetoric finds himself caught between the horns of a dilemma: either he sides with "Socrates" against the Sophists and rhetoricians, but then he discovers that what he is actually doing is subscribing to a rhetorical analysis; or he takes the side of the more loosely organized discourse (Lysias'), only to find out that what he thought was a move for naturalness and spontaneity puts him on the side of the rhetoricians who are attacked.

The responsibility for this dilemma, at any rate, lies not with the modern reader but with Plato—the problem is in the contradictory nature of his criticism of rhetoric. This imprecision, moreover, is as functional to Plato's strategy as it is inevitable: functional, because it creates the curtain of ideological fog beyond which the army of metaphysical assertions can march up to the assault; and inevitable, in any case, because any analysis of rhetorical structure which does not recognize its intrinsic necessity and its presence at every level of discourse is out of focus no matter how technical its vocabulary, how detailed its debate.

But, once it is clear that rhetoric coincides with the whole structure of human discourse in its functional aspect, then the technical analysis of discourse structure, and the technical performance realizing that structure, appear not only to be serious and useful things (something that almost every humanist would be ready to admit—albeit often grudgingly and in a condescending tone): they moreover reveal their full intellectual dignity.

It is this perspective that can make us appreciate the significance of the continuity of this tradition. We have just seen how it is taken seriously even by the alleged anti-Sophist Plato; I add that this continues through the Latin tradition: in the rhetorical treatise "Ad Herennium" (by unknown author), 1. 3–17, 2. 1–31, 3. 5–10 (see F. Marx 1964, and Caplan 1954), in Cicero's *De inventione*, 1. 14–56 (see it, together with the *De optimo genere oratorum*, in Hubbell 1949), in Quintilian's *Institutio oratoria* (cf. Butler 1922, Winterbottom 1970), and so on.

The task of the contemporary rhetorician, when confronted with data of this kind, is doubly dialectic. He must reconstruct the dialectic interaction between each of these structures and its semiotic, social, and historical context, in order to show that the diachronic development of these partitions is not the effect of a fad substituting another fad, but a matter of serious changes and conflicts in history. But the task of the rhetorician does not end here (and to believe that it ends here leads straight into what I described above as the historicist fallacy): for the rhetorician really fulfills his task only when he describes, in painstaking detail, the dialectic interaction at a given time between any one of these structural partitions and a specific text. In fact, no important text (literary or nonliterary) is reducible simply to a mechanical reflex of this structure—rather, it modifies it to a certain extent at the same time as it realizes it.

Just one example. Untersteiner correctly remarks (U 2:112) that the fourth section of the basic partition, that of the *antikatēgoríai* or 'counteraccusations,' was not filled out in Gorgias' *Apologia of Palamedes*, "so that Palamedes' magnanimity was better emphasized." This is right, of course, but there is more to it than that. This is Palamedes speaking: "Although I could counter-accuse you [the reference is to Ulysses] of numerous and grave evils, both old and new, I will not do it; for I want to be absolved from this accusation not thanks to your evil deeds but thanks to my good deeds; this, then, is all with regard to you." A structural description must analyze this paragraph as a rhetorical tagmeme (a rheme) which, at the level of Inventio (*heúresis*) fills the slot 'counteraccusations' with a zero unit, *but* which, at the same time, fills the slot of a specific figure of speech at the level of Elocutio (*léksis*) in such a way that this figure is generated by the quoted zero unit. This figure of speech, in this rheme, is an occurrence of the figure of Praeteritio (*paráleipsis*), which is realized "when we behave as if we leave something aside, but in effect we say it" (see *HR* 1960: pars. 882–86). What occurs, in other words, is *not* a hole or laceration in the rhetorical web, a moment of arhetorical "purity" of speech, in which the speaker, although he has spied a possible advantage for himself, chastely (or, clumsily) refuses to seize it.

Rather, what really happens is that the speaker/writer decides that, at this point in the text, it would not be functional to fill out the slot in a straightforward way (we need not concern ourselves here with the possible reasons for this decision, nor with establishing whether the decision looks—now, to us—like a good or a bad one). What the orator does, then, is to skillfully intermingle rhetorics with rhetoric, that is, the metalanguage of the analysis of discourse structure with his own performing language. By the very fact of stating that he will not dwell on the adversary's faults, *and* by the way in which he says it (Ulysses' faults are described by no less than four adjectives), Palamedes in fact draws attention to them.

I hope that it is clear, now, that it is the dialectic interaction which distinguishes the theory proposed here from other theories of rhetoric. The interaction is in effect triple, rather than double: I have mentioned the interaction between rhetorical analyses and their whole context of situation, and we have just seen a concrete example of the interaction between the general structuring and the specific organization of a text—but this example has shown us also something else: the dialectic interaction between theory (rhetorics) and practice (rhetoric) in the work of one and the same author.

The further look at some of Gorgias' statements which will conclude this overview of the Sophist contribution will permit us to see these interactions more and more clearly. I want to emphasize the seminal value of the Sophists' work—work that we, unfortunately, can merely have a glimpse at; for the later intellectual establishment treated their writings with neglect, and probably with something more malicious than that (censorious repression).

Gorgias, we are told, "wrote up the praises and the blames of single entities, since he considered that what was above all distinctive about the orator was the capacity to enlarge a given topic with his praise, and on the other hand to diminish it with blame" (fr. 25, cf. U 2:28). The real importance of the topoi, then, turns out, already at this time, to be not that they provide us with lists of mechanical devices, but rather that they orient our perception and expression of the world; which means that the topoi, like all other components of rhetorical structure, have not only technical, but also ontological, implications.

Here I must pause before going back to the specific quotes. We face a basic choice, because our view of rhetorical history and analysis is inextricably bound together with the way according to which we perceive society, and the world in general, today. Do we believe that there are criteria for the distinction of truth from falsity that are independent from linguistic statements, and that these criteria are crucial for understanding what these statements mean? If we believe this, then we will see rhetorical activity as an *optional de*formation of entities endowed with an independent existence. In doing this, we may appear to be realistic; and indeed in a certain sense we are—but only in a Platonic, metaphysical sense of the word. For we believe in the possibility of perceiving and evaluating "things" outside of "words," whereas our real world is nothing more than a semiotic world—a world, that is, in which we can "touch" only words.

Or do we believe, instead, that there are no absolute criteria of truth and falsity, and indeed that there is no way of getting at any facts outside of their linguistic interpretations? Do we, therefore, believe that our world is a world of signs (linguistic and nonlinguistic), not of objectively seizable entities which are then linked up to signs? If we believe this, we see rhetorical activity (that is, linguistic activity at the maximum of cultural integration) as a continuous process of *necessary trans*formation: all the facts that we perceive are, insofar as we perceive them, transformed and transformable. They never, so to speak, stand still, allowing us to perceive them as something more solid than semiotic structures. This attitude is, I think, the adequate one, and the one which fully deserves the attribute of realistic.

The realism, in this latter case, is not a cult of metaphysical objects, but an attitude which is realistic in the current sense of the word: it is the view of man as he actually manifests himself in actual society. It is only in this framework that a theory of rhetoric can be constructed, that is, that we can try to understand how human discourse really works. But let us first see what the consequences of the first view are for the data that we are now examining.

This view may best be symbolized by the ideological translation which I did *not* write, in rendering Aristotle's description of one of the basic tenets of the Sophists. I translated the sentence reported by Aristotle (*Rh.* 2. 24. 140ᵃ. 24) literally: 'making the weaker argument the better (*tòn héttō dè lógon kreíttō poieîn*)'. It looks simple, but the sentence actually implies a whole ontology of language—which is, here, a realistic one in the current and most apt sense of the word. But to show that the matter is actually far from simple, let us see how this sentence can be translated—and is actually translated, for instance in the quoted Rhys Roberts version: "making the worse argument *seem* the better" (emphasis added). This latter version, as is clear by now, implies the other ontology of language, the one criticized above.

Such an ideological translation was, in fact, tried very soon; as we can see if we look at Plato's passage which the editor appropriately quotes in connection with Cicero's statement about Gorgias and the topoi; what is described there, among other apsects of Tisias' and Gorgias' procedure, is how "they view the probable as more estimable than the true, and they make (*poioûsi*) the small things appear (*phaínesthai*) big and the big things, small, through the force of discourse (*dià rhōmēn lógou*), [and make] new things appear old, and the contrary, new; and who found, apropos of any topic, how to shorten speeches or lengthen them without precise boundaries" (*Phaedrus* 267ᵃ⁻ᵇ).

The key word here is *phaínesthai*—which expresses all the difference between a *poieîn* that is an actual transformation of topics that cannot even be perceived as existing by themselves (the realistic view which explains rhetoric) and a *poieîn* conceived—as here—as a subjective intervention on entities that can be perceived in themselves, outside of sign systems (the metaphysical view, whereby one keeps stumbling against the actual organization of discourse as against an incomprehensible obstacle).

Other passages, from the same dialogue, can be added to the one quoted by Untersteiner. Earlier in the text Plato, personifying *tôn lógōn tékhnē* ('theory'—or 'technique'—'of discourses'), imagines it stating: "This I say loud and clear, that without me the person who has knowledge of Being (*tà ónta*) does not have any particular advantage as far as the technique of persuasion (*peíthein tékhnē*) is concerned"; and he opposes to this personified force the dictum of a mysterious "Laconian" (the choice of character evokes the moralistic connotations of the Athens/Sparta debate, which we saw above as elaborated by Montaigne). This personage states that: "An authentic (*étumos*) *tékhnē* of speech which is not fastened onto truth neither exists nor can ever arise" (ibid. 260ᵈ⁻ᵉ).

Here we can see the beginnings of that rhetoric of authenticity which, in the wake of the Romantic and Existentialist experiences, still plagues us (see cf. Adorno 1963). Faced with a fully developed *tékhnē* the existence of which he cannot deny, and to whose efficacy his own writing pays indirect but continuous homage, the ideologist finds nothing better to oppose than the denial that this actually existing theory/technique is *étumos*—an appreciation so vague that it cannot be disproved or proved.

Another significant statement in the same context is Socrates' "rhetorical" question:

> Wouldn't then rhetoric (*rhētorikḗ tékhnē*) be a way of leading souls (*psukhagōgía tis*) through discourses, not only in courts of justice and other such public gatherings, but also in private meetings, a way which remains the same both for small and for big topics—and one that, provided its use is correct, does not become more respectable when it deals with weighty topics than when it deals with paltry topics? (ibid. 261ᵃ⁻ᵇ)

The mode of the rhetorical question persists in what follows: What, asks Socrates, do the parties in a suit (*antídikos*) do but debate with each other (*antilégein*)? And do not they debate "on the just and the unjust"? And "therefore, the one who does this according to the *tékhnē*, will he not make the same things appear to the same persons at one time just [and], and when he so desires, unjust? . . . . And when speaking in the public assembly (*dēmēgoría*) [will he not make] the same thing appear to the state now good, now the contrary of good?"

Also—alluding ironically to some typical representative of Eleatic philosophy—"don't we know that he spoke with such a *tékhnē* that the same things appeared to the listeners similar and dissimilar, unitary and manifold, in a state of rest and on the other hand moved around?" Socrates' conclusion:

> Controversy (*antilogía*), then, does not take place only around courts of justice and assembly speeches; but, it seems, there is one *tékhnē* (admitting that such a thing really exists) which concerns everything that is said. And this is the *tékhnē* whereby one will be able to assimilate everything to everything else, in the domain of the possible things and with regard to those for whom this is possible; and [he will be able], if another one performs such assimilations in a mystifying way, to bring them to the light. (ibid. 261ᶜ⁻ᵉ)

Not everything is clear in this Platonic characterization of rhetoric: what does it mean to confine this activity of assimilation to the "possible" things? And what is it that is supposed to be brought to the light: improperly constructed assimilations that are, therefore, unmasked—or simply relations that are expressed in a confused manner (in good faith) and that the more sophisticated interlocutor is able to express better? This latter ambiguity between the subjective and the objective side evokes the broader ambiguity whereby I translate, in a context such as this, *rhētorikḕ tékhnē*, as "rhetoric" rather than, according to my own stipulations at the beginning, as "rhetorics." I do this because the clear distinction between the objective structure present in all discourses (rhetoric) and the account of this structure (rhetorics) is possible only in a modern theory of rhetoric, which recognizes the universality of rhetorical structures as objective components of human language. Any theory, on the other hand, like the one sketched by Plato, which regards rhetorical structure as an optional, ultimately superfluous addition to a deeper structure—any theory of this sort is flawed from the beginning precisely because of this failure to distinguish between rhetoric and rhetorics, and the translation cannot but reflect this confusion, using the ambiguous cover term "rhetoric." In any case, the general drift is clear: rhetoric is so clearly delineated according to the Sophists' insight (here as in other Platonic passages: the dialogue *Gorgias*, and others) that Plato's dialogic technique backfires; that is, the supposedly false science appears as much more solid and convincing than its ideological alternative.

In conclusion: Plato's setting up of a *tékhnē dialektikē* as the true discipline which will defeat the *tékhnē rhētorikē* fails to convince. The Platonic dialectician is eminently adialectic if we think of dialectic in post-Hegelian terms. But in fact we do not have to perform this anachronistic overlapping of ancient and modern in order to criticize Plato's dialectics; for the Platonic strategy is not something that must be "historically understood" (as historicism in its apologetic variant continually asks us to do when we are faced with delicate choices); it cannot be apologized for as a concept which was then still not fully developed and of which it would be unfair to ask, before the modern achievements, such a full development.

The fact is that the "modern" interpretation of dialectic is older than Plato: at least, that is, as old as Gorgias (485/80–380, *terminus post quem*) and the other Sophists. It is in this perspective that I dare claim that the loss of Gorgias' ontological—that is, antiontological—treatise (except for one longish fragment) is one of the most serious gaps in the history of "Western" philosophy. The oft-quoted central portion of the fragment (which I cite here in one of the available versions) is a clear proof of the importance of this loss. Gorgias wrote (the "pseudo-Aristotle" tells us): "that nothing exists; and that even if it exists it is unknowable; and even if it exists and is knowable it cannot however be signified (*ou dēlōtón*) to others" (see fr. 3bis in U 2:57–58).

This statement is made more precise, in terms of linguistic analysis, by the following specification:

> neither does vision know the sounds (*phthóngos*), nor does hearing hear the colours, but sounds; and, the speaker does indeed speak, but he does not speak a colour or an experience (*prâgma*) . . . thus nothing exists, and even if it existed nothing is knowable, and even if it were knowable nobody could signify it to another person, because experiences are not utterances (*dià te tò mē eînai tà prágmata lógous*), and nobody thinks the same intellectual content (*tautòn ennoeî*) as another person. (see the end of the same fr. 3bis, in U 2:70–2)

It is, of course, dangerous to express philosophical appreciations on the basis of book titles; yet I cannot help noting that the difference between a book on non-Being and a book on Being (say, Heidegger's masterpiece) can be taken as the symbol of a peculiar experience, which runs counter to the optimistic and gradualistic ideology of progress. What I mean is that, in the case of ontological discussions, instead of progressing from naive beliefs to systematic criticism, we have traveled on an opposite path: at the beginning there was penetrating criticism, and the decisive step was taken—to the realization that the only way of talking of Being was to explain that one could not say anything about it; later, the philosophers' efforts were to a large extent spent in trying to exorcize the threat constituted by this radical critique. Thus, ideological ways of talking about Being were constructed, in order to reintroduce a principle of conventional order and ultimate respectability.

In the face of this situation, let me reiterate here what has emerged from this discussion of the Sophists and from the previous analyses: *rhetoric is the key to ontology because it is the most concrete and precise tool that can be used in order to show that every positive ontology is an ideological construction.* As such it must be carefully studied, to be sure, but in order to take apart and de-mystify this construction.

A last remark, apropos of the dialectic interaction between the rhetorics and the rhetoric of creative rhetoricians. The form of Gorgias' statement quoted above is only a little less interesting than its content; for such a form realizes a well-defined and effective configuration—which however is difficult to situate in the current taxonomies of figures of speech. It is a structure which combines elements of the Gradatio (or *klímaks*)—for which cf. *HR* 1960: pars. 623–4—with an often-commented-upon example by Demosthenes, interesting for us because the Gorgian technique here described may lie at its origin—and an informal version of the Sorites, that certain authors (cf. Perelman-Tyteca 1958: par. 54) call "Chinese sorites" in order to distinguish it from the logically tighter type called "Greek sorites."

In both structures (the gradatio and the sorites) the distinctive feature seems to be the close linkup of successive strings/statements, such that the last term of one string becomes the first term of the immediately following string. The difference is that the definition of gradatio insists on the string as a morphosyntactically concrete structure (a sentence), and on the formal side of this repetition; while the definition of sorites concentrates on the string as statement, and on the logical relationships among the successive statements.

What I want to show here is that this figure is an important characteristic of Gorgias' rhetoric, for the quoted passage (which must have been a crucial one in Gorgias' corpus of writings) must be supplemented at least by the following, from the quoted *Apologia of Palamedes*: "Neither would I have been able if I wanted, nor would I have wanted to put my hand to such [evil] things, if I had been able" (fr. 11ᵃ in U 2:116).

Both quoted passages cumulate negative statements; the following, on the other hand, passes from the negative to the positive: "The events which did not take place are impossible to witness, while with regard to those which did take place, not only it is not impossible, but it is also easy [to witness them]; nor is it only easy, but it would have been possible for you to find, not only [honest] witnesses, but also false witnesses."[8]

The task of the critic who is aware that he can be such in a systematic and serious way only if he is first of all a rhetorician, is, then, that of being always ready to animate the past with the sense and experience of contemporary life, and on the other hand to recognize the archetypes at work in contemporary life. (It is this balance—the difficult balance that makes a real critic—in which Kenneth Burke has distinguished himself; and it is a sad comment on the scarcity of principled traditions and lack of a sense of history and perspective in American criticism that this name is conspicuously absent from certain fashionable books—like Goffman 1971 and 1974—which deal in part with the same problems.)

Between the Greek and Latin classics and the direct verbal (and generally semiotic) experience of contemporary life there is, of course, a rich literary tradition; so that it would be equally unrealistic (and arbitrarily ideological) to forget the classics as to always juxtapose them directly to contemporary experience, without taking into account the stratification of successive literary variations through which they come down to us.

One instance, from an author I have quoted before, follows. It shows, not surprisingly, the enduring attraction exerted by the sorites construction illustrated above with the pioneering periods by Gorgias: "Pour juger des apparences que nous recevons des subjects, il nous faudroit un instrument judicatoire; pour verifier cet instrument, il nous y faut de la demonstration; pour verifier la demonstration, un instrument: nous voilà au rouet" (Montaigne, *Essais* 2. 12; cf. Rat *ed. cit.* 1: 677).

As usual, no sooner is the similarity recognized than we become aware of the differences appearing against that background: Gorgias' structures do not go back to the first link in the chain, whereas in this example the chain is closed—*instrument* is the starting point and to *instrument* we return (whence Montaigne's image of the *rouet*—we could say, the 'vicious circle'). This is but an inkling of a broad field of study; but the importance of this field should not obscure the need for data taken directly from contemporary experience.

When, for instance, I am stopped in the Bowery (as has happened on several occasions) by men who ask for strange sums of money like eight cents or eleven cents, it is not enough that I have a sense of the mechanism which is being crudely applied, namely, the calculation that the passerby will not stop to count out penny after penny, but will—if he agrees to give something—round off the proposed amount to a dime or a quarter.

What a rhetorician must do is to recognize the rhetorical archetype at work here: the Minutio (or *meíōsis*), that is, the "verbal expression (*lógos*) which makes the referent (*prâgma*) appear smaller" (*HR* 1960: par. 259). And he must also recognize the ethos of the figure (see Dubois et al. 1970 for a revival of this term, which I apply here in a somewhat different way); that is, the complex of connotations, endowed with ideological functions, that accompany each figure.

The ethos here is one of humble captivation: no matter how easily one sees through that realization of the figure, a halo of discretion is projected around the request, and—although it is naive to hope that this will be sufficient to persuade the passerby—one should recognize its existence and its significance in order to have both a synchronic and a diachronic understanding of the act of communication which is involved here. Note that this figure is the contrary of that of Amplificatio, or *aúksēsis* (see *HR*); we thus are confronted again with that process of continuous transformation of *prágmata* and of establishment of dialectic tensions about which Gorgias theorized and which Plato ideologically rejected.

Dialectic reasoning (as already pointed out) is constantly threatened by vagueness—that is, by ideological abstraction or obfuscation. The preceding discussions of statements by Aristotle and by the

Sophists have gone a long way, I trust, to satisfy the need for concreteness in dialectic analyses. What should be emphasized (all the more strongly because of the archaeological connotations that unfortunately tend to be attached to intellectual developments in classical antiquity) is that these statements and counterstatements reflect the atmosphere of debates in real society; these eristic confrontations are important struggles for power.

What emerges, in short, from a realistic analysis of discourse is that rhetoric gives access to *the political dimension that every discourse possesses as such*—which has nothing in common with the simplistic pretense of finding in certain discourses, as distinct from certain others, the reflex of political actions, where "political" is taken in its current, shallow, sense (so shallow and narrow, indeed, that it becomes a mystification: what the current jargon mislabels as "politics" is actually, in most cases, one or another form of ideology, whose function is precisely that of forbidding access to politics).

We must go further, and recognize that rhetoric *is* the political dimension of discourse, literary as well as nonliterary; but the relevance of literature must be especially emphasized, against vague statements about the relationship between literature *and* politics. The point is that there is *always* politics *in* literature, as an intrinsic component of the literary discourse—and this politics is rhetoric.

I will come back to this concept; but it was necessary to state it now in order to make clear in what sense descriptions like the ones presented here are to be viewed as concrete. To be sure, quotations of only one or two paragraphs' length inevitably contain an element of ideological abstraction; their brevity does not allow the reader to situate all the points in the proper perspective and relationship with the rest of the text; but this is the necessary price to be paid for any analysis like this, which elaborates a general theory and therefore cannot be confined to the treatment in depth of a single text.

However, the long illustration that follows tries to redress the balance somewhat: though still far from including a whole text, it goes beyond a couple of paragraphs.

> He that should chuse, whether it were best to keepe his souldiers richly and sumptuously armed, or only for necessitie, should seeme to yeeld in favour of the first, whereof was *Sertorius, Philopoemen, Brutus, Caesar,* and others urging that it is ever a spur to honour and glorie,

for a souldier to see himself gorgiously attired, and richly armed, and
an occasion to yeeld himselfe more obstinate to fight, having the care
to save his armes, as his goods and inheritance. A reason (saith *Xeno-
phon*) why the *Asiatikes* carried with them, when they went to warres
their wives and Concubines, with all their jewels and chiefest wealth.
And might also encline to the other side, which is, that a man should
rather remove from his souldier, all care to preserve himselfe, than to
increase it unto him: for, by that meanes he shall doubly feare to haz-
ard or engage himselfe, seeing these rich spoiles do rather encrease
an earnest desire of victorie in the enemie: and it hath beene observed, that the said respect hath somethimes wonderfully encouraged the Romans against the Samnites. (Montaigne, *Essais* 1. 47)

Interestingly enough the title of this essay reads—in the English of
Florio 1603 [1967], here followed throughout—"On the uncertaintie
of our judgement." Both poles of the antithesis are described with
equal concern, and they are presented without any attempt to choose
between them on the basis of some criterion of evaluation that would
transcend these terms. This basic rhetorical structure appears even
more clearly a little below:

Among other reproaches, that *Pompey* is charged withall in the battell
of *Pharsalia*, this is one speciall, that he idlely lingred with his Armie,
expecting what his enemie would attempt; forasmuch as that (I will
heare borrow the very words of *Plutarke*, which are of more consequence than mine) weakneth the violence, that running gives the first
blowes, and therewithall removeth the charging of the Combattants
one against another, which more, than any other thing is wont to fill
them with fury and impetuosity, when with vehemence they come to
enter-shocke one another, augumenting their courage by the crie and
running; and in a manner alayeth and quaileth the heat of the Soul-
diers: Lohere what he saith concerning this. But had *Caesar* lost, who
might not also have said, that contrariwise the strongest and firmest
situation, is that, wherein a man keeps his stand without budging, and
that who is settled in his march, closing, and against any time of need,
sparing his strength in himselfe, hath a great advantage against him,
that is in motion and disordered, and that running hath already con-
sumed part of his breath? Moreover, that an armie being a body composed of so many several parts, it is impossible it should in such furie
advance it selfe with so just a march, and proportioned a motion, and
not breake and disranke, or at least alter her ordinance, and that the
nimblest be not grapling before his fellowes may helpe him. In that
drearie battell of the two Persian brethren, *Clearchus* the Lacedemon-

ian, who commanded the Graecians that followed *Cyrus* his faction, led them faire and gently without any hast-making to their charges; but when he came within fifty paces of his enemies, he bad them with all speed to run into it; hoping by the shortnesse of the distance to manage their order, and direct their breath; in the meane time giving them the advantage of the impetuositie, both for their bodies, and for their shooting-armies. Others have ordered this doubt in their armies after this manner: If your enemies head-long run upon you, stay for them and bouge not: If they without stirring stay for you, run with furie upon them.

Aside from the main point they illustrate, these passages are of interest as the object of an informal but effective test to determine two basic levels in the rhetorical structure of a text; one could also speak of macrostructure and microstructure (a distinction which would reflect, in part, the traditional one between "figures" and "tropes"). The former structure, usually, is not lost in the translation while the latter, in most cases, is. Here, the basic dialectic structure can be fully perceived also through the filter of the English version; but I reproduce the French text (according to Rat's edition) in order to show the microscopic but significant rhetorical structures involved:

> ... qui auroit a choisir, ou de tenir ses soldats richement et somp-tueusement armez, ou armez seulement pour la necessité, il se presen-teroit en faveur du premier party, duquel estoit Sertorius, Philopoe-men, Brutus, Caesar et autres, que c'est tousjours un éguillon d'honneur et de gloire au soldat de se voir paré, et un'occasion de se rendre plus obstiné au combat, ayant a sauver ses armes comme ses biens et heritages: raison, dict Xenophon, pourquoy les Asiatiques menoyent en leurs guerres femmes, concubines, avec leurs joyaux et richesses plus cheres. Mais il s'offriroit aussi, de l'autre part, qu'on doit plus tost oster au soldat le soing de se conserver, que de le luy accroistre; joint que c'est augmenter à l'ennemy l'envie de la victoire par ces riches despouilles; et a l'on remarqué que, d'autres fois, cela encouragea merveilleusement les Romains à l'encontre des Samnites.

And:

> A la bataille de Pharsale, entre autres reproches qu'on donne à Pompeius, c'est d'avoir arresté son armée pied coy, attendant l'ennemy; pour autant que cela (je desroberay ici les mots mesmes de Plutarque, qui valent mieux que le miens) 'affoiblit la violence que le courir

donne aux premiers coups, et, quant et quant, oste l'eslancement des combatans les uns contre les autres, qui a accoustumé de les remplir d'impetuosité et de fureur plus que autre chose, quand ils viennent à s'entrechoquer de roideur, leur augmentant le courage par le cry et la course, et rend la chaleur des soldats, en maniere de dire, refroidie et figée.' Voilà ce qu'il dict pour ce rolle; mais si Caesar eut perdu, qui n'eust peu aussi bien dire qu'au contraire la plus forte et roide assiette est celle en laquelle on se tient planté sans bouger, et que, qui est en sa marche arresté, resserrant et espargnant pour le besoing sa force en soymesmes, a grand avantage contre celuy qui est esbranlé et qui a desjà consommé à la course la moitié de son haleine? outre ce que, l'armée estant un corps de tant de diverses pieces, il est impossible qu'elle s'esmeuve en cette furie d'un mouvement si juste, qu'elle n'en altere ou rompe son ordonnance, et que le plus dispost ne soit aux prises avant que son compagnon le secoure. En cette villaine bataille des deux freres Perses [i.e., Cyrus and Artaxerxes], Clerchus Lacedemonien, qui commandoit les Grecs du party de Cyrus, les mena tout bellement à la charge sans soy haster; mais, a cinquante pas près, il les mit à la course, esperant, par la briefveté de l'espace, mesnager et leur ordre et leur haleine, leur donnant cependant l'avantage de l'impetuosité pour leurs personnes et pour leurs armes à trait. D'autres ont reglé ce doubte en leur armée de cette manière: si les ennemis vous courent sus, attendez les de pied coy; s'il vous attendent de pied coy, courez leur sus.

The length of this quote is justified both by the importance of the configurations based on Antithesis, and, in terms of this theory of rhetoric, by its dialectic perspective.[9] The first antithesis shows us directly a rhetorical structure; the second, more richly developed, is even more significant because we see in it the juncture between rhetoric and rhetorics. First the author presents one point of view, quoting from an authority (Plutarch); then he explicitly builds up the opposite point of view, as an experiment ("mais si Caesar eut perdu, qui n'eust peu aussi bien dire . . . ?"); and in this context, it is significant that Montaigne chooses—to indicate Plutarch's position and his own—the term *rôle*, with its theatrical, exhibitionistic connotations.

One of the most difficult temptations to resist, when discussing dialectic, is that of trivializing it into nice trinitarian schemata of thesis–antithesis–synthesis. In fact, the notion of dialectic used here is fully based on the configuration of antithesis; and, as will become clear, it is not by chance that the very structure of dialectic opposition is designated here in rhetorical terms. However, the trinitarian temptation is almost irresistible in the quoted passage: we have the thesis (soldiers should come up to the enemy), followed by the antithesis (soldiers should wait resolutely for the enemy), and then the contrast is nicely wrapped up by the synthesis (soldiers should keep their order and compactness until very close, then run up to the enemy). Fortunately the author makes us perceive that the actual situation, even within the narrow boundaries of the topic he chose, is more complex; for he destroys the reassuring symmetry of the synthesis by presenting us with yet another synthesis. Synthesis$_1$ is the one just quoted, whereas synthesis$_2$ is contained in the final sentence, which illustrates the figure of Chiasmus: "si les ennemis vous courent sus, attendez les de pied coy; s'il vous attendent de pied coy, courez leur sus."

The faintly mundane tone of the whole passage, its flair of armchair strategy, should not make us underestimate the basic seriousness of the strategy of discourse which is revealed here: by duplicating the possible synthesis any irenic hope of settling what is, once and for all, true is destroyed; moreover, synthesis$_2$ is actually, in its own terms, an antithesis, whose surface manifestation is the chiasmus.

Finally: doesn't this antithesis bear a striking resemblance to the Sophist technique as reflected in Aristotle (quoted above)? "If any one speaks as the expert reasoners do, lead him into opposition with the majority, while if he speaks as do the majority, then into opposition to the reasoners." This is indeed the important result of rhetorics (as of any other realistic methodological approach to a vast complex of apparently heterogeneous data): to show the underlying structural similarities—as here, between philosophical speculations couched in Ancient Greek and seemingly lighthearted digressions elegantly expressed in Middle French.

In both cases, what emerges is the primacy of antithesis as the rhetorical figure that best expresses the dialectic nature of rhetorical systems. There is another reason why Montaigne's passage seemed a particularly appropriate illustration. As noted, its lightheartedness is only apparent; also, we should not be misled by the cold and detached appearance of Aristotle's statement. Indeed, the contrast described by Montaigne aptly emphasizes the hard basis of rhetorical structures: these are not the optional ornaments of idyllic reflections, but the inescapable ways of expressing conflicts in real life—struggles for power and control.

At the beginning of this analysis, I was on the verge of an apology;

for I took pains to note that the frivolity of these texts is only apparent. But at this point there is no need for such defenses, for it is clear that the implications of all these statements are serious. However, if some nostalgia for dramatically solemn examples should persist, let me point out that some of them will be briefly touched upon in the description of the various levels of dialectics (Sec. 3.2). Whether the concentration is on the semiotic background of the texts (the "real events" described) or on the linguistic structures of the text, the similarity of the dialectic mechanism at work is what essentially matters.

Fears, prejudices, thirst for power, search for social prestige and so forth, play as strong—and as *respectable*—a role in building an argument as does the search for the good and the true; for naturally (and let us recall the quoted passages from *Feuerbach*) these two complexes of forces are not absolutely opposed.

I have so far treated one out of the three areas in which linguistics presents us with an interpretative grid for analyzing the domain of rhetoric (that is, one of the three areas in which linguistics textures rhetorics). This area, in sum, is the one in which the radical descriptivism of modern linguistics appears as the best tool for making the ontology of rhetoric emerge in its dialectic structuring.

Linguistics in this first aspect, then, describes the ontology of rhetoric in its peculiar combination of two different processes: the stylization of the referents by means of the *koinoì tópoi*, and the dialectic relationship between the semantic nuclei in contrast within the rhetorical discourse. It is now time to move to the two other linguistic grids.

It was pointed out above in what sense certain ideas of historical materialism clarify what is the image of human language that rhetoric presents to us: language as a general structure, transcending the performances, motives, and intentions of the single speakers or writers. This underscores a basic point: rhetoric and linguistics cooperate, on the same level, in the task of adequately representing the structure of language-in-culture; it is not, then, a matter of linguistics colonizing the wilderness of rhetoric. For, if linguistics furnishes the descriptive method, rhetoric offers a complex of already structured discourses that are indispensable if this method is to be correctly applied; furthermore, if linguistics has elaborated a detailed (although far from complete) picture of the grammatical structure of language at all levels (from phonology to semantics), rhetoric encourages linguistics to look for the implementation of this grammatical structure even in the most apparently "free" and "individualistic" discourses—thus leading linguistics out of the impasse of modern stylistic criticism.

But, if this is the case, the images in these last pages describing the interaction of rhetoric and linguistics should be made more sharp and precise. The actual relationship, in fact, is not one of intersection and tangential contact; rhetorical structure is an indispensable component of the overall structure of language, and without it no general view of language could be satisfactory. No general linguistics, then, is possible without rhetorics.

The other two points about linguistics are the natural extension of what has just been remarked. Rhetoric shows us the limits of language—the point up to which language can go without breaking communication. In this sense, rhetorics is essential for psycholinguistics, because it shows us the possibilities of the human mind in its range of linguistic expressions.

It is because of this (and here we come to the last linguistic point) that rhetoric can be used as the test enabling us to choose between different linguistic theories: transformational-generative grammar (in its different current varieties), tagmemics, stratificational grammar, etc. That theory will be most adequate that will accommodate, in the clearest and most systematic way, the rhetorical structure of discourse.

But what has just been said obliges us to go back and have a second look at the dialectic relationship. Dialectic is a notoriously difficult concept to define and to apply systematically. In fact, any impression of excessive optimism with regard to this matter that might have been given must be dispelled here; for the breadth of analysis that the reference to dialectic relationships gives to any description in the human sciences must be weighted against the danger of vacuity that constantly threatens such analyses.

I must, indeed, go further than that in my disclaimer. Dialectic is a cluster of revealing concepts, and a source of crucial insights on the way language and every other structure for interaction in human society work (it is a moot point whether what has just been said could also be applied to processes in nature). But it does not seem possible to speak of a dialectical method as something that actually exists today. What, then, about dialectical materialism, which constitutes the background of my remarks on dialectic? There is, to be sure, a general theory of dialectic, which is at present codified as an ideology; but the relationship between the largely aprioristic statements in that theory and actual scientific method and praxis are still, by and large, to be worked out.

We have thus come to a crossroads: either we pretend (trying hard to convince ourselves–an effort which is detectable in many presentations) that there is such a thing as a full-fledged theory of dialectic satisfactorily realized in a coherent method, or we do not commit ourselves to such a view. In the former case our path soon becomes (as I have suggested) a cul-de-sac: pious verbosity and wishful thinking dominate the scene, with much bark (usually up the wrong tree) but no bite.

In the latter case, on the other hand, our path is that of constructive empirical analysis: we soberly accept the fact that there still is no fully articulated dialectical method, and we try to give a more precise form to this almost shapeless concept as we go by, through a continuous confrontation with the hard data (and of course, this back-and-forth movement is in itself the most concrete and rewarding realization of dialectic). This path has been traveled in the preceding pages, and it is certainly more fruitful than the former one. But the question, at this point, is: should we stop at this level? More precisely: are these two the only available alternatives?

The answer is no: there is another alternative, namely, a rethinking of dialectic along new lines.

3.3 THE TORTUOUS PATH TO DIALECTIC

It is always refreshing, before embarking on the analysis of a cluster of recalcitrant problems, to get rid first of what looks like a problem but really is not. In the case of dialectic, the pseudodifficulty is that of the multiplicity of meanings which the word "dialectic" has acquired, and which allegedly would make it useless as a philosophical concept. That this word has a multiplicity of meanings is true, but irrelevant; is there any philosophical concept—more generally, any abstract word—that is in a different situation today? And yet we go

on using words like "society" and "soul" and "self" and "science" and
"system"; like "being" and "bad" and "believe"; like "law" and "learn"
and "literature"; like "property"; and so forth (we even persist in ex-
changing tragically worn-out coins like "God" and "love"). Why, then,
all this uneasiness with "dialectic"? For a mundane and not an abstractly philosophical reason, I suggest: this word is the symbol of the
most innovative link between theory and praxis in the history of modern culture—Marxism.

To try to exorcise this uneasiness would mean to fall victims to it;
no such attempt will be made here. Neither will I concentrate on a
historicosemantic account of the vagaries in the use of this word in
what we can call the premodern period—from ancient Greek philosophy to Hegel—although this would be an interesting task.[10] I also
cannot present a diachronic-synchronic review of the basic implementations of the concept of dialectic from Hegel to us.[11] Moreover—
although Marxism will be the main element in the background of this
discussion—no effort will be made here to elaborate a Marxological
analysis in the sense of a specific analysis of the seminal writings.[12]
Also, I will not attempt to summarize the *status quaestionis* of modern
debates—especially, but not exclusively, in a Marxist perspective—
about the validity and limitations of Hegelian-Marxist dialectic; but I
will take some of these contributions into account, and indeed the
present analysis is meant as a modest contribution to such a debate
(but to have put a general balance sheet of ideological positions before this specific discussion would have required a separate booklet).[13]
The perspective explored here is rather that of a "dialectic of"; that
is, an applied dialectic, which moves back and forth between general
frames and those concrete situations which are favorite topics in the
humanities—and which too often are left in the care of a rigid, adialectic kind of humanism.[14] To begin with: not only will I not deplore
the multiplicity of senses now attached to the term "dialectic"—I will
welcome this multiplicity, and accept this broad semantic constellation
as the natural background of the whole discussion which follows. I
will, however, discard—or better, push farther back, into the wings—
the degraded, or banalized, senses of the word: dialectic, first of all,
as designating a particular interest for, and skill in, verbal intercourse—especially the game of repartees with one or more themes in
a dialogic situation.

Also, we should not be too concerned with the notion of dialectic as dynamic, searching mental attitude never satisfied with any single stage in the process of reflection, and never acquiescing in a statement as in something that has been definitely proven without any need for revision. Both, of course, are actually existing attitudes—in the best analyses in the humanities and the sciences—and are highly commendable. But to use the term "dialectic" to designate these basic attitudes would really be a needless inflation.

What is, then, the basic constellation? I take dialectic to designate, mainly, the following phenomena and attitudes:

a) The mental and verbal discourse which proceeds by an alternation or antithesis of opposite statements—or intellectual and psychological movements in general (whether these movements are directly opposite—inverse—or contrary, or contradictory); this discourse may be seen as reflecting the inner contradictions of objects and phenomena in the world—the strife between contrary elements (old and new, yes and no, life and death) which is the motor of change and which transforms quantitative changes into qualitative changes. (In this perspective see my analysis, in chapter 4, of a fragment by Heraclitus.)

b) The collocation of every object of reflection into this concrete context (with all its accompanying fluidity and variability) and its historical tradition, with an emphasis on content over form; and the consequent rejection of any clear-cut boundary between this conditioned object and its conditioning elements, between what is posited and constructed as an object of thought and what (or who) posits and constructs it as such an object.

c) A reflection which takes shape through the confrontation of opposite statements which are, at least partially, integrated into a broader synthesis.

d) A view of the world as a complex of processes where everything is in a state of flux, becoming, and transcendence, so that laws or trends of development—rather than constancies—are what matter. The problem is that of identifying a concrete yet many-sided object and at the same time transcending it.

e) A view of the world—nature and history—as a coherent whole, where all phenomena are connected and condition each other; the search for the proper object of analysis, therefore, is the search for something that is at the same time concrete and total.

This seems to be the basic constellation of dialectic—in a description which integrates Hegelian and Marxian elements. Too eclectic? Hardly; dialectic—as I am going to propose—cannot be a unitary concept, and at any rate the concern here is that of identifying the main points of the constellation that is current today, not to super-impose some sort of unity on them. (Lefebvre 1970—a lucid and compact account, still useful—and Foulquié 1966—which oscillates between the acute and the fairly banal—proved of help in organizing these elements.)

All this is good as far as it goes, but the question at this point must be: is it possible to go further? That is: can we shape these elements into a coherent set of methodological instruments? The answer, in my opinion, is no; and not a "no" marking a temporary setback and by this very fact inviting further exertions in order to surmount the obstacle. The point is, it is intrinsically impossible to fashion dialectic as a consistent methodological *instrumentarium* until (unless) we completely revise its ontology.

For what happens when one tries to define more rigorously the domain of dialectic without questioning the traditional ontological frame? Usually one ends up in a naive realism, asserting that the peculiar logic of the dialectical method is something that "we can discover only in the things themselves, in reality, not in our mind."[15]

This kind of simplistic realism is, in effect, the negation of what constitutes the deeper strength of dialectic. But we do have more sophisticated answers to the problem, such as the one which makes use of the concept of overdetermination (which is said to be "the most profound characteristic of the Marxist dialectic"). Overdetermination "reflects in it its conditions of existence, that is, the specific structure of unevenness (in dominance) of the ever pre-given complex whole which is its existence. Thus understood, contradiction is the motor of all development." (This whole statement is italicized in the original, Althusser 1965:223).

However, what is the outcome, even in this more interesting and refined view by Althusser 1965 [1970] (217 et passim)? "If . . . the dialectic is the conception of the contradiction in the very essence of things, the principle of their development and disappearance, then with this definition of the specificity of Marxist contradiction we should have reached the Marxist dialectic itself" (ibid.). But the fact is, we didn't; *generic* calls to specificity do not make dialectic in gen-

eral, or Marxist dialectic in particular, more specific. And the tortuous and tortured analyses of statements by Marx and Engels purporting to prove the deep originality of Marxian dialectic with respect
to Hegel end up by realizing just those negative features—of abstract
ideological construction—that Althusser and other critics in the same
position so brilliantly criticize when they are not "blinded" (to echo
Adorno) by their excessive vicinity to what they keep considering ca-
nonic texts.

Thus, between a detailed study purporting to show that the famous
Marxian phrase about the rational kernel and the mystical shell is
really deeper than the facile opposition it seems to be (Althusser
1965:87 ff.) and Adorno's appreciation that "Marx the dialectician
did not have a fully developed concept of dialectic, with which he
thought he could confine himself to 'flirting'" (Adorno et al. 1972:35);
between these two attitudes, I think that the latter points in the right
direction whereas the former would push us to erecting systems at all
costs, in a triumph of ideology. I am aware that on the one side we
have merely a hint, while on the side of the French scholar we find a
well developed analysis, which remains a very interesting example of
methodical text study. Yet the general perspective seems to be the one
just sketched.

Let us pause for a moment. At the beginning, I denied that dialectic could be successfully expressed as a set of systematic concepts—
and what has just been noted seems to me to confirm that evaluation.
On the other hand, it was also noted that a succession of purely empirical notations would be equally unsatisfactory. We are now in a
position to understand why it would be so: not because we have no
use, in the humanities, for empirical analysis of dialectical relationships—on the contrary, there is an urgent need for them, and the
pages that follow will concentrate on this aspect. To quote Adorno et
al., 1972 again—on p. 38: "Hypostatized dialectic becomes a-dialectic
and it needs to be corrected by that *fact finding* [English in the original
text] whose interest is perceived by empirical social research—which
in its turn, then, becomes incorrectly hypostatized by the positivistic
theory of science."

No, the real reason why this approach would not work, ultimately,
is that it would bespeak a sort of false humility: it would seem to
imply that, waiting for the general system of dialectic to be worked

out, one should rest content with refining and polishing the little details. But this is not the case; in fact, what was suggested is that there is no general system of dialectic which can be plausibly elaborated. It seems, then, that only one path is left open: to conclude that dialectic must be the object of an asystematic intuition—dialectic can be intuitively put to work, it cannot be explained.

This position is, in fact, adopted by some thinkers (some aspects of this attitude I find in Adorno 1973, for instance), but it seems unacceptable. Such an irrationalistic view of dialectic is only a few degrees higher than the above-criticized defensive reaction to the effect that dialectic cannot be seriously used because the term has too many different senses. In both cases, we renounce coming to grips with an idea—we do not take the responsibility of saying where we stand, whether we think that this concept is viable or not; and this responsibility cannot be evaded.

3.4 THE NATURE OF DIALECTIC

Fortunately, there is still one other path open, one which, as it turns out, is the decisive one. It was evoked above when it was noted that there was no way out of the impasse except by revising the ontology of rhetoric. Dialectic cannot be seriously used until one gets beyond the illusion that it reflects processes actually taking place in reality. Traditionally, dialectical statements are ultimately based on a simplistic realism which contrasts with the sophistication of the analyses built on it. This realistic scaffolding must be laid bare and dismantled.

But, if we are consequent in the critique of this realism, we are faced with the conclusion that what confines and weakens dialectic is nothing less than that materialist foundation which became an integral part of the most acute and consistent development of dialectic after Hegel—that is, of course, the Marxian one. (Marxian: what I am talking about here is the seminal period, not the modern bureaucratization—to a certain extent, inevitable—usually associated with what are currently designated as Marxist positions.)

This conclusion is indeed inescapable. But if this is the case, one could object that my proposal would set dialectic back, pushing it into the lap of idealism once again—whether of the Hegelian variety or of some other kind. Now, Hegel's system is still every bit as elegant to flirt with as it was in Marx's time—perhaps even more so today. But, once the heady excitement of such a courtship has waned, are we really much better off? No, indeed; however, there is no intrinsic reason why the refusal of a materialist basis for dialectic should push us right back into the arms of idealism; the conviction that this is unfailingly the case has been spread by the shallow and dogmatically repetitive interpretation of Marxism which is still too current today, and from whose awe we need to free ourselves if we want to make real progress in cultural criticism, *especially* progress in *Marxist* cultural criticism.

But, if we do not cling either to materialism or to idealism, what is left? The *bête noire* of both Hegel and Marx—as well of innumerable thinkers before and after them—the concrete alternative (strong and realistic just because it is not ontologically realist) that these thinkers have desperately tried to ward off: skepticism. Let us go back for a moment to the constellation of dominant senses of the word "dialectic." There I arranged the different senses in a roughly decreasing order of importance: the core of dialectic is the reference to a discourse (either in the sense of silent reflection or of verbal utterance) which proceeds through an antithesis of opposites.

This is essentially all that counts for dialectic, and if we stop here we have an instrument which is at the same time elastic enough to be used in all the different situations of empirical research, and sufficiently systematic to give a principled foundation (rather than a vague aura of eclecticism) to these different analyses. But, as soon as we go beyond this characterization, this flexible method (politically realistic, in the above-specified sense of the word "political") becomes rigid and abstract—a means of caging thought and action rather than liberating them: in short, it becomes an ideology.

The first (but not the only) path of ideologization in our constellation is, as noted, the one which is followed if we claim that this process reflects objectively existing contradictions, contradictions within "things." To claim this (as all modern Marxist analyses seem to do) is almost as absurd as objecting, as do many critics of dialectic (Popper and many neopositivists, for instance—See Pilot in Adorno et al. 1972:300), that facts cannot be contradictory. The latter statement encourages us to cultivate a peaceful, nonproblematic view of reality

in which, once one understands them properly, facts go happily together like parts of a well-oiled mechanism. (To be sure, there is no
logically consequential link between the claim that the feature of contradiction cannot be applied to facts, and a mechanistically stable view
of the facts of human society; but there are several psychological,
historical, and cultural links between claims of that sort on the one
hand and this view on the other.)

The statement that facts are contradictory, for its part, has the advantage of expressing a problematic view of the world. But the objectionable presumption which still persists in it is that it is possible really
to observe the facts out there—as clear objects independent of language—and then to compare them with their linguistic representation. In this respect, dialectic appears to be enmeshed in the same
empiricist and pragmatist positions that it usually attacks. But once
this illusion is dispelled, the nature of dialectic becomes clear: *dialectic
is not a complex of laws concerning processes in the world; rather, dialectic is
the best characterication of how perception is linguistically constructed.*

All facts are accessible to us only as linguistic constructions; all extended linguistic constructions are rhetorical constructions; the way,
then, in which the rhetorical structure (i.e., the functional, discursive
structure) of any utterance is revealed in all its effectiveness is usually
through the confrontation of, and balance between, opposite elements; an uneasy and constantly shifting balance, to be sure, endowed with tension, and with a continuous back-and-forth movement
between these elements. It is this confrontation which constitutes dialectic: dialectic, then, is *the dominant form in which rhetorical structure
manifests itself*; nothing more (and nothing less) than this.

From at least the time of Heraclitus dialectic has been the strongest
weapon against any excess of entrenched certainty: it has dissolved
constancies and ideological ossifications. But philosophers have too
often (and with too much success) tried to tame this process of disso-
lution, harnessing it in such a way that it would work against the theories of their immediate predecessors and rival contemporaries, but
stop short of a dissolving critique of their own ossifications.

Thus Marxism, which starts with a merciless, radical critique, is
soon preoccupied with setting itself up as one of those traditional
philosophical systems which it had promised to bring to an end; in
this case, a variety of materialism. For this is the basic point: the re-

curring generic pleas for a "literal," "tolerant" variety of this philosophy miss the point, as does every such call to tolerance within a philosophical system if it is not accompanied by a new perspective on it.
The problem is not dogmatism as such—the problem comes before,
so to speak; in accepting assertions of materialism as a basic criterion.

No available variety of materialism, no matter how sophisticated
(and Marxism is the most sophisticated one), is adequate to express
the actual creativity of language (creativity being here interpreted
neither in a vague, aesthetic, and individualistic sense *nor* in the technical sense of transformational-generative grammar, but rather with
reference to the capacity that language has to construct what we call
reality). At least, this is true of all varieties of materialism that share
what seem to be sufficient criteria for defining a given philosophy as
materialistic: realism (being exists independently from thought), ra-
tionalism (this being can be known), ontologism (thought is determined by being), and autonomism (being is independent from non-
human forms of consciousness, such as divine consciousness). This
list is one of the few specific points made in Apostel 1972—a booklet
which actually is a rather vague programmatic article.

I suggest that these features, although *sufficient* to define traditional
materialism, are not *necessary* in order to define a priori the scope of
materialism. More precisely: it seems possible to speak of a materialist
attitude which is not qualified as such by *any* assertion about being
and matter. Such assertions would inevitably be metaphysical—for
those "physical" aspects of the world around us about which we sometimes, in our flights of optimism, feel so sure are actually not clear-
cut objects clearly visible over there, but phenomena inextricably
bound up with our perceptions (in which, in turn, ideological structuring is present at every step).

The materialist attitude suggested here, on the other hand, would
limit itself to stating that man is perceivable only as a totally social
being: *his consciousness is determined by his total social context, and even his
unconscious is bound to collective patterns.* Could such a view still be
called materialist? This is not the place to develop a discussion of this
problem; suffice to have sketched it in the background of the present
analysis.

Back to dialectic and rhetoric: we have just seen that what is called
for is not an *application* of dialectic to rhetorical analysis, but a reali-

zation that dialectic *is* rhetoric—more precisely, dialectic is the favored mode of manifestation of rhetoric, which in turn is the way language manifests itself and functions at the level of discourse. Dialectic, then, should not be looked for either in "things" or in "ideas"; dialectic is *the main* mode of manifestation of language, which in its turn is *the only* mode of manifestation of the world.

What has been just presented is at the same time the strongest assertion of the importance of dialectic in human life and the sharpest limitation of any pretense of dialectic to present itself as an autonomous philosophical method. This limitation of dialectic (whether of the idealist or of the materialist type) moves—as noted above—from skepticism. A long discussion is impossible here, but at least one should say a word about what is perhaps the most familiar objection to skepticism.

Skepticism—this hoary argument goes—fails as a method because it cannot be properly skeptical about itself. This objection has become the battle cry of that respectable fellow common sense, which was introduced by Engels in the passage quoted in section 3.1; but the weakness of this objection has been known for a long time (See, for instance, Popper 1968:68). However, at this stage, even this objection becomes more refined than its current version. For the tone of the usual objections to skepticism is one of ontologic realism—they amount essentially to saying: "If we doubt of every object or event in the world, shouldn't we doubt also of our doubt?" But the thesis presented here is that the relevant relationship is not that between the observer and "reality," but that between the speaker and his own rhetoric.

The antiskeptic objection, then, cannot afford any longer to be straightforwardly realistic: it must, so to speak, take a step back and address itself to semiotic structures rather than to immediately perceivable *realia*. Its form, then, could be as follows: "You say that everything is rhetoric, but your very statement—isn't it rhetoric, too?" But it is enough to formulate the objection in this way to see that rhetorical theory has deprived it of whatever force it might originally have had. For when there is a clear-cut separation between language and reality, with the consequent distinction between discourses that faithfully reflect the structure of reality and discourses which do not; when this is the choice—and the challenge—it may be disquieting to note that a given discourse, which presented itself as a way of clearing the underbrush away and getting really close to the hard wall of reality, should actually be considered as merely another instance of oblique and misleading verbal variation.

But when the theory at issue stipulates from the very beginning that there is no such clear-cut hierarchy, and that we have to do only with different rhetorical constructions, then it is clear that the problem is not a black-and-white one, a dilemma between truth and error. The real empirical problem to which the scholar must devote his energies is that of elaborating an analysis which satisfies two exigencies: to make every step in the description as explicit as possible (which means that the rhetorician—in a fruitfully dialectical move—studies the connection between his rhetoric and the rhetoric he describes, and how they affect each other); and always to make sure that the rhetorician moves up along a scale of more and more comprehensive rhetorical frames.

This latter point is basic: all we can reasonably aim for is for the rhetoric we put most trust in (within a given historical and cultural situation, and for a given text or group of texts) to be broader than the rhetorical structure it examines. From rhetorical structure to rhetorical structure . . . isn't it an infinite regress? Yes, but perhaps we should call it a *pro*gress. Actually, this is as much progress as we can hope for in the nonexact sciences (i.e., the humanities); the only danger to be on the lookout for is that of using a rhetorical frame which is more narrow and more shallow than the structure which is being studied. If, through painstaking collecting and sifting of the relevant data, we avoid this danger, then there is no fatal objection to the positive skepticism which is proposed here.

In his discussion of ideology Veron 1971 appropriately accepts without qualms the idea of *regressus ad infinitum*. But his way of dealing with this problem in the field of ideology is slightly different:

> The scientific character of the construction of a descriptive and explanatory language about reality expresses itself through the introduction of elements *denoting the operations themselves, which have been carried out by the sender*. This does not eliminate the ideological nature of the decision made, but neutralizes its "ideological effect" . . . If a set of theoretical decisions cannot, in the present state of the social sciences, be justified by means of the formal rules of "scientific

method," the resulting discourse has been constructed under ideological conditions of production: it is impossible to neutralize these
conditions by "fiat." What may certainly *be* neutralized is its ideological
consumption. (italics in original)

The difference stems essentially from the two different levels of
discourse which are at issue here. When analyzing those (more or
less) de-forming elements of discourse that are the ideologies it is
important to try and neutralize (as far as possible) their effects. On
the other hand, analyzing the actual politics which underlies these
ideological strata (that is, in terms of my theory, the actual rhetorical
structure of discourses), our aim cannot be that of neutralizing the
rhetorical effects—for, in doing this, we would blur the features of
the real politics in favor of the ideological deformations. (Finally,
while the quoted article is concerned with scientific discourse, my
concern here is mostly with nonscientific, literary or nonliterary, types
of discourse; but this is not a crucial difference, since the present
rhetorical theory concerns all types of discourse—with due recognition, of course, of the relevant divergences within the general framework.)

As noted, the list of the main senses of "dialectic" is organized in a
decreasing order of importance, from the most concrete and fruitful
sense to the least usable, which also means the most ideological. In
this perspective it may appear strange that dialectic as antithesis, in
sense (a), put at the beginning as the most relevant, is separated by
the sense which is usually associated with it: (c), the idea of dialectic
as synthesis.

But (as indicated in the preceding section) that of synthesis is the
most dangerous concept in dialectic analysis: the search for synthesis
opens the way for all sorts of ideological legerdemains—looking for
a synthetic conclusion at all costs, it is easy to superimpose a "nice"
façade on an underlying situation of tension and conflict. Nor is the
synthesized dialectic more dynamic than the one which insists on antithesis.

The concept of dynamism is vague at any rate; but, insofar as it
might make empirical sense of rhetorical analysis, it refers to the effort to capture a given situation in all its variety and mobility, and to
express it with a linguistic richness adequate to its fluid complexity.
In this sense, there is no a priori reason why a dialectic that privileges

synthesis should be more or less dynamic than one that gives antithesis the pride of place.

A good part of the linguistic debate in the last twenty years (but more generally, all along our century) has been couched in the rhetoric of "dynamic" (good) versus "static" (bad)—a rhetoric which straddled the otherwise conflicting fields of traditional and structural linguistics, and which played (within the latter field) a large role in the debate between "traditional" structural linguistics and transformational-generative grammar. But there can be no real dynamism if the discussion is kept at the level of partial relationships between minor units—and this quite apart from the fact that the rhetoric which makes of "static" a dirty word is a highly objectionable one.

Linguistic description will become something which may usefully be called "dynamic" only when the peculiar dialectic nature of its units (especially of its larger ones) is clarified, and when the analysis of the synchronic dimension fully merges with that on the diachronic dimension; the two tasks are not sharply separated, at any rate, since an adequate comprehension of the synchronic–diachronic nexus is based on a general dialectic view. In this perspective, it seems no accident that modern linguistics has yet to come to grips with both tasks.

A skeptical dialectic does not apply only to literary and stricto sensu linguistic problems; in fact, such a dialectic turns out to be a systematic response to the dream (shared by Marxist scholarship with widely divergent trends in political analysis) of a real science of politics. The most important single reason why this project has until now been a hope rather than a concrete plan is that too often the attempt has been made to create a science of politics without creating the proper distance with respect to the subject matter; the attempt, in other words, was to create a science on the thin basis of an ideology (an error which inevitably also includes a large part of Marxist scholarship).

A science of politics cannot be a science of political *realia*; political description begins to be scientific when it treats—not only political discourses—but all political *events* essentially *sub specie orationis*. This simply reaffirms the idea that events both political and nonpolitical exist for us essentially and primarily as *complexes of signs* (particularly, and of special interest to us in rhetorics, linguistic signs; but also as signs of a nonlinguistic type).

It would appear that the authors on whose work the present insistence on dialectic is based (Hegel and his successors, mostly on the left) are also those who implicitly oppose the view expressed here, because of their insistence on objective reality (be it spiritual or material). Once again, the only response, in general terms, is that my approach is frankly revisionistic. It is also necessary to add that this revisionism has nothing to do with the current connotations of that word—a kind of shiftiness, a lack of scruples, a timid concern for maintaining diplomatic niceties and balances. On the contrary, the revisionism of this rhetorical theory is of a different, and more energetic, kind—it is a revisionism which aims at innovating, at cutting through the maze of ideology; it is a revisionism which (well aware of the inevitable errors and misunderstandings it may unwillingly commit) is ready to face the conflicts which this procedure evokes.

Dialectic must be constantly turned against itself (if this were not so, it would be too easy—and too facile—to perform the work of a dialectician). Any use of dialectic which is based on axiological assertions is to a large extent an ideological mystification; and synthesis (to repeat) is the path preferred by hollow axiologies.[16] What I am warning against is not the concept of synthesis as pointing out that the two opposite poles in a given situation still share several important elements; this concept is indeed indispensable to dialectic. What is too vague is the idea that the synthesis somehow "transcends" the elements of the antithesis.

The dialectic approach advocated here aims at being scientific (insofar as this adjective can be applied to the human sciences) not so much because of its promises as because of its cautions and qualifications. It is scientific, then, insofar as it makes the basis of dialectic more precise and less broad, and shows it as an inescapable de-formation, rather than a way of access to a deep and mysterious level of being; and in particular, its dialectic is based on nontranscendent antithesis. It is scientific also because it implies a rigorously descriptive attitude.

It is not at all easy to be descriptive at this level, because it is difficult (indeed, it is painful) to be constantly on guard against the tendency (so "natural"—like common sense) to rush into moralistic and gnoseological commitments. Skepticism is basically severe—it has very little to do with the smirking laziness of popular caricatures.

Thus this rhetorical theory must firmly deny that "'Error/truth' constitute a fundamental philosophical pair in every discourse, *in every type of discourse*—indeed, even more than 'appearance/reality', it constitutes the really fundamental pair" (Preti 1968:191—italics in original). All that has been said until now explains why such assertions are untenable. "Appearance/reality" is a dialectic antithesis—provided it is made clear that it is not an absolute one: "reality" is merely a deeper stratum of "appearance." The functionality of this antithesis is illustrated by the apparently humble world of idioms and proverbs (but Aristotle, not to mention others, already saw their importance); thus, for instance, "things are not what they seem," or, in Italian, "*l'apparenza inganna*," and so forth.

Indeed, this antithesis should encourage us not only to look for what lies behind appearances, but also to appreciate the structure of appearances—the *gaietta pelle* or 'dappled skin' (if I may borrow Dante's phrase) of the world; after all, how else would literary creation and analysis be possible? For it is clear by now, in the post-Marxian human sciences, that superstructures are perhaps even more in need of detailed consideration than structures.[17]

But "error/truth" is not a dialectic antithesis: it is too rigid and absolute to be any such thing. Of course the rhetoric (i.e., the functional structure) of discourses is full of *apparent* implementations of such an antithesis. But a careful linguistic analysis, in the full sense of the word, will show that in such antitheses there is no criterion for a clearcut opposition of truth to error; they are but variants of the "appearance/reality" antithesis, in the sense clarified above.

The lineaments of a really contemporary rhetorical criticism have begun to emerge. This criticism must be systematic—and as such must apply to all types of discourse without opting exclusively for the "hothouse" variety (that is, a certain kind of literature, commented on in a "strictly literary" way—as if such a thing were possible), or for the juridical and political genres; it must be urgent and contemporary—which does *not* mean limited to contemporary texts (my choice of illustrations should dispel this interpretation). "Urgent" means that such a rhetorical criticism looks in all texts (ancient or modern) for the burning issues revolving around the fight (the symbolic fight) for positions of power; and it is contemporary because it does not avoid—on the contrary, it welcomes and develops—the tension between the values and historical conditionings of the contemporary critic and the different historical conditionings when the texts are not contemporary. Finally, this criticism must be descriptive—not simply in the sense of trying to avoid unmediated value judgments but above all in the sense of being developed according to a rigorous methodology, which at every step clarifies the relations between the ideology of the text and the ideology of the analysis developed on that text.

We thus go farther than the surmise that "it is not at all beyond discussion that these sciences [i.e., the human sciences such as rhetoric—*PV*] cannot be *wertfrei*, and cannot be handled with fully scientific methods—and in fact they *are* handled in this way, at least tentatively" (Preti 1968). The basic aim of this book is to develop such a method for rhetoric. Thus it is hoped that another gap will begin to narrow: "from Bacon till today the productions of work on the methodology of science, on epistemology and on the logic of the scientific discourse is immense; whereas . . . parallel research on the form of rhetorical discourse is almost non-existent" (ibid.:177).

Let us—before showing some aspects of this criticism at work— bring together in a general sketch the elements of the view of dialectic expounded here. A diagram may be of use:

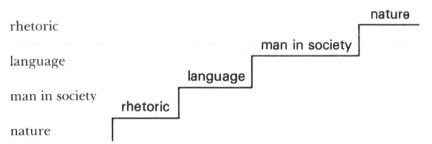

rhetoric

language

man in society

nature

What this is meant to show is the rhetorical nature of dialectic. In the traditional, ontological view of dialectic, we are implicitly told that there are certain processes at work in nature which also operate in society, are then reflected in language, and may be polished and embellished by rhetoric. What is proposed here is the opposite: these processes exist essentially as rhetorical structures, which are extended to all linguistic manifestations, and through them imposed on society and nature as the only ways of perceiving and describing phenomena in these domains.

Any object can be perceived only in antithetical terms—as both equal and nonequal to itself. This dialectic pattern emerges also, *a contrario*, from those descriptions which insist on the necessity of developing a sense of the continuity of objects through time and space:

> If, for instance, we say that a heated iron bar becomes red, we presuppose that the object "iron bar" remains identical although some qualities (color, temperature) are different. . . . Certainly, formal elements are at work in constituting the object . . . they are of the same nature as those which are called "categories" when what is at issue are general objects (regions) and concepts: . . . the unity of every individual object is constituted through a sort of individual category. (Preti 1968:182ff.)

I suggest that this "individual category" is a dialectical linguistic construct; otherwise, why would we need to reassure ourselves on the persisting identity of the object? In plain words: the very fact that we insist so much that a certain object remains the same through its several different states means that we perceive it, at the same time (and in varying degrees), as different. Thus physics "might point out that a table, for example, is a composite of processes or motions of molecules, atoms, electrons, and so on, or that in terms of a period of time the table as a whole is subject to decay and hence constitutes a process" (Pike 1967:199).

A suggestion like the following, then (advanced with caution, to be sure), cannot be accepted: "The contradictory aspect of a given temporal society might even conceivably be traced back to its source, being taken as the outgrowth or social externalization of initial biologic contradictions" (Burke 1973:250–51). Biological "dialectic" is the outgrowth of rhetorical patterns. The realistic path (which should be applied to all "contradictions") is this one instead:

> Some contradictions may be considered as purely subjective phenomena, depending for their existence upon the "point of view." . . . The glands of internal secretion "cancel" the effects of one another, but from the standpoint of the body as a whole they may be said to "collaborate." Newton talked of planetary motions as a synthesis of centrifugal and centripetal forces, but he himself warned that the synthesis was the real event and the two contradictory concepts were purely mathematical conventions used in plotting it. (ibid.)

Of course, caution should be exercised at every point: each putative dialectical relationship should be scrutinized, verified, tightened up in terms of relevant, updated scientific information. The following sketch seems more cogent than the Newtonian allusion; it also leads us back to the contemporary social problems around us, when we consider the "'philanthropic' activities by which the predatory frequently attempt to convert the fruits of their conquests back into social services." Here the dialectic view alerts us: "But this makes two antithetical stages of a process which is normally sound only when it is synthetic. It is not normal to seize and give back—it is normal to convert the act-of-seizure itself into an act of symbolic benefit" (ibid.:317–18).

This synchronic—or better, panchronic—dialectic is integrated by a diachronic (or genetic) dialectic, recognized since the beginning of philosophical reflection, for which the Classical term of *enantiodromia* is perhaps the most apt: "the play of opposites in the course of events—the view that everything that exists turns into its opposite" ("Definitions," Jung 1971:425–26). Jung provides his own interpretation of *enantiodromia*: "the emergence of the unconscious opposite in the course of time. This characteristic phenomenon practically always occurs when an extreme, one-sided tendency dominates conscious life; in time an equally powerful counterposition is built up, which first inhibits the conscious performance and subsequently breaks through the conscious control" (ibid.).

3.5 STRUCTURES AND DISCONTINUITIES

If dialectic is in its essence a complex of rhetorical patterns, and if human language—insofar as it is viewed at its most integrated level (that of discourse) and in its functions—is rhetoric, it is not a long step to the conclusion that language is essentially dialectic. Which means (to get out of purely formal deductions, and into concrete characterizations): *language is dialectic insofar as it manifests itself under the form of discourses, which are essentially constituted by antithetical statements*—implemented in various ways, and at various degrees of sharpness and directness, as far as the antitheses are concerned. But this is far from being the whole picture.

Language is dialectic also because of the continuous tension between its general design (whose reflex in the speaker is often called competence) and its implementation (performance). But the competence/performance pair is not to be interpreted in the narrow sense (current in contemporary linguistics, and especially in its transformational-generative variant) by which what is at issue is, basically, the lack of overlapping between the underlying grammatical structure of the language and its realization in this or that series of utterances by this or that speaker. The competence/performance nexus is dialectic insofar as there is *a constant struggle between the language as institution and the sociolinguistic behavior of the single speakers*—and it is out of this dialectic tension that linguistic history is born.

As an important book by Vološinov [or Baxtin?]—1973 [1927] puts it:

> The individual motives and intentions of a speaker can take meaning-ful effect only within limits imposed by current grammatical possibilities on the one hand, and within the limits of the conditions of socio-verbal intercourse that predominates in his group on the other. . . . His [i.e., the speaker's—*PV*] subjective intentions will bear a creative character only to the extent that there is something in them that co-incides with tendencies in the socioverbal intercourse of speakers that are in process of formation, of generation; and the tendencies are dependent upon socioeconomic factors.

To be sure, this passage (typical of the rest of the book) is not a specimen of stylistic brilliance (at any rate, it comes to us through a translation). And stylistic liveliness is a *substantive* issue—for all the recurring reappearances of the old, adialectic dichotomy of *fond* and *forme*. As Adorno et al. 1972:30 notes:

> The stylistic negligence of many scientists, which may be rationalized by a tabu on the expressive aspect of language, betrays a reified con-sciousness. Since science is dogmatically transformed into an objectiv-ity which is not supposed to pass through the subject, linguistic expression receives minimal attention. For the person who always handles facts as a reality in themselves, without subjective mediation, the way of formulating them becomes indifferent—in favor of the thing, which has become a fetish.

An important insight, certainly, and one that imposes a heavy bur-den on the writer; but an unescapable burden for any writer who strives toward something more than a "reified" consciousness of his work. Qualifications, however, are necessary. On the one hand, the excitement of works like "Baxtin" 1973 comes through clearly even if the text is less than overwhelming in stylistic elegance. And on the other hand, many brilliantly written texts age quickly: their epigrams fade, their points lose their sharpness.[18]

This antithetical structure of discourse has found a privileged expression in that type of discourse which has, through the ages, become institutionalized as "literature"; and we must indeed speak in terms of ages, since these antitheses are archetypes of all eloquent and problematic discourses—from the antiquity of Greece to that of India, and so forth in all languages and literatures (it seems). Consider:

> Often mentioned (in alchemical treatises) is dragon's blood or blood of the lion. The dragon and lion are early forms of Mercurius manifested as passion and concupiscence which must undergo extraction and transformation. The ancient mythological parallel is the blood of the Centaur, Nessus, whom Heracles killed when Nessus attempted to rape Deianeira. This blood was capable of generating erotic passion and when Deianeira later gave Heracles a shirt soaked in Nessus' blood in an effort to restore his attraction to her, it produced a fiery agony that ended only on his funeral pyre. Thus, like Mercurius who can be either poison or panacea, the arcane substance symbolized as blood can bring either passion, wrath and fiery torment or salvation depending on the attitude and condition of the ego experiencing it. (Edinger 1973:151)

And let us listen to a statement from the Brahmanic *Laws of Manu*: "in order to distinguish actions, he [the Creator—PV] separated merit from demerit, and he caused the creatures to be affected by the pairs of opposites, such as pain and pleasure." This passage is from Jung 1971 [1921]: par. 327ff. [pp. 195ff.], who does not use systematically the term "dialectic," but is constantly concerned with this phenomenon, as in this comment on the quoted passage and other similar ones: "It is external opposites such as heat and cold, that must first be denied participation in the psyche, and then extreme fluctuations of emotion, such as love and hate. Fluctuations of emotions are, of course, the constant concomitants of all psychic opposites, and hence of all conflicts of ideas, whether moral or otherwise." This is— in the terms of the present theory—an essential linguistic (rather than psychological) fact, but it is at any rate a fact unavoidably to be faced, whether or not we accept the religious (and ideological) synthesis that some superimpose on it: "Although Brahman, the world-ground and world-creator, created the opposites, they must nevertheless be cancelled out in it again, for otherwise it would not amount to a state of redemption" (ibid. par. 329 and passim). The following perspective is the natural frame of a rhetorical theory, *provided* that the elements described here are reinterpreted as linguistic constructs, rather than as objective psychological (or cosmic) facts:

> Every energic phenomenon (and there is no phenomenon that is not energic) consists of pairs of opposites: beginning and end, above and below, hot and cold, earlier and later, cause and effect, etc. The inseparability of the energy concept from that of polarity also applies to the concept of libido. Hence libido symbols, whether mythological or speculative in origin, either present themselves directly as opposites or can be broken down into opposites. (ibid.: par. 337 [p. 202])

(All this prepares the background for the analysis of Heraclitus' fragment in the chapter which follows.) And literature? But I have been talking of literature all the time! Let us, however, come closer both to properly literary discourse and to the historical period from which the most extended illustration up to now has been drawn: the Renaissance, which with its rediscovery of ancient Skepticism and many other critical theories of the past, is one of the crucial moments in the literary development of the language most apt to describe the psychological fluctuations between pairs of opposites, which have been just shown to be one of the basic ways of perceiving the world.

What is particularly important to capture, for a history of ideas (that is, essentially, for historical rhetoric), is the more mundane and, so to speak, soft inflection of a theme which had often been evoked (in the classic past) in a more solemn, sacral tone. Witness this concise and acute statement by one of Castiglione's characters, in one of the basic books of mundane strategies in the Renaissance: "ché non solamente a voi po parer una cosa ed a me un'altra, ma a me stesso poria parer or una cosa ed ora un'altra" (Cortegiano 1. 13. (203); see Maier 1964).[19]

This concise hint is elaborated—with the usual, almost morbid, care for refinement and *variatio*—in that essay, "De l'inconstance de nos actions":

> Si je parle diversement de moy, c'est que je me regarde diversement.
> Toutes les contrarietez s'y trouvent selon quelque tour et en quelque
> façon. Honteux, insolent; chaste, luxurieux; bavard, taciturne; labor-
> ieux, delicat; ingenieux, hebeté; chagrin, debonaire; menteur, veri-
> table; sçavant, ignorant, et liberal, et avare, et prodigue, tout cela, je
> le vois en moy aucunement, selon que je me vire; et quiconque
> s'estudie bien attentifvement trouve en soy, voire et en son jugement
> mesme, cette volubilité et discordance. Je n'ay rien à dire de moy,
> entierement, simplement et solidement, sans confusion et sans mes-
> lange, ny en un mot. *Distingo* [sic] est le plus universel membre de ma
> logique. (Montaigne 2. 1.; cf. Rat 1962, 1:369–70)[20]

It is interesting to see this theme developed later in a softer, more
sentimental and less cogent way, in passages like the following:

> Le bonheur est un état permanent, qui ne semble fait ici-bas pour
> l'homme. Tout est sur la terre dans un flux continuel qui ne permet
> pas à rien d'y prendre une forme constante. Tout change autour de
> nous. Nous changeons nous-mêmes et nul ne peut s'assurer qu'il aim-
> era demain ce qu'il aime aujourd'hui. Ainsi tous nos projets de félicité
> pour cette vie sont des chimères.[21]

What I called "softness" can be more specifically identified: the
statement just quoted transfers to the world at large those problems
that Montaigne firmly anchored in the psyche of man; and when it
does deal with man, it is not the alternation of strengths and weak-
nesses that is critically and soberly faced—the contrast is instead pret-
tified by having recourse to a self-indulgent notion (changes in love
feelings) to which no blame accrues. It is perhaps excessive to jump
directly from these two passages to a general characterization of the
difference between Renaissance and (Proto-) Romantic rhetoric: yet
the described features of these passages should be seen on this
broader background.

But it is not only in the direction of abstract reason that dialectic
statements are amplified; it is also in the sense of an analysis of the
politics of everyday interactions among men—that is, of politics in
the only concrete sense of the word (the other senses having to do, as
noted, with ideology). A significant example is in the quoted treatise
by Castiglione. Messer Gasparo, who plays the role critical of females
in the debate on women, is, at a certain point, warned not to persist;
for, says messer Ottaviano, "parmi vedere che v'acquistarete non so-

lamente tutte queste donne per inimiche, ma ancora la maggior parte degli omini" ['It seems to me that you will make enemies not only of all these ladies here, but also of most of the gentlemen']. The reply is an apt dialectic rebuff to this conformistic, timid (thus adialectic) warning (risking anchronism, one could say that a liberal fear of unpleasantness speaks through that warning): "Rise il signor Gasparo e disse: 'Anzi ben gran causa hanno le donne di ringraziarmi; perché s'io non avessi contradetto al signor Magnifico ed a messer Cesare, non si sariano intese tante laudi che essi hanno loro date'" (Cortegiano 3. 51 (410); cf. Maier 1964).[22] At one level, this could be interpreted as a glib pleasantry which "does not mean anything." But let us be careful not to be naively anachronistic, mixing the faded and degenerated style of modern bourgeois etiquette with the still powerful and ascending style of mundane strategies, at a high level of ideological debate, in a Renaissance court (we face here the same danger, of making a Renaissance nobleman into a post-Victorian petit bourgeois, that I already criticized with regard to some modern readings of Cordelia in 2.3). If one reads closely and critically the whole context, one notes that the speeches of the two defenders of women have an emphatic quality—they are abstract flights rather than concrete defenses of the status of women in specific terms. The most plausible interpretation of what Gasparo is saying, then, is the following: he makes them understand that he is aware of having, through his critical posture, radicalized the situation, of having goaded his interlocutors into assuming an abstract stance that they will probably not be able to sustain in any meaningful way. Dialectic, once again, proves concrete but not trivial; it is not pleasantries I am talking about, but the politics of living (and see, for instance, Bourdieu 1972 and 1976).

This example has evoked one of the main themes in Renaissance literature—the debate about women. The passage that follows shows a particularly interesting connection of one aspect of this psychological debate with a different, philosophical, problem. The interest stems from the fact that what unifies the two heterogeneous points is dialectic, inflected in a clear-cut rhetorical antithesis. The passage is from I capricci del bottaio by Giovan Battista Gelli (a writer who is representative of mid-sixteenth century Florentine literature). It is the soul of the protagonist Giusto, his Anima, who speaks here:

Hai mai inteso d'uno che domandava consiglio a un altro di tòr mog-
lie? E quando egli diceva: 'Ella è bella', e colui diceva: 'Tòla'; e di poi
quando egli diceva: 'Ella è di cattivo sangue,' egli rispondeva: 'Non la
torre'; e così seguitava sempre di dire sì o no, secondo che colui gli
proponeva innanzi nuove ragioni. E così fa propiamente Aristotile di
me: imperò che, quando e' mi considera unita col corpo, e' dice che io
son mortale; e quando e' mi considera come intelletto agente, e che io
posso operare senza quello, e' dice che io sono immortale; sì che, fi-
nalmente, chi lo legge non è mai certo se io sono mortale o immortale.
(Gelli:6, pp. 76–77 of Tissoni 1967)[23]

This is a caricatural version of dialectic, to be sure, but it would be a
mistake to neglect it; first of all, as noted, it clearly shows the rhetorical structure functioning as a joint between two different domains of
discourse. In the second place, it has a particular importance in literary history: for what else is Rabelais' brilliant *Tiers Livre* if not one
gigantic expansion of this antithesis about marriage? (And see Thirlwall 1833 as quoted in 3.1., on the irony implicit in the position of the
judge between two parties in a dispute.)

   Let me quote, after this instance of direct (*in praesentia*) antithesis,
an instance of antithesis at a distance, between the two opposite implementations of one and the same theme. The theme is that of Ulysses—one of the most lively cultural images during the Middle Ages
and the Renaissance. Dantes' famous lines stress the adventurous aspects of Ulysses' life—his courage in leaving his family and fatherland behind in his search for knowledge and new experience. But
there is an opposite aspect in Ulysses' experience: the love of family
and fatherland, which draws him toward home, through perils and
adventures. This is what is foregrounded in a fifteenth-century ora-
tion by Cristoforo Landino: "Come dice Omero, Ulisse uomo sapien-
tissimo, Itaca sua, benché come nido di rondine in asprissimi sassi et
massi posta fosse, non dubitò all'immortalità preporre."[24] To be precise: what is foregrounded is patriotism of a specific, local variety
(which makes particular sense in the political situation of Florence
and the rest of Italy at that time—thus, Ithaca rather than the whole
of Greece); the family theme is absent here. This remark points to a
research topic which should occupy first place on the agenda of empirical rhetorical studies: systematic gathering of themes. These
themes should be listed period by period, and—more importantly—
they should be systematically classified, in their topical structure and

in their dialectic relationships. This would provide the most effective tools for the full development of a rhetorical theory like the one presented here, simultaneously in the synchronic and in the diachronic dimension—for the "map" of themes in a given period contains the seeds of future developments as well as the traces of past situations (certain themes arise, others disappear, still others are combined together in new ways, and so forth).

But a serious, contemporary rhetorical analysis must be problematic in its use of dialectic; that is, it must devote at least as much attention to antidialectic positions, and especially to cases in which dialectic is imperfectly applied and falls short of its mark, as it does to dialectic applications which may be considered well-rounded and successful. Let me quote a fairly simple example of adialectic, or antidialectic, position from an already cited author. In another series of dialogues by Gelli, Ulysses is one of the characters, and at a certain point he is presented as worrying about the consistency of certain proverbial dicta:

> se quel proverbio il quale è in uso per la nostra Grecia, che 'egli è impossibile che quel che dicono molti sia al tutto falso,' fusse vero in tutte le cose, io potrei far da questo giudicio, che lo esser degli animali che son privi di ragione fusse assai miglior che il nostro. Ma e' debbe esser solamente vero nelle cose che appartengono a la vita attiva dell'uomo; perché, quando e' si parla de la cognizione dell'intelletto nostro circa a la verità e a la natura delle cose, ho io sentito spessissime volte usarne un altro contrario al tutto a questo, il quale dice che 'si debbe saper come i manco, se bene si debbe parlare come i più' . . . . Onde non potremo salvare che tutti e due fussino veri (e la natura de' proverbi è pure d'esser per la lunga esperienzia veri), se non intendendo l'uno delle cose pratiche, e l'altro delle speculative. (Tenth *dialogo*, "Ulisse, Elefante" in *La Circe*; see Tissoni 1967:269)[25]

This "double truth" solution is a very important one, which transcends the relative modesty of the specific literary occasion: what we witness here is nothing less than a classic move of scholastic compromise, which has played—and still plays—a large role in the history of ideas, especially in the history of religion, and also in the history of politics. The view of proverbs defended here is a rigid and abstractly idological one: experience is seen as one, therefore the truth of proverbs must be univocal. This unrealistic notion can only lead to a mechanic compromise: and everything mechanic is antidialectic. (Every great dialectic experience has its mechanistic movements, and every master dialectician *quandoque dormitat*; for instance, Jesus' famous distinction between what must be rendered unto Caesar and what must be rendered unto God is rigidly adialectic and not helpful.) It is not difficult to imagine what Rabelais, or Montaigne, or Ariosto, or any other writer of the same dialectic bent would have done with two contrary aphorisms like these just quoted in Gelli: they would have played the one against the other in a fluid context of moves and countermoves, without intellectualistic distinctions. It is differences like these that historical rhetoric must explore and clarify, thus attaining a broad and at the same time concrete typology of literary discourse.

Continuing with this study of problematic moments in dialectic performances, let me quote an example which, however small, has a strategic importance because it brings together several of the elements discussed and illustrated above. It contains one of the earliest formulations of that strategic dilemma between taking certain military initiatives and waiting for the enemy to take them which we saw in its Renaissance developments in Montaigne; furthermore, it combines this problem of military strategy with a dilemma in sexual strategy, thus confirming the deep link between the basic politics of living and the ideologized politics in the traditional sense; finally, it is from an author who is one of the basic sources of the several themes which have been illustrated in the preceding pages. Not the least interesting element in this example is that it fails, falling short of a full dialectic balance; and its failure is perhaps more revealing than its stylistic success would have been.

In one of the short paragraphs (the 37th) of his pamphlet "Advice on marriage" (one of the several essays traditionally gathered under the title of *Moralia*) Plutarch parallels the already described military choice with the behavior of the wife in marriage: "Their generals commanded to the Greeks serving Cyrus: if the enemies attacked shouting to wait for them in silence, but if they kept silent to advance against them with shouts. Now, women endowed with good sense . . . "

But let us interrupt Plutarch's discourse for a moment, and ask ourselves how we would expect it to be concluded. We would expect, at this point, symmetry: wives should respond to husbands' aggressiveness in a quiet way, and on the other hand should be aggressive when the husbands themselves are not. To be sure, this would not be an idyllic image of the married status: but after all, it was Plutarch, not we, who began with a military simile. Moreover, this picture would be a refreshingly anticonformistic one, and it would represent in a realistic fashion a strategy which is indeed an important part of everyday contacts between husband and wife, and more generally between lovers. But the actual continuation of the statement is *not* in the expected direction: "Now, women endowed with good sense will—faced with the outbursts of their screaming husbands—keep still; but if they [the husbands] are silent, they will talk to them and soften them with soothing words" (see Bernardakes 1888–1896, I:350).

In plain words, women are never supposed to shout! There has been some legerdemain here, a slight shift from one linguistic register to another, which is sufficient to weaken the tension of the simile: whereas in the military example the *quantity* (to use an old logical terminology) is the same (in both cases the same form of behavior—shouting—is at issue) and only the *quality* changes, in a complementary relationship (when one of the two partners shouts, the other does not, and vice versa); in its counterpart in married life the quantity changes as well as the quality: we have *two* quite different forms of behavior—angry shouting and peaceful conversation; they are, to be sure, both opposed to silence, but they remain divergent enough to destroy the symmetry. The result, clearly, is not merely a formal lack of balance, but a psychological and social difference. The ideology of female subjugation is superimposed on the actual, free flow of the politics of relationships between the two sexes; thus the cutting edge of dialectic analysis is blunted, and what comes out of the description is the defense of the status quo rather than its questioning—conformism rather than criticism.

Let us go more deeply into this phenomenon of repressed dialectic with a more developed illustration. I know of few instances where real dialectic and its moralistic mystification are so strikingly set side by side—better, intermingled in a mixture which is difficult to clarify—as in the long footnote that Jean-Jacques Rousseau inserts toward the end of his well-known pamphlet (already quoted in section 2.1; see Rousseau 1758, and see also Launay 1967), and which I will quote in its entirety.[26] The author—as is well known—has been developing a critique of dramatic representations, accompanied by an exaltation of its alternative, that is, of participatory celebrations like dancing—and interspersed with some rather cavalier comments about women. Then he notes:

> Il me paraît plaisant d'imaginer quelquefois les jugements que plusieurs porteront de mes goûts sur mes ècrits. Sur celui-ci l'on ne manquera pas de dire : 'Cet homme est fou de la danse', je m'ennuie à voir danser : 'Il ne peut souffrir la comédie,' j'aime la comédie à la passion : 'Il a de l'aversion pour les femmes', je ne serai que trop bien justifié là-dessus : 'Il est mécontent des comédiens', j'ai tout sujet de m'en louer et l'amitié du seul d'entre eux que j'ai connu particulièrement ne peut qu'honorer un honnête homme. Même jugement sur les poètes dont je suis forcé de censurer les pièces : ceux qui sont morts ne seront pas de mon goût, et je serais piqué contre les vivants. La verité est que Racine me charme et que je n'ai jamais manqué volontairement une représentation de Molière.... Si mes ècrits m'inspirent quelque fierté, c'est par la pureté d'intention qui les dicte, c'est par un désintéressement dont peu d'auteurs m'ont donné l'example, et que fort peu voudront imiter. Jamais vue particulière ne souille le dèsir d'être utile aux autres qui m'a mis la plume à la main, et j'ai presque toujours écrit contre mon propre intérêt. *Vitam impendere vero* : voilà la devise que j'ai choisie et dont je me sens digne. Lecteurs, je puis me tromper moi-même, mais non pas vous tromper volontairement; craignez mes erreurs et non ma mauvaise foi. L'amour du bien public est la seule raison qui me fait parler au public; je sais alors m'oublier moi-même, et, si quelqu'un m'offense, je me tais sur mon compte de peur que la colère ne me rende unjuste. Cette maxime est bonne à mes ennemis, en ce qu'ils me nuisent à leur aise et sans crainte de représailles, aux lecteurs qui ne craignent pas que ma haine leur en impose, et surtout à moi qui, restant en paix tandis qu'on m'outrage, n'ai du moins que le mal qu'on me fait et non celui que j'éprouverais encore à le rendre. Sainte et pure vérité a qui j'ai consacré ma vie, non jamais mes passions ne souilleront le sincère amour que j'ai pour toi; l'intérêt ne la crainte ni sauraient altérer l'hommage que j'aime à t'offrir, et ma plume ne te refusera jamais rien que ce qu'elle craint d'accorder à la vengeance![27]

A moving, eloquent passage, certainly; but is it "true" or "false?" Let me state, once and for all, that there is no debunking intention here: indeed, the already-noted descriptivism of this approach prohibits any negative evaluation of rhetorically coherent discourse. But this is the point: the refusal—here and elsewhere in the book—to adopt an axiological type of criticism does not imply that one should renounce critical analysis of the structures involved. The problem is not one of truth versus error but—I repeat—one of coherence.

In the opening sentences the author brilliantly and elliptically evokes the appropriate dialectic relationship (but will this suffice to discourage the clumsy exhibitions of common sense, which tears away, like a persistent and slightly obtuse little dog, at the fabric of the text?). The man loves theatre, respects great artists like Molière and Racine, is bored by naive spectacles like balls; but the moralist—and, above all, the politician—in him take it to be their task to develop, at a deeper and more general level (going beyond the immediate existential data) a critique of dramatic literature and an exhortation to simpler amusements.

So far, so good: we do not have contradiction here, but dialectic tension. However, a glimpse of uneasiness and incoherence appears, in his comment about women: here the circle is too easily closed, since the existential experience (obscurely evoked—a flash of *argumentum ad personam*) is used simply to confirm—rather than to establish a fruitful antithesis with—the possible objection.

Another revealing glimpse is this: as anticipated, Rousseau explicitly denies disliking great authors of the past (like Racine and Molière), but he does not respond to the other critique that he evokes—namely, his bitterness or irritation with *contemporary* authors. What we have in both cases is a strange rupture of the rhetorical symmetry that the author himself had established: we expect a sarcastic denial of the accusations concerning women and contemporary authors (along the lines of the other denials he makes—as we have seen—in the same passage); what we get instead is an explicit acceptance of the appreciation about women, and an implicit admission of the one concerning contemporary authors. This dissymmetry is an irruption of uncontrollable personal emotion into what would otherwise have been a cool and polished performance in the classic mode.

These slight lacerations in the consistency of the text (in its texture) become a gaping hole with the paean to the *sainte vérité*: this *captatio benevolentiae* is too rough and too arrogant to be swallowed. There will be other occasions (the "Quatrième promenade" in his *Rêveries*—see Voisine 1964) when the proud motto *Vitam impendere vero* will reveal some glimmer of dialectic, albeit in a tortured context in which self-righteousness still, unfortunately, wins the day; but here, dialectic distantiation has been completely forgotten; and the result, as was to be expected, is a lack of coherence in the rhetorical structure.

It is through a consideration of coherence that one can make it clear in what sense rhetorics is critical: not in an axiological, but in a structural perspective—not in the name of prescription, but in that of description. A last example of this, from the same text. D'Alembert in his article "Genève" in Volume VII of the *Encyclopédie* had characterized the dominant trend of thought in the clergy at Geneva as "Socinian" (a historical heresy within Christianity whose substantive elements need not be described here).

Rousseau does not like this characterization—more seriously, he senses a political danger in it. He does not want to rock the boat by making certain theological divergences public, at least not at this moment; it seems that he does not want a political debate to be sidetracked into a theological dispute. There is no quarrel with that here, but one must point out the adialectic nature of his defense. However, before doing so, it is methodologically useful to submit a tamed paraphrase of D'Alembert's argument and Rousseau's response (which is to be found in Bloom 1960); not in order to engage in polemics for the bittersweet sake of polemics, but to show a recurring danger of literary criticism and historical exposition that deal with brilliant works by famous authors. This is the danger of adopting an apologetic attitude, one that smooths over all asperities, and that consequently does not allow any distinction between coherent and incoherent rhetorical structures. In this way the fatal confusion, between the current sense of dialectic, referring to the mere surface of the rhetorical structure, to its general impression of copiousness (the *copia verborum* of Classic and Humanistic rhetoric)—and the more systematic sense which has been discussed here, is compounded.

But let us look at the concrete case. Bloom writes, "The effect of d'Alembert's imputation that the pastors of Geneva were Socinian was to separate them from the pious fundamentalists and to put them willy-nilly in the camp of the more liberal citizens who wanted a theatre. The pastors were thus made to appear heretic to their traditional supporters, besides being intimidated into thinking that the only way to be reasonable and enlightened was to be Socinian."

Let us not quibble about this presentation of d'Alembert's move, although it is not simply a summary (as it tries to appear), but the beginning of a counterattack ("imputation," "intimidated into thinking"—these are not neutral statements). What is Rousseau's response? Rousseau—we are told in this same text—protects the pastors "against the charge of heresy, but in such a way as not to force them to be strictly orthodox or fundamentalists. He wishes the clergy to be freed from the necessity of making a choice between reason and revelation, a choice forced upon them by the conflict between the traditionalists and the Encyclopedists."

Doesn't this look too nice to be true? I am not trying to split hairs and make a parade of pedantry; after all, we are not dealing here with the innocuous nuances of *belles lettres*, but with burning political and ideological issues—so that the delicate distinctions we must be concerned with are not "des purs jeux."

For isn't the kind of critical language of which an example was just given already called into question by Rousseau's own language, so much bolder and more sweeping, even when it is less than persuasive? But let us go on with Bloom's summary. Rousseau

> tries to lend the authority of philosophy to a religious teaching based on the belief in revelation; for, if the religious rationalism of the Encyclopedists is accepted, then it is hard to find a defense for the moral commands of the revealed religion which appear to the many to be the only source for obedience to severe laws. Rousseau only touches on this delicate subject in attempting to establish a doctrine which, while incorporating the concern of the Encyclopedists for tolerance as over against fanaticism (a concern that he considered more than legitimate), would not destroy the meaning of the particular religions. He takes a stand for the national religions as over against cosmopolitanism. (Bloom 1960:xxiv)

All of this looks polished, dignified, and solemn—like a discourse which should pacify everybody. But, fortunately, Rousseau's actual text is a much more heady mixture: a combination of the noise and dust of the arena with the exhilarating dizziness which overtakes one in certain moments during a chess game.[28] Let us, finally, allow Rousseau to speak in his own voice. However, to quote at length without any intervention would be—in the situation created by the preceding remarks—an apparently respectful, but actually irresponsible, gesture.

Plusieurs pasteurs de Genève n'ont, selon vous, qu'un socinianisme parfait. Voilà ce que vous déclarez hautement, à la face de l'Europe. J'ose vous demander comment vous l'avez appris. Ce ne peût etre que par vos propres conjectures, ou par le témoignage d'autrui, ou sur l'aveu des pasteurs en question.[29]

What is most fascinating in chess (at least for a rank amateur) is that every move is a constraint on the player himself who performs it—a constraint whose implications may escape him. What Rousseau has done here is to choose the topos of Size and Division, and in its most venerable articulation, the ternary one. (I have already commented on the archaic nature of trinitarian schemata in rhetorical analysis in 2.1.)

The writer's problem, now, is that of transforming this topos into a well-functioning *argument*. Am I too rash in assuming the following as the path that most readers, at this point, would expect to be asked to walk along? D'Alembert's conjectures are unreliable, the testimony of third parties suspicious, the *aveu* of the pastors nonexistent; therefore, d'Alembert's characterization is groundless.

I am comforted in reconstructing this process by the awareness that this is the structure used by Aristotle in the illustration of this topos (no. 9 in his list in *Rhetoric* 2. 18ff. 1391[b]ff.): "All men do wrong on account of one of three things—either this, or that, or that; now [in this particular case] two of them are impossible [as motives for the alleged crime], and as for the third, they [the accusers] themselves do not propose it" (*Rh.* 2. 23. 1398[a], 30–32). The fact that Aristotle does not give any specific exemplificatory content to the three motives emphasizes the general nature of his illustration. But what does actually happen in Rousseau's discourse? The first two points of the division are treated according to this time-tested technique:

Or dans les matières de pur dogme et qui tiennent point a la morale, comment peut-on juger de la foi d'autrui par conjecture? Comment peut-on même en juger sur la déclaration d'un tiers, contre celle de la personne intéressée?[30]

Other statements follow, embroidering on this theme, but what matters here is the basic structure. However, when it comes to the third alternative, the author does *not* rule it out, and thus he abandons the safety of the traditional position. This, of course, is not a negative fact in itself; however—before rushing into a Romantic celebration of the freedom from classical models—let us see whether the result of this deviation is convincing or not.

> Il resterait donc à penser, sur ceux de nos pasteurs que vous prétendez être sociniens parfaits et rejeter les peines eternelles, qu'ils vous ont confié là-dessus leurs sentiments particuliers; mais si c'était en effet leur sentiment, et qu'ils vous l'eussent confié, sans doute il vous l'auraient dit en secret, dans l'honnête et libre épanchement d'un commerce philosophique; ils l'auraient dit au philosophe, et non pas à l'auteur. Il n'eut donc rien fait, et ma preuve est sans replique; c'est que vous l'avez publié.[31]

Isn't this a lamely captious move? And, insofar as it reveals a certain functionality behind the sentimental appearances, isn't it an insidious one, opposing *philosophe* and *auteur* in a way which, as Rousseau well knows, is impossible to implement at this time—when the *philosophe* is not a solitary figure in Hellenic garb, and can survive as an intellectual only insofar as he makes himself known as *auteur*?

But this is not all: Rousseau wants now *both* to say that the pastors are not Socinian, *and* not to commit himself to this denial; *both* to say that he does not even know what Socinianism is, *and* to characterize this theological position (he is not the first, and certainly not the last, in a long line of thinkers of the modern period who, when faced with the great challenge of theology, want to have their intellectual cake and eat it too).

Logically impossible? Maybe, and yet this is just what the writer does. Let me report the lines immediately following the quote above:

> Je ne prétends point pour cela juger ni blâmer la doctrine que vous leur imputez; je dis seulement qu'on n'a nul droit de la leur imputer, à moins qu'ils ne la reconnaissent et j'ajoute qu'elle ne ressemble en rien a celle dont nous ils instruisent. Je ne sais ce qu'est le socinianisme, ainsi je n'en puis parler ni en bien ni en mal et même sur quelques notions confuses de cette secte et de son fondateur, je me sens plus d'eloignement que de goût pour elle. . . .[32]

The *New York Times* recalled (in an article published in January, 1975) the case of a well-known movie star who, during the grim period of the "witch hunt" in the fifties stated in front of an inquisitorial committee: "I do not know what Communism is, but I hate it." The "logic," as we see, is the same as what we are observing at work here. (The only difference—albeit a significant one—is that the American performer's statement is, also because of its shortness—at least in that reported version—less articulated than the French author's tortuous argumentation, which continues after the passages just quoted; and yet, that very brevity has a rhetorical effectiveness of its own.)

In both cases, a possible dialectic confrontation is avoided, and covered up with a metaphor. My purpose in analyzing this movement (let me note it once again) is not to ridicule the authors, or to perform a gratuitous exercise in logical emendation (noting that the quoted American statement is contradictory—an obvious, and basically irrelevant, fact). The purpose is, rather, one of descriptive analysis, pointing out that even incoherence may have a rhetorical function.

But this awareness does not free the analyst from the responsibility of indicating that incoherence (hence my critique of "conciliatory" summaries, which gloss over the actual rhetorical—i.e., political— problems in the structure of the text). To extract the relevant metaphors and to paraphrase them adequately is a very delicate task. In the case of the anti-Communist statement, its paraphrase should be something like this: 'I am against any problematic view of politics; what I passionately reject in Communism is, above and beyond its specific content, the fact that it has the arrogance to be a system of critical ideas about society.' In short, anti-Communism is revealed here as a variety of antiintellectualism. Thus the apparently naive, seemingly apolitical, statement turns out to constitute a quite skillful political move.

And what else is Rousseau's contention if not a form of antiintellectualism—with the accompanying faint (more than faint) demagogic exaltation of straight simplicity, of no nonsense? "Monsieur, jugeons les actions des hommes, et laissons Dieu juger de leur foi." An antithesis that still has a strong appeal—indeed, it seems the quintessence of meek reasonableness, and it casts its would-be opponents in the unpleasant role of dogmatics, trouble-makers, fanatics (hence its enduring rhetorical effectiveness, not without venom—its constant force of appeal to any silent majority).

But, in order to see the antidialectic nature and the fragility of such statements, it is enough to hint at two or three questions: are judgments that are brought on actions any simpler, more reasonable, humbler, than judgments pronounced on ideas? Indeed, is it even possible to distinguish between the two? Actions and ideas present themselves to our perception as inextricable complexes. At any rate, is the wish that certain evaluations be left to God enough to create such a reality—or is what we are actually saying, when we utter this pious wish, that we delegate ideological judgments to whatever happens to be the ruling establishment at the moment, and wash our hands of it?

Indeed, in a long footnote (which here I cannot quote *in extenso*) Rousseau clearly makes his move in favor of the establishment, and the negated theology sneaks in through the window: "Il faut se ressouvenir que j'ai à repondre à un auteur qui n'est pas protestant . . . Tel est le dogme de l'existence de Dieu; tels sont les mystères admis dans les communions protestantes. Les mystères qui heurtent la raison, pour me servir des termes de M. d'Alembert, sont tout autre chose."[33] So much for leaving theological distinctions to God!

But, to conclude the analysis of this text, Rousseau's stance is more complex than that evoked by the anti-Communist ejaculation quoted above because, in the former case, the author wants to leave all his options open until the very last moment.

> Si un docteur venait m'ordonner de la part de Dieu de croire que la partie est plus grande que le tout, que pourrais-je penser en moi-même, sinon que cet homme vient m'ordonner d'être fou? Sans doute l'orthodoxe, qui ne voit nulle absurdité dans les mystères, est obligé de les croire : mais si le socinien y en trouve, qu'a-t-on a lui dire? Lui prouvera-t-on qu'il n'y en a pas? Il commencera, lui, par vous prouver que c'est une absurdité de raisonner sur ce qu'on ne saurait entendre. Que faire donc? Le laisser en repos.[34]

Thus the circle is closed, in complete confusion: for what has just been quoted is an indirect apology for Socinianism (cf. the preceding remark about the have-my-cake-and-eat-it-too tendency), and a veiled declaration of solidarity with it. Isn't there something petulant, and slightly childish, in this Rousseauian defense? But only a pedant could think that such an admission of petulance—in the context of this general criticism—would be irreverent or diminishing. On the contrary: one of the reasons why I feel that it is worth our while to concentrate on this passage is that it and the others like it, by Rousseau and many of his contemporaries, lie at the root of a great part of modern political and moralistic writing.

Let me emphasize the role of such considerations here. In fact two exigencies (which, at least potentially, contradict each other) are felt in a research like this: on the one hand, the need to base the theory on the broadest possible scope of data, both qualitatively (different languages, genres, stylistic registers) and quantitatively; on the other hand, the need—or at least, the desirability—of giving some sort of cultural coherence to the discussion. The balance proposed here is the following: to draw the data for discussion from some key periods and literatures, both in the history of rhetoric and in that of European literature in general (which does not imply, of course, that these are the *only* periods worth considering, or that the literatures of Europe are the only ones relevant to this kind of research).

We have already seen these key periods, in the passages examined so far: Ancient Greek; Classical Latin; Italian, French, English in the Renaissance and in the late eighteenth century, which prepare the way for modern politics. In this way, it is hoped, the need for abundance and variety of primary linguistic data will be satisfied while at the same time the linguistic analysis will be anchored to a relatively coherent cultural base.

One example of extension, showing the strategic character of these periods and texts: An evening at the theatre made one spectator think that a modern classic, Bertolt Brecht's *The Good Woman of Szechuan* is one of the best parallels one can think of to Diderot's work, especially to the brilliant "schism" of the dialogue which has been commented on above. The very title of the play is an indication of its dialectic ambiguity: the usual translation "woman" is too explicit, and thus does not do justice to the functional ambiguity of the German word *Mensch*. Perhaps the place where the dialectic dimension most clearly emerges is at the end (in the tenth and last part of this *Parabelstück*), where such dimension is made clear *a contrario*; that is, the reader or spectator feels the need for it because the pat answers of the gods to Shen Te's anguish are so obviously unsatisfactory.[35]

But this modern literary example might have been counterproductive: rather than confirming the broad scope and general relevance of rhetorical analysis, it might have evoked the gap (cultivated by the tradition of literary criticism) between theological wrangles like that discussed in the Rousseau example and "properly" or "purely" literary texts, allegedly the sole concern of the literary critic (a limitation which linguists have shown themselves, in general, only too eager to accept).

An implication, however, of the whole analysis so far is that such a gap is an ideological deformation whose function is to protect the acritical nature of much of traditional literary criticism. The more one insists on the separateness of literature, the less insight one gets into the literary process—not to mention the lack of understanding of the links between the literary discourse and all other types of discourse. It is because this theory of rhetoric insists on the similarities rather than on the differences between literary discourse and other discourses that it can serve also to construct a new perspective on literary analysis. Indeed one of the first tasks of the still almost non-existent Marxist criticism of literature (as distinct from the current brand of ideological digressions under the rubric of Marxism) is that of making explicit the ideological conventions that have led to the strict delimitation of the field of literature, and to show that such conventions have as a result that of mystifying the process of literary production as well as the processes of discourse production in general.[36]

All of this becomes dramatically clear when the theological discourse implicit—as a partial and informal component—in a literary discourse comes into conflict with explicitly, officially, and punctiliously theological discourse. This happens, for instance, when Giovan Batista Gelli speaks (in the "Ragionamento sesto" of his *Capricci del bottaio*) of the Schoolmen and in particular of "que' teologi che son chiamati della scuola parigina." Both Giusto (the cooper who is the protagonist of the dialogues) and his sole interlocutor, his Soul, argue that fortunately these philosophers are now out of fashion ("queste cose loro non passan più"). Why?

> *Anima.* Mercé de' Luterani, che non prestando fede se non alle Scritture Sacre, hanno fatto che gli uomini sono stati forzati a ritornare a legger quelle, e lasciare stare tante dispute.
>
> *Giusto.* Vedi che egli è pur vero quel che si dice : che spesso d'un gran male esce qualche bene. (Gelli in Tissoni 1967:77–78)[37]

Sound innocuous? Not to the censors of the Council of Trent, who cut out this passage, with the following explanation: "—Taxat scholasticos, et nominatim scholae Parisiensis. —Commendat Lutheranos, de quibus dicit . . . "; and the statement, quoted above, by Anima follows, from *Mercé* to *dispute*; but Giusto's reply is *not* mentioned (Tissoni:497).

This is significant in terms of text analysis and of its ideological implications. The first censure, apropos of the critique of the Schoolmen, is straightforward and—in structural terms—unobjectionable: whatever we modern readers may think of this, it is a fact that the author criticizes the Schoolmen, and in an explicit way.[38]

To be sure, the censorship overdramatizes the reference to the Schoolmen in Gelli's text—a reference that is informally and lightly touched upon; and this can be said of all censorial interventions in this text, which distort and weigh it down with their ponderous attention. (To a certain extent, this is a feature of all censorial interventions in literary texts: they create a peculiar rhetorical relationship by which the very gesture which strikes out certain passages draws dramatic attention to them.)

But it is the second intervention—the "Commendat Lutheranos" remark—which is inconsistent in its internal structure; for it ignores both the *dialogic* and the *dialectic* form of the passage at issue. The dialogic form: because the censors quote Anima's sentence out of its context—whereas if we put it back into the context we note that the Lutherans are treated as "un gran male," and it is only the development of a more modern philosophical style that is considered as "un qualche bene." The dialectic form: for this exchange amounts to a textbook example of dialectic analysis.

It is also a quite plausible historical evaluation, which must have been widespread among the most liberal Catholic thinkers of that time (Gelli does not show great originality in his writings). The "evil" of the Reformation has—from the Catholic point of view—a positive effect: to stimulate a fresher and more direct contact with the Scriptures. In the face of all this, the censorship displays rigidity and the incapacity to enter into the movement of a dialectic reflection.

And yet . . . is sufficient to treat the censors as crude, and unaware of the actual complexity of human discourse? Certainly not: for the very rigidity of the response should be read, in part, as a proof that these specialized readers were indeed aware of the peculiarities of dialectic thought. What they attributed a special importance to was that aspect of dialectic by which the boundary line between opposites is blurred.

In other words, they perceived (and quite correctly, I think) that the very fact of mentioning a good result coming out of the Reformation movement was dangerous for the simplified polemic view which they needed; they felt dialectic as something soft, diminishing the will to fight and weakening the firmness of simple loyalties. In this sense, it is their remark itself which must be dialectically interpreted. At first inspection, it appears not to be the case that Gelli "commendat Lutheranos," and the antithesis to that evaluation points out that such a censorial critique mutilates the dialogic exchange and misunderstands its dialectic content; but the antithesis of the antithesis indicates that this censorial interpretation is a rationally and politically functional one—which sees the *commendatio* as a matter more subtle than a straightforward declaration "pro" or "con." For this exchange may indeed be interpreted as a qualified *commendatio*.

Chapter IV

THE STRUCTURE OF
THE RHEME

4.1 THE THICKET OF SYNTAX

The system of rhetoric is built on topoi; but these topoi (as we have begun to see) are not ordered one alongside the other or one on top of the other, as if they were boxes in a storeroom or construction blocks: they are dialectically opposed the one to the other, whether the dialectic opposition is *in praesentia* (syntagmatic) or *in absentia* (paradigmatic). Let me quote a concrete case, which functions both as a metalinguistic statement *on* dialectics (in the field of human behavior) and as a realization *of* rhetorical dialectic.

It is a significant example also because it shows that philology—enriched by the modern advances in linguistics, cultural history, etc., and on the other hand continuing its brilliant tradition—is indispensable to rhetorical analysis. It could, indeed, be said that an insufficiency of a minute and patiently detailed philological work has been one of the major limitations in modern rhetorical research—a limitation which has often made empty, if not slightly demagogical, the insistence of modern rhetorics on the alleged sophistication of the techniques with which it is implemented. The example is one of Heraclitus' fragments, which must (for reasons which will become clear presently) initially be reproduced in its original Greek form:

Tòi oûn tóksōi ónoma bios, érgon dè thánatos.

Current translations do not satisfy fully, because—although they clarify the meaning of the sentence—they do not give us, in themselves, an adequate idea of the syntactic and lexical ambiguity that is essential to the interpretation of the rhetorical structure (hence the reference above to the indispensable role of philology).[1]

It is not fully adequate, for instance, to translate: 'The bow (*biós*) is called life (*bíos*) but its work is death.'[2] For this translation gives the impression that Heraclitus uses only the word *biós* for 'bow,' and that this word (with the different accentuation) is repeated twice, while a look at the Greek text is enough to show that neither of these impressions is correct. Of course, the ancient text does not carry the accent markers and other diacritical signs (a—necessary—addition of modern editors); but in cases like this it is the *lack* of accent marks which is essential to the semantic interpretation of the sentence: this is why it is better to transcribe the word without marking the accent.

This eight-word string has already turned out to hide a small forest. We must proceed very carefully, for in investigating a complicated cultural and linguistic cluster like this one we cannot avoid facing one of the following three risks: frivolity, mad confusion, or pedantry. Frivolity if we simple sketch the "play on words," implying that it is no more than a play and that its structure can be simply and intuitively perceived; madness (and I do not exaggerate—see Valesio 1971) if we go into the ideological ramifications of this statement without taking proper care of the linguistic description; pedantry, finally, if we develop a methodical linguistic analysis.

Of these, the third seems the most worthy risk. I propose, then, to concentrate on this Greek sentence as an illustration of the nature of the objects which are the main concern of the theory of rhetoric here developed. Let me repeat the Greek text:

Tôi oûn tóksōi ónoma 'bios', érgon dè thánatos.

I have made another alteration (besides the zero accent mark on *bios*) with respect to the Marcovich transcription: namely, placing quotation marks around the word. The latter graphemic device sets the word off as an instance of *hypostasis*: "the bringing to attention or the repeating of a unit outside its normal emic context" (Pike 1967*a*:107).[3]

The notion of hypostasis is, by the way, a good example of the need for closer interchanges between rhetorical and strictly grammatical terminology: hypostasis is not usually listed among figures of speech, yet it is—as the definition above shows—essentially a rhetorical configuration, and as such should be recognized and classified. But I do not want to start "at the top," that is, with the directly perceivable linguistic material, the figures; for the concreteness thus gained is only apparent, and quickly ends in confusion. I intend, rather, to start "from the bottom," giving a more precise idea of the internal articulation of a rhetorical unit.

This whole linguistic structure is based on a topos whose Latin name is *Notatio* (while Aristotle does not label it in a specific way). The term *Notatio* is employed by Cicero ("quia," he explains, "sunt verba rerum notae": *Topica* 8.35; see Tissoni 1973, and Bornecque 1924), who says that the topos takes place "cum ex vi nominis argumentum elicitur" (ibid.; his earlier definition—in 2.10—is the same: "cum ex verbi vi argumentum aliquod elicitur"). A better term for it today is that of topos of Iconicity, which I propose to define in the following way:

The linking of the references of the thematized words on the basis of the etymological and/or formal (nonetymological) synchronic relationships between the words implementing these references, without necessarily making an issue of their morphosyntactic structures and related variations.

The present realization of the topos of Iconicity (the token of this type) is the suggestion that there is some connection between the referent of the oxytonic noun *biós* 'bow' and that of the paroxytonic noun *bíos* 'life'—two semihomophonous items; two words, that is, whose morphosyntactic and segmental-phonological structure are identical, with only a suprasegmental phonological feature (oxytonic versus paroxytonic stress) distinguishing them formally. As for their etymology and their meaning, they are unrelated.[4]

This has been a linguistic characterization, but at this level we are *not* dealing with actual linguistic structures; rather, we are examining the psychocultural structures underlying them. This is why I spoke of the *suggestion* that there is some connection between *biós* and *bíos*, and not directly of the connection between them; and this is why I do not define the linguistic relationship *biós/bíos* with a specific term. (Once again, terminology—or the specific renunciation of it—is not a frill, but a substantially significant issue.) The topos here is implemented as an Argument, specifically as one of the two main types of argument: that subtype of the argument Enthymeme which is called Maxim. For the moment I will adhere without further discussion to the Aristotelian classification; and I will confine myself to saying that—among the four kinds of Maxims identified by Aristotle (*Rh.*

2.21. 1394^{a-b}, and passim)—this seems to belong to those which "are enthymematic in nature, but not [presented as] part of an enthymeme; they are the most appreciated ones. Indeed, they are those where the reason for the statement made is shown indirectly, as it happens in: 'Do not, being mortal, nourish an immortal wrath'" (ibid. 1394^{b}).

At this level too we are considering a psychocultural structure, keeping it aside (for the moment) from its actual linguistic shape; it is only at the next and last level—the surface—that we deal with actual linguistic structures. This is the level of Figures, and it is only after having examined their scaffolding that we are able to perceive how many they actually are, and how intricate their relationships; and to see also that they are merely the tip of the iceberg: for what has been said already is enough to show that figures are only one component of the rhetorical unit—that is, of a unit constituted by the three-layered combination of topos, argument, and figure(s).

But let us leave figures aside for the time being and consider the strictly linguistic structure rather than its rhetorical integration; specifically, let us look in detail at the syntactic implementation. This argument is, like any other argument, embodied in a syntagmeme; and to describe the peculiarities of this syntagmeme is as a good a way as any to give an idea of the linguistic structuring of this theory of rhetoric. (This analysis is based mainly on Pike and Pike 1975 and related texts; specific references will be provided en route.)

The syntagmeme at issue is a compound sentence, made up by two coordinated clauses. More technically, what we must account for is a clause coordinate complex, filling the nucleus of a sentence. Schematically:

Clause coordinate complex : +	Nucleus $_1$	Independent clause
	Statement	(?)

+	Link	Coordinating conjunction
	Coordination promised	Anaphoric (it points back to Nucleus $_1$)

Each four-celled tagmemes indicates: Slot (upper left cell), Role (lower left cell), Class(es), in the upper right cell, and Cohesion—in the lower right cell. Thus the general shape of the tagmeme is:

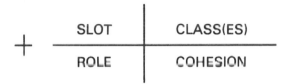

In other words, each tagmeme shows: *where* the relevant item is situated, and the contrast in its nuclear versus marginal position in the wave or sequence of linguistic items at issue (Slot cell); *why* the item is in the wave—what its purpose or function is, what the relevant contrasts, connected to this function, with other items, are (cf. the Role cell); exactly *what* it is that is carrying such a functional load in this wave, and what the relevant contrasts are that are realized by it, as a member of a given grammatical class, with respect to other members of the same class and to the other classes which together with the one at issue may constitute a grammatical hyperclass (and this is the content of the Class cell); finally, *how* the item in question relates to others within the wave, and specifically how it contrasts with them (is it marked or unmarked with respect to them, does it govern them or is it governed by them, does it constitute their presupposition or do they constitute its, etc.?), and this pertains to the Cohesion cell.

But if we were to stop here, the clarity of description offered by this structural model would be offset by its vague generality. What we must do is to dig into it, bringing the implicit structures to light. The most natural move (which will not be avoided here) is to start from the first clause, which, on the other hand, is also the more complicated of the two, because it realizes the merging of *two* different underlying clauses. The difference is realized only partially at the morphophonemic level (with an implicit suprasegmental contrast), but it is relevant to the different lexical implementation which may be given to the morpheme filling the slot of the predicate attribute—which, indeed, *has* to be given if these clauses are to make sense as a coordinate complex; thus, as the filler of a compound sentence nucleus, rather than as two disjointed clauses.

But first—in this web of *concordia discors*—the *concordia*; let us look at the elements of similarity. For this slot, no matter how it is filled out, is part of one and the same frame. The frame at issue is that of a nominal clause—which, as such, is (so to speak) thinly disguised as a phrase. (A realization of what in tagmemics is often called *level-skipping*: when a tagmeme is realized, "not by a set of syntagmemes from the next lower level, but by a set which includes a tagmeme from still a lower level"—Longacre 1976:264.)

In fact, all three clauses involved in this sentence (the two merging into the initial one, and the second one) are nominal, and the lack of any verb form is perhaps the main stylistic feature in the sentence. The fully nominal sentence is frequent in Ancient Greek as well as in Classical Latin, and this case confirms what is generally the effect of the nominal rhetoric: namely, an aura of solemn concision, in the manner of a pithy epigram. Here we come, again, to a crossroads. Indeed, rhetorical analysis brings out in a particularly vivid manner the difficulty—better, the tension, the harsh exercising of the mind— present in every critical movement. It must constantly be on the lookout for choices; at every step, it must choose how to restrict its own procedure at the very moment when it becomes aware of a variety of fruitful perspectives.

Let us look into the syntactic and lexical structure of this text, trying to describe, as clearly as possible, what this structure actually is.

Morphological and syntactic structures on the one hand, lexical and semantic relationships on the other, cannot be kept separated in absolute, sharp terms—either as two groups or within each one of these groups (hence my frequent use of compound words; morpho-syntactic, syntactico-semantic). However, a relative separation is not only feasible but necessary for a clear analysis. I will start, therefore, with a description focusing on the syntactic structure (but not, as noted, to the exclusion of other components). The technique will be based on a reelaboration of tagmemics, especially as described in Pike and Pike 1975 and Longacre 1976. The details of terminology and notation will be clarified as the analysis proceeds—and the same will be done for the theoretical modifications (which are not insignificant) characterizing the present theory of rhetorical description vis-à-vis tagmemics.[5]

It would seem that we move now on an easier ground, after the forest of symbolic actions and counteractions connected to notions like that of Maxim. But it appears immediately that the problems, although apparently of a more humble nature, are very intricate. What less controversial, at first sight, than assuming that we have to do, here, with a sentence? And yet, of the two assertions implicit in this statement, one is certainly untrue, the other doubtful. It is doubtful that this is an autonomous sentence, certain at any rate that it is not *one*—there are here (at least) two sentences, because the initial clause is in reality a blend of two clauses. Briefly (and each step of this description will have to be retraced in more detail): in one version the predicate attribute slot is filled by the lexical item *biós*. We thus have the following sentence:

(1) *Tôi (oûn) tóksôi ónoma biós, érgon dè thánatos.*

'The name of the bow: "arbalest," and its work: death.' (We will see later what is implicit in the parenthesis temporarily excluding the form *oûn* from our consideration.)

Arbalest is not, of course, a current word in English; but that is precisely what makes of it an appropriate rendering for *biós*—an ancient item of the epic lexicon, later used in tragedies, but destined to become obsolete in Greek, and thus to constitute as such an object of philological curiosity (as we shall see). At any rate, what we have here is a synonym of *tókson*.

In the other version, the predicate attribute slot is filled by the word *bíos* 'life':

(2) 'The name of the bow: "life"; but its work: death.'

I leave aside for the moment the morphosemantic problem of the paronomasia, and the metaphor (both will be treated below); and I will concentrate on the syntactic aspect. What we have here are two different combinations of predications. The first is a disjunction—or weak antithesis—by which a concept, that of 'bow', is divided into two different aspects: its linguistic representation on the one side, the effect of its referent on the other.

This disjunction can be seen as the effect of the application of the topos of Size and Division—which then would be the third topos active here, beside that of Iconicity and that of Authority (this last referring, of course, to literary authority). But note that "here" applies to *this version* of the sentence, and it cannot be transferred *tout court* to the idea of the sentence as a whole (for it would not be exact to say that the Heraclitean sentence in its version (2) displays a realization of the topos of Size and Division).

We begin to see, at this point, a phenomenon which will be one of the leitmotifs of this whole analysis: every technical problem of linguistic analysis leads to an ontological question; no issue is too minute or marginal for that. On the other hand, this realization is disquieting, because it forces us to abandon any scientistic optimism about the possibility of describing a section of linguistic structure (*any* section) as a closed and autonomous system. Also, we are haunted by the intricacy of speculation, by the vertigo of abstract thought—of philosophy, in short. No more fond hopes, then, for linguistics as a refuge from the abstract intellectual strife, as a welcome excursion into the realm of hard facts! All this may be, as remarked, troubling.

On the other hand, I find it heartening that all the minute discussions which a seriously detailed analysis of a sentence like this makes necessary are not an end in themselves—a pure technical exercise: they are directly related to questions about our basic ways of perceiving the world and human history.

I sketched above the structure of the tagmemes constituting this sentence. Between that movement of general presentation, and the movement (which I will follow presently) of detailed analysis of these tagmemes—between these two movements I want to situate the sketch of the general syntactic profiles at issue, going back now to version (1) as a realization of disjunction. It can be represented as follows:

$$(1) \quad P \; a \; b \; b' \; \bigwedge \; Q \; a'' \; [b] \; c.$$

Where: P and Q are predicates, the symbol $\bigwedge$ marks the disjunction, and a and b are the terms of the predicates: here, 'name' (a), 'bow' (b), 'arbalest' (b'), 'work' (a''), and 'death' (c) respectively. (The prime sign, as in b', marks a relation of synonymy, whereas the double one, as in a'', indicates a relation of antonymy; the brackets around [b] symbolize that, in the second clause, 'bow' is understood.)[6]

This formula (which might be too coarse grained for the logician's extra-delicate sieve) is at the right level of abstraction for us: it shows us the general syntactic balance before we enter into the analysis of the several tagmemes. It justifies my calling this antithesis weak (which is *not*, here, a gnoseological or an aesthetic evaluation, but an objective structural indication—with implications, to be seen presently, for the choice between different interpretations of this text). The antithesis is weak because the antinomic contrast does not concern here the nuclei of the two clauses, which are the predicate attributes (*biós* and *thánatos* are here heterogeneous lexical items, b' and c), but only the margins of it, that is, the subjects of the two clauses; moreover, the tension in the sentence is not, here, stretched to the possible limits. This sentence is, so to speak, heavier in its body than in its tail: for there is a structural link of solidarity in the first clause (the synonymic relation between *tókson* and *biós*—b and b') which is absent in the second.

But what about version (2)? It represents a strong antithesis, for which the topos of Size and Division is no longer relevant. Its formula is the following:

$$(2)\ \ P\ a\ b\ c \bigwedge Q\ a''\ [b]\ c''.$$

This time, not only the margins but also the nuclei of the two clauses (that is, as indicated, their predicate attributes) are antonyms one of the other: there is, then, a tension and a tightness which is absent in the other syntactic construction.

But, with all this, we have still barely skimmed the surface of the structural relationships present in this string. However, in order to see what they are, it is necessary to examine in detail the tagmemic structure of the various clauses. The first clause can, in version (1), be represented as follows:

(1)

	Indirect Object	Noun Phrase
+	Range (Synonymic Identification)	Governed by a Noun
	tôi toksói	nominative

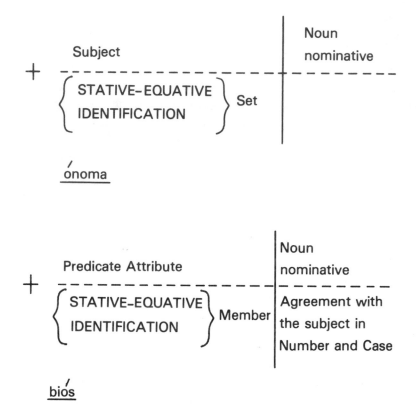

The embedded Noun Phrase, in its turn, is articulated as:

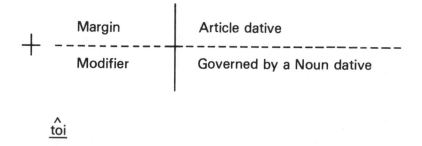

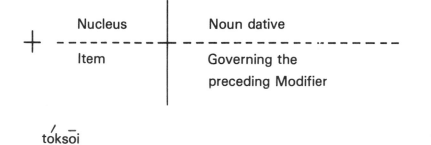

$+$	Nucleus		Noun dative
	Item		Governing the preceding Modifier

tóksōi

A few words of explanation are called for. The upper left cell of each tagmeme contains the functional slot, or Function (within which the terminology is usually that of traditional grammar—still perfectly adequate for this task—like: Subject, Indirect Object, Predicate Attribute, etc., plus some terms which are more characteristic of tagmemics: Margin, Nucleus). The upper right cell identifies the grammatical Class (or Category) which realizes that function (and the terminology used is the current one, combining morphological with syntactic indications). As for the lower right cell, it indicates the elements of grammatical (syntactic and morphological) Cohesion between the tagmeme at issue and other tagmemes in its close context (of phrase, clause, sentence)—and here again, the terminology used is not in need of clarification.

The (relatively) new kind of cell—and the one therefore which is most in need of explanation—is the lower left one, representing (as noted above) the grammatical Role of the tagmeme. I specify this role with the concept of Case, and I indicate it through a case frame, where the braces enclose the features identifying the predicates relevant to the various cases; and to the right of the braces there is the indication of the role of the relevant noun.

In this version of the sentence, it seems that the most adequate analysis consists in viewing the Subject Noun and its Predicate Attribute as being both in the Identive case; that is: an equation of a stative character (hence the "STATIVE–EQUATIVE" label) is established between the Subject Noun and its Predicate Attribute such that the latter noun is identified as a member of the set designated by the former noun. The Indirect Object, in turn, specifies the range to which this identification is relevant: a range, as noted, of synonymic identification between itself and the Predicate Attribute. (We see from this, as well as from indications like Modifier and Item in the tagmeme of the Noun Phrase, that the concept of role is broader than that of case frame; more precisely: those roles which express directly relationships of predication can—and should—be formalized in terms of case frames, while this does not seem advisable for the other roles.)

The Indirect Object has essentially the same structure (although the content and quality of the kind of Range it establishes is different with respect to that in (1), since the case relationship it serves as the background for is—at least in part—different); however, the case relationship has—within the same broad frame of equation between two states—changed subtly, but in a significant way.

Here the Predicate Attribute is not a synonym for the noun which establishes its range; rather it contributes, within this range, some new information—a new way of referring to (of considering) objects in the world; and, with respect to the Subject, it occupies a strategically different position: it is no longer simply a member of the general set indicated by the Subject (the set of nouns, or more specifically—embracing the following Noun Phrase—the set of "names for the bow"), as in (1); rather, it is the goal to identify, of which the name is but an instrument. In other words, the relevant relationship here is not one of synonymic identity, but a new reference; or, if you wish, it is not an essentially solipsistic passage from one word to its synonym, but a commitment to a different, and controversial, view of the world. The latter statement, then, breaks out of the structure of language, whereas the former represents a mere variation within this structure.[7]

The category of case, as a specification of the general notion of role, is particularly important, because it constitutes an ideological structuring of semantic relations. More on this later—but meanwhile, let us recall that no characterization of roles is "innocent": the description of roles must go hand in hand with an analysis of what this description means as an ideological evaluation of relations among men in society. Every detailed semantic analysis becomes willy-nilly (better to do it willingly, then) also an analysis of ideological stratifications.[8]

The second (and final) clause has a structure analogous to the sec-

ond version of the first clause, but with interesting differences. It can
be represented as follows:

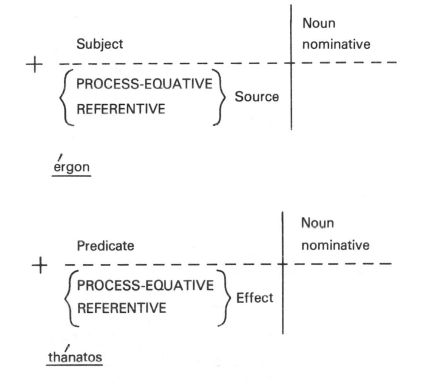

The differences in the case frames with respect to version (2) of the
initial clause are two, and they are interrelated: in the first place the
equation is based on process rather than on state; and secondly, the
relationship is not one between designation and its designated referent, but a direct one of cause and effect in the "real" world. We can
thus detect a gradience in realism, or a movement out of language
into reality.

In this sentence, the first interpretation of the first clause, with its
Identive case frame, is internal to language (I spoke of solipsism); but
the second interpretation of this first clause begins to move out of
linguistic tautology into the realm of innovative attribution; and finally, the second clause is not concerned with naming, but with processes in the world.

A detailed analysis such as the one developed here inevitably evokes the role which word order plays in the sentence. So much has been written about word order in general, and Ancient Greek word order in particular, that I will confine myself here to some remarks which are indispensable with respect to this sentence. If we accept the idea that the Greek sentence tends to follow, in general, an ancient Indo-European pattern by which the determiner precedes the element it determines, and in particular, that the sentence subject ordinarily does *not* occupy the first place in the sentence (see Humbert 1954:93, 95); if we retain this framework, then it appears that the word order in this sentence does not show anything strikingly unusual, and that consequently the position of the Indirect Object is *not* emphatic. (Such a framework—I must recall—is not beyond dispute: "In Greek prose of the fifth and fourth centuries B.C. the subject tends to precede its verb"—Dover 1960:25; on the other hand, the relevant relationship here is not the subject/verb one—Dover does not give statistical data about nominal sentences—and besides, the Heraclitean sentence is a century older.)

The notion of "emphasis" is an ambiguous and complicated one (see, with respect to Ancient Greek, ibid.:32ff.). What I want to note here is that the idea of emphasis as the effect of an unusual formal collocation in some linguistic structure (say, a sharp difference with respect to the normal word order) is not the same thing as the focus on this or that linguistic constituent deriving from the position of this constituent in a given syntactic structure: the latter phenomenon is connatural to syntactic structures—every constituent occupies, of course, a position, and every position possesses certain semantic associations. Focus, then, is always to be accounted for, whereas emphasis may or may not take place.

In our case it does not seem possible (for the reasons noted above) to speak of emphasis, and we are left with the task of determining what kind of focus exists here. What we see is a topicalization of the "things" pole in the "things-vs.-words" opposition which characterizes the semantics of this sentence: the focus is on the fact that *the bow* is called by a certain name. If *ónoma* had been in initial position, we would have had a topicalization of the "words" pole. In both cases, at any rate, the topic would have been the same (*tôi tóksōi ónoma*) and the comment (*'bios'*) would have been the same too; or, in another terminology (see. Valesio 1976) the motif (= topic) and the theme (= comment) would have been the same and what would have varied would have been the peak of the motif (topic) wave—a variation which, as we just saw, is still significant for the semantic characterization of the sentence. The actually implemented topicalization generates a rhetorical effect of realism; that is, it displays a picture of firmly identified substances.[9]

The lack of emphasis in word order is confirmed by the absence here of a figure which Heraclitus frequently employs—cf. frs. 21, 25, 26, 36, 67, 92, etc., and which could easily have been used here: namely, Chiasmus. (The numeration of the fragments, here as elsewhere, is as indicated in Note 2, that adopted in Diels–Kranz 1966.) The role of chiasmus in Heraclitus' text must be underscored because this figure has been sometimes bypassed in an objectionable way.[10]

On the other hand, the notion of chiasmus has lately (see Bollack and Wismann 1972) been used in a rather vague way with respect to Heraclitus. It is well to remind ourselves, then, that chiasmus—*and zero-chiasmus*—have always existed as alternative ways of expressing antitheses, and that the presence of chiastic structures in texts written on ancient Greek boundary stones (thus, in texts which are not *stricto sensu* literary, not sophisticated) shows that chiasmus is not only a literary figure (see Dover 1960: 53–54); and this is confirmed by its absence in such a sophisticated literary structure as the one which I am examining.

4.2 AT THE FRONTIERS OF LINGUISTICS

Let us pause for a moment and take stock of the figures which we have identified so far in this sentence. There is in the first clause, by the first interpretation, a figure of synonymic variatio, or dittology; and, in the second version of this same clause, a figure of metaphor (more on this below). Moreover, I distinguished two levels or degrees of antithesis, ranging over the sentence as a whole, according to which interpretation of the first clause is adopted. This antithesis must now be seen in more detail. Indeed, we come here to a web of relationships so thin that ordinary linguistic analysis rarely captures them, and yet so subtly strong that the whole connotation of the sentence is lost if they are not identified (it is precisely the identification of such relationships which is the task of rhetorics).

Remaining within the domain of the weak antithesis—that of "words" versus "things" which I pointed out above in the context of a distinction between motif and theme—we must note that this contrast is more complicated. There are two levels of motif/theme relationship in this sentence: one at the level of the simple clauses and the other at the level of the whole sentence.

The level of the first clause has been already shown: the motif is the *tôi . . . tóksōi ónoma* cluster, and the theme the '*bios*' noun phrase. As for the second clause, the motif is the *érgon* noun phrase, and the theme the *thánatos* noun phrase. But: at the level of the sentence, the whole of the first (blended) clause—*Tôi oûn tóksōi ónoma 'bios'*—is the motif (topic), whereas the whole of the second clause (*érgon dè thánatos*) constitutes its theme (comment).

Now, the semantic relationship pertinent to the idea identified above is the following: the indirect "words"/"things" contrast in the clause adumbrates (and, in a sense, mimes) the full-fledged "words"/ "things" contrast which works at the level of the whole sentence, thematizing the *ónoma* noun phrase in the sentence motif and the *érgon* noun phrase in the sentence theme as the key lexical items expressing that contrast.

Nor is this all, for there is a subtle but significant relationship between this configuration and the topos on which the sentence as a whole is built. In effect, the topos of Iconicity (on an instance of which, we recall, this sentence is built as a rhetorical object) by its very nature calls into question the relationship which is assumed to exist between "words" and "things." I keep putting these terms within quotes because they are not evoked here in a logical sense (a logical account would have to discuss at length the relations between meaning and reference). The point here is not a problem in the metalanguage of linguistics, but a dialectic opposition in verbal folklore. Indeed, the "words"/"things" dialectic is widespread in the verbal lore of different languages. Suffice it to quote here the male-supremacist version (if I may use that jargon for an instant) of this dialectic which is to be found, for instance, in a folksy expression like the Italian *I fatti sono maschi, le parole sono femmine*: 'facts are males, words are females'; or, on the other hand, in the supercilious statement attributed to Dr. Johnson that "words are the daughters of the earth, but facts are the sons of heaven."[11]

This antithesis is reinforced by grammatical parallelism, which strengthens it as a rhetorical figure: for both *ónoma* and *érgon* belong to the neuter gender in Ancient Greek. That this is not a mere linguistic anecdote is proved by the fact that the other two lexical items in the nominative case constitute their own, so to speak, separate parallelism: *biós* and *bíos* on the one hand, and *thánatos* on the other, are nouns of masculine gender. Thus, in the two-to-three clauses making up this sentence, both subject slots are filled out by neuter nouns, while both predicate attribute slots contain masculine nouns.

While the lexical side of the *ónoma–érgon* parallelism remains the same (in the perspective of the above-sketched oral folklore), the other two pairs present a more complicated situation (as was to be expected, because of the *aequivocatio*). Before sketching this picture let me note that, in this as in most other cases, the linguistic distinction is relative rather than absolute; that is, what I called "formal" parallelism is—more exactly—a combination of morphophonemic features (the two realizations of the -*os* morpheme cluster; for both -*o*- and -*s* are morphemes, above and beyond their existence as phonemes) and grammatical meanings (since in both cases the morpheme cluster marks the masculine gender).

The distinction of "form" versus "content," in this case, is not a sharp one: it is simply a way of opposing, *grosso modo*, the "upper" to the "lower" part of the lexeme (in the terms of the schema which will be shown below): the morphophonemic string and the grammatical features on the one side, the lexical features (denotative and connotative) on the other. But let us go back to the "equivocal" pair.

The (relatively) formal parallelism of *biós* and *thánatos* is supplemented by a metonymic relationship whose space is carved within the general domain of the topos of Cause and Effect: for *thánatos* is frequently an effect of the use of *biós*, thus envisaged as cause (or immediate source). On the other hand, the formal parallelism between *bíos* and *thánatos* is accompanied by a lexical relationship so deeply embedded in the code that it is rarely perceived in its original strength as a figure: I mean the relation of antonymy (which is also a dialectic relationship—see the discussion above). Antonymy, as noted, is as rhetorical in nature as metonymy is; and only the schizoid state

of much of contemporary grammatical lore is responsible for the fact
that the former structure is usually ensconced in the lexical chapters
of grammar books while the latter is reserved for stylistic appendices.
Also, antonymy is here functioning within the broader scope of a
topos, as it is metonymy: only, in the case of this antonymy, the relevant structure is the topos of Time Sequence.

This might seem a very (excessively?) detailed analysis of the nouns
in this sentence; actually, it is a rather concise examination—for there
are several other relevant characteristics present here which should
be taken into account. For instance, in this sentence, all the nouns
which are involved in one or the other schema of parallelism are also
nouns in the nominative; also, each one of them fully coincides with
a noun phrase (at the next higher level), without being articulated in
a cluster of: determiner + noun. The only remaining noun in the
sentence underscores *a contrario* this cluster of grammatical features,
because it brings together the two features which are *absent* in the
just-identified cluster. In fact, *tôi tóksōi* is, in the first place, a noun
phrase articulated into: determiner + noun; and in the second place,
it is not in the *casus rectus* (as are the other nouns), but in the *casus
obliquus* (here, the dative). Also: both subject nouns are neuter, while
both predicate nouns are masculine—another feature of balance in
the sentence.

There is, by now, an ample body of literature devoted to the minute
study of these formal structures, especially in short poems (see, for
instance, Jakobson and Valesio 1966 and the critical discussion in Valesio 1969*b*). Doubts have often been voiced as to the significance of
these manifestations of *concordia discors*—doubts which are usually
construed as an expression of skepticism with regard to the usefulness of such detailed gathering and sifting of data. What is submitted
here is that, while the doubts are not unjustified, the conclusion usually drawn from them is wrong. It is in the direction of *more*, and
more *detailed*, research, not in that of haughty overviews that progress
must be looked for. The dialectic intuition (sometimes optimistically
christened as "law") that quantity is converted into quality is relevant
here.

For instance, let us look again at the general configuration of balance ranging over the whole sentence, in the terms of which all nouns
in the nominative are—two by two—homologous of each other. Like

all rhetorical configurations, this one is the extension of a basic grammatical process. Pike 1967a:218–19 gives as an example a sentence which he sets up as a proportion: "John : ran home : : Bill : ran home," and he observes:

> John is here a homologue of Bill, while Bill is a homologue of John. Two morphemes which are proportionate in filling the same tagmatic (or tagmemic) slot, then, are homologous; homologous items fill a comparable space in the next layer of the hierarchy of which they are a part . . . whatever the meaning is, or whether or not there is any detectable meaning, the relationships are parallel between the utterances, and between the elements substituting one for another within the tagmemic slot.

Of course, it is not a surprise that Heraclitus' actual sentence does not conform exactly to this *exemplum fictum*; yet the structural differences are significant enough to deserve attention. In the quoted example from Modern English there are two balanced pairs of phrases, as in our Greek sentence, but: the two homologues are not antithetical, and the other pair (the two predicate verb phrases) does not show homologues, but the rhetorical configuration of full Repetitio, or Epanaphora. On the other hand, the Greek sentence shows two pairs of homologues (as noted), and furthermore, in both the meaning is relevant to the analysis, since it shows that both are (in different degrees of strength) antithetic. Degrees of semantic strength cannot be measured exactly, at least in the context of research like this, but they are intuitively felt, and pertinent: the *bíos/thánatos* antithesis is stronger than the *ónoma/érgon* antithesis.

A last point on antithesis. Its strongest degree seems to be Oxymoron, and already here, in the *bíos/thánatos* contrast, we have an oxymoron (see the definition and discussion in 2.2, and see also Büchner 1951). Perhaps the clearest criterion of distinction between the general notion of antithesis and the more specific one of oxymoron is a combination of syntactic and lexical criteria. Thus, one can speak of oxymoron only when the opposite semantic nuclei are implemented within a very close framework—as close as that constituted by one and the same phrase or one and the same clause; whereas, when the opposition ranges over more than one clause, then it is more justified to speak of antithesis. Moreover, oxymoron implies the confrontation of one or more antonyms, while the lexical opposition which must exist in order to speak of an antithesis can be defined in less strict terms.

Of course, this is not a foolproof recipe to be mechanically applied; but, also obviously, progress can be made only combining detailed empirical analysis with the elaboration of general guidelines: we cannot go much further if we jump into the data neglecting formulas and general definitions, or if we refine these formulas always using the same old handful of examples. For instance: what defines oxymoron as such is the *combination* of the above-described lexical and syntactic criteria, rather than the isolated presence of one of them. Thus in our example, *bíos* and *thánatos* are antonyms in terms of the general linguistic code (although the importance of this sentence lies precisely in its questioning this codified semantic and ideological relationship). But two antonyms which, like these, confront each other out of two different clauses do not seem to constitute a sufficiently close syntactic framework to qualify for an oxymoron. This sentence, then, must be considered as realizing an antithesis. We can see the fruitfulness of this criterion if we compare this with another Heraclitean sentence (possibly a later imitation; see Bollack and Wismann 1972:344), whose general sense and ideology are parallel to those of our fragment, but where instead the notion of oxymoron seems to be the appropriate one:

> *Tà psukhrá théretai, thermòn psúkhetai, hu ⟨grón⟩ auaínetai,*
> *karphaléon notízet ⟨ai⟩.*[12]

Here we have a clear-cut series of oppositions within one and the same clause—so actually we have four immediately successive oxymora, which fill out the whole of this compound sentence. This sentence also displays a feature which—although not yet established so firmly as to become a criterion of definition—is interesting enough to be mentioned: there is at least a tendency for the oxymoron to imply the opposition of different parts of speech (typically, noun vs. verb), whereas the antithesis tends to be realized through homogeneous parts of speech; which means, also, that there is a peculiar link between oxymoron and figura etymologica. Also, we find here the figure of chiasmus already discussed (end of 4.1, and note 10).

The general construction of the sentence, in fact, illustrates chiasmus; but what is of special interest is that it shows us that the notion of chiasmus is more complex than what might seem at first sight, and that we should distinguish at least two levels in this figure: the lexical and the morphological one. The feature which is necessary and sufficient in order to define chiasmus is the semantic one: thus here, within the compound sentence, the four clauses are structured into two groups of two by the back-to-back collocation of the basic semantic nuclei, which constitutes enough of a link to enable us to say that they are joined by chiasmus. However, the chiasmus of the first couple of clauses is stronger than that of the second (and my translation tries to reflect this characteristic) because in the first two clauses (but not in the latter two) the link in meaning is doubled by a link in form (the same two roots being used for all words):

Noun		Verb			Noun		Verb
psukh(r)-	:	ther-	:	:	ther-	:	psukh-
'cold'		'to become hot'			'hot'		'to become cold'

As we see, the semantic structure is complemented here by the morphological structure, and the only Variatio is provided by the non-chiastic implementation of the grammatical categories realizing the semantic level; whereas, in the second couple of clauses, the effect is not one of full parallelism but rather of total Variatio: four diffferent roots are used; and this morphological difference has a lexical implication. For, while in the first couple of clauses we have to do with the same semantic nuclei (the only difference being the different semantic modality implemented by the nouns with respect to that implemented by the verbs), in the second couple what we have are synonyms, which are not fully overlapping.[13]

The moral of all this? That there is just no substitute for painstaking empirical analysis; and that our anatomy of this fragment so far, far from being too minute, is still not detailed enough. The only condition (but it is an important one) for this kind of analysis to be fully significant, and an instrument for better understanding man in society, is that it be integrated into a critical analysis of the ideologies built around the lexical structure at issue—as is being done in this analysis (and see Valesio 1976b).

It is high time to turn to the particles: they have been left out until now, in this otherwise detailed analysis of the syntactic structure of the sentence. What follows will show that they have *not* been discarded as marginal elements which do not contribute anything really

significant to the analysis; on the contrary, I left them behind in order
to deal with them more systematically, and thus to do justice to the
peculiar nexus of meanings and formal relations which they evoke. I
will go against the linear order of the signs in the sentence, starting
with *dé* rather than with *oûn*, and this for two reasons. In the first
place, the former particle is clearly a constituent of the original text—
something which is far from clear in the case of the latter particle, as
we are going to see presently; secondly, *dé* evokes relations within the
sentence, while the other particle leads us to discuss the problem of
the links between the sentence and its context.

This latter is a distinction which I (unlike Halliday and Hasan
1973) do not codify into a sharp separation between structural relations and cohesive relations. Indeed the tagmeme, in the format
which has been described and which is going to be used again for the
particles, makes of cohesion just one among the categories describing
structural relations. In the *biós* version of the sentence (version (1)
here) the tagmeme relevant to *dé* can be represented as follows:

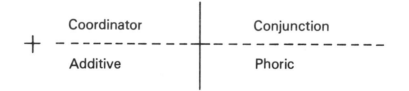

$$\underline{\text{dé}} \text{ 'and' } (= \text{ version (1) })$$

This might seem a proliferation of overlapping terms, but it is not
so: the distinctions are functional, both to a general analysis of the
function of particles like *dé*, and to a specific appreciation of its value
in the linguistic system of Ancient Greek. The most interesting conception of textual grammar is the one which insists that textual relationships are *not* simply the usual kind of structural relationships (the
only difference, allegedly, being that they take place beyond the sentence rather than within its framework), but that there instead is a
qualitative jump, an essential difference, between intrasentence and
intersentence relations; similarly, the best way to make sense of traditional grammatical labels like "Conjunction" (which I put in the cell

of Class—traditionally, Part of Speech: the one in the upper right cell of the tagmeme) is to recognize that conjunctive relationships are not simply coordinations at the sentence level (operating, that is, between clauses)—which would then be a purely mechanical extension of the same relationships as they operate at the clause level (i.e., between phrases). This is but one aspect of a broader phenomenon: traditional grammatical categories like "Conjunction" are not so much faulty as they are merely suggestive; they do not define a given phenomenon, but rather, they circumscribe the general area within which a serious analysis can take place. Briefly: in coordinative relationships the syntactic aspect predominates, whereas additive relationships can be recognized as such only if the formal assignment is integrated into a semantic analysis of the coordinated clauses.[14]

I account for both levels by the two left cells of the tagmeme. The upper one (representing the syntactic slot) reads "Coordinator," thus focusing on the almost completely formal link (no relationship at this level is fully formal—that is, completely devoid of semantic implications), whereby *dé* links up one clause with another, stringing them along at the same level, in a paratactic succession. The lower cell, on the other hand (which stands, we recall, for the Role), is labeled "Additive" and indicates a deep relationship, whereby the second clause as such (and here the linear, temporal succession is crucial) adds an idea, such that it is only the addition of this idea which fully justifies the first clause and gives sense to it. We see confirmed here what was noted above—namely, that the category of Role is broader than that of Case and includes it; for the latter is relevant to nouns, verbs, and adjectives, while the former can be applied to any lexical item.

Finally, as far as the lower right cell, the one representing "Cohesion," is concerned: I saw no other choice but the neologism "Phoric"; for I needed both to indicate the similarity of this relation with the one traditionally labeled "anaphoric" and with the other one more recently baptized as "cataphoric," *and* its difference with respect to these two concepts. If anaphoric is the linguistic item which presupposes (in order to be fully interpretable) a preceding item, and the item which constitutes the presupposition justifying a following item is cataphoric—then a linguistic item which is *fully and equally divided* between a function that points backward (which Halliday and Hasan 1973:236 call "retrospective" or "retrojective") and one that points forward, can reasonably be called "phoric."

Of course, there are several linguistic items in any text which are such that, in order to be fully analyzed, they must be described both in their relationships with one or more preceding items and in their effects on one or more following items. Indeed, the majority of items in any given text must be investigated in this way (thus, the problematic use of notions like "anaphoric" and "cataphoric" is one of the many instances in which strictly linguistic analysis, for all its apparent refinements in technique, reveals itself as coarse-grained with respect to the real complexity of the text).

But it is a different matter when these relationships merely round up the analysis of a linguistic item which can essentially be defined by itself, and when—as in our case (whence my underscoring of the definition above)—the simultaneous presence of an anaphoric and of a cataphoric relation is indispensable to understand the sense of the lexical item at issue, and also it is *all there is* in it—so to speak. This is why the notion of phoric is not superfluous; indeed, it is indispensable. And I submit (as a contribution to the linguistic theory of texts) that *all conjunctive elements are phoric*, and that this is indeed one of their crucial distinctive features.

Coming back specifically to the Greek conjunction, we note that it occupies the second place in the clause—which is its normal position in Ancient Greek (Denniston 1954:162ff.); thus it constitutes a typological opposition with respect to languages like Italian or English or French, etc., where its normal position is the first one.[15]

What is the tagmeme of *dé* in version (2) of the sentence, the one centered on *bíos* 'life'? The difference is interesting just because it is not large: it is precisely limited, a fact which underscores its importance. In the four-cell tagmeme the only cell with a different content is the lower left one, pertaining to Role:

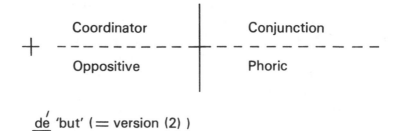

dé 'but' (= version (2))

Thus: *dé* in the second version of the sentence fills out the functional (or syntactic) slot in the same way as in version (1), as a Coordinator, and (just as in the first version) it represents a Conjunction within the cell of grammatical categories; and it is also Phoric, in the same sense. But its role now is that of Oppositive, as against its Additive role in version (1). Once again, an apparently negligible terminological variation is the cue to a significant difference. Conjunctions of the 'but' type are usually subsumed under the category of 'Adversative' (Halliday and Hasan 1973, for instance), but a conjunction like Ancient Greek *dé* reminds us of the necessity of distinguishing (as Humbert 1954:402 does) the "Adversative" from the "Oppositive" function.

However, the terminological simplicity of Halliday and Hasan is compensated for by the delicacy of their semantic appreciation ("in addition to the meaning 'adversative', *but* contains within itself also the logical meaning of 'and'; it is a sort of portmanteau, or short-hand form, of *and however*"—p. 237); while on the other hand the terminological subtlety of the French syntactician is partially obfuscated by his mechanic dichotomy ("Since French makes a very broad usage of the conjunction *mais*, we are not well prepared to perceive exactly the difference separating *oppositive dé* from *adversative allá* . . . "—Humbert 1954:402).

The typological contrast/similarity, then, should be viewed as follows: in languages like English (*but*), French (*mais*), Italian (*ma*), etc., the 'oppositive' and the 'adversative' semantic nuclei coexist, as different senses within the meaning complex of one and the same morpheme; in other languages, like for instance Ancient Greek and (apparently) Modern Russian, the 'oppositive' meaning is associated with a specific morpheme (Greek *dé*, Russian *a*, and so forth) while the 'adversative' meaning is neatly detached from it and comes to be identified with another morpheme (Greek *allá*, Russian *no*, etc.).[16]

The picture is complete when we notice that *dé* is halfway between the purely additive conjunction *kaí* 'and' (cf. Russian *i*) and the purely adversative conjunction *allá* in Greek. Thus we may grasp the balance: *dé* in version (1) is close to *kaí*—but it is not a full synonym here, and probably never is; while *dé* in version (2) is close to *allá*.[17]

In other words: the essentially additive role of *dé* in (1) still is tinged by an element of opposition or contrast which is enough to make it different from *kaí*, whereas the basically oppositive role of *dé* in (2) is nuanced by an additive element which suffices to forbid its identification with *allá*. A last point, which is not absent from Halliday and Hasan's description of 'and' versus 'but' and is dimly evoked when Humbert, continuing the passage quoted above, notes that with the oppositive *dé* the parataxis is based on "la coexistence de deux réalités affirmées l'une et l'autre, mais avec une force inégale."

One cannot establish a crucial distinction between the 'and' forms and the 'but' forms by opposing them in absolute terms as additive (connective, copulative) versus adversative. But this does not mean that there are no other distinctions—not immediately crucial perhaps, but such that they cannot be ignored; they are there, but the area of meaning in which we must look for them is a different one. The divergence is that the syntactic parataxis with 'and' is a fully homogeneous semantic parallelism, with equal force of the coordinated statements; at the most, the second clause, when it concludes the sentence (as in our case) represents a slightly stronger assertion. On the other hand, the 'but' form does more than coordinate—albeit in an oppositive (or contrastive, or adversative) way: it underscores an irregularity in the force of the two coordinated statements, such that the second assertion is supposed to semantically win over the first—not merely to be slightly more emphatic by virtue of its syntactic position. Thus the semantic parallelism with the syntactic parataxis is destroyed, or at least damaged: semantically we have a slight *hypo-taxis*, that is, a subordination of the first statement to the following 'but' statement—in short, a hierarchy between the two statements.

Thus, the additive *dé* in version (1) represents a full coordination or parataxis (semantic as well as syntactic) whereas the oppositive (or contrastive) *dé* in version (2) is the symbol of a counterpoint: a syntactic parataxis superimposed on a semantic subordination. The statement about death, then, is—in version (2) of our fragment—slightly stronger than the statement about life: not in the sense that the former refutes the latter, but in the sense that it underlines the 'death' theme as being *slightly* more important than the 'life' theme. Slightly, I said: for the subordination is not such as to destroy the delicate dialectic balance of this statement. Above, I described *dé* as specifying a full parataxis in one area, a parataxis semantically tinged with hypotaxis in another. It is not the case that this characterization of the meanings of the two clauses derives from an analysis of their connecting particles; since the connecting particle is the same, it is not it which determines the semantic difference. Rather, the conjunction *dé* has different values because the clauses it connects have different meanings.

Enough of *dé*; what about *oûn*? If the role of *dé* is complicated and delicate in a general way—in the sense, that is, in which every linguistic unit, if analyzed with the proper care, is complex and delicate—the case of *oûn* is not only complicated but obscure, and it evokes not only one aspect of a general linguistic code, but a local problem, with several intricate clusters. First of all, its etymology is not, as it is the case with *dé*, irrelevant to the structural analysis of the sentence. More precisely: the etymology of both *dé* and *oûn* is obscure, but while—in the case of the former—obscurity is like a thick blanket, the darkness surrounding the latter is interrupted by a tantalizing crack: it seems that *oûn* (variant: *ôn*) is originally a participial form of the verb *eimí* 'to be'.

If this etymology is accepted, then we should have a situation in which a statement of being is smuggled into a sentence which (by virtue of its nominal structure, already analyzed) firmly excludes any explicit use of verbs of being. This is significant also in view of the fact that *oûn* possesses a meaning which contains both a confirmative (strengthening) component (of the type of English 'actually') and a conclusive, stock-taking element, in the line of English 'now, as we may conclude,' *et similia*; a semantic field, then, which is rooted in the confirmation of reality within the framework of time (Humbert 1954:424–32).[18]

But this is the third and latest stage in the semantic development of *oûn*, coming after an early (Homeric) phase when its meaning is essentially temporal, and a slightly later phase when the idea of "actuality or essentiality" predominates—this later phase being that of the above-sketched usage, which can be characterized as "inferential or progressive" (Denniston 1954:416); and this third stage, as noted, becomes current only beginning with the writings of Sophocles. But this raises a problem: since the appropriate meaning here seems to be the conclusive or inferential or progressive one, rather than the temporal one, what is this tagmeme of the middle of the fifth century B.C. doing in a text which belongs to the sixth century?

The distinction is important beyond the local specification, and it has to do with what certain authors (like Halliday and Hasan 1973:239–40, and passim) express as a difference between external and internal structural relationships. In the former dimension, sentences are related to one another as steps in a temporal succession of events or actions; in the latter, sentences are related as steps in an argument.[19] It is important, then, to understand precisely at what level of textual structure this internal semantic relationship belongs. In investigating this, we reach a new dimension in the study of this fragment: namely, the real understanding of it *as a fragment*, rather than as an autonomous sentence.

4.3 THE FRAGMENT

In order to give an adequate idea of the actual complexity of linguistic structure I have been exploring this sentence, until now, as if it were an autonomous utterance. But of course we know that it is a fragment. What is not a matter of course, and therefore must be underscored, is that the concept of fragment evokes not one, but two, distinct sets of problems: the relationship between the actual surviving sentence and the authorial discourse originally surrounding it, insofar as we can reconstruct anything of it; and the relationship between this actual sentence and its actual context, that is, the text which explicitly quotes the fragment as such. The first set of problems is prevalently formal, while in the second group what emerges is the ideological element.

The existence of the problem has been recognized even in such abstract philosophical discussions as Heidegger's, on another fragment by Heraclitus ("Aletheia [Heraclitus Fragment B 16]" in Heidegger 1975*b*). Apropos of the fragments, he notes that "a close examination of their place of origin in the writings of subsequent authors yields only the context into which the quotation has been placed, not the Heraclitean context from which it was taken." Right; but no sooner is the real problem evoked than ideological obfuscation sets in: "The quotations and the sources taken together, still do not yield what is essential: the definitive, all-articulating unity of the inner structure of Heraclitus' writings."

Here a certain kind of existentialist thought, apparently very far from structuralist reflection, joins structuralism at the weakest point of the latter's chain of concepts: the a priori assumption, namely, that important texts must be unitary—an assumption which is ideological and mystifying. The difference is that, while structuralism makes at least an effort toward empirical interpretation, this kind of thinking exploits the fragmentary nature of the text in order to construct an ideology of vagueness: "Only a constantly advancing insight into this structure will reveal the point from which the individual fragments are speaking, and in what sense each of them, as a saying, must be heard." It does not take much forcing to paraphrase such a statement as follows: Since complete contextualization is ultimately impossible, insofar as we cannot reconstruct the full original context, let us renounce philology and empirical research, having recourse instead to an abstract meditation on what the fragment could be made to mean.

Such an ideological escape is rejected here: each text is an object of material production, and a description which does not address itself to this process of production is a mystification. Better to face final obscurity at the end of a determined effort of empirical investigation, than to construct artificial concretions on the text. The concern here is with a materialist theory of textual production—which is what philology objectively and always prepares, whether or not its practitioners care to develop its inner core explicitly.

We face, then, a cluster of dialectic relationships: the one linking this piece of text to its original, Heraclitean context, and the one connecting/opposing this fragmentary text to the later context which quotes it as a fragment; furthermore, each one of these two relationships is doubled by another link—the one connecting it as a text to the broader context. This is what goes beyond the context as a syntactically determined structure which immediately surrounds the fragment: it is the context of *ideological and social* signs which ultimately condition, and give sense to, the *verbal* signs (making up the strictly linguistic text-cum-context).

Since the social and ideological (con)text of Heraclitus must be distinguished from those of the later scholars quoting his discourses as fragments, and since one and the same fragment by him is usually quoted by more than two sources (each one having its verbal and social-ideological context), clearly we have to do with several relationships clustered together. From what has just been noted it follows that the minimum number of such dialectic links is found when the fragment at issue is quoted by only one source—we have then four links.

Just because I vindicate throughout this research the idea that, without philological integration, no linguistic theory (rhetorical, as the one presented here, or otherwise conceived) can lay claim to any basic seriousness; just because of this, the movement of general linguistic description must be clearly distinguished from that stage of philological localization or contextualization which alone will give it sense, and a place in the world of knowledge. Thus I must make clear that the implication of what I have been saying is that there are *four* alternative syntactic-semantic interpretations of *oûn*: a tagmeme with the meaning 'then' in a temporal sense (possibly correlating with a particle like *epeí* or *ōs* in the original, lost discourse); or: a tagmeme with an asseverative sense, 'actually' (as a near-synonym of a particle like *dĕ*—not *dé*!—and usually presupposing a preceding particle like *gár*, *oúte*, *eíte*, *mén*, or *dé* in the original discourse); or: a tagmeme with the meaning 'then,' but (in this case) in an inferential-progressive, rather than temporal, sense (compare one of the senses of the adverb 'now' in English); or, finally: a zero tagmeme—more precisely, a tagmeme which is to be rejected from the original, Heraclitean sentence, and considered instead as representing an interference between that sentence and the local context of its quotation. Here are, more schematically, the alternatives (in the order of their mention):

(1)

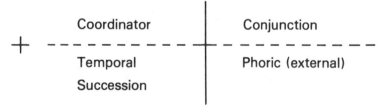

In agreement with what has just been noted, the phoric cohesion (in this case) does not take place between this clause and the following one within the context of our sentence (if this were the case, the label "phoric" would not be justified, and "cataphoric" would be the adequate definition); rather, the cohesion takes place (if this tagmeme is accepted) between the initial clause of this sentence and one of the clauses making up the immediately preceding (and irremediably lost) sentence in the original discourse.

Now for the second alternative:

(2)

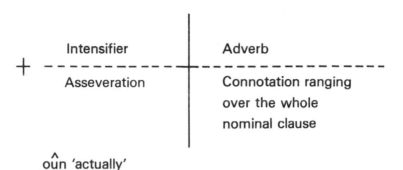

| Intensifier | Adverb |
| Asseveration | Connotation ranging over the whole nominal clause |

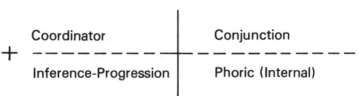

oûn 'actually'

The asseveration which defines the role of *oûn* in this interpretation makes the statement embodied by the first clause cohere at the level of its connotation—in the sense that the statement is (in this interpretation) made with a connotation of particular earnestness (which is what I meant to indicate by using the term "asseveration"). This interpretation implies a grammatical framework quite different from the others, for in lieu of a coordinating conjunction, we have here an intensifying adverb. Thus its cohesive force exhausts itself within the clause, and it does not link it up explicitly with the preceding or following clause.

As for the third interpretation:

(3)

| Coordinator | Conjunction |
| Inference-Progression | Phoric (Internal) |

oûn 'then, therefore, now'

The terms of this interpretation have been already explicated and its nexus of similarity/distinction with respect to (1) is clear by now. What must be emphasized is the difference between the external cohesion (between acts or events) established by tagmeme (1), and the internal cohesion between steps in an argument, represented by this tagmeme.

Finally, the zero tagmeme interpretation should not be designated with a separate number: it is not (4) with respect to the preceding three, because it does not imply a different tagmeme. What it implies is a different level: in this interpretation *oûn* belongs to another clause (and thereby to another sentence) which in turn represents a different text superimposed on the original text; namely, the quoting text, which *frames* the quoted text—in two senses of this word.

For the quoting text frames its quote in the sense that it encloses or encircles it like a wooden frame which encases a picture, and thereby discreetly and efficiently borders it. But the quoting text also (and always, albeit in different forms and degrees) frames its quote in the more slangish sense of the verb: namely, it manipulates the evidence surrounding it so as to deform its meaning. This latter sense designates the *inevitable* ideological de-formation (a noun used here in a strictly descriptive sense—which I have tried to symbolize by the hyphenated spelling—without derogatory connotations.) And this act of framing has the following peculiarity: that, whereas in the current idiomatic sense the act of framing always has an incrimination as its aim, ideological framing is much more sophisticated; its de-formation is never unequivocally an "incrimination" of the text (in a broad metaphorical sense, of course)—it is always as much an "exculpation" as an incrimination. For the boundary is never sharply delineated between the moment in which the ideological framing depresses the text, impoverishes it, brings it down several pegs in its value as a cultural object, and the moment in which ideology raises the text above its normal value, inflating its price. In literature as in all other artistic and literary endeavors, the immobile solemnity, the sacred seriousness of the museum of high culture is misleading. This atmosphere hides a constant movement of the waves of conflicting and changing evaluations; in other words, every museum is the congealed compromise between numerous separate auctions.

Thus, in this last interpretation, we have three possibilities doubling up the three which have been already described: 1^1, 2^1, 3^1. Since this shift in level has introduced us to the philological contextualization of the text, we may ask ourselves whether the general linguistic analysis can tell us anything more before the philological concretization. It can, indeed: interpretation (1) can be excluded on general semantic grounds; for the statement contained in this sentence is "internal"—concerning steps in an argument—rather than "external" (designating successive events taking place in the world).

If (1) is excluded, can (1^1) be excluded, too? Not right away, since it is possible to have the temporal 'then' interpretation of *oûn* in the frame sentence: which first reports one statement by Heraclitus, then another one—the one which is being analyzed. But the context excludes this possibility. It is high time, then, to turn to this context.

The basic source for this fragment is the *Etymologicon Magnum*, whose frame sentence—more precisely, the part of the frame which precedes our sentence (I will come back to it) is, s. v. *biós*: "It seems that the ancients designated homonymically (*homonūmōs*) as *biós* both the bow (*tò tókson*) and life (*hē zōē*). Anyway [or: thus] (*goûn* or *oûn*) Heraclitus the Obscure: *Tôi oûn tóksōi* . . . " (Gainsford 1848:198).

As we can see, no linguistic level is safe from variation. Even the language layer which serves as a metalanguage delimiting a specific linguistic structure is not completely lucid and stable. Thus, one tradition of this passage reads *oûn* (whose meaning we already analyzed), but another textual tradition of the same passage (preferred by Marcovich 1967:190ff.) has *goûn*, which I rendered as 'anyway'.[20]

We are here at the thin line between realistic structural analysis and ideology. The appearance of *oûn* in the Heraclitean sentence immediately after *(g)oûn* in the frame sentence is suspicious, and it makes us think that the copyist made a dittology—dittology, this time, in the philological rather than in the rhetorical sense. Or rather, to be more precise, dittology not in the internal, linguistic sense in which this concept has been used above (actual repetition of equal or similar lexical items), and which pertains directly to rhetoric, but in the external, metalinguistic sense: erroneous transcription of a linguistic item—which comes to be repeated two or more times, whereas it is present only once in the original message; this phenomenon too, although it is usually discussed by philologists, is of concern to rhetoric (as we are seeing just now). The dittology is a full one if we retain the *oûn* reading in the metatext, while it is a close echo rather than a dittology stricto sensu if we adhere to the *goûn* variant.

I commented above on the general difficulty that the presence of *oûn* poses for the semantic interpretation of the sentence; and I just noted that this item in the text is almost completely identical to an immediately preceding item in the metatext. Is this combination of a semantic difficulty with a textual ambiguity sufficient to reach the conclusion that *oûn* does not belong in the original Heraclitean sentence? I do not think that this is enough for that conclusion; but there is one more piece of evidence, and a quite significant one.

If the *Etymologicon Magnum* quote (to which, as noted, I will return) can be considered as our basic source, still it is not the only one. The other source is Tzetzes' *Exegesis in Iliaden* (Hermann 1812)—also a text to which it will be necessary to return: " . . . and that it [the bow] was also called *bios*, says Heraclitus the Obscure: '*tôi dè tóksōi ónoma* etc.'"

Marcovich (1967:190ff.) remarks that this *dé* "might be genuine." We have, then, the same text quoted by two different sources with an identity which is the best (the only) guarantee of its consistency and authenticity—with one exception: *oûn* versus *dé*; a variation which, after my analysis of the particles, I trust will not be treated as a trivial one.

It is only against this background that a fact which, by itself, would not be decisive acquires a particular weight: the fact, namely, that in all the Heraclitean corpus (as segmented and available for inspection in *indices verborum* such as those compiled by Marcovich 1967:623–32 and Bollack and Wismann 1972:371–85) there is no other instance of *oûn*.[21]

As noted, this by itself is not an argument against the authenticity of *oûn*, which could very well be an *ápaks legómenon*; yet, when this absence of *oûn* from the rest of the fragment is considered together with the facts listed above, it contributes to reinforce our doubts about its authenticity here. This reflection is important also for a more general reason. I pointed out above that there are at least two contexts with which we have to deal, when we consider this sentence as a fragment: the context of the original discourse by Heraclitus (irremediably lost, but which at any rate is by definition a context), and the context in which the fragment has the specific status of a quote—

this latter being actually a series of different contexts, as we just saw.

Now, this apparently simple act of checking out a lexical item against the index of Heraclitus' words reminds us that the actual situation is even more complicated than that. The two contexts which I just recalled are not only syntactic, but specifically *syntagmatic*; that is, they both pertain to the strings immediately preceding and those immediately following the string at issue. But what I have just been discussing points to another context, this time a *paradigmatic* one: the context constituted by all the other fragments by the same author—which give rise to a whole web of relationships, a *concordia discors* (in lexical choices, types of metaphor, sentence types, etc.) with the fragment at issue. This is the closest kind of intertextuality relevant here.

Finally, since I am on the subject, let me anticipate something that will be more fully treated below: the two first contexts evoked are deeper than their syntagmatic aspect; or, alternatively, we could add in each one a broader semiotic context to the strict syntagmatic context. For neither the original Heraclitean context nor the series of quotation contexts are limited to strings of lexical items: each one of them comprises the complex of ideological and social signs which ultimately give a sense to the discourse; and the crucial problem of rhetorical analysis—as an analysis built upon linguistics but which goes beyond linguistics—is that of reconstructing and evaluating these broader contexts.

This, then, is definitely the only weak link in the textual chain, as far as the text as a philologically (re)constructed object is concerned. But to speak of a weak spot is not the same as speaking of an inauthentic lexical item which should be lopped away from the text. Indeed, what I argue is that it is, in most cases, impossible to decide which items are authentic and which are nonauthentic (thus philology, if consistently applied, leads us back to the principled necessity of a skeptical position); and even in the cases where such a decision is possible, what matters most is the family of variants, the constellation of alternative possibilities, that the analysis reveals. I propose the name *glosseme* for the family of variants clustered around every lexical item in every text (as soon as the text begins to be transmitted).[22]

What the reader is usually faced with is, not the glosseme as a structure or a set of analytic steps (such as the one detailed above) leading to this structure—but the result of the editorial decision to reduce the glosseme to one only of its members. In other words, the reader usually deals with ideological constructs. The task of rhetorical theory, then, is that of recovering—in each concrete case, and insofar as it is possible—the glosseme behind the ideologeme. The present case is a particularly good illustration of this problem, because no clear-cut decision about the authenticity of the lexical item at issue is possible; thus the real task—reconstructing the glosseme—appears more clearly.

Thus, it is ideological to quote the sentence (as, for instance, Bollack and Wismann 1972 do) without putting the *oûn* form in, and without warning the reader about its peculiar kind of presence/absence in the text. It would be equally ideological, on the other hand, to transcribe the sentence with *oûn* but without any notation on its marginal status with respect to the other linguistic items in the sentence. The best solution, within the unavoidable limits of a traditional philological presentation, is the one by Marcovich, who quotes the sentence by printing *oûn* in smaller type—thus showing that its status is different from that of the other constituents of the sentence—and gives the basic information (the *goûn/oûn* variation in the quoting text, the *dé* variation in the quoted text).

To Marcovich we also owe the distinction—crucial from a general linguistic and ontological point of view—between degrees of literality in the quotation: the one closest to the original text is the one represented here by the *Etymologicon Magnum* and the Tzetzes' quote (the level Marcovich calls *Citatio*); here we can assume that we have to do with the original text—or more precisely (I would say) with one of the glossemes of the original text, within the very strong limits in which this notion has a serious sense. The degree below this is called *Paraphrase*, and it implies just what its name suggests; thus, it is one further step removed from the original text. The third and furthest step, finally, is what Marcovich calls *Respicit* ("no more than a reminiscence or reference to the fragment").

It is interesting that all three steps are illustrated by our example. The two *Citationes* we saw already; as for the level of Paraphrase, it is represented by Eusthatius *in Iliadem*: " . . . and it was with elegance (*asteíōs*) that the Obscure Heraclitus said as how (*ōs ára*), about the *bios*, verily: '*Toû tóksou, tò mèn ónoma "bios," tò dè érgon thánatos*.'"

I will return presently to this passage; for the moment, I note that

I am aware of the clumsiness of my English translation: its justification is that it aims at showing, as precisely as possible, how the text is fitted into the metatextual frame, by insisting on the phrasal idiom of conjunction (ōs) + adverb (ára) which in Ancient Greek is typically used to introduce some other person's words, for which one disclaims full responsibility.[23]

Also, I wanted to reflect in my version what looks like an intricate pattern of word order in the Greek metatext, and which raises a problem of interpretation. If we take that as the genitive form of *bíos* 'life', then the word order is less than perspicuous, since there is no reason for the "distantiating" idiom ōs ára to govern the noun phrase 'life': it is not the reference to life in itself, but the peculiar characteristic which he predicates of it, which makes the originality of Heraclitus' statement, and which therefore must be assigned to his responsibility.

On the other hand, if that form is interpreted as the genitive of *biós* 'bow', then the collocation of words is semantically justified: the very idea of focusing on this lexical item is what makes Heraclitus' statement provocative—his predication, therefore, must be distantiated by the very text which quotes it.

Nor is this all: this delicate choice emphasizes an important (and usually neglected) feature of paronomastic paradigms (see Valesio 1974b, and below): that, for any pair of lexical items, one cannot reconstruct a paronomastic paradigm once and for all, based solely on the forms in which such items are usually listed in dictionaries; for every inflectional form of each of the two items (if the language at issue possesses inflectional paradigms, of course) may modify the paronomasia, or even lead to the appearance of a paronomasia where the dictionary forms did not show it, or conversely destroy the existing paronomasia. Thus, *biós/bíos* is—as we are going to see—a semi-homonymic paronomasia (the difference being at the suprasegmental level, in stress position, while all the phonic segments here are identical); but if we switch to the genitive, (the paronomasia *paradigmatically* evoked in the metatext of quotation), we have a fully homonymic paronomasia. This confirms, once again, the wisdom of transcribing unaccented *bios* wherever possible in order to respect the ambiguity in the texts, which is strictly functional to the statement that they are making.

Finally, the *Respicit* degree of textual framing is represented by a passage in Hippocrates' *De nutrimentis* (cf. Heiberg I, 1:81): "Nourishment, not nourishment—if it cannot be eaten [safely]; ⟨non-⟩nourishment, nourishment—if it is such that it can nourish. The name, 'nourishment', but not the work; the work, nourishment, but not the name."

A close translation is—in the framework of all this analysis—such an obvious necessity that to keep apologizing about the stylistic clumsiness of the English versions would be coyly inappropriate. It was necessary, in fact, to reflect the Greek text especially in its nominal structure. (I cannot go into further details, but it is interesting to note that the antithetical structure of the text made the transcriber's task difficult, so that emendations and corrections were necessary; in particular, "non-" enclosed in angled brackets—⟨ ⟩—reflects Diels' appropriate addition of *ou*, without which the opposition loses its sense.)

It bears repeating that these are *not* technicalities: they are the basic determinations of the text as a concrete entity—for which purpose a detailed description of its glossemic structure is indispensable. One could still object that this—interesting as it may be to the philologist—*is* a technical detail. But how could this be considered a technicality when it deals with nothing less than the establishment of the ontology of the text? Far from being a technicality, then, it is *philosophy*: philosophy *in concreto*, philosophy as a systematization of philology; a step forward in the philological procedure, to be sure, but a step forward which takes place in the same direction and has the same nature. Thus the condescending tone of Bollack and Wismann 1972 toward the previous philological research—and especially, albeit indirectly, it seems, toward Marcovich 1967—reveals all its fragility: the philosophy displayed in their work is, by and large, ideology.

But, it is time to resent the glosseme—or at least, the glosseme which most interests us here; its structure, and position within the sentence, can be preliminarily represented as follows:

$$\textit{tôi} \quad \begin{matrix} \textit{oûn} \\ \varnothing \\ \textit{dè} \end{matrix} \quad \textit{tóksōi ónoma bios, érgon dè thánatos.}$$

This transcription is significant not as a formal innovation, but as a substantive claim on the nature of texts. Usual linguistic characterizations of sentences—including the ones elaborated by transformational-generative grammar—turn out to be too simplistic, for even the distinction between underlying formative and surface morphemes must be enlarged in such a way as to take place, not once and for all for every lexical item, but for every member of the relevant glosseme.

A sentence, then, must be analyzed into glossemes before anything can be said about the lexical items which one chooses to analyze out of each glosseme. The glosseme is the locus where the dialectal variants of the sentence constituents are brought together. This description has several implications, which cannot be developed here. But an aspect of this proliferation of glossemes (which destroys every surviving ideological illusion on the structure of the text as a unified structure) must be noted: every sentence not only is constituted by the sum of a series of glossemes (an obvious consequence of the way in which the glosseme has been defined here), but is itself a member of a glosseme, and *not* in the sense resulting from the simple mechanical sum of its glossemes.

This has to do with the different philological genesis of the structures in the text, as we just saw: the variants making up the glossemes come down to us, either as variants of isolated items (*dé* and zero—symbolized as Ø—as variants of *oûn*) or as variants of larger structures—phrases, clauses, or, like here, the whole sentence: for it is the whole sentence that is involved in Eustathius' variant (*toû tóksou*, etc.).

The final version of our sentence (final *at this point*, pending a full collation of all the variants, which is not possible here) is, then, the following:

	oûn										
tôi	Ø	tóksōi	Ø	Ø	ónoma	bios,	Ø	Ø	érgon	dè	thánatos
	dè				oúnoma						

| toû | Ø | tóksou, | tò | mèn | ónoma | bios, | tò | dè | érgon | Ø | thánatos |

(I tentatively consider Hippocrates' *ounoma* as an actual variant of Heraclitus' text in this sentence, rather than as an indirect echo.)

To conclude on the glosseme, by making clear the difference between glossemic reality and ideological abstraction which has been hinted at above: the most important *cognitive* result of the analysis by glossemes is the principled justification of an *agnostic* attitude with respect to the variants. A paradoxical conclusion? Only if we were to neglect that this theory of rhetoric has been explicitly inscribed in the perspective of a contemporary renewal of skeptic thought. Thus, the refusal to choose between *oûn* and *dé*, as well as between any of these two full slots and the empty one, is not a manifestation of indifference, or a narrowly positivistic diffidence toward principled reflection (the last would be an antiphilosophical attitude which has been rejected here from the start); neither is it a way of expounding a fully irrationalistic philosophical approach.

This refusal is not meant as a destructive, but rather as a constructive, gesture: it insists that the reality of the text—its concrete, material ontology—is faithfully reflected only in a *prima facie* "unreadable" transcription like the one proposed above. In the local situation just described, to write only *oûn*, or only *dé*, or only nothing, is a basically arbitrary decision, an aprioristic way of cutting a knot whose interest lies in its very intricacy; in short, it is an ideological decision. This local case, in fact, illustrates a much broader lesson about literary texts: the price of readability is, very often, the performance of (or the tacit complicity in) an act of ideological deformation. Never mind how slight this act is (as here), and how far removed it is from burning issues of a political, social, or religious nature.

The philosophical concern of the present theory of rhetoric is to point out the genesis and phenomenology of such de-formation, whatever its justification (which, in certain circumstances, can be very good and—within a context clarifying it—can be maintained as a legitimate component of the text). The concern is also that of pointing out the ways to construct an analysis complicated by a mininum of ideology (a completely unideological analysis is impossible). The analysis by glossemes is one of these means.

But there is another way of making the delicate interpenetration of basic rhetorical patterns and ideology—within one and the same linguistic structure—come alive; and this way also is available here, indeed, it shows itself as a path which must be explored if we want to do justice to this linguistic structure: I refer to the analysis of the metaphor which is presented here.

4.4 THE METAPHOR

A distinction must now be underscored, which is relevant to all aspects of grammar and rhetoric, but is particularly important (because it is usually obliterated) in the case of metaphor: the distinction between examining the ideological components of rhetorical-linguistic structures, and examining those structures without any general view or specific awareness of the role of ideology—thereby falling victim to ideology as acriticism—even if this acriticism is posing as an example of allegedly objective and neutral analysis. The fact is that the analysis, or critique, of ideology is very different from an ideological analysis.

Metaphor has received great linguistic attention of late; but we have now come to a grave impasse. The fleet of studies on metaphor is in disarray: some of the ships have been lost in the high seas of generality, while others have run aground against the reefs of mere technicalities. In both cases, although the methodological stances are opposite, the cause of the impasse is the same: the reduction of critique to ideology.

In one case, this ideological reductionism means a decrease in depth and precision of analysis. The ideologization here consists in this, that metaphor becomes little more than a generic label for various elements of dynamism and ambiguity in language. What we have then is a general appreciation about language, rather than the study of specific linguistic structures (see the special issue of *New Literary History*: "On Metaphor," 1974, and Ricoeur 1975, among others).

At the other extreme, we have several technical studies on metaphor (see, for instance, several articles in *Poetics*, especially in vol. 4, 1975, and vol. 5, 1976). Most of these studies have the opposite defect from the one just described: they focus on a purely technical typology of metaphorical phrases or sentences, severing them from their connections with broader cultural-linguistic patterns, and especially from the ideologemes, which are at the root of the persisting fascination and ambiguity of metaphors. But perhaps the most glaring flaw of these studies is their lack of interest in the empirical data. For there is nothing particularly scientific in the current practice of juxtaposing a few sentences (either made up or belonging to literary texts—usually modern texts) and some experimentation with descriptive tools. All these remain intellectualistic exercises, which do not help us much in advancing our knowledge of linguistic structures as they actually function in culture and society.

In view of all this, "theoretical" studies of metaphor (and of metonymy) must be put in a seriously critical perspective: they are, at this point, ideological exercises. The wheel is, indeed, come full circle. At the turn of the century, the positivistic style encouraged collections of data on metaphor, with little methodological elaboration. As a reaction against this attitude, an interest for general discussion of metaphor set in—an interest which has lasted until today, and which by now constitutes an embarrassment, because the insights which this reflection has produced are far from being numerous. The time has come, now, to turn back to the gathering and sifting of primary data.

One has to have recourse, to be sure, to all the resources of linguistic analysis which have been developed in the meantime. But a moratorium should be proclaimed on all general claims and appreciations about metaphor which do not grow out of a corpus of first-hand data empirically analyzed; *or at least*—when the structure analyzed is one only—out of a detailed textual and contextual study of the form at issue. This latter is the task which I have assigned myself here (for this, obviously, is not the place for analyzing a corpus of metaphors). In trying to fulfill this task one finds something that always happens in active research but that, every time it takes place in a given local situation, provokes a fresh effect of surprise and excitement: namely, that theoretical insights emerge out of the empirical analysis and demand to be accounted for, forcing themselves on the analyst.

Thus, this metaphor, which is based on the blending of *bíos* and *biós*, calls into question several current notions about metaphor as soon as we start looking at it more closely. First of all, when we analyze the actual criss-crossing of semantic features between these two lexical items we realize that terms like "metaphor" and "metonymy" have by now outlived their usefulness as significantly opposite notions (and the difficulty of establishing clear boundaries between metonymy proper—whatever that is—and synecdoche should have warned us about the inadequacy of this excessively coarse-grained taxonomy). What we face is a continuum of semantic processes, where the terms "metonymy" and "metaphor" can still be used in, so to speak, a modest role—that is, as the labels of the two poles around which these semantic processes tend to cluster, in a movement which is one of continuous shading rather than of clear-cut opposition.

Moreover, metaphor—which has completely overshadowed metonymy in the tradition of studies on figures of speech—turns out on closer inspection to be such a fleeting configuration that its definition can only be negative: metaphorical relations are those which are constituted by those semantic relations (whose nature will be made clear presently) which cannot be expressed in a clear-cut grid of hierarchic connections. On the other hand, those semantic relations which can be expressed in the terms of such a grid characterize the pole of metonymy; and the best way to describe the grid—within a theory such as the one put forth here—is to have recourse to the basic topoi. They are, in most cases, the topos of Cause and Effect and the topos of Size and Division (this latter subsuming such relations as genus/species, part/whole, container/contained, etc.—every relationship representing also its inverse: thus, species/genus, and so forth). Thus, at the metonymic pole, the internal structure of the lexeme is *a replica—on a smaller scale—of the topical relationships which take place at the broad scale of the paragraph or discourse.* As far as I know, this structural parallelism between two different levels of rhetorical structure—the figural level (metonymic process) and the topical level—has not been noted until now. An indirect anticipation of some such picture may be found in Bally's remark (it is not clear who he is quoting) that "in the majority of cases, what are called metaphors, synecdoches and metonymies rest on 'paralogisms of simple inspection'" (1951 I: par. 198). But this is presented there, it seems, as a negative factor (in keeping with Bally's misguided attitude toward rhetoric), and it is not developed into anything like the analysis of topical structures which is presented here.

Metaphorical relationships, then, are those which do not reflect clear-cut patterns. At the most, we can generalize to the point of saying that the nonhierarchic, analogical relationships clustering around the metaphorical pole are often such that the lack of hierarchy is manifested by the components of the metaphor being at the same semiotic level, as in the species-to-species relationship (cf. Homer's "Drawing the life with the bronze" [*II*. 2. 272]) or in a relationship which I would call antipredication, by which the referent is alluded to with a negative periphrasis (for instance, 'a cup that holds no wine' as a metaphorical designation of the shield). But, on closer inspection, at least, this latter generalization does not work, because not every negative definition of this kind is a metaphor (see for instance, a defining sentence like: *it's a car because it isn't for carrying heavy loads*, used as a frame to test semantic contrasts—in this case, a contrast between words like *car* on the one hand and words like *truck* on the other [cf. Nida 1975:59–60]).

The reader will have recognized traces—including the two examples just quoted—of the famous Aristotelian classification of metaphors in *Poetics* 1457^b (which is referred to also in *Rhetoric* 1405^a ff.). But he will also have noticed that I divide between the metonymic and the metaphoric poles what Aristotle assigns exclusively to metaphor, assigning two of his four + one categories, namely the genus-to-species and species-to-genus ones, to metonymy; the other three (species-to-species, analogy, and, tentatively, what I call antipredication) I assign to metaphor. I speak of "four + one" rather than five categories because the last one is merely hinted at as an afterthought by Aristotle, after the presentation of the four categories. Besides, as we just saw above, antipredication as criterion for identifying metaphor does not work, at least in the generic terms with which Aristotle presents it.

But I am falling into the danger I just denounced, that of the too-general discussion; it is time, then, to focus on the *bíos/biós* metaphor. However, the point is that the preceding pages *as well* have been about this metaphor—commenting on the way in which this specific linguistic phenomenon forces on us a rethinking of metaphor. Indeed, I cannot even start describing the basis of this particular metaphor without being forced (even against my initial, unconfessed desire to develop a "safe" application) to call into question a distinction which seemed to have persisted until today as one of the few clear points in any analysis of metaphor: I refer to the well-known differentiation (introduced by Richards 1936) between "tenor" and "vehicle." Whatever names may be used (and several have been employed) as variants of these two, the fact remains that metaphor has most often been described as born out of the tension between a linguistic item *in praesentia* in the text, the "tenor," and an element (linguistic and/or extralinguistic—let us say, a semiotic entity) which is *in absentia,* and which makes its effects felt in the linguistic form at the surface of the text.

One flaw of this characterization which, I suspect, has by and large escaped notice is that such a description considerably (better: excessively) simplifies the structure of metaphor right from the start. For it assumes that all the problems in the description of metaphor are concentrated at the semantic level, while the formal basis of this semantic configuration is treated as if it were simple and straightforward. But, as we look at our example, we see that this is not always the case: for here the basis of the metaphor is the most complicated among the figures of speech—at the morphophonemic level, and as far as the calculus of the formal relationships between the items at issue is concerned. This figure, which has been briefly touched upon already, is Paronomasia.

The tradition of rhetorics on paronomasia is a scattered heap of details, with much overlapping and confusion with other figures. But, building on recent work (cf. Valesio 1974*b* and 1976*b*) it is possible to put some order into it and to come out with a definition which (to my knowledge) is the first attempt in the literature to be explicit and systematic. We identify paronomasia when: *given a list of two or more lexical items, there is a sequence of phonemes which shows up in every item in the list, such that the number of phonemes in that sequence is more than half of the total number of phonemes in each other item in that list.*

At least two specifications must be added. The first—already hinted at above—is that the list relevant to the identification of paronomasia changes as the inflectional forms of the lexical items in question change.[24]

The second specification which must be appended to this definition of paronomasia is that the sequence of phonemes at issue may include all the phonemes, and all suprasegmental features, of all the words in the list. That is to say: paronomasia may include full homophones or (as noted above) semi-homophones, in which the only element of difference is the stress contour.

BIOS, then, is no autonomous form, but merely the graphemic label for the paronomastic paradigm:

$$
\text{BIOS} \quad \left\{ \begin{array}{ll} /\text{biós}/ & \text{'bow'} \\ /\text{bíos}/ & \text{'life'} \end{array} \right\}
$$

Actually, it appears that the paronomastic paradigm at work here is richer than this. It seems to have escaped critical attention until now that the graphemic cluster BIOS can stand for yet another lexeme (beside 'life' and 'bow') in the lexicon of Ancient Greek: namely *Bíos* as a man's name. (Most dictionaries, unfortunately, do not list names together with nouns—as if the former would not be as linguistically interesting as the latter; and Liddell and Scott 1940 is no exception; but Stephanus' *Theasaurus* 1572—thorough and downright precious in this as in other respects—lists *Bíos* as 'nomen virile'. The two dictionaries just named are the basis for the lexical description which follows.) Thus we have:

$$
\text{BIOS} \quad \left\{ \begin{array}{ll} \text{/biós/} & \text{'bow'} \\ \text{/bíos/} & \text{'life'} \\ \text{/bíos/} & \text{'Bios'} \end{array} \right\}
$$

This addition is not only interesting for a phenomenology of paronomasia—showing that, while most paronomasias (especially those based on homophones or semihomophones) include no more than two lexical items, there are those which include three or more such items; the addition is also interesting for the semantic analysis of our specific context. In fact, the sentence is now seen to involve *a two-layered word play on the act of naming*. On the already described level, the ambiguity is between an act of synonymic labeling and one of metaphorical creation, both involving common nouns. But now we see that both these acts are made to allude to the conventional social act of giving an entity a proper name. That the entity thus designated is an inanimate object rather than a human being does not constitute a damaging break in the pattern—for it is part of a schema of personifying metaphor.

Moreover, this is part of a large and widespread system in verbal folklore: that of giving names to weapons. This semantic interpretation, then, casts around the sentence the thin web of a heroic connotation—which is however a slightly anachronistic one, for it evokes the rhetoric of the Middle Ages rather than that of ancient Greece. But if we look at this heroic connotation on a larger scale we see that its implication is broader. The idea is that of treating a weapon or an animal as the companion of the warrior rather than his tool: it is, then, the same "logic" at work from Achilles' talking horses to Durendal brandished by Roland.

In any case, something must be underscored which is more strictly pertinent from a linguistic point of view: this interpretation presupposes a change in the semantic-syntactic value of the definite article, a change which assigns it to another class in the general typology of the values or functions of the definite article. We saw above (in the wake of Halliday and Hasan 1973) that the definite article, in the basic interpretation of this sentence, identifies the individual entity at issue as the representative of its whole class—in this case, the class 'bow' (*homophoric* is the label I accept for this function).

In the proper-name interpretation, however, it is highly improbable that a proper name is here assigned to the whole class of bows (this would make of *Bíos* a special synonym of *biós*). The most plausible interpretation, of course, is that the article (insofar as it identifies the common noun within a proper-name predication) specifies a particular individual within the class, and this individual is such as to be identifiable in the given situation. This latter element, it must be noted, is not the effect of the article; rather, this usage of the article presupposes that this form of identifiability exists, no matter how it came about.

Something more should be noted on the latter point. *Both* usages of the article that we discussed (the homophoric as well as the present one, which I will tentatively call *individualizing*) belong to the broader class of *exophoric* uses of the article; where exophoric means that the information necessary to specify the reference of the article is assumed to be given by the situation, or better by the semiotic context (or context of situation).

The alternative to the exophoric use of the article—its *endophoric* usage—represents the situation in which what is implied is that the information necessary to identify the referent comes from the text, in the sense of *immediate linguistic context*, in which the article appears (as opposed to the broad semiotic context surrounding the whole text to which the article belongs).[25]

Now, one of the ways in which a sentence, once identified as a fragment, conditions the linguistic analysis which can be made of it is precisely the one we are considering: it is hermeneutically impossible, by the very definition of "fragment," to explain the identification performed by a definite article as an endophoric procedure, because, of course, we do not have the con-text.

As for the proper-name interpretation: I am *not* suggesting it as an alternative interpretation which would clarify the "mystery" of *bíos/ biós*. What I am saying is that the proper name interpretation exists as a hermeneutic possibility, which is not developed, but which however is left in the morphosemantic (paradigm of the paronomasia) and syntactic backgrounds of the sentence, in such a way that it colors it with a peculiar connotation.

But, one could object, isn't this still too much to accept? Isn't the connotation of this name-giving a faintly grotesque one, rather than the heroic one alluded to above? To which the best answer is: Yes, but what is wrong with all this? In fact, side by side with the vaguely heroic connotation of the weapon-with-a-name, there is a quite different connotation, oscillating between the absurd and, as noted, the slightly grotesque: an ontological interrogation on different forms of being (what is the essence of life?) is degraded to the process of nicknaming an instrument. This observation does not constitute an objection, for the Heraclitean text has shoulders broad enough to carry with elegance also a connotation of grotesque.

The absurdist allusion in this fragment is in keeping with what we know about the real complexity of this ancient reflection; and to make such a complexity and manysidedness explicit is an essential task of rhetorical analysis as a procedure to demystify the ideological curtain of hieratic solemnity often thrown on these ancient utterances.

Actually, the paronomastic paradigm is even richer than noted until now:

$$
\text{BIOS} \left\{
\begin{array}{ll}
\text{/biós/} & \text{'bow'} \\
\text{/bíos/} & \text{'life'} \\
\text{/bíos/} & \text{'Bios'} \\
\text{/bía/} & \text{'strength, force'}
\end{array}
\right\}
$$

But showing that it is reasonable to assume the presence of *bía* in the paradigm leads us into problems of relationship between metalanguage and language, as well as of the relationships between ideology, connotations, and denotations. These problems (within the limits of this section) will be dealt with in the course of my analysis of the metaphor realized here.

To sum up what I have established—or rather, what I have tried to disestablish—about metaphor which is crucial for the analysis which follows: metaphor does not exist as a clear-cut, autonomous rhetorical configuration—rather, it is a complex of several subsystems of semantic processes whose distinctive feature is essentially a negative one: metaphors are *not* expressable through a grid of sharply profiled, hierarchical relationships (as happens for metonymies); also, the tenor/vehicle dichotomy is *not* a necessary distinctive feature of metaphor. We are, indeed, going to anatomize a metaphor where neither of the (at least) two lexemes involved, *bíos* and *biós*, can be said to be the tenor or the vehicle of the other.

Another characteristic of metaphor which is, in a sense, connected to the one described above can be expressed by saying that addition and modification, rather than substitution, are the key concepts of metaphor. A lexeme (or lexical entry, or term) is here viewed as the combination of a morphophonemic structure with a complex of semantic features—more precisely, a complex of bundles of semantic features. Each bundle of semantic features constitutes a sense; the complex of all senses constitutes the meaning of the lexical entry.

Semantic features include grammatical as well as lexical features. That grammatical processes have semantic implications is well known; but it is not usually discussed—as far as I know—whether the distinction between denotative and connotative holds for features of grammatical meaning as well as for the features of lexical meaning. I tend toward an affirmative answer; but in any case it is not necessary, in this example, to debate this technical point, for the connotations with which I will have to deal pertain to the lexical features.

This is not to say, of course, that the problem is thereby made easy: the distinction between what is denotative and what connotative is a notoriously difficult one. Here as elsewhere, the issue is one of empirical research rather than of theoretical debate. I confine myself to this: a theory of rhetoric like the present one encourages me to adopt, among the various current ways of using the concept of connotation, the broadest one. If denotative features are, as currently assumed, those which have a diagnostic value, that is, those which serve to define the so-called referential meaning of a given lexical item, then all the features which, in a given time, are not strictly functional to this purpose should be viewed as connotative.

This is not a new idea (cf. Nida 1975:36–37). But the view, and use,

of connotative elements here presents two features (one relatively restricted, the other of broad import) which are new. In the first place,
I do not treat the denotative/connotative distinction as an absolute,
paradigmatic one. One and the same semantic feature within one and
the same lexical item may be connotative in one context and denotative in another. The indications, then, like the "d" and "c" which accompany features in my lexical entries below, should be interpreted
as being, in large part, contextual indications.

In an abstract and formalistic view, this broad definition of connotation and its sensitivity to variations in con-text and context could be
seen as flaws; but in an empirical and functional view of language
such as the one embodied in my theory of rhetoric, these features
constitute an advantage. They allow us to list connotative features in
the lexical matrices without burdening them excessively. Appended
comments and developments will, then, take care of the necessary
specifications: which of these connotative features represent presuppositions for the appropriate use of the item in question, which are
the locutionary effects of it, which ones are bound to iconic elements
in their morphophonemic shapes, which ones are strictly dependent
on the context and which ones are largely independent from it; and
so on and so forth.

In the second place and above all, the importance of connotative
features does not lie in a generic emotional coloring which they allegedly give to the lexical item. What is at stake is much more serious:
*connotative features are the material out of which ideological stratifications
are constructed.* Connotations, then, do not express evanescent emotions: under their misleadingly frivolous appearance, they weave a
supple but strong web of ideologies. Thus the study of connotations
has important consequences on both sides, for the critical understanding of culture. As the contribution of empirical linguistic analysis to the critique of ideologies, it is one of the few ways available to
give a solid foundation to this critique, freeing it from that purely
ideological status which it is supposed to criticize. On the other hand,
as the contribution of critical theory and ideological awareness to linguistic analysis, it gives a broad and more serious framework to the
latter, going beyond the intellectual poverty of semantic techniques
such as that of componential analysis (cf. Nida 1975) in the very act
in which it makes use of these techniques.

Finally, connotations (in my view) should be described as being ordered in a rough hierarchy of importance, from relatively central to
relatively peripheral. What happens, then, when what we call a metaphor takes place? That the meanings of two (sometimes more) lexical
items—like *bíos* and *biós* in the Heraclitean sentence—become conflated into a third meaning which cannot be identified with the meaning of any one of the two separate items (addition, as noted, is the
key word, rather than substitution). In this third meaning, each semantic feature of the three separate items enters into one of the following relations with a semantic feature of the other item: it either
(a) overlaps with it, or (b) is added to it without conflict, or (c) is added
to it with some concomitant semantic tension (which is often ex
pressed as a complementary relation of opposition, or reversion, or
conversion).

Furthermore, in any of these three cases a feature, if it is connotative, can: (a) remain at the same hierarchical level, or (b) be promoted
to a higher level, or (c) be demoted to a lower level. Now, the following comparative descriptions of the two lexical items involved are not
exhaustive (no such description can be exhaustive, at the present state
of our knowledge), but they do go a long way toward a complete
description of their basic structure and of its rhetorical ramifications.
At least, they show that no rhetorical analysis of texts, from now on,
can afford less than this detailed and systematic description, whose
implications go far beyond mere technique. (Once again, what we
have here is the philosophy of philology—which is still in its beginnings.)

These descriptions constitute an internal analysis of the meanings
of the lexical items at issue; as such they are different from analyses
like that of *run* and similar verbs (Nida 1975:79ff.), or of the lexical
system of Italian *cavallo* 'horse' (cf. Alinei 1974). Both these descriptions constitute broad characterizations of semantic features associated with several lexical items, while the effort made here is that of
digging deeply into the semantic and ideological makeup of a pair of
lexical items.

One point more: what is presented in Fig. 1 as the lexical matrix of
biós is normally introduced in the dictionaries as the matrix of *tókson*,
for *biós*—in a standard Ancient Greek lexicon—would have to be presented as a rare and obsolete synonym of *tókson*, and so subordinated

FIGURE 1

bió̱s

noun
singular
masculine
common
count
concrete

ḏ

entity
I   inanimate
manufactured
curved structure

ii   weapon
offensive

c̱

of ii:

> means of providing food (CONTEXT: hunting)
>   vs.
> means of deadly destruction (CONTEXT: war)

of I, ii:

elegantly shaped

of I, ii:

locus of tension

to the latter as far as lexical description is concerned. But *biós* probably did *not* have such a "marked" dialectal/stylistic status at the time of Heraclitus. This is why I put the relevant features under *biós* (which is thus equalized, without further qualifications, with *tókson*), and I do not indicate here diacritic features like 'rare' and/or 'obsolete'.

As usual here, I consider a running gloss on these skeletal indications as an integral part of the analysis, rather than as an optional addition. For the criterion of elegance for a study in the human sciences should be sought after in the direction of detailed and varied exposition (adhering to the empirical complexity of its manifold object) rather than in the aping of the diagrammatic style of the exact sciences. We could say that elegance in the human sciences means not to cultivate any "elegance" of formulation.

This is also why a less formalistic style should be adopted in the presentation of the semantic features. First of all, the binary representation (± concrete, etc.) should be abandoned because it gives only the illusion of exactness, while the semantic differences which really matter are differences of degree, and should be expressed in an *n*-ary system (when necessary, then, the features should be accompanied by raised numerals indicating relative degrees of strength of the feature in the given meaning: concrete^1, concrete^2, etc., as is currently done in the representation of stress patterns). Secondly, and more significantly: the criterion of redundance should be clearly subordinated to that of explicitness in the representation of hierarchical relationships.

This latter point is important enough to warrant some further comments, for it is the whole movement of the researcher's attention which is at issue here. Is it more important to offer an allusively economical representation, in which the mere mention of a feature like 'weapon' is enough, since it is implicit that a weapon is 'manufactured', that a manufactured object is 'inanimate', and that an inanimate object is some kind of 'entity', and all these features therefore should not be written out—or is it more important to detail the route through which these features move, so as to make the underlying semiotic hierarchy emerge in its explicitness?

The drift of all that precedes should not leave doubts about my answer: it is the second path which is the right one, for a realistic rhetorical analysis. But let us go back to the beginning, and see what is the nature of the semantic features in this theory of rhetoric. The essential point is that this theory rejects the myth of a unified and "pure" metalanguage, and it squarely faces the fact that no such metalanguage is possible in our field. The task: to show the ideological conditioning of the metalanguage in the very act of using this metalanguage. The apparent eclecticism thus points in reality to the coherence of a radical critique. But, all this has to be shown in the concreteness of our matrix.

The solid double line separates the grammatical meaning (above) from the features relevant to lexical meaning; and, within the latter set, the single solid line separates denotative features (see the abbreviation "d" at the head of the list) from connotative features ("c"). As for the dotted lines within each set, they represent the rough hierarchy of importance which was mentioned above: the features above the line occupy, *under normal conditions*, a more central position than those below the line in determining the meaning of the item at issue. We touch the concrete problems which we mentioned above when we try to establish the nature of the metalanguage employed in these sets.

The first set does not present special problems here: it reflects the metalanguage of linguistics. This is not to say that such a metalanguage is absolutely and fully adequate (suffice it to think of the ambiguities implicit in a notion like that of "concrete" which, if we take it seriously, involves a series of problems, from the physiology of perception to metaphysics); it simply means that the ideology implicit in this metalanguage is the one which is least disturbing and mystifying within a rhetorical analysis (while it might produce obfuscation if applied *tout court* to, say, sociological research).

The case of the second set is more complicated: its ideology is only partially (cf. "inanimate") the described one, of codified linguistic terms; for the rest, it is an ideology of positive (and positivistic) determination of *realia*, an objective taxonomy of the world as machine. The advantage of this taxonomy is the clarity of its overall design and the absence of immediately evident philosophical implications. Its weakness? It could be expressed in almost the same words: it lies in the illusion (typical of positivist ideology) that this taxonomy creates, of being "natural," virgin of philosophical elaboration. But here as elsewhere in this book, the question is not one of all-or-none choices: once we are aware of the ideological conditionings at work, and once we try to characterize them as clearly as we can in their limits *and in their insights*, we should not feel apologetic for making use of them.

Let us briefly see what is at work here, before turning to those semantic features which represent my analysis of the meaning of this lexical item. This hierarchy of denotative features reflects a taxonomy currently used for the preparation of a dictionary of the Greek New Testament (cf. Nida 1975:178–87); a hierarchy where one climbs down the several ladders, in order to arrive at 'bow', as follows: (I.) "Entities," (A.) "Inanimate," (2.) "Manufactured or constructed entities," (a.) "Artifacts (nonconstructions)," (4.) "Armor," (a.) "Offensive." The main bifurcations at which one has to make a choice are, step by step, the following: (II.) "Events," (III.) "Abstract," and (IV.) "Relationals" vs. "Entities"; and, within "Entities": (B.) "Animate entities" as against "Inanimate," (1.) "Natural" opposing "Manufactured," etc., (b.) "Processed substances: foods, medicines, and perfumes" facing the "Artifacts" category; and then: (1.) "Generic: 'object', 'thing', 'goods'," (2.) "Vehicles," (3.) "Tools," and other such categories flanking that of "Weapons"; and within the latter: (b.) "Defensive": 'helmet', 'shield', 'breastplate', etc. versus the quoted "Offensive": 'weapon', 'club', 'sword', 'arrow', 'bow', 'spear', etc.

The limitations of such an ordering are now, I trust, clearer, and some of them have been already indicated in the already-quoted, brilliant book (Bally 1951), a book which decries the limitations of what is called there *l'ordre des matières* because—while it is necessary to "leave to it" all "the concrete words devoid of metaphorical or symbolic value, it is, on the other hand, useless for the determination of abstract ideas" (par. 137; and cf. par. 140 and passim). Actually, Bally's criticism is too limited, and a more radically critical view is needed, one which goes beyond this artificial distinction. For, as we saw, a theory of rhetoric is made necessary, among other things, by the fact that there are just no such things, in any language, as "concrete words devoid of metaphorical or symbolic value." This is, of course, what I am showing here in the case of just one such apparently "prosaic" word, *biós*.

A distinction such as the one discussed above, exists—as we are going to see when we sketch the lexical matrix of *bíos*—but it is much more subtle than what is suggested by the quote above: it has to do with the *different* symbolic (i.e., rhetorical) connections of these two different types of words, not with a simplistic opposition of symbolic vs. nonsymbolic. Such a sharp opposition is an ideological construct. (By the way, it is significant—in this perspective—that the traditional name of the lexical taxonomies I am criticizing/using here is "ideological dictionaries"—*dictionnaires idéologiques*, and so forth in the other languages.)

But let us go back to some of the available alternatives. The most richly articulated is probably Hallig and Wartburg 1952, toward which Nida 1975 is less than fair (true, their essay is listed in the final bibliography—but the reader has no idea of how much Nida's quoted classification owes to it since that text is not discussed in what would have been the most logical place, namely when the taxonomy to be used for the Greek dictionary is introduced). Hallig and Wartburg's contribution is considerable, and the authors try to bring the *ordre des matières* aspect together with a philosophical dimension such as the one developed in Bally 1951 (on which see below). Yet, all in all, the ideological conditionings on their taxonomy are heavier and more compromising than those at work in the above-used grid.

Let us climb down to 'bow' (or to the word closest to it—'bow' is absent from their list) along the ladders provided by Hallig and Wartburg (remembering that the actual lexical items in their taxonomy are French): (B.) "L'homme," (IV.) "L'organisation sociale," (f) "La défense nationale," (1.) "L'armée de terre," (dd) "Les armes et les armures," (2) "Les armes anciennes"—and under this latter category, only 'flèche' and 'arbalète' are exemplified. The main oppositions are the following: "L'homme" is contrasted with (A.) "L'univers" and with the synthesis (C.) "L'homme et l'univers," while within "L'homme" category, "L'organisation sociale" is preceded by (I.) "L'homme, être physique," (II.) "L'âme et l'intellect," and (III.) "L'homme, être social"; and so forth.

This schema tries to incorporate a general time dimension when, for instance, it distinguishes (1.) "Les armes modernes" from the quoted "Les armes anciennes"—whereas the schema in Nida 1975 is fully contained within the framework of the ancient world; thus, for instance, it does not problematize the chronology of its more clearly dated objects, like weapons. This limitation, however, is not very disturbing for the present analysis, whose background is Ancient

Greece—thus, roughly speaking, a background which is not very dissimilar from that behind the grid in Nida 1975 (but we will see later the ancient Greek lexicographers' awareness of time distinctions in the description of lexical usages).

On the other hand, just because they try to straddle different epochs, the ideological conditionings stick out more clumsily in the Hallig and Wartburg schema. An impressive illustration of these conditionings is contained in our example: superimposing the designation of ancient weapons with such a modern category (typical, at the earliest, of late eighteenth-century political thought) as "La défense nationale" is a clear instance of ideological deformation, by which the straightforward destructiveness and the clear strategies of power and conquest connected to the ancient terminology of war are hidden by a justificatory and "respectable" label ('national defense') which is typical of the apologetics of modern empires. (Semiotic and rhetorical history repeats itself just like history at large: a straightforward designation like "Department of War" becomes obfuscated later by the euphemistic label "Department of Defense," in the terminology of United States institutions; it would be interesting to make a comparative study of these sorts of designations, as part of a general examination of the rhetoric of euphemism.)

The dotted line between the first three features and the following two is very important for the internal articulation of the meaning. For we see, once again, that rhetorical figures are not something superimposed on basic linguistic realities: they are instead part and parcel of the basic linguistic reality. Thus it is impossible to describe the meaning of a lexical item in its literalness, "before" it becomes involved in figures.

Every reasonably detailed description of the meaning of one and the same lexical item is also the description of metaphorical and metonymic relationships within this item. This confirms that configurations like metaphor do not obtain between words or word-meanings but between *semantic features*, cutting across words; and it also indirectly confirms that the vehicle—tenor pair is *not* a universal characteristic of metaphor. Finally, figural relationships do not involve only lexical features: grammatical features are often indispensable in order to describe them. All this is shown concretely in the semantic microcosm of 'bow'.

One sense of this word rests on the substitution of the grammatical features 'count' and 'concrete' with the feature 'abstract'; thus is generated the sense: 'bowmanship, archery', which implies a metonymic relationship by which a *pars* (the object *bow*) comes to designate a *totum* (the general complex of techniques and lore of 'bowmanship'). Another metonymic sense is generated by substituting the feature 'plural' for the feature 'singular', thus obtaining the sense: 'bow and arrows'. (A *pars*—'bow'—once again is assumed in order to designate a *totum*: this time, the concept of 'bow + arrows'; more on this later.)

There is a difference (which should be emphasized) between saying that the feature 'plural' is substituted for that of 'singular' in the basic matrix of the lexeme and saying that this lexeme is pluralized. The latter phenomenon is, of course, what normally happens to every noun (in a language with singular/plural inflection), including 'bow'— and naturally the regular plural of this noun designates several 'bows', not a 'bow-and-arrows' complex. The former process, on the other hand, implies that in this version, the noun becomes a *plurale tantum*, i.e., here the feature 'plural' *excludes* the feature 'singular' rather than presupposing and including it, as in the case of the regular plural.

But the actual landscape is even more richly dotted with intricate clumps of trees and complicated byways. Let us not forget that I introduced a simplification at the beginning—justified for the purposes of analysis, but still a simplification. I transferred on the lexical item *biós* the complex of senses that Greek dictionaries normally describe with relation to *tókson*. Thus the *plurale tantum* for 'bow-and-arrows' of which I am talking about is actually *tóksa*, and we will presently see this plural implemented in some passages by Sophocles relevant to this analysis. This raises a problem into which it is impossible to dig too deeply here. Suffice it to evoke its two most significant aspects.

On the one hand, what is at issue here is the ontology of lexical items—the real foundation with respect to which metaphor, metonymy, etc. are inflated epiphenomena: what does it mean to identify a given bundle of features (phonological, semantic, etc.) as a lexical item—and, where does one lexical item end and another lexical item begin? On the other hand, this posits once again the problem of synonyms, in the sense of: what does one actually say when one considers *biós* and *tókson* as synonyms? Does one mean that (aside from the features pointing to different registers, like 'rare', 'obsolete', 'typical of certain literary genres', *et similia*) whatever semantic analysis is developed for *tókson* can be transferred to *biós*, and vice versa? Or are there irreducible local differences even between the closest synonyms?

The analysis above shows that I favor the first alternative over the second, but this is a problem which requires further investigation. One point should be noted, in this connection, specifically about *biós*—a point showing how intimate is the presence of figures in any meaning; indeed, it could be said that every meaning is continually eroded, or stretched outside of its conventional boundaries, by the workings of figures within it.

The quoted *Thesaurus* discusses (even if it is only to reject it) the possibility that the difference between *biós* and *tókson* is that the former designates the 'bow-string' (generally *neûron*, or its metonymic plural); this would be the synchronic reflex of a diachronic development, if we accept the above-mentioned etymology of *biós*, deriving it from the same Indo-European root whence also Latin *fīlum* 'thread, string'. And what is interesting is that, in order to question this metonym (in which a *totum*, 'bow', would be assumed for a *pars*: 'bow-string')—the quoted lexicon opposes another metonym (this time with the *pars→totum* movement), by which apparently *biós* designates, in certain contexts, both *biós* proper and *pharétra* 'quiver' (a fortiori, then, *biós* would designate the whole bow rather than a part of it); which brings us back to the 'bow-and-arrows' sense of *tóksa*, thus confirming the closeness of the two synonyms. Actually, this explanation of *tóksa* is the one I advance, and at least another possibility (accepted by Liddell-Scott—apparently as *the* explanation) should be recalled. In this interpretation, the metonymic structure justifying the plural *tóksa* is a different one—an internal metonymy, so to speak, as opposed to an external one. That is: *tóksa* is plural perhaps because the bow was made with two different pieces (generally, it seems, pieces of horn) joined by a center-piece (*pêkhus*). (This tripartite composition is, as far as I can see, still the basic structure of bows as sold in sporting goods shops in Europe and the United States.) But these two metonymic interpretations do not exclude each other.

The other figurative ramifications within the meaning of 'bow' have to do with the denotative semantic features, and they are metaphorical. (It will be, on some other occasion, worth looking into the problem, whether one can establish that there is a general tendency of metonymic configurations to operate on grammatical features, versus metaphorical processes, which have to do with lexical features.) They combine the first section of denotative features (the core ones) with the connotations of 'curved structure (more or less elegantly shaped)', generating the senses of: 'arch', and 'support, cradle (used in certain medical operations)'. Further investigation of the semantic field of 'bow' would probably reveal other such ramifications; but the present analysis is full enough to give an adequate idea of the background against which the central senses of the word are profiled. They are centered around the features 'weapon', and 'offensive' (the latter opposing 'bow' to other items in the field of which it is a part, like 'helmet', 'shield', etc., and on the other hand putting it in the same series as 'sword', 'spear', and so forth).[26]

We are, as noted, at the core of this semantic field—where the study of connotations introduces, at one and the same time, an in-depth structural analysis and the critique of ideologies. In an ideally complete lexical matrix, every connotation should be accompanied by a contextual indication, and in fact the boundary between textual and contextual within connotations cannot be sharply defined. But contextual indications are indispensable when the connotations are in antonymic (or, opposite) relationships, as here. One connotation reflects what can be called an economic ideology, where *biós* is the sign of one of the fundamental relationships between man and nature; in this ideology, what most interests us is that *biós* is in a *metonymic relationship* with *bíos* in one of its dominant senses (as we are going to see presently), namely, that of 'livelihood'. Not only, then, is there no opposition between *biós* and *bíos* in this interpretation, but the two terms are closely linked, the former being—in a sense—a label for the domain identified by the latter (in the same sense in which—to use the venerable examples of the tradition, considered by Aristotle as metaphors but actually identifying metonymies—the 'shield' labels the godly domain of Ares, the 'cup' represents the area of activity of Dionysos, and so forth). This connotation is implicitly dialectic, for what such an ideology implies is that death (*thánatos*) is brought about by the *biós* in the service of livelihood (*bíos*): the dialectic, then, is here objectively inscribed in the code.

The second connotation, on the other hand, reflects a clearly opposite ideology, a warlike one; consequently, an ideology where death has a totally destructive aspect. This in itself is, of course, a special conditioning which is being applied to the width of possible readings; for the war ideology can also be one which asserts itself as something constructive, speaking the language of glory and of civic realizations. With respect to this latter ideology, one can take a straightforward—and inadequate—stance: that is, criticize it as mystifying and obfuscatory (cf. the quoted case of the "Défense nationale" category), denying it a place in a modern critical analysis. But this procedure would be much more ideological than the ideology it is supposed to criticize (and its movement would be antidialectic).

We do not need to take a stance on this problem here. What I submit is that the nomenclature of single weapons (like 'bow') is not usually employed to convey metonymically an ideology of war as glorious assertion; rather, these terms are used to connote an ideology of battle and conflict as destructive operations. Thus, I can confirm this connotation as the opposite of the preceding one: 'bow' here is metonymically linked to *thánatos* and it is the opposite of *bíos*.

Finally, the third ideology is an aesthetic one, which emphasizes the component 'elegantly shaped' in the general mental image (a concept which is used here unabashedly, without any behavioristic apology) of 'curved structure'. Within this aesthetic ideology, the 'bow' occupies a series together with all other curved objects produced by a skillful technique of some sort (for instance, the lyre, as we are going to see), or natural entities which convey an image of dynamic beauty and tension; for instance, the meandering course of a river (whereas a river with a straight and narrow course is, within this aesthetic ideology, traditionally associated with the shape of an arrow).

No wonder, then, that—as part of this ideology—the bow becomes an important aesthetic image, and as such the central component of a whole iconographic lore—to which it is not possible here to do justice. Suffice it to recall the metonymic cluster around the Zodiacal figure reflecting this image: whose traditional stylized symbol looks like an arrow, whereas the current Latin terminology (*Sagittarius*, or *Arcitenens*) points to the *totum* (the 'archer-with-bow-and-arrows'). But it should not be forgotten that other traditions focus on the bow as the Zodiacal figure: in Arabic for instance, the heavenly figure equivalent to the Latin *Sagittarius* is *qáus*, i.e., 'bow'. Nor is the folklore of the bow limited to this—as witness, for instance, the alliterating phrase naming an American racing horse *Beautiful Bow.*

This can suffice as a characterization of the ideological structures connecting the field of this lexical item *provided* that we insist on the necessity of gaining an adequate "feel" of the way ideological movements, structuring the connotations which make up a lexical item in its peculiarity, thematize certain aspects and leave others in darkness. This complex of thematic adjustments is what really deserves the name of *semotactics* ("the significant combination of meaningful units"—Nida 1975:67; yes, but it is necessary to clarify what is meant by "significant", something that componential analysis does not make fully explicit; for what is at issue is, as I am showing, the full ideological scope and cultural sense of linguistic structures, not just an arrangement of technicalities).

The semotactics changes in the course of linguistic history: ideologically thematized connotations are confined to the background or obliterated, previously neglected connotations are brought to the light of ideological emphasis, and so forth. This is why a synchronic analysis of texts, especially of literary texts, is ultimately an ideological mystification; the only structural analysis which has a chance of adequately criticizing its own ideological conditionings is the one which takes place in a historical dimension.

Concretely: the ideological thematizations which have been identified for the lexical item 'bow' acquire their full significance when the spaces they fill up are compared with some of the gaps which are left—the absences being as significant as the presences. For instance, the primitive-economic ideology (hunt for livelihood), the war ideology (death and destruction), the aesthetic ideology (beauty of the tense, curved shape) could have been accompanied by an ideology of labor, i.e., by an advanced economic ideology insofar as it is an ideology which thematizes the process of standardized manufacturing of tools, and thus reflects a more systematically articulated social structure (and awareness of social structure) than one which thematizes the tool as such.

What do I mean by this? I mean that there is space, in the matrix of this lexical item, for an ideological thematization of the 'bow' as the *result* of a craftsman's laborious application, of an *érgon—not only* as an instrument whose *érgon* is this or that process (the latter being the sense in which this key word is used in the Heraclitean sentence).

What is missing, in other words, is an ideological thematization of the productive work which *went into* the bow, as against the thematization (described above) of the uses which, so to speak, *flow out* of the bow.[27]

This empty space does not seem to be filled out if we consider the mainstream of the semantic development of the Ancient Greek word *tókson* and of its synonym *biós*. But (aside from the fact that further empirical research on the history and use of these two lexical items could considerably modify this picture) the empt space thus identified docs not simply stand there, as an embarassing accident—it constitutes, by its very existence as an empty space, an element of tension in the semantic field of our word.

If we have spent so much time on the analysis of the lexical matrix referring to a relatively simple concrete object like 'bow', how are we ever going to deal satisfactorily with such a richly complicated and abstract concept as 'life'? The problem is delicate indeed, but it should not be exaggerated, for an essential aspect of this theory of rhetoric is to pierce through concrete empirical analyses the halo of mystery which often obfuscates certain words and concepts, making of them threatening weapons to stop critical reflection, rather than instruments for thinking. There is, however, one way to simplify the problem which turns out to be an unacceptable shortcut: namely, to locate the meaning of 'life' within the same taxonomical grid of semantic features which has just been used to describe the meaning 'bow'. It would seem that this consistency is a minimal prerequisite to be respected, that, indeed, it is the only way to offer a serious confirmation of an analytic method; but this is so only within a conception of linguistic analysis which impoverishes its own object and renounces actual insight in the name of a superficial and trivializing order.

As hinted, to think in terms of a grid which is universally valid *in its single contents* is essentially an ideological illusion. But I do *not* think that to establish a grid whose *form* is universally valid is an ideological deformation. Hence the reelaboration, presented here, of tagmemic and other structural concepts which lead to matrices of equal form for all lexical items ('life' as well as 'death', 'bow', and so forth). To renounce this would mean to sacrifice, once again, the proverbially bathed baby; without permanencies like these, the critique of ideology would be deprived of concrete tools, and it would fall down to the level of an ideology battling another ideology.

As we just saw, the grid appropriate to the description of 'bow' is an empirical and positivist taxonomy, which starts from a nonproblematic concept of entities in the world and then proceeds to subdivide them in various categories. But such a grid is not adequate for the description of the meaning of the lexical item *bíos*. The proof, aside from the general considerations of method sketched above? The lexical item 'life' is absent (unless I am mistaken) from the taxonomy in Nida 1975, who lists only 'die', under the subcategory (B.) "Physiological" of category (II.) "Events." Hallig-Wartburg 1952 is more systematic: indeed we find 'vie' under the subcategory (j.) "La vie humaine en général: la naissance, les âges de la vie, la mort" of the already-mentioned category (I.) "L'homme, être physique" within the general category (B.) "L'homme."

But this way of filling up the lexical gap shows the inadequacy which the gap itself concealed (although this form of concealment is a clumsy and short-lived one): namely, the limitations of an acritically materialistic taxonomy, which pretends to take care of a semantic nucleus like 'life' (and 'death', for that matter) by putting it down as just another piece of equipment in the physical appurtenances of man.

What we need is a taxonomy which makes perceivable the dialectic tension between the movement in which life appears as matter—or better, as materiality concretely articulated into forms which are not only physiological, but psychological and sociological as well; and on the other hand life as, so to speak, the bursting forth of existence: a movement, this latter, which (whether we interpret it in religious terms, in general spiritualistic terms, or even in terms of materialism) is different from the perspective on life as a mere datum, an entity among other entities.

The necessary balance is a precarious and delicate one: if we neglect the former aspect (the materiality of life) we give a blank check to an ideology of mystery and obfuscation which tries to scare us off from the linguistic analysis of culture by setting up picket fences around certain ideas alleged to be ineffable, beyond words and scrutiny. If, on the other hand, we become too complacent with the just-described awareness and disregard the complexity of life as a primary phenomenon which tests our ideas about being and existence—if we thus scorn the latter of the two aspects described above, we fall prey to an ideology oscillating between vulgar materialism and a shallow form of "linguistic philosophy."

Is all this argumentation too philosophical? The only way to reply to this possible objection is with another question: Too philosophical with respect to what? Certainly not with regard to the objective needs of any serious linguistic analysis; for philosophy chased—in a burst of acritical delight in details—out of the door will creep back through the window under the guise of one or another ideological presupposition (as we just saw).

The "Tableau synoptique" proposed by Bally 1951 (II: pp. 225–64) goes a long way toward answering the needs which have been sketched in the case of a word such as ours: a word which appears, as indeed is fit, at the beginning of the whole taxonomy, rather than being ensconced in one of its minor subcategories. Within the general category (I.) "L'a Priori," the first item to occur is 'Vie', heading the list of words which fills out the subcategory "Existence: Inexistence" (note the antithetic—or, in lexical terms, antonymic—form of representation, which is particularly useful for a realistic lexical analysis, reflecting the dialectic way in which discourses are structured). Let me transcribe the paragraph in full (but for the cross-references): "Existant: in-; réel: ir-. Être, exister; ne pas être, ne pas exister; il y a (un Dieu); il n'y a pas de (Dieu). Réalité: ir-; néant: présence: absence. Sujet (: predicat). 'Vie', in its turn, cross-refers to the antonymic pair 'Vie: Mort' under the subcategory (A.) 'Création; Vie et Mort' of the other main category following 'L'a Priori': namely (II.) 'La Matière. Le Monde Sensible'. The 'Vie': Mort' paragraph reads as follows: 'Vivant, en vie: mort; animé: in-; (nature) organique: in-. (Naître:) vivre, exister: mourir, périr: (survivre: resusciter). Vie, existence: mort, décès (: survivance, résurrection). Donner la vie: l'ôter (engendrer); ranimer, resusciter. Donner la mort, faire mourir, tuer; assassiner, égorger, pendre, empoisonner, etc.; se tuer, se suicider. Meurtre, assassinat, etc.; suicide. (Funérailles; tombe, cimétière, etc.).'"

It is, as we can see, a rich series of semantic connections, and deftly sketched (how different from the plodding kind of listing found in the other list quoted!) Yet the description of the lexical matrix which follows (Fig. 2) will have to add a significant aspect to this analysis (an aspect unaccounted for here probably because of Bally's neglect of the structures of rhetoric). Here, then, is the proposed core of the lexical matrix of the Ancient Greek word for 'life'.

A comparison with Figure 1 quickly reveals a double contrast in the

FIGURE 2

<u>bíos</u>

	noun
	singular
	masculine
	common
	mass
	abstract

<u>d</u>

	principle of existence
I	animate
	natural
ii	material sustenance (how$_1$)
iii	style (how$_2$)
iv	time span (when)
v	place (where)

<u>c</u>

of I, iii

    positive assertion, construction, energy

of ii

    hardship, struggle

of iv

    brevity, elusive rapidity, regret

of I, ii, iii, iv, v

    locus of tension

set of grammatical features: *bíos* is a "mass" noun whereas *biós* is a "count" noun and, while the latter word is "concrete," the former is "abstract."[28]

But (as in the case of *biós*) a rhetorical transformation can change some of these features, generating one of the senses of *bíos*. In this case, it is the metonymic transformation which, changing the two just-mentioned features ("mass" into "count" and "abstract" into "concrete") generates the sense 'personal life, biography'. But the core sense of *bíos* is that identified by the combination of the nontransformed set of the grammatical features with set I of the denotative lexical features: the result is the concept or mental image of 'life' as a general principle of existence which embraces men and animals, without any specification as to the manner, the place, the means of such existence—thus, the notion of 'life' as an antonym of 'death' (*thánatos*). In this sense, the lexeme *bíos* is, to a point (that is, to the point in which the categorical differences locate the two lexemes on different planes) the opposite of *biós*, for the former term is "animate" and "natural" whereas the latter is "inanimate" and "manufactured." The assignment to different planes, with a consequent effect of heterogeneity rather than of opposition, is connected to the fact that *biós* is one of the "entities" occupying that general space of "existence" of which *bíos* is the "principle."

One might express this relationship by describing *biós*, insofar as it is an-object-in-the-world, as metonymically related to *bíos* which is the general principle describing the-world-in-its existence. This in fact points to the *reductio ad absurdum* of the too-famous metaphor/metonymy contrast, pointing out that *there is no item* in the lexicon of any language which does not fall, under certain points of view, under the category of metonymy, and under certain other points of view, under that of metaphor. Every item in the language, in its capacity as representative of some subcategory, can be described (as we just saw) as metonymically related to some other item representing a higher category; and these vertical relationships are integrated, for *every* item, by horizontal (or lateral) relationships, making of it a substitute for some other item, and thus constituting a metaphor. This is the definite proof of the fact that metaphor and metonymy are simply the two basic ways of semantic integration of a lexical item into the structure of the lexicon.

Thus, a mere indication that a given structure represents a meta-phor or a metonymy is never sufficient, and every dispute about the two definitions is ultimately vacuous: what has to be done is to empir-ically describe the widest possible variety of such integrations, keep-ing in mind that the isolation of these figures as marginal, exceptional effects is one of the devices by which rhetoric becomes the ideology of itself, fragmenting itself and obfuscating its own possibilities.

The senses which follow represent particular rhetorical operations on the basic set. (Let us recall the difference between the capital Ro-man numerals and their small counterparts: the former indicate the basic set of features, while the latter designate those features which can be understood only with relationship to the basic sets—they, then, need the basic set in order to be implemented, while the reverse is not true).

The second most important sense is the one which I identified, in parenthesis, with one of the basic rhetorical categories for the defi-nition of topoi, the "how"—and here this adverb is implemented in the one among its senses which may be called *instrumental*; that is, as designating the idea of: 'in what way, through which means?' (hence the subscript numeral, distinguishing it from another sense of the same adverb which will be discussed presently).

The relationship between the sense identified by feature ii and that defined by set I is, once again, a metonymic one: feature ii ("material substenance") identifies the 'livelihood, means of living' sense of *bíos* (that is, the feature should be considered as the basic component, or from another point of view the exponent, of this sense). Such a sense is a *pars* of that *totum* which is 'life': 'livelihood' indicates the complex of means, goods, resources by which 'life' is sustained—thus (to be more precise than in the mere indication of a *pars/totum* relationship), 'livelihood' is the basis of 'life', or, the instrument to sustain 'life'. In this 'livelihood' sense, *bíos* is used as synonym of other Ancient Greek lexemes like *zōḗ* and others. *Thánatos* is *not* the opposite of *bíos* in this sense. It is not clear whether or not this sense of *bíos* has clear-cut opposites; in any case, one should look for them in the semantic field represented by lexemes like those for 'poverty', 'deprivation', *et similia*.

The relationship between *bíos* and *biós* is also changed when we consider this sense: while in the sense identified by set I *bíos* is the antonym of *thánatos* and is thus distinguished from *biós* which is met-onymically connected to *thánatos*; in the 'livelihood' sense, *bíos* is (as noted) metonymically connected to *biós*. Which is another illustration of how the boundaries among lexemes are conventional (and largely ideological), not qualitative: for the same rhetorical processes are at work between the senses which constitute the meaning of some lex-emes, and between the meanings associated with different lexemes. Thus, the sense ii ('livelihood') of *bíos* is metonymically associated with sense I ('life'), the former being the instrument for the preservation of the latter. And in its turn, the lexeme *biós* is metonymically associ-ated with *bíos* in sense ii, for (once again) the former is the instrument to gain the latter: through the 'bow' one gains one's 'livelihood', and the 'livelihood' keeps up 'life'.

Less crucial—but significant, and important in order to complete the description of the lexical matrix—are the other senses: feature iii generates another metonymy, which is symbolized by the adverb 'how' in what can be called its *stylistic* sense (hence, 'how$_2$'), that is, the adverb 'how' implemented as asking the question: 'in what state, shape, condition?' This application generates the metonymic sense 'manner, way of living' (or, in the worn-and-torn jargon of pseudo-modernity, 'lifestyle'). Another metonymic application is the one gen-erated by feature iv, answering that other staple rhetorical question, 'when?'—which results in the sense of life as 'life span'.

With respect to *bíos* in this sense iv, *thánatos* is still an opposite, but in a temporal sense which brings it closer to one of the basic semantic relationships alternative to that of opposition, namely to *reversion*; moreover, the antonyms of *bíos* iv are balanced: on the one side (of the time continuum) there is *thánatos*, and on the other *geneá/geneé* 'birth' (used here as the head of a list of quasi-synonyms: *genéthlē*, *génesis*, etc.); cf. the 'naître, donner la vie' connections in Bally's quoted taxonomy.

The last main sense of *bíos* completes this list of basic rhetorical questions by answering the query: 'where?' In yet another metonymy, feature v implements the lexeme for 'life' to designate, more nar-rowly, the place where life exists as a natural phenomenon, that is, the 'world' (cf. a similar metonymic movement in the Latin word *sae-culum* 'century', which acquires—in Christian Latin usage—side by side with its basic temporal sense, a local sense: 'man's world'). In this last sense *bíos* v has as its antonyms the lexemes designating all those parts of the universe which are not the human world. But this leads us to that aspect of the matrix which was discussed also apropos of *biós*: namely, the gaps in the matrix—those aspects of the meaning which could be filled out but which seem to be left undeveloped, and whose shapelessness helps, *a contrario*, to shape the semantic field of the lexeme at issue.

In *biós* as it comes to us via the mainstream of the classical tradition there seem to be two main blind spots—two forms of absence which, by their facing each other at the two extreme poles, end up by filling out, in a peculiar way, a semantic space. At the most general pole, the cosmic one, the specific opposition of 'supernatural, spiritual life' vs. 'mundane life' is not, it seems, implemented within the basic semantic field of this lexeme (cf. on the other hand, in Bally's taxonomy, the antonymic reference: "il y a (un Dieu): il n'y a pas (de Dieu)" which, in its apparent naiveté, in effect cleverly identifies the semantic possibility of sharp opposition between two different dimensions of life within the semantic field of this word).

At the opposite pole, that of the individual, a thematization of the sense of 'life' in which it is the environment shaping the perception of the individual—where, in sum, life is seen as a manifestation of the 'self' (cf. once again, Bally's connection with "sujet") is missing. One could compare here, in order to make the gap visible *a contrario*, the polysemy of the Standard Literary Arabic word *nafs* where (all the senses are quoted from Wehr 1971) the senses of 'life, essence, nature' are accompanied by senses like: 'soul, psyche, spirit, mind, human being, personal, individual, self'.[29]

The two opposite poles share, probably, the characteristic of being both products (or at least, radical rediscoveries) of the Judaeo-Christian ideology; their absence, then, would shape the described lexical matrix of *bíos* as a coherent reflection of a pagan ideology. Whatever the ultimate reality of this hypothesis (which would require a more extended study), this leads us straight into the analysis of ideology, which is the crucial point of this whole description. We already saw, in the case of *biós*, the inner workings of ideology—how it works itself into the meaning of any lexeme; but it is time now to be even more precise about it, for a critique of ideology which does not express itself as a systematic structural analysis is ultimately powerless with respect to its own object. Since such an object is, by itself, a subjective representation of the world (every ideology, no matter how crude, is nothing less than that), it cannot be criticized merely by putting an alternative representation side by side with it; rather, the metalanguage analyzing this representation must be sufficiently analytical and detached to be able to analyze its object in a really critical way.

Thus, the first caution to apply in the critique of ideologies (and one which has been clearly brought home by the preceding pages, I hope) is to reduce macroscopic constructions to microscopic structures. This is the basic way of demystifying ideologies. *In the absence of microscopic analyses, demystification is but an empty slogan.* This implies the necessity of a dialectic double movement for the critic, who must be ready (in the face of the impatience and blame of the more traditionally minded critics) to systematically shift grounds, thus seeming (but only seeming!) to change topics in order to surprise the reader. When confronted with large-scale ideological pronouncements the critic should break them down in their ultimate components (paragraphs, sentences, phrases, lexemes) and then analyze them in detail. When, on the other hand, the data with which he has to start are (as in the present case) sentences and their components, then what the critic should do, while analyzing them, is to point out their integration into broader ideological constructs.

As we can see, this strategy can seem contradictory only at a superficial examination. In both cases, what matters is not to accept the *illusory compactness*, which is ideology in its most negative aspect (a false structural perspective within the text which falsifies the reader's perception); the task, then, is to analyze this apparently compact object into the mechanisms actually at work within it. Only, in the first case the compact ideological discourse is there to start with, and the effort which must be made is, then, the effort of making explicit the smaller parts which make it up; while in the second case, the necessary effort is that of avoiding to posit a sharp separation, in absolute terms, between the small syntactic components one has under one's eyes and the large ideological text "out there" in the wide world; on the contrary, the analysis must show how the smaller components fit into the larger ones.

At this point, it is almost superfluous to note that the present theory of rhetoric is designed to found and to articulate just this kind of integration. The meaning, then, of the adjective "contemporary" qualifying my theory of rhetoric can be paraphrased as follows: a theory of rhetoric is contemporary when it focuses *both* on the rhetorician-as-critic (the good rhetorician has always been a critic—of literature, of writing in general, *of society*), *and* on the critic-as-rhetorician. The latter insistence means that: the critic today, faced with a plethora of ideological claims, and in particular with separatist delusions, must (in reaction to all this) reaffirm the dominant role of rhetoric if the literary *connoisseur* wants to be really a critic, that, is if he wants to analyze ideological constructs systematically.

But it is high time to go back to our metaphor. There are at least three ideological spheres which have been more or less directly uncovered, in the preceding pages, as relevant to the analysis of a text, and the preceding discussion has begun what the following pages will complete; namely, an analysis of the ways in which these spheres partly overlap and partly diverge. First of all, there are the ideological elements embodied in the connotations of the matrix of each lexeme—we can view them as internal elements. These internal elements move toward the outside, without however becoming fully external to the lexical items at issue (the internal/external, or inside/outside, distinction is a relative one), when they are combined together in a given rhetorical configuration, like the '*bios*' metaphor here (and this is the second ideological sphere). Finally, all these connotations and combinations of connotations are linked to the broader ideological contexts in which the lexical items are actually used, and these are the external elements (constituting the third ideological sphere), which are closely linked to the internal ones.

We have seen the internal ideological sphere of *biós*. As for *biós*, its elements have already been listed: the general sense of 'life' as 'principle of existence' (I) and antonym of 'death', as well as (probably) the sense which refers to 'life' as a complex of concrete ways in which the self presents itself in society (iii), seem to be normally linked to a connotation of 'positive assertion, constructive efforts, energy'. This is not the same as the connotation of 'hope, happiness'; the latter may or may not be present in this or that context, whereas 'positive assertion, etc.' usually accompanies the lexical item 'life' in every context, *no matter how* this assertion is inflected—in a mood of joy and serenity, or in a mood of conflict, of polemics, of harsh struggle.

Let me recall, at this point, what has been noted above: namely, that there is no clear-cut boundary between textual and contextual, when it comes to identifying and defining connotative features. What I give in the matrices are what seem to me to be the basic connotations—the textual ones, in the sense in which the lexeme is viewed as *a mini-text in itself*; those, in other words, which are least dependent from the accidents of the contexts in which the lexeme is used. But even there traces of contextual presuppositions are often present which limit their general validity, and a constant empirical work of checking and rechecking is called for, to make of the lexical matrices an adequate way of representing the balance between what the connotations of a given lexeme *put into* the context (no matter what the context), and what they *draw out* of contexts (with actual contents which vary from context to context).

Back to our connotations. 'Life' used in the sense of 'life span' (v) seems usually to imply a connotation of 'brevity, elusive rapidity, regret'. The most significant fact for our analysis is that, when 'life' is used in the sense of 'livelihood'—thus with the metonymic application of the feature 'material sustenance' (ii)—it seems to be usually accompanied by a connotation of 'hardship, struggle'. The inflection of 'life' ii is thus quite different from that of 'life' I—a fact that has far-reaching hermeneutical consequences.

Finally, all these senses share a connotation of 'tension'—the same connotation shared by the senses of *bíos*. And here we can see one of the basic processes at work, which define metaphor as such: the new lexical entity which results from the merging of *bíos* and *biós*—and which cannot be identified any longer with any of the two matrices but constitutes a third, enriched matrix—"raises" (or "promotes") the connotation 'locus of tension' to the same level as the other connotations. In each of the two separate lexical matrices, this connotation (along with the many others which could be added) occupies a secondary position: it is in the background of each semantic field, and under normal circumstances (i.e., when the respective lexical item is not used within a special rhetorical configuration like metaphor) this connotation is not active—that is, it does not qualify the semantic behavior of the lexical item at issue. The importance of metaphor lies

FIGURE 3

BIOS (=conflation of bíós 'bow' × bíos 'life')

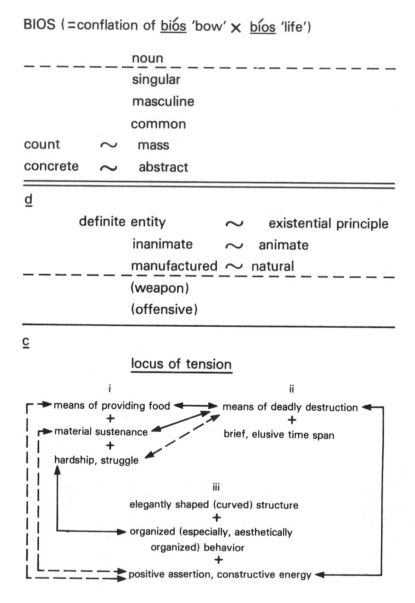

```
_ _ _ _ _ _ _ _ noun _ _ _ _ _ _ _ _ _ _ _ _ _ _ _
                singular
                masculine
                common
count      ~    mass
concrete   ~    abstract
═══════════════════════════════════════════════════
d
      definite entity          ~      existential principle
            inanimate     ~   animate
_ _ _ _ _ _ _ manufactured ~ natural _ _ _ _ _ _ _ _
            (weapon)
            (offensive)
───────────────────────────────────────────────────
c
```

locus of tension

```
          i                              ii
┌─►means of providing food ◄────► means of deadly destruction ◄─┐
│          +                              +                     │
│ ┌─►material sustenance ◄────         brief, elusive time span │
│ │        +                                                    │
│ │ hardship, struggle ◄─                                       │
│ │                                                             │
│ │                          iii                                │
│ │              elegantly shaped (curved) structure            │
│ │                          +                                  │
│ └──────────► organized (especially, aesthetically            │
│                 organized) behavior                           │
│                          +                                    │
└ ─ ─ ─ ─ ─ ─► positive assertion, constructive energy ◄────────┘
```

precisely in the fact that, whenever it takes place, it makes active, and promotes to a higher position within the lexical item at issue, one or more of the secondary connotations (cf. Valesio 1975*b*).

Let me sum up, via Figure 3, the conflated lexical matrix representing the metaphor which I have been describing.

To be sure, this representation could be enlarged and made more precise—although I do not know any description of a single metaphor as detailed as this one, in the available literature on the subject. It could also be made more tight formally, but I do not think that this would be an unmixed blessing. For, in a large part of the linguistic literature on metaphor and similar phenomena, the formalistic discussion of alternative notations gives the illusion of exactness without really contributing to sharpening our perception and empirical description of certain objects.

What I did (as already remarked) was, rather than expand on the desiderata of an analysis of metaphor, to submit such an actual analysis; further descriptions of similar and different configurations will show which features of the description are confirmed, and which ones will have to be modified. In the interest of such developments, let me explicate what I tried to mark out symbolically in my representation of the matrix. The features written in the center of the column ("noun," "singular," "masculine," "common," "*locus of tension*") are those shared by both lexical matrices without conflict. The last of the quoted features is underscored in order to mark its importance in the economy of this new matrix—for, as noted, it is its raising (implicitly indicated by its position at the top of the list of connotations, as against its position in the two separate matrices) which basically defines the function of this figure.

The remaining features of grammatical meaning, as well as most of the lexical denotative features, are arranged in pairs: the symbol ~ marks their opposition. This also is a relatively novel feature in the representation of metaphor. There has been a school of thought recognizing that in metaphor the dominant phenomenon is the tense coexistence of different senses rather than the substitution of one sense to another. But the present one is, to my knowledge, the first attempt at an empirical presentation of some of the modes of this coexistence. This actually is the second process which characterizes the peculiar function and value of metaphor (the first being the raising of formerly secondary connotations): the dialectic, or conflictual, coexistence of opposite semantic features (*complexio oppositorum*, to borrow a phrase rediscovered by Jung).

Now to the other features in Figure 3. The two in parentheses on the left side in the center are thus distinguished in order to point out that they represent a direct trace of one only of the lexical items (*biós*), in its separateness (they are neither shared by *bíos*, nor dialectically opposed to corresponding features of *bíos*). But the crucial area is the following one down the column: the set of the connotations. I already explained about the '*locus of tension*'. But there is a more general methodological problem which should come before the discussion of the single items in the list: some features which were classified as denotative in the separate *bíos* matrix are now put among the connotations. Does this change mean anything specific? If yes, what is its import?

It has to do with that effect of blurring the meaning which characterizes a metaphor. Such a blurring has been observed throughout the history of studies on metaphor (and the characterizations which are apparently opposite are not really so different: pointing up the liveliness, the vivid quality of metaphor is, usually, just another way of characterizing the peculiar semantic imbalance which—looked at from another angle—can be called blurring). In fact, it is because of this blurring effect that metaphor constitutes a problem.

What I try to do here is to present a structural explanation of this blurring effect: the *complexio oppositorum* is not the normal state of a lexical matrix; the conflated lexical matrix which shows such clusters of warring features also shows, as a consequence, a loss in the sharpness of its references. Put another way: a conflated lexical matrix is always one in which there is a loss in the clarity of denotations—a loss which is compensated for by an enrichment of its connotations. This is exactly what we see at work in our conflated matrix, where we also witness the phenomenon opposite to the one described above: namely, the connotative features of the two lexemes tend to combine, rather than to oppose each other (hence the symbol +, against the symbol ~ of opposition, used above). Opposition, however, is far from being absent from the network of connotations.

Here, the listing and the arrows roughly translate the various relationships involved, connecting features originally belonging to *biós* (like the two opposite ones in the first row, respectively under i and ii), and features originally belonging to *bíos*. As for 'material sustenance': 'bow' is the instrument, 'life' is the goal. In 'destruction etc.' and 'brief, elusive time span', 'bow' is, once again, the instrument, and the goal or result is 'death', as an antonym of 'life'. As for the 'aesthetically organized behavior': both 'bow' and 'life' can be viewed as objects of aesthetic organization—with the difference that in the former case the result is a well-delimited object, while in the latter, the reference expatiates broadly, ranging from the organization of behavior to the organization of the whole environment of this behavior.

But the situation becomes more complicated when we consider the relationships across the semantic fields. i is opposed to ii by a sharp contrast in the function of the 'bow', which serves 'life' in the first case, 'death' in the second. As for the third block, it is—because of its aesthetic aspect—equidistant from the preceding two, *if* we do not ideologically refuse to see the potentially aesthetic aspect of destructive actions (suffice it to recall the Homeric image of Apollo coming with his bow and arrows to sow death).

But we can see more precise relationships if we look at the single connotative features. Thus, starting from iii: its feature of 'aesthetically organized behavior' is opposed to the 'hardship, struggle' feature in i (opposition being symbolized here by the solid double-pointed arrow, which is the equivalent of ~ used to describe horizontal relationships); whereas the 'positive assertion' feature from iii is opposed to the 'death and destruction' feature in ii, but complements the 'providing food' and 'material sustenance' features in i (this relationship of complementarity is symbolized by the dotted double-pointed arrow, which is the vertical equivalent of the + used in horizontal notations).

Let me recall, at this point, what was said about the three ideological spheres: in the terms of that distinction, the connotations I have been describing constitute the intermediate sphere, straddling the inside sphere of the connotations peculiar only to each lexical item taken separately, and the outside sphere of the connotations spreading over the various cultural contexts (or frames, layered one upon the other) which ultimately determine the function—and thus, the significance—of the sentence in which these items appear.

There are essentially no limits to the study of these broader connections, and I do not pretend to describe them in full here, as far as
the Heraclitean sentence is concerned. On the other hand, the difference between an analysis which sketches some of the connections and
an analysis which leaves them aside is crucial. The only way to avoid
this ideological obfuscation under a scientific guise is to follow the
path of empirical study.

The other problem is that of making full use of all the instruments
of formal analysis—*but*, to use them not only on the linguistic structure but also on its social context (semiotic integration).

Let us sketch, then, the third ideological sphere surrounding the
Heraclitean sentence. The study of this sphere is the necessary, basic
justification of the denotative and connotative features which the linguist identifies in the lexical matrices; it is basic, because such features
can be accepted as a contribution to knowledge about language only
insofar as they ultimately reflect some aspects of the broader historical and cultural reality surrounding linguistic structures. We really
acquire knowledge about language, in a serious sense, only when we
come to know language as language-in-the-world.

4.5 THE CRITIQUE OF IDEOLOGIES

Let us start with the compound connotative feature: 'means of providing food + material sustenance + hardship, struggle', where the
first two features are linked (as indicated) by a metonymic relationship (to understand which it is necessary, of course, to keep in mind
that all three sentences linked by the + sign are syntactically autonomous; thus 'material sustenance'—actually a phrase rather than a
sentence—is *not* governed by the phrase 'means of etc.').

Why, first of all, start with this feature rather than with the one
about 'tension' which opens the list? Because the ideological frame of
this connotation seems to come chronologically first in such philological documentation as we possess (which does not necessarily imply, of course, that this connotation actually was the first among those
in the list to make its appearance in the history of Greek).

At a certain point in the action of one of the classic tragedies of
ancient Greece we witness the conflict between an older warrior—left
for ten years in a desert place where, weakened by a grave wound, he

gains his livelihood by hunting with his bow and arrows (a bow which has an exalted status: the warrior inherited it from Herakles), and a younger warrior, who has the difficult task of convincing the older man to go back to the army and collaborate with some men he hates; the young man steals his bow in order to pressure him into yielding to his request.[30] The old warrior is in despair: "I am ruined, miserable, I am betrayed! What did you do to me, stranger? Give me back right away my bow and arrows."[31] And a little later, Philoctetes explains (131–33): "You stole my life (*tòn bíon*) having seized the bow and arrows (*tà tóks'*). . . . Do not take away my life." Still later, in the melancholic interlude of the *kommós*, Philoctetes lingers on the image of Neoptolemus, "brandishing in his hand the nourishment (*trophán*) of miserable me."

The metonymy here is so striking that a Scholiast felt the need to explain this use of *trophá*, noting: "he means the bow and arrows." Isn't this metonymy the clearest proof of the well-foundedness of the connotative feature which I established? Actually, the preceding translation could have been less ambiguous, focusing on one of the listed senses of *bíos* and thus translating specifically (foregrounding the metonymy) 'livelihood', or 'means of livelihood', rather than generally 'life'.

This translation would be a perfectly legitimate move, *provided* the linguist, integrating his own work with that of the rhetorician, realizes that the rhetorical structuring is significantly different, so that the two translations—with their different rhetorical functions—point to the ambivalence of the original text, which blends two contrasting ideologies. They are the ideologies already identified in my analysis of the connotative features: the foregrounding of the metonymy as such unveils a no-nonsense ideology of struggle with nature, a grim concentration on material needs; on the other hand, to leave the metonymy in the background (using what can be called the archilexeme 'life'—as against the various specific senses listed above into which this archilexeme is articulated) means to implement an ideology of the "poetic effect" which *melo*dramatizes the event (all this, of course, is noted without any ironic condescension), transporting it into a vague atmosphere.

Actually, to be precise, in both cases we have to do with a foregrounding of the metonymy—with a difference in the aspect of the metonymic configuration that is foregrounded; and this explains the ideologically significant difference in rhetorical effect. (Let me note that, at this point, I am dealing with the lexical matrix of *bíos*, not with the conflated matrix of the '*bios*' metaphor.) In the first case what takes place is a componential translation, which renders a Greek (ar-chi)lexeme (*bíos*) with the English version of one of its semantic fea-tures—a feature which is metonymically linked (in the original Greek matrix) with the basic set of denotative features.

What, then, the foregrounding of the metonymy really means here is an analysis—in the etymological sense of dis-solving operation (we could speak of a demystification)—of the metonymic link. That is: the *totum* is *not* used in lieu of its *pars*; instead the *pars* is clearly shown in its (so to speak) partiality. This is why I feel justified in speaking of demystification; it is a slight demystifying move, of course, and this term might be felt as disproportionate to what is actually taking place—*until* one realizes that the broader and polemic sense of "de-mystification" is built on hundreds of such smaller processes.

The task of the rhetorician is precisely that of showing in detail what the basis of these vast structures actually is: all the small mecha-nisms, like the one just described, which constitute their only reality. Demystifying demystification, then? Exactly: this indication is neither a pun nor a paradox; it describes the peculiar nature of the rhetorical enterprise.

The second case is different: here, the Greek archilexeme is ren-dered *at the same level*—by a translation which is not componential but, so to speak, holistic: it uses, that is, the corresponding English archilexeme, 'life'. Here, foregrounding of the metonymy means em-phasizing the metonymy as such, in its *totum pro parte* mechanism. The mechanism concealed in Greek is concealed also in English, and this is the root of the poetically solemn effects, in terms of rhetorical structuring.

To follow up systematically the metaphorical, and especially the metonymical, ramifications branching out around the lexeme *tókson* (or *biós*) would be a job worthy of a separate monograph. Consider the Variatio in Neoptolemus' speech on this topic. When he gives the precious object back to Philoctetes he refers to it metonymically by designating only one *pars* of it—the arrows (*bélē tàde*, on l. 1287), and here the metonymy verges on synecdoche; the objects to be thrown are designated in lieu of the complex constituted by: thrower + objects to be thrown. Almost immediately afterward, the same character designates the same object by using another kind of metonymy—one which displaces the reference up to the archilexeme symbolizing the general group of which 'bow' is only one component class (cf. the taxonomies discussed above): *tôn sôn hóplōn* 'your weapons' (1292—the singular form *hóplon* exists in Greek, but this lexeme is used mostly in the plural, *hópla*, as in the genitive phrase just quoted). And still later, Neoptolemus reverts to the metonymy previously employed by Philoctetes himself: *tà . . . tóks'* (1308); this latter (I did not specify it above) is yet another kind of metonymy. It represents the most frequently mentioned type of metonymy: namely, that involving relationships among lexical features. *Tóks(a)*, on the other hand, is metonymic insofar as it problematizes a grammatical feature: the use of the plural number against the singular number.

Once again, the difference must be underscored between a core structure which is prevalently "grammatical" (more precisely, not directly rhetorical *at the level* and *in the function* which are at issue—no element of linguistic structure is absolutely nonrhetorical); and a structure which realizes a specific rhetorical configuration. In our case: *hópla* is the normally used grammatical form—it has almost (but not quite) the status of a *plurale tantum*; thus, its use does *not* imply a metonymic fragmentation of the reference between 'bow' on the one hand, and on the other hand, 'arrows'. On the contrary, *tókson* in the singular *is* the grammatically normal form for 'bow', so that the use of the plural *does* fragment the reference, separating 'bow' from 'arrows', and also—so to speak—separating 'bow' from itself (by the emphasis on its composite structure).

The interest of such distinctions goes beyond mere technicality, and it points to different ways of using language to perceive—and to structure—the world. For instance, the analysis sketched here reveals that at least two different typologies of metonymic processes are possible, each one of them underlining a different way in which rhetorical strategies give shape to human culture and articulate its ideologies. One possible typology is of a formal nature, and it is closer to the extensional pole in the intensional/extensional dichotomy (although these two typologies do not fully overlap with this dichotomy in its strict logical sense). It can be represented by a cluster of concentric circles, the smallest marking the terms which *directly refer* to the smallest class of objects, the largest, the term which points to the largest; thus:

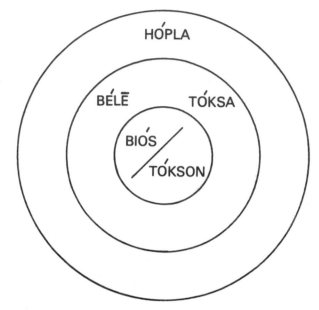

The figure is certainly not a complicated one: the synonymic pair *biós/tókson* points to the smallest class, that of the objects called 'bow', while *bélē* and *tóksa* point to a larger class, or class complex—'bow' + 'arrows'—but they are not, of course, synonyms. On the contrary, they point to the two opposite sides of the "package": *tóksa* designates the *pars* 'bow' for the *totum* 'bow-and-arrows', while at the other pole, *bélē* designates the *pars* 'arrows' for the *totum* 'bow-and-arrows'.

The two metonymies, however, are not symmetrical. There is a significant difference between them, a difference which brings grammatical and lexical meaning together. The plural form of *bélos* is a "natural" one (it is more normal to refer to arrows, in connection with a bow, as a bundle of two or more arrows—and at any rate, the most plausible interpretation in this context is the one which implies a bundle of arrows: Philoctetes' bow—as his threat to Ulysses' life, later on, proves—is at the ready). Thus, what is rhetorical here (and implements the metonymy) is *not* the plural form per se, but only its *use* to designate both the bundle of arrows and the bow. Put it another way, the grammatical meaning of this lexeme is not rhetorically implemented; only its lexical meaning is.

On the contrary, the pluralization of *tókson* is, so to speak, "innatural" (to use the antonym of a much-abused term in contemporary linguistics). Whether or not it is more normal to focus on one 'bow' at a time than on more than one is a question which, in these generic terms, cannot be usefully answered. What matters is that the whole context clearly requires that only one bow be focused upon—the powerful bow once owned by Herakles (whether or not Neoptolemus, Ulysses, and the other characters in the play sport their own bows is semiotically irrelevant here: the semiotic context, even before the specific intervention of the linguistic context, makes a selection of the elements in the "real" world which are going to be relevant to the particular world projected by the work at issue).

Thus not only the use of the lexeme, but also its grammatical form, implement the rhetorical configuration, because the plural here cannot be a "literary" reference to two or more bows; the metonymy, then, is shared by the grammatical and the lexical meanings of the lexeme, and it is not located exclusively in the latter, as happens with *bélē*. We see at work, in this area of grammatical meaning, a process analogous (not equal, of course) to that which characterizes, in the grammatical meanings of verb forms, oppositions like the one between "inclusive *we*" (where *we* = 'I + others + you') versus "exclusive *we*" (i.e., *we* = 'I + others, but not you').

Where does the similarity lie? In the possibility of distinguishing different internal articulations of what is, in a more general (less "delicate") perspective, the same grammatical meaning. The grammatical meaning 'plural number' in *bélē* is articulated as: "1 arrow (*bélos*) + 1 arrow + 1 arrow, etc.' (the notion of 'bow' is not present at this level—it appears only at the level of lexical meaning, as the result of an application of the rhetorical configuration of metonymy). But the grammatical meaning: 'plural number' in *tóksa* is *not* articulated as: 1 *tókson* + 1 *tókson* + 1 *tókson*, etc.'. Rather it is *empty* as a grammatical meaning and filled out only at the lexical level as: '1 horn of the bow + the joining center piece (*pĕkhus*) + the other horn of the bow' and often (as in the present case) also as: 'the three preceding pieces (constituting a bow) + 1 *bélos* + 1 *bélos* + 1 *bélos*, etc.' One can also view this structure in a different way: rather than analyzing the grammatical meaning as an empty slot, one can reconstruct a situation in which the barrier between grammatical meaning and lexical meaning has fallen: the former is filled out by the latter. But the difference, as we can see, is slight; it is, this time, really a problem of notation.

Finally, *hópla* designates the largest class, which includes all other weapons beside 'bow' and 'arrows'. What about the second typology? This typology is (as noted) nearer to the intensional pole: but the general logical notion of intensionality is here made both more precise and less formal by anchoring it to what is the crucial process at work here—the tension between the construction and the unveiling of ideologies. The movement of this typology is, in a sense, the opposite of that of the first: for what in the former typology is the simplest nucleus (*biós/tókson*) is, in this typology, the locus of complication and concealment.

Essentially, what happens here is the parallel on the "outside" (among lexemes) of what we saw above happening on the "inside" (within one and the same lexeme—*biós*). The lexemes *hópla* and *bélē* demystify (in the sense discussed above) the metonymy. They show the, so to speak, *disiecta membra* of the cluster of objects at issue: *hópla* demystifies the cluster from above (showing that 'bows' and 'arrows' are separate members in a long series of different classes of objects), while *bélē* demystifies it from below—it shows that this is not a unitary object by focusing on the individual pieces of equipment which make it up.

By contrast, the form *tókson* steps away from his demystification and moves on the path of ideological layering: the grammatical meaning points to the complex articulation of the object at issue, while the lexical meaning creates an illusion of unity. Apropos of the complex articulation, I have written until now as if the referents pointed out by these words were two classes of objects: a 'bow' and a bundle of 'arrows'. But it is not otiose to point out that one must take into account at least a third class of objects: the 'quiver' (*pharétra*) which holds the arrows. That this is not irrelevant is proved by the fact that, in discussing the extension of the notion 'bow' Stephanus' quoted *Thesaurus* discusses cases in which the word *biós* could point also to the *pharétra*. In its turn, this relates to another problem (also mentioned in the *Thesaurus*, and evoked above when I hinted at the etymology of *biós*): namely the distinction, not only between the two horns and the center-piece of the bow, but also between these solid structures and the bowstring (*neûron* or its metonymic plural).

I cannot pursue these lexicological problems here, aside from adding to standard dictionary descriptions the observation that the plural *tóksa* (and, a fortiori, *hópla*) includes, at its broadest, references to: the two parts or horns of the bow, the center-piece, the arrows, and the quiver. But these problems had to be mentioned in order to show that even the present analysis, which might seem excessively detailed, is instead—if anything—simplificatory with respect to some aspects of this semantic object. The lesson is not only a local one (that is: what is called for is a full-scale lexical investigation, monographic in size, of the semantic field of 'bow' in Ancient Greek, and on this model in other languages); there are also, here, a methodological lesson and a theoretical lesson which should be explicitly drawn.

Methodological lesson: any "formal" analysis of any linguistic structure (whether it belongs to a "dead" language or to a "living" one, whether or not it deals with literary texts) which does not delve into the minute infrastructures and local details of this structure is essentially sterile.

Too broad a conclusion for such a limited case? Not really; in fact, one must go further than this and develop (as noted) a theoretical lesson, which is the following. The critique of ideologies in broad (i.e., *ideological*) terms has given, by now, all that it could offer; to continue along this line would not bring us further. The only path open for a serious development of the critique of ideologies is to analyze ideologies into their microscopic components—which is what is done here. The apparent ideological "irrelevance" of these components (and consequently of their analysis) is, in reality, the guarantee that the research is done at the proper level, and thus will result in new insights rather than in tautologies.

Back to our second typology, the one on ideological veiling. In this typology, *biós* and *tókson* represent the point of thickest veiling: the metonymy triumphs insofar as it conceals its own structure; the singular form and its traditionally straightforward lexical gloss give the illusion that we are dealing with a unitary structure, and thus sweep the "messiness" of the actual ramifications involved under the lexical rug: the frame (horns centerpiece) vs. the string in the bow, the bow vs. the arrows, both vs. the quiver.

Until now I have discussed only the semantic aspect of the Sophoclean (con)text, showing how it illuminates and justifies the connotations of the term at issue. But of course, the reason why this particular context is quoted goes deeper than that: it is one of the proofs that the metaphoric paronomasia of *bíos/biós* was part of the general verbal folklore (the other alternative—to presume, namely, that Sophocles is specifically quoting Heraclitus—is not very plausible). The difference is that, while the paronomasia in the Heraclitean sentence is *in praesentia*, here it is *in absentia*, because (cf. the quote above) two different forms are used: *bíos* vs. *tóks(a)*.

The opposition, however, must be qualified on both sides. In neither of the two cases (nor in any other context, as far as I know), is the paronomasia really implemented *in praesentia*; to be thus developed, both lexemes (*bíos, biós*) should be present in the same syntactic environment. What happens instead is (as we saw) a conflation in the Heraclitean text, a formal opposition in the text by Sophocles. One can still talk, however, of a *praesentia* in the former versus an *absentia* in the latter insofar as the former context, making a straightforward translation impossible (hence all this elaborate analysis), draws attention to the rhetorical structure it contains, whereas the latter—allowing for a direct, unproblematic translation—conceals the rhetorical structure at work.

The difference is not merely technical, because it situates the two texts in quite different positions with respect to linguistic history—which is the basic concern here: for, these texts are not examined for their sake but in order to critically illustrate a theory of rhetoric. Now, Heraclitus' text, insofar as it shows up its own rhetorical structure, sketches a critical perspective on itself, and thus makes of its language, up to a point, a *meta*language. No such thing happens in Sophocles' text, which indirectly uses the rhetorical structure at issue, but it does not show it up, and thus does not develop a metalinguistic perspective on itself.

As a consequence, Heraclitus' text is *both* an object of linguistic history and a subject of it, insofar as it constructs the language with which we can talk of a certain paronomasia (*bíos/biós*) and follows its development throughout history—including Sophocles' text, which for its part is only an object of linguistic history. This, however, is not the whole story, for we can see in this case how texts and contexts are connected by a subtle and intricate web of reciprocal relationships, in which they exchange their roles, depending on what perspective of analysis is chosen. Thus text A may serve as the explanatory context of text A′ from one point of view, while from another point of view it may be an object of contextualization on the part of A′.

We can see here how this works *in concreto*: if we look at our problem in its aspect of identification of a paronomastic structure, Heraclitus' is the critical context, Sophocles' its object text. But the lexical analysis in the preceding pages had a different aim: what was at issue is—we recall—identifying the ideological framework of the semantic features making up two specific lexical items. From this point of view—which is also the point of view of what follows—texts like that by Sophocles (and that by Aristophanes, which will be quoted presently) function as the *contexts* of the semantic features discussed.

But—to finish with the promised qualification—our paronomasia is not as absent from Sophocles' text as it looks at first sight. True, in the quoted passage there is the clear-cut formal opposition of *bíos* and *tóksa*, an opposition which reappears later:

" . . . you stole the bow and arrows (*tà tóks'*) . . . " (1272)

" . . . you who having grabbed it with tricks stole my life (*tòn bíon*) . . . " (1282–83)

However, if we look at this last passage more closely, we see that it essentially presents the same conflation as the Heraclitean one. the key is in the way in which it repeats, and yet does not exactly repeat, the previous statement. That one (931–33—quoted above in translation) read: *apestérēkas tòn bíon tà tóks' helṑn . . . tòn bíon me mē aphéléis*. The passage immediately above (1282–83), on the other hand, is: *hóstis g'emoû dóloisi tòn bíon labṑn/apostérēkas*. The clue here is in the verbs, rather than in the nouns (a new proof, if another was needed, of the crucial importance of context). I scrupulously paralleled, in my translation, with different lexical choices in English, the Variatio in the original text (alternative translations are, as always, possible; but what really matters is to preserve the Variatio as such): *apósteréō* ('to steal'), *airéō* ('to seize'), *aphairéō* ('to take away') in the first passage, *lambánō* ('to grab') and again *apósteréō* in the second.

The crucial structural difference is that in the first passage each verb is associated with an object noun, and with one object only (*apos-*

teréō goes with *bíos*, *airéō* is paired off with *tóks(a)*, *aphairéō* is joined with, again, *bíos*), whereas in the second passage both verbs (*lambánō* and *aposteréō*) are associated with the same object, *bíos*. This is essentially another syntactic way of creating the metalinguistic effect discussed at length above for the Heraclitean text—once we get rid of the illusory (ideological) reassurance provided by the accent mark (added by the modern editors, of course): while Heraclitus problematizes '*bios*' by his use of contrasting predications for it, Sophocles problematizes '*bios*' by making of it the object of two different verbs at the same time. This is, then, a realization of one of the most important rhetorical figures operating on syntactico-semantic structures: the figure of *Zeugma*.

To be sure, the contrast here is weaker; for, whereas in Heraclitus it is impossible to translate the text as it stands, one can render Sophocles' text by implementing a unitary reading, *bíos*: 'you grabbed my life and stole it with your tricks'. But the historical tradition as revealed by Heraclitus' text (historical context) *and* the relation between the two verbs employed here with one and the same object and the verbs divided, in the passage quoted above, among many different objects (local context) make it most plausible that what this sentence actually does is to bring to the surface of the linguistic structure the paronomasia which until then was concealed.

I have used this text as a context of ideological clarification for the metaphor at issue in two different senses: to give a concrete foundation to one of the main connotations in the conflated lexical matrices (and the process of this analysis has shown the metonymic ramifications of these matrices in all their complexity), and to show that Heraclitus' paronomasia is not an isolated invention; on the contrary, it is solidly rooted in verbal folklore and in the history of the language. The two movements have the same effect: to give a solid foundation to the linguistic analysis, rooting it into a critical materialist theory. Thus rhetorics verifies the activity of philology on a deeper level, clarifying its claims and giving the appropriate breadth to its procedures.

Going back to the analysis of the connotations of *bíos*: one might doubt that the *bíos-biós* nexus is primarily connected with 'livelihood'. Couldn't it be that when Philoctetes links the possession of the bow to his life, he is thinking primarily of its usefulness as a weapon to defend himself against his enemies? While the doubt is, in general terms, not implausible, the concrete contextualization dissolves it, for Philoctetes himself makes the connotation explicit when he exclaims: "Killing neither wingéd bird nor mountain-ranging beast with this bow-and-arrows (*tóksois . . . toisíd'*), but myself wretchedly dying, I will provide food to those on which I fed, and those which I chased before will chase me now; I will, wretched that I am, pay with my blood as a reprisal for [shed] blood" (955–58).

The passage is interesting also because of its thrice-repeated (with a semantic *Variatio*) conceit, based on a dialectic of life and death which is close to that in Heraclitus' fragment. A last element must be pointed out, which is found in this very stretch of discourse: it enlarges the foundations of the paronomastic field and at the same time it provides grounding for another feature in the lexical matrix.

When Philoctetes exclaims, with sad irony: "He drags me by force (*ek bías*) as if he had seized a man in his strength, and he does not know that he is killing a dead man . . ." (945–46), his discourse objectively evokes, in terms of textual structure, a third member of our paronomastic paradigm: *bía*, related both to *bíos* and *biós*. The connection is all the more cogent because *bía* is actively present both at the formal level (we just saw this) and at the semantic level: it embodies that feature of 'tension' whose "promotion" (as noted) is the most distinctive trait of this metaphor.

The rhetorical configuration on which I just commented became so famous as to receive perhaps the most refined form of literary recognition: a parodistic citation. About a decade later (the play seems to have been first performed in 392), Aristophanes in his *Women at the Assembly* (*Ecclesiazusae*) has one of his characters cry out: "No way, by the gods, don't do that! Do not take away my life!" (562–63).

Essentially, what he is doing is quoting line 133 (discussed above) of Sophocles' tragedy. The parody resides in the lowering of the register (which also clarifies in what sense parody may be regarded as a form of demystification of ossified ideological concretions). The desperate invocation originally uttered by a great warrior is here misplaced with careful calculation, being put in the mouth of Blepyros the *sukophántēs* (or professional, paid informer): he is concerned about losing his 'livelihood' if a law is passed which forbids informing.

This connection is interesting in terms of literary history, but it casts some light on our lexical problem only *a contrario*: it is like experimenting with a chemical combination by taking away one of its components. For the context makes it clear that only *bíos* 'life, livelihood' is present here: there is neither formal nor semantic (con)fusion with *biós*. The interest of the passage then is (as noted) to show the metonymic feature of 'material sustenance' characterizing the lexical item in the absence of a metaphorical extension of this item. But the case is different for a slightly later Aristophanic play, *Plutos*.[32]

There, one of the characters marches off to consult a god—but not on his own behalf, for he does not have any illusion left: ". . . believing to have already shot my life away (*ektetokseûsthai bíon*) . . ." (34).

Here the allusion is clear (although it is obfuscated by editors who substitute *ektetolupeûsthai* 'to bring to an end' for *ektetokseûsthai*): the *bíos/biós* paronomasia is taken up again, in the framework of an elegantly structured metaphor. There is not space to expand on this, save for noting that the elegance of the metaphorization here stems from the fact that the two lexical matrices at issue are kept in balanced opposition by having one of them (the one pertinent to *bíos*) fully emerge on the surface of the sentence, in the object noun phrase, while the other (the one associated with *biós*) is doubly concealed—and doubly revealed: concealed morphologically by the stem *tóks-* which reflects a synonymic word, *but* revealed by the very fact that this word is a synonym; and again, concealed syntactically by its appearing embodied in a representative of a different part of speech (a verb phrase rather than a noun phrase), *yet* at the same time syntactically revealed by its being put in direct contact with the other lexical matrix, which is contained in the direct object of this verb.

But what is most fruitful, for the definition of the field of this research, is that this manifestation of the paronomasia serves as the ideological background of two other features in the lexical matrix: the 'locus of tension' one and the one about 'brief, elusive time span' within an atmosphere of 'regret'. The latter feature is reaffirmed by the prefix *ek-* of this verbal compound, with its semantic implication of, so to speak, 'done away with'; and the former is underscored by this metaphor of living one's life as one shoots an arrow.

One should try and strike the right balance, here, between the minute detail and the general effect. What I mean is that it would not be correct to claim that here 'life' is assimilated to an 'arrow' (thus, *bélos* or some other synonym) rather than to the 'bow'; what is at stake is really the whole connotation of tension implicit in the functioning of the bow (and at any rate, we saw clearly enough, in the preceding analysis of the intricate metonymic ramifications within the word(s) for 'bow', that 'bow' refers to a complexly articulated set of tools rather than to a unified object).

Thus the groundwork is laid for the ideological contextualizations generated by the later texts, the ones which were already briefly evoked above as the citational contexts of Heraclitus' fragment. (In what follows, I will use as a base Marcovich 1967.) Let us look at the metatexts, or texts-contexts, more closely. (They are not contexts, because they do not belong to Heraclitus; neither are they contexts, in the sense of semiotic contexts—hence my calling them texts-contexts.)

The *Etymologicon Magnum* provides two alternative explanations, which reflect the elements already made explicit in my analysis of the matrices at issue. After Heraclitus' quote, that erudite text states:

> Either the weapon (*tó hóplon*) has been called like this [i.e., *biós*] because of the strength of the tension (*tền bían tês táseōs*), because it takes strength to tend it; or, because the ancients obtained through it, using it on the wild beasts, the things necessary for life (*tà pròs tòn bíon*); for they procured themselves the things necessary for life shooting down with arrows (*tokseúontes*) the wingéd creatures and the four-footed animals.

Despite its slightly naive, encyclopedic tone and repetitive style, this passage is important because it makes explicit the two basic ideological frameworks which structure the connotations of the word: the aesthetic ideology of 'locus of tension' and the economic ideology of 'means of sustenance'. In describing the latter, the text reads like a paraphrase of Sophocles' quoted passages in *Philoctetes* (and indeed, this passage might very well be an implicit but fairly straightforward quotation from that tragedy); while in characterizing the former, the text makes explicit what the quoted texts by Sophocles and Aristophanes merely represent and evoke indirectly. We see, then, the very different sense in which the two sets of texts (*Philoctetes* and *Plutos* on the one hand, *Etymologicon Magnum* on the other) contextualize this lexical item. The first two are, so to speak, unprogrammed metalanguages: that is, they can serve as metalanguages in order to understand either the metaphor in itself or the whole sentence containing it, only insofar as a third party assumes them as metalanguages.

Thus, the texts-contexts do not try to explain or even to comment on *biós* through *bía* and/or *bíos*. They merely establish a proximity (of images and connotations) among these words.

On the other hand, the *Etymologicon Magnum* presents itself explicitly as a metalanguage, as a device for interpreting a text. Should we, then, draw the conclusion that a statement like this represents the passage from a prescientific to a scientific attitude? Actually, this would be a rather shallow evaluation. Throughout this book I insist on the importance of tradition, and I criticize often the inflated view that modern linguistics tends to have of itself. Thus, I cannot be accused of arrogant scientism when I note that modern linguistics has indeed shown us what is wrong with linguistic statements like the one quoted above from *Etymologicon Magnum*. But let us make a careful distinction.

The ancient philologist correctly identifies some areas of the world in which the referent of the problematized word (*bíos*) is used. I believe that the identification cannot aim directly at reality, but only at the structure of signs which we perceive—thus what are actually identified here are, as noted above, ideologies within whose systems the lexical item is used; in general, what post-Marxist critique correlates to linguistic signs is not a direct perception of society, but systems of societal signs. This distinction however, important as it is in general terms, is not crucial at this point.

But then, the ancient goes too far for the good of his description; for he establishes a *causal* and *genetic* relationship between lexical items central to these ideological fields and the items at issue. Thus: a certain object in the world has been called *biós* (according to him) *because* it takes *bía* to handle it, or *because* it is useful for *bíos*.

We can call this the etymological fallacy, for we know that etymology, as a sphere in linguistic history, *partially* but not *completely* overlaps with other spheres.

On the other hand, an element of critical sophistication in this statement is what can be called its historicism: writing in a period when the economy, and in general the organization of society, had already reached a high degree of complexity, the compiler of the

Etymologicon Magnum realizes that the dominant position of the feature 'livelihood' in the lexical matrix of *biós* implies a relatively primitive degree of socioeconomic organization, where hunting is one of the primary motors of the economy. Hence, his indicating that the connection is relevant to the world of the 'ancients' (*hoi arkhaíoi*); which is, as noted, an interesting trait of historical (or anthropological) integration of the lexical analysis.

Another ideological contextualization is the one evoked by the gloss in Tzetzes' Homeric commentary; according to which the *tókson* is called *biós* "with a view to an oppositional distinction (*antidiastolé*) with respect to *bíos*, which signifies 'life' (*zōé*)." Here the characterization of the semantic relationship as an *antidiastolé* is enough to show that it is the connotation 'means of deadly destruction' (rather than the 'means of providing food' one) which is foregrounded, so that *biós* is treated here metaphorically as an antonym of *bíos* rather than (metonymically) as a component of the world of *bíos*.

Yet another ideological contextualization is sketched in the Homeric commentary by Eustathius, where the metalinguistic dimension is evoked. In fact, the citation (or paraphrase) of the fragment is introduced here as an illustration of how a change in accent (*allagé . . . toû tónou*) can be connected to semantic differentiation. Heraclitus is appreciated as having expressed his thought 'elegantly' (*asteíōs*), and the process involved is specified as one of creating a paronomasia (*paronomázō* is the verb actually employed).

The adjective *asteîos* 'urbane, witty, elegant' (as an antonym of the lexical item *ágroikos*), is one of the key terms in Aristotle's *Rhetoric*, which provides a further specification for the aesthetic contextualization of Heraclitus' discourse. Aesthetic, insofar as Aristotle's appreciation of Heraclitus is concerned, should be more precisely understood as: aesthetic-philological; and it is not, in this case, the notion of *asteîos*, but a divergent one (a connotation of hard obscurity, albeit not its antonym, pointing to uncouthness) which is at issue here.

For, what interests us here is less the particular fragment (the opening passage of Heraclitus' lost treatise—see Diels–Kranz 1966, fr. 1— almost a symbol of the lost text), than the way Aristotle introduces the discussion of it. "In general," he writes, "the written text must be easy to recognize (*euanágnōstos*) and to enunciate (*eúphrastos*). This [ease] is precisely what the presence of numerous connecting elements (*súndesmos*) does not allow—nor is this allowed by the texts which are difficult to punctuate (*diastízō*), like those by Heraclitus."

A specific passage by Heraclitus and a more general appreciation follow, which I will present because of their interest for modern rhetorical theory (refraining of course, since space does not permit it, from entering the forest of problems connected to this fragment— number 1 in the Diels-Kranz ordering, to repeat—which marks the tantalizing entrance to the tantalizingly lost book).

> To punctuate Heraclitus' writings indeed is quite a task, because it is not clear [given two or more clauses] to which one [a given connecting element or particle] is joined, whether to what comes later (*tò hústeron*) or to what comes earlier (*tò próteron*), as for instance right at the beginning of his book. In fact he says there: "Such being the truth always un-understanding men turn out to be"; now the "always" is not clear, with which one of the two [clauses] it ⟨should⟩ be joined through punctuation.

A point which has been made already emerges here with particular clarity, and it bears repetition; indeed—at this still primitive stage in the development of rhetorical theory—it will never be repeated enough. What the quoted statement reflects is yet another episode in the century-long conflict, which it is not exaggerated to call a life-and-death struggle, between rhetoric*s* as a realistic and fully descriptive account of rhetoric, i.e., of the actual structure and functions of discourse (rhetoric*s*, then, as scientific knowledge of the politics of discourse, as a human and social project); and, on the other hand, rhetoric*s* as an ideological mystification of *rhetoric*, as a normative and intellectualistic approach which erects a particular, conservative literary taste into the sum and model of all possible forms of expression. This latter approach implants the fatal equivocation (still very much alive) which refuses to see that rhetoric*s* is a matter of understanding rhetoric for what it actually is, scrutinizing it without the blinkers of ideological prejudice; rather, this equivocation presents rhetoric*s* as a set of externally assigned rules, which label certain types of discourse as acceptable, nay even elegant, and discard certain others as shapeless, such that they should be rewritten.

Clearly, then, it is no hyperbole to speak, in this context, of a life-and-death struggle: the former view, or attitude (for here it is not simply a matter of looking at cultural constructs, but of doing things, in the social praxis of criticism as performed today), is the life of rhetorics; the second, its death (with a first-class funeral at the expenses of academic conservatism, which sees in this kind of *rigor mortis* its chance to subtract criticism from the world of praxis and to erect it into something innocuous and respectable). That major writers (like, in this case, Aristotle) are often ready to defend this deadly view of rhetoric is perhaps the best explanation of why such intellectualistic normativism is so readily accepted, even when the victims of such misguided judgments are, as in most cases, the best passages of the strongest writers. It is a case of one among the possible implementations of the topos of Authority (the Critic-as-Judge) winning over another version of this same topos (The-Writer-as-Arbiter-of-Literary-Taste).

But the timid reader, and more specifically the modern critic who interprets his heritage from the classics (that heritage which marks the richness and the obligation of us all who work in these fields) in a repressive way, is not well advised when he shows himself too ready to conform to such authoritarian (rather than seriously authoritative) *dicta* and rushes into a complacent repetition of such stylistic censures. For, in the cultural praxis of the major readers and shapers of critical opinion, such as Aristotle, the apparently formal condemnations hide complicated ideological maneuvers, which lend seriousness to their pronouncements, however narrow and misguided they are. But, once detached from their hidden roots, these condemnations turn, in the hands of the epigones, into merely formalistic pronouncements, devoid of what made their deeper interest. Thus do the flowers of stylistics soon wilt when pulled from the soil of ideological struggles out of which they were born. More prosaically: this is the heavy price that any neglect of history sooner or later has to pay. In order to see Aristotle's ideological strategy, and at the same time its bearing on the aesthetic contextualization of our fragment, more clearly, let me complete my quote, citing the rest of the paragraph:

> Besides, the following leads to commit solecisms (*soloikízō*): the fact of not restoring [the full connection] if you do not yoke together (*epizeúgnumi*) what fits with both [components of a given syntactic unit], as for instance, for the [designation of] a sound and a color [the verb]

'to see' is not a shared element, but the perceiving [i.e., the verb 'to perceive'] is shared. And, it is obscure (*asaphēs*) if you talk without placing [certain sentence components] before, [but on the contrary] you pretend to put many [such components] in between, as for instance: "For I intended, having conversed with him about this and that, and thus, to go," but not: "For I intended, having conversed, to go, then this and that and thus happened." (*Rh.* 2. 1407^b 11–25)

It is objectively ironic, in the anti-iconic sense characterized in 2.2, that this passage in which Aristotle criticizes examples of alleged linguistic obscurity is itself elliptical and obscure. (Hence, the necessity of frequent editorial interventions in brackets.) What is interesting, moreover, is that this concise, fragmented, allusive mode of expression is far from being an exceptional feature of this particular passage; on the contrary, this paragraph is typical of Aristotle's style, at least in the *Rhetoric*. The irony is even more complicated than the above-described contrast between pretense and reality in the metalanguage presenting alleged *specimina* of obscure language. What is more ironic is that Aristotle-as-theoretician-of-style is blind to his own style as a writer; more precisely, he does not care to make explicit that his style is as *asaphēs* as the examples he criticizes, and that *just because of this* it is lively and effective, exactly as those criticized passages are lively and effective. I said: "he does not care to make explicit" rather than: "he does not see," or "he cannot see." The former expression would be condescending, the latter excessively dramatic, and above all, both would be misleading.

For what happens here, in these apparently stylistic analyses, is that Aristotle chooses ideology over realism. The rhetorical level at which he speaks is not that of Elocutio (where, as noted, he would easily be proved wrong, so clearly is what he writes belied by his very way of writing it), but the underlying semiotic organization. In other words, he has to say what he says because of the general ideological balance of *aurea mediocritas* which he is constructing in order to protect and organize his whole book. We have seen above why and how this balance is constructed, and presently we are going to see some further specifications of it.

Tantalizing: a realistic analysis of the functional aspect of utterances is no sooner evoked that it is obfuscated by a generic condemnation; a rhetorical analysis, then, must restore the structures which ideology has heavily painted over. Starting from the end of Aristotle's statement: we must not allow ourselves to be intimidated by the syntactic condemnation of embedding—which will become a commonplace of ideological syntactic-stylistic pronouncements through the centuries, in so many languages and literatures. Writers will, of course, ignore such condemnations and go on (fortunately) constructing varied and complicated sentences (cf. Valesio 1974a on complicated versus complex sentences).

This particular censure, at any rate, makes less sense than most because the two sentences are not exact paraphrases of each other, so that it is not clear in what sense the second sentence is viewed as the correct version of the first, or even if this is indeed the hierarchy that Aristotle means to present. (The situation is such that—even though this is only the very last resort, to which one should have recourse most sparingly, when everything else fails—one cannot help suspecting a "corruption" in the Greek text as it has been transmitted to us.)

More to the point for the analyst of rhetoric: the structural contrast evoked here adumbrates a figure of speech, *Hýsteron Próteron*, which is hinted at—as we saw—earlier in this same passage, apropos of Heraclitus' fragment. Let us, tentatively, define hýsteron próteron (or *hysterología*) as the configuration where the syntactic order contrasts with the normal semantic interpretation of the succession of events described by that syntactic structure (cf. the vague definition in HR 1960: par. 891; and a systematization in Valesio 1975a). Neither of these two configurations fully implements the hýsteron próteron, but neither of them can be understood outside of the frame of this figure. The anonymous utterance realizes hýsteron próteron at the level of clause interchange within a sentence. Heraclitus' fragment, on the other hand, evokes (but does not really implement) hýsteron próteron at a lower syntactic level: possible interchanges in the position of a word (the quoted *aeí* 'always') within a phrase.

This leaves us with the middle case, that concerning the problem of associating nouns for 'color' and 'sound' with verbs of 'seeing' (an allegedly incorrect linking) versus the association with verbs of 'perceiving' (which, we are told, is the grammatically correct solution). The correctness of the latter connection is not, of course, to be denied: but if we rashly accept the condemnation of the former one we miss a functional rhetorical configuration which, far from violating grammar, enriches it. Actually, this is a cluster of two different figures of speech: the already familiar zeugma and synaesthesia, or more precisely, synaesthesia with a coloring of zeugma. The first figure (already defined and exemplified here) points to the syntactic side of the possible implementation of this linking: presumably, in a clause or sentence which links a noun or adjective for some 'sound' and a noun or adjective designating one or other 'color' to a verb of 'seeing', the verb itself will appear only once. But the dominant configuration is that of synaesthesia, which here I take as any linguistic expression in which a given sense modality is described in terms of a different sense modality (see cf. the note under synaesthesia in Preminger 1966; strangely, the term is absent from *HR* 1960).

Any clause or phrase in which a verb 'to see' is applied to a noun or adjective for 'sound' implements a synaesthesia (while the coexistence of a noun or adjective for 'color' in the same phrase or clause would be the contribution of zeugma). Synaesthesia, of course, is a universal phenomenon in literature, including Greek poetry from Homer on (no examples are really necessary), so that the ideological character of Aristotle's stricture emerges with particular clarity. But I did not linger on this case for the perverse pleasure of waging a pedantic attack on the Philosopher's pedantry in this matter: the interest of this observation lies in the fact that, as a description (aside from the unwarrented censure), this appreciation comes very close to describing the *bíos/biós* cluster in our fragment.

This blend cannot realize a zeugma in the strict, traditional sense because such a figure requires a verb and (as it was discussed at length) Heraclitus' sentence is a nominal one; on the other hand, the pair does not constitute a synaesthesia because the two nouns at issue do not designate sense perceptions. And yet, this blend does belong to the same semantic area as the two described figures, and any linguistic description which failed to point this out would not be sufficiently "delicate" for its object. In fact, it is not only because (as we saw) the verb *epizeúgnumi* is used in the above-quoted passage to designate the 'sound'/'color' cluster that I feel compelled to insist on the relevance of this configuration to a broad view and definition of the figure of zeugma.

Indeed, this is an example of the dialectic interaction between actual linguistic structures and the configurations generally defining

such structures (the dialectic, that is, between rhetoric and rhetorics):
on the one hand, a figure like zeugma helps us to understand more
clearly what takes place in cases like the yoking of 'sound' and 'color'
words together with the verb 'to see', and with the Heraclitean sentence; but on the other hand, it is just a concrete linguistic structure
like our fragment that shows how the traditional linguistic definition
of zeugma (see the quoted HR 1960: pars. 692–708, 745, and passim)—focused on syntax—is insufficient; we need a semantic characterization of this figure.

For what else is the yoking together of a description of the work of
the 'bow' and description of the workings of 'life', if not a species of
zeugma? A certain clause (the nominal clause: 'its work—death') is
linked, as a predicate, to a clause containing the noun 'bow' *as well as*
to a clause containing the noun 'life'. This is a zeugma, where the
only differences with respect to the traditional definition of zeugma
are, in the first place, that it operates with clauses at the level of the
sentence, rather than (as in the standard illustrations) with verb
phrases at the level of the clause; secondly and above all, that one of
the clauses at issue is "understood," or more precisely, it is blended
with the other one—so that the process is a semantic rather than a
syntactic one. But such differences do not appear sharp enough to
justify cutting off this configuration from the general domain of
zeugma.

The present theory of rhetoric, then, contains (in its, still virtual,
development into a full list of definitions of figures of speech) a
broader definition of the figure of zeugma. Finally, synaesthesia is not
totally absent from our fragment, even if (as noticed) the nouns at
issue do not designate sense perceptions; for a distinction must be
made between sense perceptions as *the semantic content* of a given word
(something which is absent here) and sense perceptions as *a way of
perceiving* the semantic content of a given word—something which is
potentially present around every lexical item (no matter how abstract).

One of the most important effects of strong poetic statements like
this fragment is precisely that of foregrounding the sensuous quality
of words which otherwise would remain abstract. Thus, the *bíos/biós*
blend has a synaesthetic aspect insofar as—by the very gesture of
blending the two words—the reader is stimulated to search for a

nexus between the way one perceives a given object in its aesthetic shape (more on this presently) and the perception of an abstract concept ('life') which now is viewed in its more concrete, sensuous aspect. The promoted and shared feature which (as we saw) defines the metaphor as such—namely, 'locus of tension'—appears, now, in this synaesthetic aspect. For, clearly, to predicate 'tension' equally of the 'bow' and of 'life' means to blend two quite different modes of perception; and this is the basic move in synaesthesia.

An improved understanding of certain figures of speech has been a bonus, in this analysis of the Aristotelian passage; but we must not forget our original purpose: to describe yet another ideological contextualization of the Heraclitus' passage. The Aristotelian frame is not, as we saw, a direct contextualization of the passage. I recorded and discussed it here, however, for its methodological interest; but I will not pursue the examination of such contextualizations indirectly related to the text because—interesting, and indeed necessary, as such an investigation would be—space obviously fails here.

Only I must underscore in what sense this Aristotelian contextualization constitutes an aesthetic ideologization of the fragment. It is aesthetic in the sense that it expresses an aesthetic evaluation of the text *qua* text—of its linguistic organization; and it is ideological because such evaluation obeys abstract a priori notions. It is *not* an aesthetic contextualization in the other, possible, sense of this term: namely, a way of contextualizing the text which focuses on the aesthetic connotations and evocations of one or more of the lexical items *contained in* the text.

The contextualizations which I am going to consider now are aesthetic in this second sense of the term: that is, they focus on the aesthetic evocations of the senses of the lexical items in the sentence—namely, those of the two synonyms for 'bow.'

In so doing, these contextualizations bring more closely together the 'locus of tension' connotation and the connotation of 'elegantly (curved) shaped structure'. In short, they concentrate on *tókson* (as well as on its synonym *biós*) the host of connotations which in modern English are distributed among three nonsynonymic words: not only *bow*, then, but also *arc* and *arch*. The latter two items reflect, of course, the Latin avatar of the Indo-European root *arkw-*; which, interestingly for our analysis, seems to have been characterized *ab origine* by the same type of polysemy which we noticed in the Greek usage of *tókson* (and *biós*) deriving from other Indo-European roots: the meaning of 'bow-and-arrows' (cf. the analysis of *tókson/tóksa* and *hópla*, above).

The critique of ideology trains the critic to constant diffidence, and makes him particularly aware of the danger of anachronism. But sometimes there is reason for optimism, when what seemed to be an anachronistic layer on an ancient text turns out to have been a contextualization as ancient as the text; this is, indeed, what happens in the present case. For, it might seem that this view of the bow as a beautiful object or structure is a manifestation of (lato sensu) post-Romantic aestheticism. In this sense, such a contextualization could be symbolized by a statement like this (attributed to a modern theoretician of dancing, Doris Humphry): "Every movement is an arc between two deaths"—an effective metaphor, which brings together (poetically) the idea of beginning and end of an aesthetically disciplined movement, and the beginning and the end of life. This, by the way, suggests yet another reading for Heraclitus' fragment—one in which *bíos* is related to *biós* not metaphorically but metonymically.

Specifically: *biós* 'bow' is the structure arching out of, and along, *bíos* and ending into *thánatos*. (After all, *tókson* does have an architectonic meaning, which legitimizes this idea of arching movement.) This semantic possibility casts a new light on the symbolic field of the Sagittarius as a Zodiacal sign (his bow can be the symbol of the basic outline of life, suspended between birth and death), and in turn shows how deep are the roots of the widespread image of human life as an arc.

But all this is historically richer and deeper (as the reference to the Zodiacal sign already makes us realize) than a post-Romantic anachronism. We confront essentially the same situation that we faced above, when what at first sight might have seemed a Romantic anachronism (the importance of the feature of 'tension' in the matrix of *biós*) turned out to be a connotation identified, in historically authoritative terms, by the original cultural context (cf. the use of the term *bía* in the ancient glosses).

Something analogous happens here; in fact, it takes place in an even more striking way. For it is not a later philologist who establishes a connection, but Heraclitus himself. We see, then, a manifestation of one of the most significant phenomena for a semiotic theory of the text: namely, *a portion of the text functioning as the critical metalanguage which analyzes another part of himself* (which can be in its immediate context or—like here—in another section of the corpus). It is, one could say, a process by which *the text contextualizes itself*.

The passage I refer to is the second part of the fragment 51: "A joining which flows back into itself, like that of the bow and of the lyre" (*palíntropos harmoníē hókōsper tóksou kaì lúrēs*). That we have here an aesthetic contextualization is clear; but (as usual, in the fragments) the sense of the statement is unclear.[33]

There is no time here to go into the local problem, but I must point out that the demons of ambiguity and variation haunt this place, too; there is no solid ground, no lexeme that can serve as a fixed point of reference. Thus, no sooner is the difficulty of translating *palíntropos* fully grasped that one discovers that this item is actually only one member of the relevant glosseme—the other member being the lexical item *palíntonos*.

The documentation of this second variant is more ambiguous, but it cannot be ignored, because the term clearly evokes the world of the bow, and its meaning is dialectically polarized: for *palíntonos* seems to mean *either* 'strung, bent' (as the bow being readied to shoot) *or* 'unstrung' (as the bow which bends back after shooting); a balanced translation of this term, then, would be one which focuses on the change of state as the common denominator, so that *palíntonos* would be said of the bow when its stringing changes from one state to another (from unstrung to strung, or vice versa).

As for the word which I translated 'joining'—emphasizing its "prosaic," technical aspect—it is something less than *harmoníē*, whose close rendition 'harmony' evokes, of course, a very different register, one of cosmic patterns. Actually, the alternatives represented by these two lexical items are related. The 'joining' version of *harmoníē* and the choice of the variant reading *palíntonos* as the representative of the glosseme reflect an ideology of technical precision and well-delimited, "realistic," representation of the world as a conglomerate of objects and of specific processes. Note, also: the (-)*tonos* morphological component in this compound word, related to the root of the verb *teínō* 'to stretch, to strain' is the parallel, at the level of language, of the connotative feature of 'tension' discussed above in terms of the descriptive metalanguage. On the other hand, the translation 'harmony' and the implementation of *palíntropos* as representative of the glosseme collaborate to build up an ideology of general suggestions— hints of elegance and of cosmic implications.

This second ideology is more aesthetic than the first one: but we can consider both—based as they are on a figure of simile paralleling the 'bow' and the 'lyre'—as parts of a process of indirect aesthetic contextualization of our fragment; where the term "aesthetic," as noted, does not point to the evaluation and editing of this or similar fragments (as it was the case for the discussed Aristotelian contextualization), but to the nature of the connotations which are being emphasized in the words making up this fragment.

We have followed a roughly chronological order, from the more ancient to the more modern contextualization; let us, to conclude this part, make a step backwards, recalling that beside the economic ideology (the bow as the means to gain one's livelihood), the warfare ideology (the bow as a distributor of death and destruction), and the aesthetic ideology (the bow as an object of delicate balance and checked tension), a fourth ideology as possible (although it could also be considered as an internal inflection of the whole ideology of livelihood): it can be called the hygienic (or medical) ideology, and it is represented by the quoted Hippocratic statement about *trophḗ ou trophḗ*, etc.

This statement is rightly considered (cf. Marcovich 1967) as nothing more than a *Respicit*: that is, the Heraclitean element in it is not even an indirect citation or paraphrase (let alone a specific quote), but simply a "reminiscence"; we could say that Heraclitus' text is here present only as an ideological echo or resonance. Indeed, the best attitude here is a conservative one, since, if we start putting in the direct context of a text like ours all *Respicits* of this sort, there is no way to stop; we would be, then, obliged to attach to such a text all the subsequent texts which appear to contain some echo of it, no matter how feeble and indirect.

On the other hand, it is very useful to record texts like these, because their very presence emphasizes an important methodological point: namely, that there is *no clear-cut line of division* between a text and its context—as we can very well expect, once we become convinced that the text does not have a separate existence as an ontologically defined unit. Thus the usual separations between texts and their contexts which make current histories of literature possible are the result of ideological decisions, which is to say: of more or less artificial cuts in the verbal and cultural continuum of text-context.

To be sure, one could propose a more specific reason why it is not inappropriate to recall this context: and this is that at least one other Heraclitean fragment—8 Diels-Kranz, a three-word noun phrase quoted in Aristotle's *Nicomachean Ethics*—indirectly contextualizes our fragment in the terms of a hygienistic ideology. The fragment reads: *tò antíksoun sumphéron*. However, this contextualization is not at all convincing as a specification of the hygienistic ideology. For there is no clear reason to translate it into medical terms—as Bollack and Wismann 1972 do, rendering it as: 'Le nuisible, salutaire'.

The two terms are much more general than that, and the phrase could be translated: 'The hostile, profitable'. And indeed, the idea expressed here might be less dialectically polarized than it seems if we recall that one of the senses of *sumphérō* is: 'to come together (or: to meet) in battle', so that the concept could be something as simple as: 'The hostile engages in battle'. (Which could be a banalization, already present as such in the Aristotelian text, of a more sophisticated sentence by Heraclitus whose structure might have been simplified in later transmissions.)

At any rate, the temptation of a direct connection between this rhetoric and that of the bow should be rejected, notwithstanding Bollack and Wismann 1972:79: "Il n'est pas exclu qu'il faille superposer a l'acception courante des mots une analyse 'étymologique'. Dans le *nuisible* s'exprimerait la tension (*anti*) des extremites de l'arc (*toxon*) et dans le *salutaire* le rapprochement qu'accomplit la *corde* (*sum-pheron*)."

But what etymology is evoked here? There would be no reason to pedantically deny attention to a folk etymology if it were an ancient one; but the fragment is not contextualized in terms of *tókson*. Nor can this be a modern etymology, since it is wrong: *antíksous* is not etymologically related to *tókson*. In fact, with this example I have concluded a section of my contextualization of this text, and opened another section (the last one in the discussion).

Until now, the ideological layers built on the text (or, in another image, the ideological frames contextualizing the text) have been analyzed as inevitable de-formations; inevitable, because the text per se is shapeless, and any structure giving some shape to it is ideological with respect to the free flow of rhetorical strategies which constitute the text. The crucial difference (as already indicated) is not an absolute one; the differences whose careful discrimination justifies the whole enterprise are matters of degree. Ideology is, *up to a point*, indispensable in order to give intellectual organization to the text; the challenge is to establish, case by case (on the basis of empirical study of the local contexts) where ideology as functionally indispensable deformation ceases, and ideology as dispensable, nonfunctional deformation mystifying the text, begins.

This amounts to saying, in effect, that there is no such thing as ideology—in the sense of a monolithic entity of some sort, definable in a simple and unequivocal way. What we find in the reality of history, culture, literature are ideologies; that is, specific ideological formations, at various levels of complexity, in various mixtures of abstract and concrete elements, of brilliant insights and evasive maneuvers, structured in varying degrees of skill and comprehensiveness. Finally, it is well to recall that ideologies are not specific contents (bundles of ideas) but structures, where a given matrix processes ideas into specific semiotic forms.

I was speaking of ideology as mystifying (de-)formation. But, even when we believe that we recognize such an ideological formation, caution is called for: deforming and mystifying are not (at least, not always and necessarily) synonyms with terms like: facile, obtuse, irresponsible. On the contrary, very often the ideological deformation is the result of an agile movement of the imagination, it is an admirable expression of sensitivity—and all this is often expressed with great skill. For instance: Bollack and Wismann 1972 comment on one of the most famous among the Heraclitean fragments (91 Diels-Kranz); it is a sensitive gloss, but it is also a deformation of its sober (indeed, stern) structure into a post-Romantic spiraling of cosmic allusions.

"To twice enter, it is not given, into the same river," or: *potamôi ouk éstin embênai dìs tôi autôi.* The syntactic strain in my English version is willed, in order to give an idea of the chiastic structure of the original, aptly noted by the quoted editors. Their comments expand thus: "Comme pour l'arc, la tension immobile des contraires identiques produit l'élan différencié du mouvement. Sans la courbure du bois que maintient la corde, les flèches ne partiraient pas. Sans la pression constantes des rives, les eaux stagneraient. Parce qu'ils illustrent également la construction logique du passage de l'opposition à la succession, l'arc et le fleuve servent de chiffre au processus cosmique."[34]

This is suggestive; it enriches the connotation of the lexical items involved; but this description also moves out of the area of careful contextualization.

The simile linking the bow with the lyre is explicitly presented as such in the original texts—whose language then gives a solid grounding to the metalanguage of the connotative features entering into the lexical matrices at issue. On the other hand, if we assume (as seems to be the case) that the simile connecting bow and river is not made explicit as such either in the original Heraclitean texts or in the ancient contextualization of them, then we face a crucial difference in the status of these two descriptions.

At any rate, the quoted discussion on the river imagery as connected to the bow is—for all its Romantic halo blurring the hard contour of the original text—closer to the actual verbal strategy than the heavier kind of direct ideological overcoating, in the mode of traditional philosophy. As for instance the following statement, which presents itself as a paraphrasis, but is actually an abstracting deformation: "the bow, seen in its similitude to other things, as an element of multiplicity, is cause of death; seen outside of this simile—outside of the multiplicity, as one, it is designated by the name for life; in the name, convergence is revealed, while divergence is revealed in the work" (Maddalena 1940).

We can see clearly, now, the opposite dangers between which this peculiarly delicate structure hovers, like a frail bridge. On the one hand, the clarity of its profile may be obfuscated by a mist of vague anachronism; but on the other hand the whole structure can crack if it is suddenly covered by a heap of philosophical bricks. With respect to such irruptions of abstract thinking, philosophical description *sub specie* of a historical and philological commentary is more fruitful— indeed, it has a demystifying effect. As when, for instance, Calogero 1936 notes that *érgon*, as meaning 'action' or 'function', is different from the same lexeme in idioms like *érgōi* 'as a matter of fact'; and that, then, the relevant opposition here (which he bolsters with Ho-

meric references) is that between 'discourse' and 'action' rather than
the one of 'fact' versus 'name'.

But this same author, and in the same text, reverts to the mystifying
stance which expresses itself in what might be called an *anxiety of edification*; the tendency, I mean, to view the analyzed discourse as a
locus of solution, of superior conciliation of conflicts. Thus we are
told that for the idea expressed in this fragment, "it is necessary that
name and function be viewed on the same level, as equally objective
determinations of reality: it is necessary to assume that what makes
itself manifest in the word also makes itself manifest in the thing—
the one and the other bearing witness, in reciprocal cooperation, to
the essence of truth. Which is to say that for Heraclitus the full adhe-
sion of reality-truth to its linguistic clothing is a positive point of departure, inasmuch as this is the only premise which explains the spirit
in which this statement is formulated."

A careful study of Heraclitus' fragments failed, as we saw, to turn
out any such "positive point of departure": such characterizations are
essentially constructions superimposed on an intractable set of texts,
in order to give them unitary and edifying direction that they do not
in fact have. Thus is the illusion generated that these conflictual microtexts are actually parts of one compact text. But: this is true, isn't
it?—since we know for sure that these are fragments out of a unitary
sungrámma (to use Aristotle's term): the (big? little?) book proudly offered by his author to Diana, at her temple in Ephesus (or humbly
offered? Or slyly offered? the sense of the gesture escapes us—because we do no longer have the relevant context in the society and
culture of the time). But this is precisely the trap into which we
should not fall: because we know that there is a book behind these
fragments, this is not a sound reason for making it up at all costs,
pouring the mortar of our ideology in between the bare bricks of the
original language (with their own conflicting rhetorical strategies).

4.6 CONCLUDING PERSPECTIVE

Thus I have concluded my contextualization of Heraclitus' microtext, as well as the critical review of the several contextualizations
which the fragment underwent through the centuries. To be sure,

this review cannot be considered exhaustive—indeed, one of the salient methodological points in the preceding exposition was that of showing that such an exhaustiveness is virtually impossible, because of the richness of links and reverberations that every utterance shows, as soon as it tries to question the cliché (which does *not* mean: to eliminate the common place completely; this, as I have been arguing all through the book, is impossible—as it is proven by this very fragment, which was shown to echo an element of verbal folklore). But, after these pages, the hope can be expressed that the horizon of reading for this text has been fully secured, so that all further explorations should be conducted in the light of the preceding analysis.[35]

Indeed, it would be essentially a matter of going back to the general picture drawn above and to continue filling in this or that detail within the already traced contours. For instance, I could integrate this morphophonemic analysis of the paronomasia with a phonological and graphemic analysis—which, among other things, would point out that the shape of the Greek letter called "beta," designating the initial stop in the word '*bios*', iconically suggests the shape of a bow (unstrung, or just relaxed after shooting its arrow).

The syntactic analysis also could be further refined, especially continuing in the line (largely developed above) of the coordinated usage of rhetorical and syntactic concepts. One such concept which is relevant here is that of *Prolepsis*—whose rhetorical definition (see *HR*: par. 855) has still to be brought in line with the syntactic definition. Here I am thinking of the relevance of this notion to the first word in the text—the determinative article *tôi* whose function has already been commented upon, but which could be further analyzed, with increased delicacy; and the definition of prolepsis pertinent here is the syntactic one, with its emphasis on the function of anticipating relationships between the sentence constituents which follow.

It is, essentially, a matter of filling up in a more detailed way the Cohesion cell (the lower right one) of the four-celled tagmeme which has been used in detail above (see especially section 4.1) as a syntactic grid for the analysis of the fragment. In prolepsis (as in most other configurations joining rhetorical and syntactic structures) lexical and morphosyntactic functions intertwine. Thus, the article *tôi* anticipates, by virtue of its dative form, the object function assumed by the word *tókson* later in the sentence; at the same time, it anticipates the presence of a noun—thus allowing the reader to go through the pause constituted by the conjunction *dé* without losing momentum—on the contrary, experiencing a sense of anticipation.

The semantic level also—as was to be expected—can be filled up further. For instance, the delicacy in the description of the role linking *érgon* to *thánatos* (cf. the lower left cell of the tagmeme) can be increased. In the analysis above (see section 4.1), the case relationship linking the two items was presented, we recall, as a "process-equative" and "referentive" one, whereby the second lexical item (*thánatos*) designates the effect of the first (*érgon*) which can then be regarded as its source.

But one could go further, exploring the finer implications of this semantic relationship—or, in more sharply profiled terms, exploring what is properly *semantic* in the relationship between these *lexical* items.

Insofar as *érgon* is considered as the source of *thánatos*, it is viewed as a metonymy of *tókson*; now, to say that the work of the bow is death, may imply either a subjective or an objective relationship between 'death' and 'bow'. In the objective relationship, the role connection described above is confirmed: death is the result of the working of the bow, that is, the bow is an artifact which spreads death (whether it is the death of animals—ultimately productive of livelihood—or the purely destructive death of human beings).

But in the subjective relationship, the roles are in a sense reversed: it is death, now, which is viewed as the power which wields the bow, rather than as the effect of it. In both cases, the bow is seen as the instrument of death. But, in what I have called the subjective relationship, this means that the bow is one among the tools handled by that general force which is death; whereas, in the objective relationship, death is the result of the operation of this tool.

Another path for a refinement of the semantic analysis lies in the direction of a more delicate analysis of the general metaphorical structure of the relationship between bow and life. I already remarked that the analysis of this metaphorical field makes us aware of how ancient are the roots of the metaphor depicting life as an arc, or parabolic movement. But this is a way of positing a problem, rather than presenting a solution. For, as in every study of metaphor, we must find—concrete case by concrete case—the right balance between the recognition of the general (universal) basis for the metaphor in natural structures, and its peculiar way of creating a conventional, cultural interpretation of nature.

Thus, to see the course of human life as an arc can evoke a variety of natural configurations: the profile of a rain*bow*, a natural structure of overarching stones, a bridge or similar architectural construction (as an imitation or extension of such natural structures), and so forth; this can then appear as a natural and universal response of human speech to nature—an unavoidable reflex of the way the world happens to be shaped. But the opposite track could also be taken: that is, one can consider this metaphor as an original way of dividing, reconstructing, foregrounding the raw stuff of nature, and look at it as a conventional image competing with other, equally conventional, images: life as a river, life as a foot race, and so forth.

Thus it is *not* an otiose question (of the chicken-and-the-egg kind) to ask ourselves: does the *bíos/biós* paronomasia reflect (in one of its several facets) an already existing and widespread metaphor of life as an arc, or is this paronomasia on the contrary one of the crucial sources for the development of this metaphor, which thus can be said to enter fully into circulation only in the wake of this paronomasia? This question can be answered only by a systematic investigation of Early Greek literature in all its genres—from proverbs and jokes to philosophy—which is obviously beyond the scope of this analysis (the Early Greek verbal folklore should then be compared with the analogous verbal folklore of other ancient literatures).

What can be pointed out, however, even in this restricted context, is that the above-quoted Aristophanean phrase (see *Plutus* 34) about shooting one's life away reflects a metaphor which is quite different from that of the arc of life: in that utterance, the basic vehicle of the metaphor is the arrow rather than the bow; and at any rate, it is not the bow as architectural shape which is evoked, but rather the bow as an object-throwing machine. The phallic aspect of this latter metaphor should not be underestimated—the suggestion is that one spends one's life as if one were spending his semen, in a series of exhausting spurts; by contrast, the arching metaphor is an Olympic one—a restful, wise overview which goes beyond sexual tension. It should be pointed out that linguistic history knows many cases where homophony has led to the interference of originally differentiated semantic fields—a process that can lead to folk-etymologies, or, as in the present case, to the possible creation of a metaphor.

Apropos of metaphors, at least one other case should be quoted, which casts a new light (and at the same time a further area of shadow) on the interactions between the curved shape of the bow and the curved meanderings of a river. This case also deserves to be quoted because it shows how the direction of study which had been evoked in section 4.1. can be pursued, apropos of the D'Annunzio passage: namely the study of all the modern "rewritings" (echoes, variations, evocations) of this text.

In one of his Latin essays (the *Intercoenales*), titled "Fatum et fortuna," the famous Italian humanist Leon Battista Alberti (1404–1472), tells, through the *persona* of a Philosophus, a dream: he is on a high mountain surrounded by a river, and a legion of shadows (*umbrae*) is moving between the mountain and the river. "Tell me, if you please, what is the name of this river?" asks the dreamer. The *umbrae* tell him that the name of the river is Bios. But the dreamer asks that "these names" (actually, only one name, Bios, has been uttered) be translated from Greek into Latin (the whole text is, of course, written in Latin), so that he can understand them better. The *umbrae* then answer: "In Latin that river is known as Vita ('life') and Aetas ('lifespan') of mortal men; its shore is Mors ('death') and—as you can see—whoever touches that shore again vanishes into a shadow" (Alberti in Mancini 1890).

This is not the place to try to establish through what philological traditions Leon Battista Alberti came to know Heraclitus' text. But it seems fairly clear that it is this fragment, indeed, that serves as a subtext to the quoted text describing the river. Alberti's sketch, then, brings together what is direct—but abstract—and what is indirect, but concrete. What is direct and abstract (of an ideological kind of abstraction) is the explicitly labeled concepts of "life" and "death."

More indirect, but also more concrete, is the metaphor of the river, with its aesthetic connotation of meandering curves: "A river most rapid and turbulent went all around this mountain, running back into itself (*in se ipsum rediens*)"—writes Alberti. And finally, still more indirect (indeed, hidden) under all these microtexts lies the metaphor of the bow—with its connotation of elegant curves and at the same time of destructive tension—which, if I am not mistaken, exerts the strongest pull on the whole microtext. Strongest, because it enlightens the whole text (the macrotext) of which this passage is a part, revealing its true nature.

This is a cold, marblelike, Humanist digression, which uses only as a cover the atmosphere of human defenselessness implicit in any dream (it is this frailty which Giovanni Della Casa probably had in mind when in his well-known *Galateo* he blamed as uncouth those who are in the habit of always telling others about their dreams). This *human* experience is the rhetorical *captatio benevolentiae* introducing the really important strategy, the one embodied in the *human-ist* subtext: which, by way of its erudite hint to Heraclitus' paronomasia (one among several such strategies in the text, to be sure) coolly selects the appropriate readers. The ideological layer represented by the Alberti text for Heraclitus is characteristic of a fastidious *gradus ad Parnassum*: a stately, refined, somewhat archaeological evocation of the classical roots.

I have thus given an idea of the basic stages in the contextualization of Heraclitus' text, from his quasicontemporaries, through the Alexandrian philologists and then the Renaissance, to the twentieth-century authors. This work may look arid and prosaic, but (as noted) it is the only path to analysis as a solid and at the same time critical activity. We have seen how the apparently compact picture is, in reality, the result of a series of coats of paint: so many successive ideological layers that must be critically identified, listed, analyzed. As noted, I consider that the preceding pages have shown how many are the layers still to be studied, and at the same time (this being their constructive aspect) that future analyses will fill out lines which have been already drawn in the preceding pages.

A last remark on this point, to show how numerous and delicate are the frames, or citational levels, which contextualize this text:[36] Heraclitus' text comes to us as part of a citation, or better, of a family of citations—and we have seen the several delicate implications of this fact. What remains to be added is that the citational text within the text may hide a depth more considerable than the one which has been described: for Heraclitus may be quoting here a statement by another philosopher. We would, then, have a philologist (a series of philologists) quoting Heraclitus quoting another philosopher; like this (in one of the already discussed two versions):

"'The name of the bow, then, ⟪life⟫; but its work: death,'"

Or alternatively (if we consider *oûn* as the citator's insertion):

"''The name of the bow,' then, '⟪life⟫; but its work: death.'"

Whereas the double quotes represent the frame of the late Greek citator, the single quotes symbolize the frame constituted by Heraclitus quoting somebody close to him in time, and the guillemets designate the hypostasis of the lexical item for 'life' which is foregrounded as such (that is, as a piece of language to be examined—thus transforming the language of the rest of the text into a metalanguage, as I have explained above).

But there is a last possibility to be considered, which does not change the notational structure of this text, but does change its cognitive and cultural situation: it might be that Heraclitus *is quoting himself*. That is, it might be the case that Heraclitus is quoting something that he had previously said or written, and that now he wants to put into a new perspective. As I said, this would not change the arrangement of the quotation marks, but it would change their semiotic value.

Finally, I repeated above the "bare" translation which I submitted at the beginning; but this is not meant to discourage more extended paraphrases. Paraphrases, rather than being revelations of the glaring inadequacy of any criticism and any commentary with respect to the uniqueness of the original text—constitute the essential instrument for a critical translation (cf. Valesio 1976*b*) and demystification of the ideological layerings on the text. One such paraphrasis is submitted here, not as being perfect, but as one among several possibilities for gathering up into a symbol (in the theological sense of *summary*—of the basic tenets of a confession or creed) most of the connotations analyzed above:

> The bow which is called "life," the bow which serves to sustain our livelihood (and actually, we also refer to it by the synonym of "arbalest," as if suggestive of "life"): indeed, death operates continually in it, and its very work is death.

Such a paraphrasis does not hide—on the contrary, it explicitly declares—its complex of heterogeneous sources, from ancient philology to modern dialectic. One could still go on, of course, but at this point really not much of significance could be added. I have concluded, then, my contextualization of Heraclitus' microtext, as well as the critical review of several contextualizations which the fragment underwent through the centuries.

Thus the theory of rhetoric I have presented here confirms its function as orientation for the semiotic analysis of discourse. In such an analysis, a new approach to literary criticism has emerged.

Notes

I. WHAT AND WHY: THE ONTOLOGY

1. I am, of course, aware that the distinctions I just proposed are reelaborations of actual English usage: they do not simply reflect it. Thus *rhetorics* seems to be a neologism, and the difference between *rhetorician* and *rhetor* is one of register (the latter term is obsolete, the former still current), rather than the semantic one I proposed. But all this was to be expected: some adjustment is always necessary between a metalanguage and its object language, and to be conservative with respect to the introduction of new words does not mean to limit oneself to a passive reflection of the current, necessarily informal and vague, use of words. The attempt here is to strike a balance between the need for consistency and systematicity in the presentation of a new theory, and the avoidance of an excessive number of terminological innovations.

As for this distinction in other languages, in Italian the only current forms are *retorica* and the agent noun *retore*—this latter with negative connotations. True, there is an old phonological variant *rettorica* (that Croce still used), and the adjective *retorico* is on record as having been sometimes used as a noun; still, this is a more restricted picture than that offered by French, whose pair *rhéteur* and *rhétoricien* is at the root of the quoted English pair, and which can boast, beside substantivized (ancient) *rhétorique*—parallel to Italian *retorico* an an agent noun—also *rhétoriqueur* (this last term having, as we shall see, a peculiar usage).

2. An example in *corpore vili* (based, that is, on the present writing): the use of the first person throughout this book raises a—still not adequately analyzed—problem of rhetorical characterization, and (transcending the personal case) evokes the diachronic depth of most of the apparently synchronic phenomena in this field. On the one hand, the use of the first person pronoun is linked to a rhetoric of egocentrism that compares unfavorably with the rhetoric of self-effacement implicit in the *pluralis modestiae*, the "we." On the other hand, this "we" also involves the opposite rhetoric—that of the *pluralis maiestatis*, with its connotation of pomposity; thus, it is at a disadvantage with respect to the rhetoric of frank simplicity, and full assumption of responsibility, evoked by the "I" (already at this stage, dialectics, as an uninvited guest, sneaks in; it will receive its full welcome later on).

3. According to Wiley 1948, "A guess could be hazarded ... that *rhétoriqueur* began to have its present-day connotation around the end of the nineteenth century," and he points to Guy (1910) as the work that definitely fixed the reference of this term.

4. Originally a two-volume work published in French in 1958, now revised as Perelman-Tyteca 1970. In the meantime, it was translated at least into Italian (see Bobbio 1966) and English with a profusion of translators

involved (two for the English text, three for the Italian one—the latter a strange figure, in view of the modesty of the stylistic results).

5. It is not surprising, however, that one should quote in this connection also that maverick in modern American philosophy who has now acquired a semimythical status in presentations of semiotics: Charles Sanders Peirce. Here, I only want to note his stylistic and ideological awareness of what it means to use the term—an awareness that is in line with what is being described in these pages. In discussing a work in which mention is made of "rhetorical evidence" Peirce notes: "To me personally perhaps the designation gives that sort of satisfaction which so many schools have manifested in adopting appellations invented by their opponents as depreciative. For although Prof. Schroeder cannot but acknowledge the value and need of this kind of reasoning, a slight shade of disesteem seems to mingle with his approval on account of its undeniable formal imperfection. Now to me this very imperfection marks the reasoning as being drawn direct from those observational sources from whence (sic) all true reasoning must be drawn; and I have often remarked in the history of philosophy, that the reasonings that were somewhat dark and formally imperfect, often went the deepest" (*Collected Papers* vol. 2: par. 333 [= pp. 190–1], Hartshorne and Weiss 1931–58).

I have no intention of making fun of Professor Schroeder, who remains a mere name for me (Peirce's editors do not identify him)—so much the more so since an irony toward this figure could be misunderstood as an homage to that obnoxious cliché, the condescending attitude toward German so-called pedantry. However, it is impossible not to notice that the attitude that Peirce describes is still alive; once again, rhetoric must carefully steer its course between the Scylla of the logicians' diffidence (rhetoric is too informal, too "soft" and loose) and the Charybdis of the literary critics' fear (rhetoric is too "tough," to formalistic and rigid). I do not know of any modern philosopher who develops a theory of rhetoric in a systematic way (thus going beyond the brilliant concepts of Burke and the programmatic hints of Peirce) and with a critical attitude (thus reaching deeper than Perelman's description). Certainly this is not the case for Richards (1936, translated in Italian late—in 1967— and needlessly, since no critical introduction is provided), whose ambitious title is the only stylistic flaw in an otherwise impeccably written essay.

6. This does not mean that rhetoric, being a contemporary theory, must deal only with contemporary discourses and texts—indeed, this confusion would be deplorable. For clearly a contemporary theory is one that strives to make good use of those contemporary achievements in the construction of critical metalanguages that help to understand its data better; and one of the basic criteria for the acceptability of a theory as such is, of course, that it be applicable to all relevant objects (here, all discourses in their functional aspect) in all periods.

In fact, it might even be argued that ancient texts (meaning, roughly, texts no more recent than the late Renaissance in Europe) are the most important test for a developing theory like rhetoric, since they require many sustained efforts in order to gather and control the relevant information—thus reducing the dangers of arbitrariness and improvisation. Be it as it may, the focus of this research will be on ancient texts—from ancient Greece to the Renaissance. However, early modern (especially, eighteenth century) and contemporary texts will by no means be ignored. And of course, the applications of the theory are just beginning: there is ample space for experimenting with texts belonging to different historical periods.

7. On narratology one can have recourse, as to summary indications on a much larger literature, to the bibliographical notes in Segre 1974:73–77 and Eco 1976:23. The points of divergence with respect to the former author's theses appear throughout this book (see also Valesio 1972). As for the analysis of functional sentence perspective: texts like Mathesius 1936 (now in Vachek 1964:306–19) and Karcevskij 1937 bring us back to the pioneering efforts (cf. also the remarks in Vachek 1964: 18, 89, 109, 176). The Prague tradition is continued in articles like Daneš 1964, Firbas 1964, Hausenblas 1964, Beneš 1968, Palek 1968 (Svoboda 1968 and Mel'čuk and Žolkovskij 1970 can be linked to this tradition). Another parallel path is that of research in England (for instance, Halliday 1967–68). Yet another parallel is that with one strand of American linguistics as it appears, for instance, in Hatcher 1956a and 1956b (the latter available now in Householder 1972), in Hockett (1958:201ff.), and Whitehall in Wermuth 1964 (also in rather vague remarks in Jackendoff 1972:29–46, and more specifically in Kuno 1975; in a sense, also in Kuroda 1973).

8. The connection between the several apparently different lines of research begins to become clear: in order to introduce the "American" discipline of discourse analysis I echoed the "British" description by Halliday 1970, explaining what he calls the *textual* function (we will see below why the term "text" is misleading in this connection), that enables the speaker or writer to construct "connected passages of discourse that is situationally relevant; and enables the listener or reader to distinguish a text from a random set of sentences." This function is flanked by two others: the *ideational* one (expressing the "speaker's experience of the real world, including the inner world of his own consciousness") and the *interpersonal* one (pertaining to "the expression of social rules, which include the communication rules created by language itself"). True, there is something too mechanic, too easily reassuring, in these partitions; and the pages that follow will try to express the actual tension behind such divisions. But we cannot afford the luxury of ignoring the existing taxonomies, and of not thinking in taxonomic terms—taxonomy has been a "dirty word" for too long, with bad results for literary and linguistic studies.

9. For discourse analysis, the pioneering text seems to have been the diptych by Harris 1952a (the first part is reprinted in Dubois and Sumpf 1969—one of the few links between the English and the French rhetorical modes of textual descriptions). The most lucid continuation of this line of research that I know of is Longacre 1958—a name that brings us to tagmemics, which has been the structuralist "school" most active in the analysis of discourse (although Pike 1967:146 disagrees with the quoted article by Harris). Let us recall: Longacre again (1968), West 1973 and Pike himself (1944, 1964a, 1969—the last two now in Brend 1972a—and 1964 in Brend 1974:289–305). Brend 1974 contains other relevant articles: by Ballard, Conrad, and Longacre; by Klammer and Compton; by Larsen. Some other articles and collections along these lines are: Gudschinsky 1959, Koen et al. 1969, and Koen 1967, Loos 1963, Powlison 1965, Rodgers 1966, Becker

1966a, and in Kreidler 1966, Jacobson in Garvin and Spolsky 1966, Reid et al. 1968, Hale 1973, Trail 1973. (Several unpublished essays and dissertations are also quoted in the articles just cited.) Bibliographical indications are to be found in Pike 1966 (on discourse analysis see pp.:372–73, 386–87, 388–89, 391), as well as in Brend 1970 and 1972b. Some anthropological parallels are to found in Fischer (in Wallace 1960), and in Dundes 1962; Doležel 1972 may also be recalled.

For all the activity in tagmemics, one should not forget stratificational contributions (like Lamb 1966 and Gleason in Makkai and Lockwood 1973, Taber 1966, Cromack 1968), contributions more explicitly connected with narratology (although these links are present also in the above-quoted essays) like Labov and Waletzky in Helm 1967, Colby in Garvin 1970, Banfield 1973, and transformationally oriented contributions, like Georges 1970 (for folklore), Sadock 1970, Smith 1971, Ruhl 1973. There are also attempts at compromises (like Belasco 1964, oscillating between tagmemics and transformational grammar), critical reviews of problems (like Bierwisch 1965 and Hendricks 1973); and several analyses that are even more difficult to label than the preceding ones, like Sprang-Hanssen 1956, Stempel 1964, Sachs 1967, Christensen in Love and Payne 1969, Kinneavy 1971, Baxtin 1971, Enkvist 1974.

10. Introductory texts and collections of readings abound: Bense (1962 and 1969), Koch (1969 and 1973), Stempel 1971, Schmidt (1970 and 1973), Petöfi (1971 and 1973, 1974 with Rieser, 1973 with Franck, Dressler 1972 (Italian translation 1975), Kallmeyer et al. 1974, Breuer 1974 and Dähl 1974. To this one should add monographs and programs (like Weinrich 1972 and van Dijk 1972), and articles (like Harweg 1968, Oomen 1969, Hartmann 1968, Kummer 1972, Bellert 1970, Lang in Kiefer and Ruwet 1974). Gardin 1974 offers intelligent criticism, although he is needlessly shrill.

11. Robinson 1972 is a good introduction to this field—but, once again, its narrowness must be corrected with the typology of parallel studies that is being presented here. To the bibliographical indications, then, contained in this work (like Davitz 1964, Ervin-Tripp in Gumperz and Hymes 1964, Vetter 1969, Fishman 1965, Schegloff 1968, Soskin and John in Barker 1963) one should add others; noting, for instance, that discourse analysis has from its beginnings (see Harris 1952b, and see now Harris 1963) been open to the study of the anthropological and social connections of discourse: and cf. now Wise, and Bock, in the quoted Brend 1974 and 1972, respectively); and Albert 1964. See also the sociolinguistic investigations in Hovland et al., 1953 and 1957, and Slama- Cazacu 1961.

12. For content analysis see the presentation by Riley and Stoll 1968, with a bibliography that, however, should be supplemented at least by: Lasswell, Lerner and Pool 1952, Bech 1955, Holsti in Lindzey and Aronson 1968, v.2), Gipper 1963, and Gerbner et al. 1969. More recently Faye 1973 offers a stimulating (and not too clearly organized) example of content analysis sui generis (with a saber-rattling rhetoric).

13. For hermeneutics, see Gadamer 1965 (and now 1975) and his American interpreter, Palmer 1969 (a critical assessment of the trend in Tatham 1973). But the danger of complacent obfuscation lies elsewhere, in the flowering of cryptic references to discourse of which Derrida—who has

moved from the diligent and very academic sobriety of his 1967 book to the narcissism of pieces like his 1975 article—is one of the best-known examples, although he is not the only representative. More controlled—but still too glad to veer into the mist at every occasion—are Chabrol and Marin 1974, and Marin 1975. There is now a whole constellation of collections of articles and essays (for instance: Léon et al. 1971, Avalle 1973, Greimas 1973, Grize 1974, *Langages* 31 (1973), etc.) on such problems. All this line of work must be considered with attention, although we are still too often confronted with ideological pronouncements that queerly oscillate between an ideology of scientism and an ideology of irrationalism.

14. If I may be allowed, apropos of such studies, a brief excursion on native grounds: Valesio 1968 is the first example in Italy of something that can be called rhetorical criticism (as distinct from stylistic criticism on the one hand, historiography of rhetoric on the other). A critically retrospective look at that book reveals (among other flaws) the limitation implicit in confining rhetoric to the study of figures. It must also be noted, however, that no other large-scale effort has yet been made in this direction of rhetorical criticism, and that this particular limitation persists also in the recent works that are related to this line of research (useful as such analyses are), like Agosti 1974 and Beccaria 1975; see also Traina 1977. Of course, such studies are not exclusive to the Italian scene—but as noted (and the reader will probably breathe a sigh of relief at this) detailed bibliographical indications on the international research along these lines will be given at the relevant points in the rest of the book.

15. Thus for the fourth time, if I am not mistaken, that crucible of fundamental experiments—Eastern Europe, especially the milieus of Moscow and Prague—comes into the picture: it was evoked apropos of narratology, quoted again for the analysis of functional sentence perspective, hinted at with respect to formalism; and now the two most recent presentations of textology I know of refer to that nucleus of experiences; from the first pages of his book Laufer 1972 locates the constitution of textology as an autonomous discipline in the Soviet Union of the first decades of this century. And on a more restricted scale, the postwar Prague school appears as one of the centers of textological works (see fn. on pp. 145–46 of Červenka's article "Textologie und Semiotik" in Martens and Zeller 1971). Once again, the function of the scholar is, first of all, that of weaving the apparently different strands of research together. I am not advocating eclecticism: I am talking, much more simply, of acquiring a reasonable range of information, against the recurrent temptation of parochialism.

Thus Laufer 1972 notes the apparent lack of communication between Russian textology and Anglo-American *material bibliography*; on the other hand, he himself (*salvo errore*) does not deal with the flourishing German tradition represented by collections like the quoted one by Martens and Zeller; and in its turn, the latter seems to be (with the exception of the quoted article) the compact expression of a German group (although the texts considered do not all pertain to German literature). At any rate, some efforts at keeping the lines of communication open are still being made: see the review article by Anglade 1972.

16. The leaves of Burke's books are indeed scattered around in some

confusion: collections are rearranged and reedited, titles overlap, prefatory remarks on these matters are either nonexistent or too vague. A useful bibliography of this author is Frank and Frank in Rueckert 1964:495–512. This latter collection is the strangest *Festschrift* I ever saw. Burke must have appeared, still at that date, as the tainted wether of the flock, because the collection includes (for "balance") a considerable amount of venom and trivialities side by side with serious assessments.

17. There are aspects of Bentham's work, like his *Book of fallacies* (Bowring 1838–43) and his analysis of political sophisms (in Crespi 1947) that are directly relevant to rhetoric (for his linguistic discussions in general, see Ogden 1932). As far as Nietzsche is concerned, see Goth 1970.

As for the psychologists: the narrow-minded concentration on Freud, in those literary and linguistic studies that deal with the deep analysis of the psyche, is a problem in itself, that would require a separate treatment (detailing, among other things, the ideological elements—a relatively more "tough" scientific aura, liberal imagery, etc.—that condition this preference). But the typological expansion of linguistic and literary studies will, I believe, soon recognize more explicitly that the most significant psychological guidelines for these studies (much as they are open to discussion) are those established by Jung. The collocation of Jung side by side with Marx may appear—to traditional secular as well as to traditional religious pieties—a much more shocking antithesis. The fact is that the times are more than mature for the comparative discussion of these two systems of thinking, not as an exercise in paradox or archaeology, but as a direct contribution to a theory of human discourse.

II. THE COMMONPLACE AS THE COMMON PLACE

1. "Implicit in a perspective there are two kinds of questions: (1) what to look for, and why; (2) how, when, and where to look for it. The first could be called ontological questions; the second, methodological" (Burke 1973:68). It is not uninteresting that these very questions, and in these shapes, belong to the equipment of classical rhetoric; they are thus particularly appropriate to designate procedures in the rhetorical perspective.

2. For instance: "Every concrete empirical objectivity, together with its material essence, finds its proper place within a *highest* material genus, a '*region*' of empirical objects. To the pure regional essence belongs then a *regional eidetic science*, or as we also say, a *regional ontology*," etc. (Husserl 1972, sec. 9; italics in original).

3 "Idealism!": one feels it hovering in the air, about to be slapped on—this label that still is capable of stirring emotions; especially in the context of the present research, which takes place mostly on Romance grounds and elaborates certain aspects of Marxist reflection. Idealism, long dominant in the history of Romance linguistics (see Iordan and Orr 1937) has been attacked in modern times (from within this field of study), and rightly so, for that aspect in it that leads to vagueness and indifference vis-à-vis the scientific analysis of linguistic structure. As for the Marxist tradition, its anti-idealistic rhetoric is more than well known. This writer's attitude will become clearer in the course of the pages that follow; but already at this point his una-

bashedly revisionistic stance is revealed by his being not particularly embarrassed by the label of Idealism.

One word more: the linguistic tradition influenced by Idealism (especially the Italian one) seems to have, by and large, watered down the strength of Idealist thought. In particular, it has taken from Croce's work one of its weakest aspects—its obscurantist hostility toward precise classifications and detailed analyses of structures; on the other hand, it does not seem to have developed enough its most interesting challenge—namely, the refusal to see a direct and simple link between language and reality. Thus, for instance, Devoto 1951 (one of the extremely few modern books on historical linguistics that is seriously committed to a general reflection on history) views institutions—linguistic and nonlinguistic—in a straightforwardly realistic way that would not be particularly strange in other philosophical traditions, but that—coming as it does in the wake of crucial Idealist debates on language—cannot but appear rather simplistic.

4 I retranslated all quotes from Aristotle, going back to Ross 1969; but I kept constantly in mind the translation by W. Rhys Roberts in Solmsen 1954. I believe that this retranslation (done with attention to the microscopic detail) was necessary—indeed, the features of what could be labeled a microscopic, or analytic, translation, will be noted at the relevant points. Here I want to emphasize that the work was done with the proper humility, and respect for the intricacy of philosophic Greek, and being aware that this is but a minuscule part of a very large forest.

5. "In the comic genre he [the poet] diminishes them [these relationships] and puts them below men; and in the tragic genre, he strains them in order to make them heroic, and thus he puts them above mankind. Thus, such relationships never are at human measure, and in the theatre we always look at beings who are not really our fellow-creatures. Let me add that this divergence is so true and so clearly recognized that Aristotle makes a rule of it in this *Poetics*: 'Comedy tries to imitate men as worse than they are now, and tragedy tries to imitate them as better.' Isn't this a well-conceived imitation, whose object is something that doesn't really exist, and that, suspended between lack and excess, discards what actually exists as if it were a useless thing?" (This, from Rousseau's *Lettre à D'Alembert*, Launay 1967:82). The lively irony of this rhetoric acquires a sadder—more self-righteous?—inflection in Trilling 1972:87 who, strangely, fails to mention that his statement there is a paraphrase of the quoted one by Rousseau.

6. One of the most common devices used in defense of the status quo in the history of rhetoric is that which consists in overwhelming the reader with a mass of bibliographical references, pointing to several historical analyses of rhetorical theories and performances, as if this would be the answer to the need for an ontologically new and critical approach. Now—aside from the fact that one should distinguish between repetitions and first-hand discoveries—it should be clear by now that such a response is not sufficient. This, of course, does not mean that such historical treatments are useless; they are actually indispensable, and the indications that follow are meant as a recognition of the large basis available even now (for all the need we still have of modern editions of rhetorical texts) for the elaboration of the new history of rhetorics *and* of rhetoric. These indications are not, of course, exhaustive;

and at any rate they exclude from the start a documentation about the various modern editions of ancient, medieval, and Renaissance treatises. Also, I will confine myself to a simple hint as to the availability of anthologies (such as Benson and Prosser 1972, Miller, Prosser, and Benson 1973) and of bibliographical panoramas (for instance, the "Bibliography of rhetoric and public address" which appeared in the *Quarterly Journal of Speech* 1947–1951, then in *Speech Monographs* 1952–1969 and, from 1970 on, as the "Bibliographical Annual" published by the *Speech Association of America*; some more limited efforts are the scanty sketch by Rastier 1972 and also Reid 1960, Haberman and Clears 1964, Serial 1969, Murphy 1971, Bitzer and Black 1971 and—more specialistic—Schneyer 1969. As for journals devoted to this field, some of them have just been mentioned; one should add to them *Philosophy and Rhetoric* (note that all these are North American journals; I do not know of a European journal, or a similar publication in other continents, completely devoted to rhetorical research—a reminder that European scholarship should not be too complacent in viewing its special link with the rhetorical tradition). As for repertories of rhetorical terminologies, I will not mention them here, for let us not forget that what interests us at this point are sketches and discussions of the history of rhetorics.

Efforts in this direction are as early as (for instance) Volkmann 1885 and 1901, Chaignet 1888 or Bornecque 1898 (1902), or Sabbadini's 1891 article, or the essay by Croce 1903 (and see Menapace-Brisca 1952), and more generically, Saintsbury 1905. Also at the beginning of the century we find Navarre 1900, Suess 1910; and then Clark 1922 and 1957, and the standard cycle by Baldwin—beginning in 1924 and 1928, concluded in 1939. Nor should one forget works like Solmsen 1931 (see also his 1941 work), Winkler 1931, and standard references—with a scope broader and more vague than that of rhetoric proper—like Jaeger 1934, and Curtius 1948 (later 1963). The next wave can be represented by writings like Fries 1940, Wallace 1943, and more indirectly Atkins 1943 (see also 1951, and 1966), and articles like Wilcox 1942, the over-estimated McKeon 1942 (in Crane 1970, then in Schwartz and Rycenga 1965) and 1946 (and before, there had been articles like Haskins 1929, Charland 1936, and monographs like Söter 1937); nor should Funaioli's 1946 essay be forgotten. In all these (as noted) erudition counts for more than originality of vision, and the following historiography—although, of course, more up to date on several technical aspects—is not appreciably more critical (Della Volpe 1954 symbolizes some philosophical possibilities). Let us recall, beside works only indirectly relevant like Marache 1952 and Wellek 1955, more pertinent contributions like Clarke 1953, Bolgar 1954, Rostagni 1955, Webster 1956, Fourny 1953, Howell 1956 (see also 1971), Barwick 1957, Perelman and Tyteca 1958a, and—more generically—Wimsatt and Brooks 1957; also, several articles, like Nadeau 1959 and Munteano 1959 (rather weak), to which others should probably be added; mention should also be made of studies like Rossi in Banfi 1953, Ong 1958.

We come now to our decades: and to writings like Michel 1960, Tateo 1960, Vallese 1962, Howes 1961 and (less directly) Weinberg 1961; to broad assessments like Kennedy 1963 and Leeman 1963, to general vistas like Marrou 1964. Barthes 1966 is (as usual) stimulating, but also (as often) rather thin; let us also recall: Dockhorn 1965 (see also 1968), Fussell 1965 and de Pater

1965. More recently, we have had: introductory, and tame, outlines like Plebe 1968 and Dixon 1971, and diligent but unoriginal reviews of problems like Seigel 1968 and Florescu 1971 and 1970. I should also mention: Davidson 1965, Pinborg 1962 and 1967, Morpurgo-Tagliabue 1968, Thompson 1968, Vasoli 1968, and (more generally) Pfeiffer 1968 (and, of course, articles and essays: Chevrier 1966, Santini 1968, and so forth). What are the developments of the seventies? Serious, well-informed essays are perhaps more numerous than ever, but we are still far from a really critical approach. Struever 1970 remains slightly out of focus, but she injects in her research a contemporary liveliness and relevance that is remarkably absent from, for instance, Trimpi's long essays (1971 and 1974); very useful, and impressive in their erudition, their approach however is rather frigid. Bonebakker 1970 and Oliver 1971 point to the urgent need for rhetorical research to get out of Western European parochialism; Murphy 1974 gives us (in line with the above-criticized tradition) a solid—but ultimately archaeological—collection of important data (cf. also, in a more restricted domain, Scaglione 1972— apropos of which, see Valesio 1974). I also want to recall: Vickers 1970, Faulhaber 1972, Sider 1971, France 1972, as well as various articles and essays (Gallo 1971 and 1974 and also: McCall 1969, Jaffe 1974, and so forth).

An "arid" list? Rather, the indispensable documentation, in order to avoid the danger of confusing the contemporary critical approach (that I advocate) with an attitude of hurried unawareness.

7. The quote is from Althusser (1965:24, et passim); here, Gaston Bachelard is indicated—without specific reference—as the source of this concept. This indication does not imply my agreement with the way Althusser employs this notion of *coupure épistémologique* for Marxist thought—and what I am thinking of is a general, not a local, divergence. In other words, it might very well be that—with Althusser's system—the *coupure* divides "Marx's thought in two essential periods: the still 'ideological' period, anterior to the break in 1845, and the 'scientific' period following this 1845 break" (ibid., 26); and so forth and so on. But what rhetorics as such calls into question is the degree to which a system like Marxism in its standard version can be considered as a science rather than an ideology. Marxism is still essentially an ideology, and any scientific development of it requires a choice among its components, with the inevitable attending sacrifices in terms of breadth and safety of positions. One has, for instance, to withstand the attacks of an oversimple structuralistic rhetoric (quite frequent in antistructuralist quarters, like for instance certain varieties of Marxist criticism), asserting that the system must be implemented and discussed as a whole—a move that, if followed, leads the scholar right back into the ideology out of which he was trying to move. For no choice can shun the burden of revisionism—on the contrary, it must gladly take it up; and the present proposal is no exception: it constitutes a neoskeptical type of revisionism.

8. Once again, this does not mean that the historical context should be ignored; and this is why I will concisely locate each one of the preceding quotes, in the order in which they appear. The "objective logic" one is to be found in *CP* 1: par. 444 [= pp. 241–2], while the tripartition of symbols is in *CP* 1: 559 [= pp. 259–60], where the other two types of symbols are the *terms* ("which directly determine only their grounds or imputed qualities") and the

propositions ("which also independently determine their *objects* by means of other term or terms"). The term *methodeutic* (together with a more suggestive label, "transuasional logic") is suggested in *CP* 2: 93 [= p. 52]; apropos of terms: in a letter of 1908, Peirce recalls that in 1867 he proposed the term universal rhetoric for the study of "the relations of signs to their Interpretants" (Wiener 1958:403). As for the statement on "pure rhetoric," it also comes at the end of a tripartition, in a passage (*CP* 2: 229 [= pp. 135–6]) that is also reproduced in Buchler 1956:99 and is taken up again—without a subsequent development—in Derrida 1967:71. On the other hand, the term "speculative rhetoric" is what appears in the Professor Schroeder discussion quoted in the first chapter, note 5. Finally, the indication of "formal rhetoric" comes in a context which—among the quoted ones—is the one most suggestive of linguistic analysis. "It would be a mistake," Peirce notes, to consider this rhetoric "to be a matter of psychology." And a little later on he notes that "the *Grundsatz* of Formal Rhetoric is that an idea should be presented in a unitary, comprehensive, systematic shape. Hence it is that many a diagram which is intricate and incomprehensible by reason of the multiplicity of its lines is instantly rendered clear and simple by the addition of more lines, these additional lines being such as to show that those that were there first were merely parts of a unitary system" (*CP* 4: 116 [= pp. 87–8]). An observation like this marks a step forward with respect to the still widespread indifference toward the aesthetic structure of scientific discourse, and similar types of discourse. On the other hand, a properly realistic and catholic appreciation of the structural variety of literary discourse (of which we already saw some examples, and will see more later) makes us avoid normative and simplificatory statements, like the abstract stipulation that an idea should be present in a "unitary shape."

9. Just one example of this kind of derivation. "The author cannot choose whether to use rhetorical heightening. His only choice is of the kind of rhetoric he will use," we read in a still much-quoted book (Booth 1973:116). True; but this insight should not be limited to literary authors, and should not remain in the area of a basically traditional kind of literary criticism. And in fact there is no reason why we should see it in such a narrow way, for this is only the echo of earlier and bolder analyses (I am not speaking here, let me make this clear, of passive imitation or plagiarism; I am speaking of the watering down of a certain critical discourse as a phenomenon that transcends the personalities of the single scholars involved, and in fact evokes a set of changes in the politics of culture, in and out of American universities).

Here is one of those earlier statements about the various ways in which one can communicate an event in real life (say, a disaster) to somebody else: "in every one of these cases I have communicated 'the fact'. Yet . . . there are many different *styles* in which I can communicate this 'fact.' The question of 'realistic accuracy' is not involved . . . I have simply made a choice among possible styles—*and I could not avoid such a choice*. There is no 'unstylized' feature here except the disastrous event itself (and even that may have a 'stylistic' ingredient, in that it may be felt as more of a blow if coming at a certain time than if it had come at a certain other time—a 'stylistic' matter of timing that I, as the imparter of the information, may parallel, in looking for the best or worst moment in which to impart my information" (Burke 1973:127; italics in the original). The scruple with which I quote this critic will, I trust, eliminate any suspect of exhibitionism if I note that I had applied the term *stylization* to the way in which the topoi structure objective reality before reading this analysis. What follows in this book is, among other things, an attempt to make this concept more systematic and precise.

10. 'Truth must be naked, and the more it is naked, the more it attracts. And in fact we saw that the apostles, thanks to naked and simple truth, were more attractive and powerful than the orators with their fine words and their speeches brimming with eloquence. Naked truth attracts men toward that against which their mere reason would revolt—and this attraction no orator could ever have worked, with his skill and eloquence.'

11. The word *dittology* is, I hasten to note, not alien to English, although its normal meaning ('A twofold or double meaning or interpretation') is different; and the same difficulty exists in the case of *dittography*, 'The unintentional repetition of a letter or word, or series of letters or words, by a copyist' (as usual, definitions not otherwise marked are taken from *OED*). Italian *dittologia*, on the other hand, has essentially the meaning described in the main text. As far as English is concerned, one could speak of a synonymic *pair* (or *couple*, or *binomial*). However, I believe that *dittology* is preferable, because of a criterion that—let me state it here once and for all—guides terminological choices throughout this book: in cases of terminological oscillations, the calques of words in the Classical languages (Classical Latin and Ancient Greek) are preferred to their more modern equivalents. Furthermore, in the case of a choice between a Latin and a Greek calque, the latter language is preferred. The reason: Classical words can provide a terminology that is more unitary and easily translatable, less conditioned by the peculiarities of the many different modern languages. Now, it is urgent to bring rhetorical taxonomy (and not only terminologically, but also substantially) to the same balance of sophisticated detail within a unified framework that taxonomies in other fields (botany, zoology, medicine, etc.) already possess. As for the preference for Greek, it might appear as a needless complication for the reader; but precisely the fact that the Greek or Greek-based terms are less familiar than the Latin ones is an advantage for a scientific, descriptive classification: for in this way one avoids the historically secondary connotations that have acquired a dominant role in many of the Latinate words, making of them current words in the language (charged with psychological innuendos and ethical judgments) rather than terms in the metalanguage of rhetoric. The latter point—one of the few clear remarks in an otherwise quaint booklet—is implicit in the choice of Chaneles and Snyder (1972:15), who correctly prefer difficult but psychologically neutral Greek terms like Bdelygmia and Aposiopesis to their Latin equivalents—Abominatio and Reticentia, respectively—that are "to close to English to avoid unwarranted meanings or feelings" (the problem is, I add, essentially the same for French, Italian, and many other languages). For analyses of the binomial structure see also Möntmann 1955, Malkiel 1959, now 1970, Valesio 1968.

12. 'Some say, that in other Cities of *Greece* they went to seeke for Rhetoricians, for Painters, and for Musicians; whereas in *Lacedemon*, they sought for Law-givers, for Magistrates, and Generals of armies: In *Athens* men learn'd to say well, but here, to doe well: there to resolve a sophisticall argu-

ment, and to confound the imposture and amphibologie of words, captiously enterlaced together; here to shake off the allurements of voluptuousnesse, & with an undanted courage to contemne the threats of fortune, and reject the menaces of death: those busied and laboured themselves about idle words, these after martiall things: there the tongue was ever in continuall exercise of speaking, here the minde in an uncessant practice of well-doing' (Florio 1603, I. 24; and in Stewart 1931:137).

13. There is no space and opportunity here, of course, for developing an analysis of the relationships between this scene and the rest of the play, much less to do full justice to the varied gamut of critical opinion on *King Lear* and its characters (see the selections appended to Furness 1880 and Quinn 1970 and, more richly, Bonheim 1962 and Kermode 1970). But I am aware that I am not the first to see in Cordelia something less (something more) than lily-white candor set against the blackness of her sisters. However, I trust that the difference is clear between the rhetorical analysis proposed here, and an approach that remains basically moralistic, and that can be exemplified by the following remarks: "She [Cordelia] is proud of being in the right, in contrast with her vulgar sisters, and this feeling she opposes to her sisters and to her old father. The weak old father has a right to a few flattering expressions from a loving child, because he needs them. She offers him, on the contrary, what he cannot bear, the truth . . . love is essentially a lie, not a truth, and Cordelia misbehaves like her sisters, only in a different way, by egoism and lovelessness. One for whom she does not tell a little lie, she does not love as she should" (quoted in Furness 1880:17).

Thus is a rich and finely textured Renaissance tapestry degraded into an embroidered centerpiece for the drawing room. Here we are at the peak of rhetorical tradition, where (behind the archaic scenery of the origins, of the mythological history of England, a scenery that should not deceive us for a moment) the real, political, struggle takes place between different and equally sophisticated rhetorical strategies—the heirs of Savonarola and Machiavelli, of the verbal–intellectual wars between Reformers and Counterreformers, and so forth. And the brilliant representatives of such eloquence are called "vulgar"! and the whole subtle fight is reduced to the banality of bourgeois admonition: oh, why could she not utter "a few flattering expressions," condescend to "a little lie"?

14. Just an illustration—from that summa of mediaeval poetry ripening into fall:

> Chi poria mai pur con parole sciolte
> dicer del sangue e de le piaghe a pieno
> ch'i'ora vidi, per narrar più volte?
> Ogne lingua per certo verria meno
> per lo nostro sermone e per la mente
> c'hanno a tanto comprender poco seno.
>
> (Dante 1. 28. 1–6; Petrocchi 1966–67)

'Who ever could, even if he were to tell it in prose, express in full the blood and wounds that I then saw—even if he would present several forms of his account? For sure, every tongue would fail, because of the limits of our language and our mind, too small to comprehend all this.'

15. In both cases it is a matter of intensifying *certain features*, and not of

intensification versus weakening; or, to put it differently, the opposition is—as noted—one of upward versus downward, not of increase versus decrease. In this case, the Greek definition of Hyperbole in *HR* 909–10 is particularly to be kept in mind, when it speaks of Hyperbole as "a linguistic expression lifting up actual truth for purposes of praise or disparagement"—which makes it clear that it is not the concepts of 'increase' and 'decrease' but, as written, those of 'praise' and 'disparagement' that should be used to translate *aúksēsis* and *meíōsis*, respectively. Analogously, it is often forgotten that all basic kinds of discourses, including the epideictic—that is usually identified only with its encomiastic aspect—have a positive *and a negative* side; we have read above how Aristotle, apropos of the epideictic genre, says that "for those who praise *or blame* (*pségousin*), the concern is for what is noble versus what is base (*aiskhrón*)" (emphases mine).

16. This folk-etymology is not more objectionable (indeed it is much more authoritative) than the one that Heidegger (1962:57), apparently spurning this and other antecedents, puts forward with assurance: "The Greek words for 'truth' (*hē alétheia, tò alēthés*) are compounded of the privative prefix *a-* ('not') and the verbal stem *-lath-* ('to escape notice,' 'to be concealed'). The truth may thus be looked upon as that which is un-concealed, that which gets discovered or uncovered ('*entdeckt*')." The dangers of this etymologizing (a realization, as we are going to see below, of the Topos of Iconicity) are made clear even by this small illustration: operating with the same morpho-lexical elements, the quoted philosophers arrive—if I understand them correctly—at opposite semantic interpretations: for the ancient one is emphasizing the 'un-concealment' as a normal, public *state* of truth—that, then, is what is normally *not* concealed; while the modern thinker seems to emphasize the laborious *process* by which truth—that therefore, presumably, is normally concealed—is uncovered! In the former case, then, we have a public, rhetorical, "commonplace" interpretation, in the latter on the contrary, a private, secretive view of truth.

Nor is this the end of the possible semantic combinations; for I do not think that I am splitting hairs when I note a still different interpretation of the Greek etymon in the following remark on one aspect of Plato's thought, apropos of "a close link between the theory of *anámnēsis* and the doctrine of manifest truth: if, even in our depraved state of forgetfulness we see the truth, we cannot but recognize it as the truth. So, as the result of *anámnēsis*, truth is restored to the status of that which is not forgotten and not concealed (*alēthés*): it is that which is manifest" (Popper 1963:10). Further discussions on *alétheia* are quoted in Vitali 1971:54.

17. The refinements with which this cluster of concepts is implemented, and which we subliminally perceive as readers even without a conscious rhetorical analysis—this is why the Shakespeare canon is perhaps the largest repository of well-worn idioms in English—should not escape our conscious scrutiny as rhetoricians. The "sharp" (in homage to the etymology of the *oksús* component in *oksúmōron*) points of this oxymoron are the two words belonging to the same semantic field: "glad" and "liking"; and the immediate succession of two almost identical sentences with the same meaning is relieved by syntactic Variatio: *I haue not* versus *not to haue* (in the same line); that is: different position of *not*, finite versus infinite form of the verb *to have*.

18. It was only when the analysis was completed that I became ac-

quainted with two articles that develop some aspects of the two rhetorics I analyzed, and I was glad to see that many of their conclusions (reached in one case through historical, in the other through psychoanalytic techniques) agree with the conclusions arrived at here through a rhetorical analysis. The analysis above has been left intact, but I think it necessary to briefly discuss here these texts. The richer and more significant analysis is clearly that by Jaffa 1957. This quote will show at a glance both the convergence and the divergence between our two kinds of analysis: "it is not impossible to ascribe to Cordelia a very shrewd selfishness in Scene i. Consider the consequences of her boldness: she was the intended bride of the 'waterish' Burgundy; but, losing her dowry, she loses a poor lover and gains a superior one, France. . . . Accordingly, Cordelia's course could be interpreted, not only as a sacrifice of public interest to private happiness, but as a clever scheme to become queen of France and England, thus defeating Lear's just policy, which is national and patriotic." Lear's "just" policy? "National and patriotic?" As we see, concrete political analysis is mixed up with ideology and simplistic moral apologetics (this is the case where the discourse of political science reveals itself as less political—and more ideological—than the discourse of rhetoric). On the other hand, we have here a concrete, really political analysis of why the two heroes had to die (a stumbling block for the emotional–moralistic criticism of the play, along the centuries): "The defeat of the French Army forces, and the unification of the kingdom under Albany is, we must observe, a political consummation which achieves all the just purposes of Lear's original plan. The survival of Lear and/or Cordelia would throw all this once more into confusion." But this realistic analysis closes with a statement where political analysis reverts to ideology, and in fact theology: "according to Shakespeare, monarchy is the understanding of the true relation of the political to the human, and of the human to the divine. Surely, such knowledge was never more needful." To go from this chilling statement to an analysis that frankly proclaims the incestuous tendencies of King Lear (Donnelly 1953) is a relief, but this line of research will have to be developed in a much more articulate way; reading psychoanalytic literature on such subjects one notes that, once again, rhetorical analysis is more appropriate and realistic. Also, a false claim must be corrected. Donnelly alleges that Freud "compares the choice of the three daughters with the situation of the suitors in *The Merchant of Venice*, but does not point out that in one case it is a man choosing a wife while in the other it is a father who is making the selection." But this is just not so, and here is Freud: "We must not be led astray by the fact that Lear's choice is between three *daughters*; this may mean nothing more than he has to be represented as an old man. An old man cannot very well choose between three women in any other way. Thus they become his daughters" (see p. 293 in "The theme of the three caskets" in 12:289–301 of Freud 1966–74).

We are thus led back to rhetorical analysis as the dominant analysis (and form of control of other methodologies) when we deal with verbal products—especially literary texts. This analysis of mine may also be seen as a response to an invitation made in Burke 1951: "Critics systematically recognized that orators employed 'topics' to 'move' audiences in the practical meaning of the word 'move' (inducing them to make practical decisions, etc.). But when they came to the analysis of poetry (with its purely aesthetic way of being 'moving'), instead of reference to topics they shifted the stress to 'imagery'. . . . 'Images,' however, are but one aspect of 'topics'. And this shift of term conceals a continuity of function. Or, otherwise put: if the topic is said to figure in the appeal when a given line of *oratory* is being analyzed, what happens to such appeal when this same line is appreciated purely as poetry? Does the *topical* appeal drop out of the case entirely? Or are such considerations retained, but in disguise, as critics focus the attention upon 'imagery', with its varying capacity for inducing moods or forming attitudes?" (italics in original). The answer to Burke's rhetorical question is clear throughout this book, in which I attempt to eliminate the "disguise" and to restore the central function of the topoi also in poetic discourse.

III. RHETORIC, IDEOLOGY, AND DIALECTIC

1. I feel justified in evoking once again this famous literary case, because modern critical treatments do not seem to me to exhaust its richness—in fact, they mark sometimes a retreat from the text. It is a pity that Burke's thumbnail sketch (now 1974b:142–45) does not refer to the philosophical tradition on this dialogue. On the other hand, the more extended and documented discussion in Trilling 1972 (27–34, 44–47, et passim) recapitulates its intellectual history, from Goethe and Hegel to Marx and Freud, but does not mention its specific development in Engels. We are informed (p. 28) that Marx made the text known to Engels, but we are not told about the brilliant development by the latter author. Even if the word "dialectical" is not absent from it (p. 47, et passim) the slim, well-written book by Trilling does not represent a dialectic approach; it rather reflects the polite frustration, the genteel refusal of the necessary brutality of any deep intellectual involvement, that are some of the most characteristic limitations of traditional literary criticism.

An example of these limitations, that amount to a strategy of antidialectic? Let me quote a case different from that of Trilling but relevant to our text. Mortier 1958–59 serves up a self-evident fact: "Engels est plus economiste que philosophe, plus politique qu'artiste." From this he proceeds to castigate the "Anti-Dühring" (see Engels 1972 [1878]) as a "texte qui confond a plaisir toutes les acceptions du mot 'dialectique'" (that, however, are not distinguished by the critic) and to note "les vues un peu courtes" of Engels apropos of Diderot. Engels had noted that "Outside philosophy in a restricted sense, the French nevertheless produced masterpieces of dialectics. We need only call to mind Diderot's *Le neveu de Rameau* and Rousseau's *Discours sur l'origine et les fondements de l'inégalité parmi les hommes*" (Engels 1882). This, we are told, is an "Analogie superficielle et jugement hâtif"; why? because, "s'il y a, dans l'oeuvre de Diderot, un corrélatif au *Discours sur l'inégalité* ce serait plutôt le *Supplement au Voyage de Bougainville*. Et comment mettre sur le même pied la critique brillante, mais negative, du *Neveu* et les tirades enflammées, la rhétorique primitiviste du *Discours*?" Even granting—for the sake of discussion—that this characterization holds, at its appropriate level (which is not the right level here), the attack fails. First of all, we are not given the context and development of Engels' appreciation, and we are going to see that they put to rest Mortier's judgment about "les vues un peu courtes" (and this by a critic who, earlier on, commenting on a passage by Marx, criticizes another author for not submitting such appreciations to a detailed analysis in their original context). In the second place, and above all: what is not understood here is the difference between a stylistic characterization, that (even if acceptable) remains at the surface of the text, and the deeper evaluation of the rhetorical structure, as sketched by Engels. The latter is not—nor did he pretend to be—an "authority" on Diderot, yet his view is more stimulating and imaginative than these pedantic specifications.

I spent some time on this article because it seems a good illustration of one of the basic defensive strategies of literary criticism in the traditional mode: faced with a broad and challenging appreciation—especially one that brings up the ideological implications of *any* form of literary analysis—the literary critic still too often tends to frantically rush and gild some lily, trying to obliterate the ideological link.

2. Italian linguistics has been particularly interesting from this point of view, elaborating what I think could be called an elegiac *storicismo*, a hothouse variety of certain strains in Idealistic philosophy. Suffice it to recall names like Giulio Bertoni, Benvenuto Terracini (on them see now, respectively, Golden 1969 and Beccaria 1970), Giacomo Devoto (see especially his little book of 1951). A systematic critique of this tradition is still needed; my book provides a system that can be used in this sense.

3. Thus in Florio, see Stewart 1931:669; see also Florio 1603 [1967]: 307 (for Montaigne's original passage, see Rat 1962:656 [*Essais* 2. 12]). Just one quibble: "weigh all, and complaine of reason" is a rather misleading translation of the original: "poisent tout, et le ramenent à la raison"—but Florio might have read this passage in a different version; and at any rate, this is but a trifle with respect to the beautiful sweep of his prose, evoking, from more than one point of view, the rhetoric of the almost contemporary Shakespearean text that I discussed above.

4. The three parameters whose misapplication produces *sukophantía*— that is, the *katà tí kaì prós tí kaì pē*—may have different translations, especially the third, which could also be translated as an interrogative adverb ('why?') or a locative adverb ('where, which way?'). Apropos of translations: Rhys Roberts (in Solmsen 1954) renders the weaker/better argument passage in a different way. He writes: "but whereas in the latter case the probability is genuine, in the former it can only be asserted in the special sense mentioned. This sort of argument illustrates what is meant by making the worse argument seem the better."

While recognizing my debt toward Rhys Robert's translation in general, I must stress the difference between the two versions here. The problem is not only with the famous dictum, which should have been put within quotes (as I did, using quotes to isolate the tradition quoted by Aristotle, and simple quotes within quotes to mark the imaginary dialogue). It is, in particular, the way the two evaluations are distributed that I find puzzling, in that translation. The *tò mèn . . . tò dè* antithesis is not unequivocal and thus it leaves to the translator the task to indicate which is which. Neither of the two translations can be proved wrong grammatically, and the only criterion is: which one is more functional to the interpretation of the text? Now, it seems clear to me that the unequivocal argument is the one concerning the weak man, while the more captious one is that which exculpates the strong assailant; whence my distribution of "former" and "latter" in the translation.

Less clear cut, but even more significant, is the translation of *hósper eíretai*. Restricting the validity of the argument to the 'special sense mentioned' is still too broad, and it makes the immediately following reference to the weaker/better tactics incomprehensible. Solmsen's alternative, proposed in a footnote: 'In the former not simply so!' is much more persuasive. With the translation I propose, on the other hand, we can better understand the role of the following sentence: what the author is saying is that the rhetorical context may make acceptable the tortuous second statement about probability.

5. As happens in some rather weak works with promising titles: for instance, Untersteiner 1950, Ramnoux 1968, Vitali 1971. This is all the more disappointing because of all the analytic work which has been done already, and which one would have hoped by now to have led to a really new assessment: general descriptions of the Sophists' activity (see Capizzi 1976), especially in its relation with rhetoric (such as Gomperz 1912, Bux 1936, Dupréel 1948, Buccellato 1950, Rostagni 1955, Buchheit 1960, Levi 1966), discussions of the relations between the Sophists (and their rhetoric) and other thinkers (e.g., Diels 1884, Bux 1941, Buccellato 1953, De Corte 1955, Adorno 1961, Coulter 1964, Elthen 1960, Sicking 1964, Brownstein 1965, etc.), analyses of their style on the background of the development of Greek prose (as in Blass 1887–98, Wundt 1903, Aly 1929, and so forth), analysis of single Sophists and critical editions of their fragments, as in the case of Protagoras (for instance, Lana 1950, Capizzi 1955), and others (see, for instance, in the case of Corax, Aulitzky 1922 and Hinks 1940)—especially, and appropriately, Gorgias (Thiele 1901, Reich 1907–1908 and 1908–1909, Sykutris 1927, Immisch 1927, Gigon 1936, Vollgraff 1952, Moreschini 1959, Segal 1962). A separate topic is that of the analysis of "sophistic" kinds of literature in later periods (as the Middle Ages: Glorieux 1925/1935, Grabmann 1940)—an analysis which deserves to be vastly increased.

6. Some works on skepticism, spanning a century of scholarship, are: Maccoll 1869, Goedeckemeyer 1905, Patrick 1929, De Lacy 1941 and 1958, Robin 1944, Dal Pra 1950, Stough 1969 (this last a detailed study of some of the main sources, which however does not offer any general perspective). As usual in this book I try—with my references—to give an idea of the vastness, richness, and long tradition of these studies—since care and respect of these traditions are the indispensable conditions for elaborating a critique which is both radical and empirically serious. However, the more the bibliographic indications, the stronger the possibility of finding lacunae. Let me repeat, then, that it is not my intention to offer a complete bibliography for each of the topics treated here—as for instance these brief allusions to the history of Greek thought, which evoke a monumental bibliography (see for some help, Adorno 1969). In particular, the history of skepticism is not, of course, confined to Greek thought: see, for instance, the historiographical work by Popkin (especially 1964).

7. Untersteiner (1949–62, 1:16) appropriately notes that such expressions should not be taken literally, but that they reflect the ancient tendency to indicate at all costs the *prôtos heuretès* ('first finder') of various sciences, techniques, devices, etc. The subsequent comment, however, that the whole history of Greek civilization had to lead, sooner or later, to the formulation of the *dúo lógoi* concept, must be qualified, for as much can be said of any notion in the history of ideas—and on the other hand, it is strange to make this

remark with regard to one of the most controversial and strongly attacked theories—beginning at least with Plato, and the series of attacks is by no means over—in the history of ideas and philosophical systems.

For my part, I note that the *prôtos heuretês* theme should be regarded as a subpart of the topos of Time Sequence; and that this sub-topos appears to be quite widespread throughout world culture—as in the case of medieval Arabic literature where (to quote one instance) an author may remark, apropos of an historical personage named Ayūb, that he was the first among the Arabs to carry that name.

8. Another interesting configuration is the one in which Gorgias seems to be a precursor also with respect to the problem of identifying the basic parameters which are necessary in order to describe, with a minimum of precision, an event: "tell . . . the place, the time, when, where, how you saw (. . . *tòn tòpon, tòn khrónon, póte, poû, pôs* . . .)" (ibid., 124). This is one of the oldest roots of such sets of questions—which are found, to name only some cases, in Aristotle (*Posterior Analytics* 2. 1. 80^b 23–25, 2. 90^2 31–34), in Cicero's already-quoted *De Inventione* (1. 8. 10 and 11. 16), in Quintilian's *Institutio Oratoria*, also quoted, with its "Sitne? Quid sit? Quale sit?" (3. 5. 5–16). Once again, differences as well as similarities should be studied in the various versions of this set. Here I would like simply to go back to Gorgias' formulation, in order to emphasize the symmetric disposition, as a linguistic implementation of the linguistic terms; and precisely: the homoeoteleuton in *tÓpOS/khrÓnOS*, and the alliteration in the last three words. Taken together, these configurations constitute what should be considered as a realization of Paromoeosis, "die höchste Steigerung der Parisosis" (*HR* 1960: par. 719 ff.)—a figure, the latter, which is traditionally associated with Gorgias.

9. Some of the ancient sources use the Greek word *antíthesis*, others the Greek *antítheton*. Lausberg's choice of the latter to designate the configuration abundantly exemplified above, while reserving the former term for phonological permutations (see *HR* index) seems unwise: for it is the term "antithesis" that is currently used to designate structures like that illustrated in Montaigne's text. As for the actual analysis of the structure, the handbook offers a relatively ample phenomenology, but the traditional treatment is inadequate, especially from the semantic point of view. For instance, none of the statements collected there is really apt as a description of the structure in the French text. It would be wrong—indeed, it would be faintly snobbish—to regard such terminological discussion as useless. In fact, given the chaotic state of terminological proliferation in the various rhetorical traditions, a minute and patient selection of the terms—choosing the most apt, weeding out duplications and confusions, and so forth—is indispensable for scientific analysis.

10. The literature on this subject is more than a century old: Janet 1848 and 1861 (the latter comparing the ancient with the modern conception), Thurot 1860. Add to these at least: Müri 1944 (specifically lexical), Rodier 1926, Goldschmidt 1947, Liebbrucks 1949, Robinson 1953, Stenzel 1972 (all concerned with Plato); while Wilpert 1956–57, Owen 1968 devote their attention to Aristotle, which is the case also with Hayden 1957 (on the theological implementation of Aristotle's thought) and de Pater 1965 (a comparison with Plato). See also Franchini 1961.

The panorama of historical research between Aristotle and Hegel seems to be less rich; let us mention: Viano 1958 (for the Stoics), Verra 1963 (on Plotinus), Preti in Banfi 1953 (for the Medieval period), Vasoli 1968 (on the Humanists), Sesmat 1955 (concerned with Christian philosophy), Salvucci 1963 (on Fichte), Vaihinger 1903 (on Kant).

11. See Michelet and Haring 1888, Adler 1927, Dürr 1938, collections like Dialectique 1956 and Dialettica 1958; and: Liebert 1929, Marck 1929–31, Sandor 1947, Heydenreich 1954, Wein 1957, Findlay 1959, Heiss 1959, Marcuse 1960, Popper 1968 [1937], Goldmann 1971. Other works will be quoted presently.

12. The standard German edition is Marx and Engels 1963, 1964–68. See references to the Marxist classics in section 3.1, and add: Engels 1941 [1888], Engels 1960, Marx 1972. A detailed bibliography is found in Rossi-Landi 1974.

13. Italy has a particularly rich tradition of analysis and discussion on dialectic, since the brilliant sets of annotations in Gramsci 1975 and the statements by Croce 1907 and Gentile 1913, to monographs and articles like: Giannantoni 1958, Della Volpe 1964, Rossi 1960–63, Dal Pra 1965, Valentini 1966, Massolo 1967, Colletti 1969, Timpanaro 1970, Corradini 1972, Luporini 1974, etc. See also Marino 1968.

But the debate is not, of course, restricted to Italy, and it does not only involve the relationship between different interpretations of the seminal concepts of dialectic, but also the relationship between the dialectical method and the several sciences. See for instance: Korsch 1966 [1923], Raphael 1934, Gonseth 1939 (whose work is also connected to the journal *Dialectica*, begun in 1947); also: Haldane 1939, Lefebvre 1947, Prenant 1948, Popper 1961 with the reply by Cornforth 1968 (and see Cornforth 1966), Gurvitch 1962, Jordan 1963, Topitsch 1964, Weil 1970, Sève 1971, the simplistic Novack 1973, and so forth.

14. French scholarship seems to have been particularly active in this concrete implementation of dialectic, probably because of the interaction between dialectic and existentialist analyses, which leads—to borrow Kierkegaard's phrase—to a lyric-dialectic attitude. Cf., for instance, Lasbax 1925–27, Bachelard 1936, Merleau-Ponty 1955 and 1956, Goldmann 1959, Sartre 1960, Fougeyrollas 1964. But see also, outside France, analyses like McKeon 1954, Merker 1971, especially Horkheimer and Adorno 1947.

15. Thus Havemann 1965—in his lively and acute pamphlet. Even more simplistic is the attempt to grasp dialectic in a unitary formulation in Sichirollo 1973:230, where (at the end of a rather too rosy outline of the progress of dialectic from the ancient Greeks to Gramsci) we are told that "reality, the social being of man" is "dialectic itself,—our being in the city of man, our willingness to understand ourselves within it, as it continually changes thanks to our activity." Thus, not only is dialectic to be looked for directly in the things—dialectic now is said to *be* the social nexus of these things. But in this way we are led back to the rather bland and generic views which had to be discarded at the beginning of this discussion. (For all that, Sichirollo's book—besides containing a bibliography which proved useful—is that rarity among introductory handbooks, especially Italian ones: a text written with flair and with a lively tone of intense participation.)

16. I hope that my zeal in criticizing the strong ideological components of dialectic in the Marxist tradition does not encourage the erroneous impression that hurriedly conciliatory syntheses are the monopoly of this intellectual trend. On the contrary, it is much easier to fall into a purely ideological compromise when the background of the research is *not* that of historical materialism. For instance, it is a little too simple to observe, of Hegelian dialectic: "Whether or not this can be demonstrated in history, it can certainly be verified empirically in individual psychology." And (to go on to the immediately following statement), it is very plausible to consider this dialectic "as one more expression of the archetype of the trinity"; but it is too rash to claim of this archetype that it "gives structure and meaning to the dynamic, temporal events of human life in contrast with the static, eternal aspect." Edinger 1973:184–85—a book that, like most such introductions to Jung's thought, although not devoid of merit, encourages a rigid and unproblematic view of a reflection which is much more deep, obscure, and irregular, so that the flaws are hard to separate from the brilliant insights; and it is just this peculiar mixture that makes of Jung's work a more important focus than that of Freud for linguistic, philological, literary, and historical studies. Is there any reason to consider trinitarian schemata as dynamic? Would this imply that quaternary schemata (whose crucial importance is clear in Jungian analysis) should be treated as static? Indeed we just saw, in the discussion of some Aristotelian analyses, how a profusion of trinitarian structures can yet be remarkably static, and very far from dialectic.

What has been said enables us to see the error implicit in reasonings like that in the quote above. It is not schemata like the threefold simplification of dialectic that offer us the necessary scientific insight into cultural structures, among which rhetorical performances; rather, it is rhetoric that allows us to understand the recurrent fascination with trinitarian schemata—because of their peculiar balance of symmetry and dissymmetry. Thus we can put in the proper critical perspective, as manifestations of discursive structuring, all such schemata.

17. Indeed, "The Marxist theoretical practice of *epistemology*, of the history of science, of the history of ideology, of the history of philosophy, of the history of art, has yet in large part to be constituted. Not that there are no Marxists who are working in the domain and have acquired much real experience there, but they do not have behind them the equivalent of *Capital* or of the revolutionary practice of a century of Marxism. Their practice is largely *in front of them*, it still has to be developed, or even founded, that is, it has to be set on correct theoretical bases so that it corresponds to a *real* object, not to a presumed or ideological object, and so that it is a truly theoretical practice, not a technical practice" (Althusser 1965:170). Yes, but the indication which immediately follows, and the similar ones in the rest of the work, are not sufficient, because they are still formulated within an assertive philosophy, i.e., in the cage (no matter how ample and well built) of an ideology. The decisive step is the one which leads, out of assertions about the world, into the analysis of linguistic structures. On the other hand, these pages should have made clear in what sense the present proposal differs from the form of linguistic philosophy developed in Great Britain, and later applied (often in an uncritical way) to contemporary linguistic descriptions, especially

in the United States. To put it briefly, and apologizing for the perhaps too epigrammatic shortcuts: on the one hand, it is difficult to imagine how one can work in these fields as a Marxist, and equally difficult to imagine how one can work if not in the wake of Marx. On the other hand, a linguistic philosophy cannot be built on such an abstract ideological figment as "ordinary language"; it is here that dialectic reveals itself indispensable.

18. A case in point is the essay on the writer in Barthes 1964; and not because he states the contrary of the thesis advanced here ("le langage n'est pas dialectique . . . ," it "ne peut dire que: *il faut* être dialectique, mais il ne peut l'être lui même: le langage est une representation sans perspective . . . "), but because he does not argue the thesis, and one has the feeling that it would have been as easy, in his discourse, to throw off the opposite contention, without caring to develop it either. This critical style (no matter how socially aware, in a general Marxian perspective) is the response of the conservative critical tradition, based on ideology, against the threat of a really critical (therefore sober, "prosaic") analysis. The ideology of the critical style represented by Barthes is an irrationalistic one—as should be clear by now, after the dazzling effect of a Marxist–structuralist display has passed. It is, moreover, a moderate and mundane brand of irrationalism, and as such it does not even have the positive features that a bolder and more consistent irrational style has (certain aspects of Heidegger's thought on language and literature, for instance—see Heidegger 1975*a*).

19. 'For, not only it may be that you are of one opinion and I am of another, but even I myself could now be of one opinion, now of another.'

20. 'If I speake diversly of my selfe, it is because I looke diversly upon my selfe. All contrarieties are found in her, according to some turne or removing, and in some fashion or other. Shamefast, bashfull, insolent, chaste, luxurious, peevish, pratling, silent, fond, doting, labourious, nice, delicate, ingenious, slow, dull, forward, humorous, debonaire, wise, ignorant, false in words, true-speaking, both liberall, covetous, and prodigall. All these I perceive in some measure or other to bee in mee, according as I stirre or turne my selfe; And whosoever shall heedfully survay and consider himselfe, shall finde this volubility and discordance to be in himselfe, yea and in his very judgement. I have nothing to say entirely, simply, and with soliditie of my selfe, without confusion, disorder, blending, mingling; and in one word, *Distinguo* is the most universall part of my logike.' (Florio 1603, in Stewart 1931:379–380).

21. This is from the "Neuvième promenade" in Rousseau's *Les rêveries du promeneur solitaire* (see Voisine 1964), and it could read in English: 'Happiness is a permanent condition which does not seem to be destined for man in this world. Everything on earth is in a state of continuous flux, which does not allow anything on it to take a constant shape. We ourselves change and nobody can be sure that tomorrow he will love what he loves today. Thus all our plans for happiness are impossible fancies.'

22. 'Signor Gasparo smiled and said: "On the contrary, the ladies have very strong reasons to thank me; for, if I did not contradict the Magnifico and messer Cesare, we would not have listened to so much praise as these two gentlemen gave to them."'

23. 'Did you ever hear about a man who asked the advice of another

about marrying? When he said: "She is beautiful," the other said: "Take her"; but then when he said: "She has a bad temperament [or: she is not of good family]," he replied: "Don't take her"; and thus he went on saying now yes now no, according as the other put forward new arguments. Exactly in the same way does Aristotle behave with respect to me: for, when he views me as united with the body, he says that I am mortal; but when he considers me as active intelligence, and such that I can act without it [i.e., the body], he says that I am immortal; so that, in conclusion, his readers are never sure whether I am mortal or immortal.'

24. 'As Homer says, Ulysses—a very wise man—did not hesitate to put his Ithaca before immortality, although it was placed among very sharp rocks and crags, like a swallow's nest.' See *Orazione facta per Cristoforo Landino da Pratovecchio quando comincio' a leggere in Studio i sonetti di M. Francesco Petrarca*, in Corazzini 1853:125–34 (this passage, on pp. 131–32).

25. 'If that proverb which is widespread through our land of Greece, that "it is impossible that what many people assert be completely false," would be true in everything, I could deduce that the way of being of animals devoid of reason is much better than ours. But this must be true only for those things which pertain to the active life of man; for, when what is at issue is our mind's knowledge of truth and the nature of things, I very often heard another proverb being used which is completely contrary to that one, and which says that "one must know as much as the minority, although one must talk like the majority. . . ." Therefore we cannot salvage both as true (and yet the nature of proverbs is that of being true, because of the long experience they reflect), except by applying the one to praxis, and the other to speculation.'

Only a look at the context of situation may explain the perplexity from which this monologue originates: Ulysses has been trying to convince several of his Greek cocitizens, transformed by Circes into various kinds of animals, to revert to the human state (a feat which Circes empowered him to perform), but all the animals interviewed up to this point have strongly refused (however, in this very dialogue the Elephant will finally be the first and only to agree to be transformed back into a man). This, by the way, is another facet of Ulysses' image: human reason embattled against the brutality of the instincts and of grossly material life.

26. The bibliography on Rousseau and the culture of his time is immense, and no attempt will be made here to summarize it, or even hint at its several components. Some texts by Rousseau have recently received new attention in a critical perspective which is often presented as rhetorical criticism (see for instance, de Man 1975). But the development of this example will, I trust, show what the differences are; for the moment, I would like simply to insist on the fact that rhetorical analysis as I see it must be empirically detailed, verifiable, and standardized in its procedures—must, in short, have the courage to be "prosaic."

27. 'Sometimes I find it amusing to try and imagine the judgments that many will utter about my tastes, on the basis of my writings. On the basis of this one, people will certainly say: "This man is crazy about dancing," whereas I get bored looking at people dancing: "He cannot stand plays," while I am enthusiastic about them: "He has an aversion to women," and there I would have very good reasons: "He is bitter toward actors," while I have every rea-

son to be satisfied of them, and the friendship of the only one among them whom I have known well is such that it cannot but honor a good man. An analogous judgment might be expressed apropos of the poets whose texts I am obliged to criticize: it might be said that the dead ones are not to my liking and that I am irritated against the ones who are living. The truth is that I am fascinated by Racine and that I never voluntarily missed a play by Molière. . . . If my writings are a source of some pride for me, it is because of the pure intentions which lie at their base, it is because of an unselfishness for which few authors have served me as models, and which very few will imitate. Never did a selfish view cloud that desire of being useful to others which put a pen in my hand, and in fact, I have almost always written against my own interest. *Vitam impendere vero*: this is the motto that I chose and of which I consider myself worthy. O readers, I can deceive myself, but I will never willfully deceive you; be on your guard against my errors, not against my bad faith. The love of the public good is the only motive which leads me to speak to a public; then I do not think of myself and, if somebody insults me, I hold my peace fearing that anger may make me injust. This line of conduct is good for my enemies, since they can harm me as they please without fear of retaliations, it is good for my readers who do not have to fear that my hatred can lead them astray, and above all it is good for me, who, remaining peaceful while people abuse me, at least experience only the suffering which is inflicted on me and not the one I would feel if I rendered evil for evil. O holy and pure truth to which I devoted my life, no, my passions will never stain the sincere love I prove for you; neither self-interest nor fear could weaken the homage that I love to pay to you, and my pen will never refuse itself to anything but what it considers a concession to vengeance!'

28. Saussure's chess metaphor has been worked to death in general linguistics, but it seems to me that the rhetorical structuring of language illustrates this image much more precisely. What is most problematic in a chess game is not so much the purely oppositional value of the pieces (as Saussure indicates). This is true but obvious; what is remarkable is, rather, the fact that every move is a direct challenge which, to a certain extent, constrains the freedom of movement of the other player. It is this dramatic aspect of language that rhetoric emphasizes, and that rhetorics must reflect, thus going deeper than traditional structuralist complacency ("human affairs being dramatic, the discussion of human affairs becomes dramatic criticism, with more to be learned from a study of tropes than from a study of tropisms"—Burke 1973:114).

29. 'Several ministers in Geneva are, according to you, Socinians through and through. This is what you loudly proclaim in front of all of Europe. I dare to ask how did you learn this. It must have been only through your own conjectures, or on the strength of other people's witness, or by admission of the ministers involved.'

30. 'Now in matters of pure dogma and such that they do not concern ethics at all, how can one judge other people's faith by conjecture? Indeed, how can one judge about it on the basis of a statement by a third party, against the statement of the interested person?'

31. 'One would then be left to think—with regard to those among our ministers whom you allege to be Socinians through-and-through and to reject

the notion of eternal punishment, that they confided to you their inner thought on these matters; but if these actually were their inner thoughts, and if they confided them to you, surely they would have told you this in secret, with the frank and free effusion of philosophical intercourse: they would have addressed, in telling all this, the philosopher and not the public writer. He, then, would have done nothing with this information, and my evidence for this does not admit of rebuke; for you did publish it.'

32. 'It's not that I pretend to judge or blame the doctrine which you impute to them; I simply say that one does not have the right to impute it to them unless they acknowledge it, and I add that it does not at all resemble the doctrine that they teach us. I do not know what Socinianism is, so that I cannot say anything good or bad about it; also, basing myself on some confused notions of this sect and its founder, I feel more antipathy than liking for it. . . .'

33. 'We must once again remember that I have to answer to an author who is not a Protestant. . . . Such is the dogma about the existence of God; such are the mysteries admitted by the Protestant confessions. The mysteries which clash with reason, to borrow M. d'Alembert's phrase, are something completely different.'

34. 'If a theologian came to me and commanded me in the name of God to believe that the part is larger than the whole, what could I tell myself, but that this man comes to command me to be mad? Certainly the orthodox person, who does not see any absurdity in mysteries, is obliged to believe in them: but if the Socinian finds absurdity in them, what is one supposed to tell him? Will they try and prove to him that there is no such absurdity? He, for his part, will start by proving to you that it is an absurdity to develop a reasoning apropos of something that one cannot understand. What is to be done, then? Leave him alone.'

35. It was, therefore, a pleasant surprise when—at a time following the moment when the spectator first thought of the Diderot–Brecht link under the sign of dialectic—it was discovered that this link had already begun to be investigated. I refer to Breck 1971 (especially his "Exkurs: Der dialektische Mensch. Zu Brechts 'Geschichten vom Herrn Keuner',' on pp. 41–59; cf. also his "Schlussbemerkung"). This criticism is more interesting than the more conventional variety, which in our case can be exemplified by Sokel in Demetz 1965. The Diderot–Brecht parallel has indeed acquired that indispensable mark of status in literary criticism: it has caused a divergence of opinions (thus, Breck quotes critically Kesting 1970).

36. The points of references are not wanting; the task is that of revising, systematizing, developing them. For instance, take this (by now) hardly novel remark: "statements about a poem's 'subject' . . . will be also statements about a poem's 'form'." What is interesting is how this assertion is developed: instead of being expanded into a paean to the poem as a totally coherent whole, this intuition is applied to broader and more vital matters. Thus: "The same point of view would apply to the analysis of the structure in the strategies of theology and philosophy. A speculative thinker is not 'frank' (when he is 'frank') through some cult of 'disinterested curiosity.' He is frank in order that, by bringing himself to admit the real nature of obstacles and resistences, he may seek to construct a chart of meanings that will help himself and others

adequately to encompass obstacles and resistences. In the course of such work, he may often seem to wander far afield. This is due partly to the fact that each tactic of assertion may lead to a problem, that tactic of its solution may lead to a further problem, etc." (Burke 1973:102). I hope to have already shown, especially with the analysis of the Rousseau passage, what I take to be the concrete implications of this statement.

37. 'Soul. Thanks to the followers of Luther, who—trusting only the Holy Scriptures—have had as an effect that people have been obliged to go back to reading them, and to leave aside many disputations. *Giusto*. As you can see, it is true what is often repeated: that often some good results of a great evil.'

38. I am not, of course, defending either the institution of censorship in general, or its specific historical realization in the Catholic Counterreformation in particular; nor am I suggesting that the censors are right in this particular case. I am simply applying what I consider a distinction and strength of rhetorical criticism: that of being an *internal* analysis, not an external confrontation of rival ideologies. What matters is not whether the discourse is, in absolute terms and for the reader "in general," right or wrong. What counts is the internal articulation of the discourse and the analyses of the junctures, as well as of the discontinuities and inconsistencies, within that structure.

But the critical reader might doubt that my "innocence" is so complete; he might remark that this descriptive analysis takes place within the horizon of a pre-judgment (even if not of a prejudice), it is connected to a general ideological choice. That is: my choice of the example is not innocent, because it is not casual; it displays, indirectly, certain opinions—let us say, it hints at a critical attitude toward Counterreformistic censure of discussions and ideological debates. That critical reader would be right—but the conflict with the method advocated here is only apparent; indeed, this potential criticism was already dealt with earlier in this section, when the *regressus ad infinitum* of ideological frames was admitted, and when it was also noted that this does not constitute an obstacle.

What the critic must do is to adopt broader and more elastic ideological frames, and make a particular effort to penetrate with sym-pathy into the ideology of the object of his analysis (no matter how alien it is to him at the beginning), while at the same time stepping out—as far as possible—of his own ideology (no matter how dearly and deeply held). That this guarantee exists here is proved by the fact that I just had to go to some lengths in order to clarify that I am not supporting the mechanism of censorship.

IV. THE STRUCTURE OF THE RHEME

1. This does not mean that it would not be interesting to trace the several translations, versions, variations, on this statement through several literary traditions in various historical periods. I will confine myself to one example, which illustrates how this image can survive, without losing its force, the transference from the philosophical ambiance of archaic Greece to the literary context of a modern novel of passionate "decadence": "Conosci tu questa parola del grande Eraclito? 'L'arco ha per nome BIOS e per opera la morte.' Questa è una parola che, prima di comunicare agli spiriti il suo signi-

ficato certo, li eccita" (from *Il Fuoco*; see D'Annunzio 1968 [1898]). ['Do you know this utterance by the great Heraclitus? "The name of the bow is life; its work, death." This is an utterance which, even before communicating its clear meaning to consciences, excites them.'] This is an acute way of characterizing the peculiar connotations of this utterance—as we are going to see.

2. This is from Burnet 1930, used for Jung 1971:426; in that text (which follows Bywater's edition) the fragment is number 66. I quoted the Greek text according to Marcovich 1967, which also includes a full apparatus with the ancient passages citing the fragment (more on it later). But, unlike Marcovich, I follow the numeration adopted in the classic edition by Diels and Kranz 1966 [1922].

3. From Pike 1967, some examples of cultural and linguistic hypostases: "A quotation, abstracted from a lecture and repeated out of context; or a quotation of one's own speech . . . a word used out of its normal distribution . . . part of a word referred to, as such, in grammatical discussion . . . the related usage of lexical elements by nongrammarians . . . each of the entries ('words') listed in a dictionary; each of the vocal sounds mentioned as such in a general lecture on phonetics; practising passing, by itself, in preparation for use of that activity in a football game; or the repeated practice of a specific medical operation on a cadaver." The last phrasing reflects the heaviness which is characteristic of most varieties of structural linguistic discourse, and which makes them slightly out of tune with the lightness and urbanity which characterizes most styles of literary criticism. Yet an advantage might be drawn out of this rather clumsy approach: that of realizing, in general, that the urbane mode is almost as mystifying as the ploddingly detailed scrutiny, as far as the peculiar nature of the literary object is concerned; and in particular, that the organicist mythology of the work of art is inadequate in *all* its inflections. That is: to conceive of the literary corpus as a corpse is no more grotesque than to regard it as a healthily alive body. In both cases, the text (or complex of texts) is viewed as *one organism*, an idea which discourages a materialist and seriously critical analysis of the text as an ideological construct, and of its radical discontinuities.

4. Both are Indo-European words. But *biós* is an item with few sure cognates in other Indo-European langauges beside Greek: it is perhaps related to Latin *fīlum* "thread, string'; the original meaning of the root in Greek is probably 'bow string.' *Bíos*, on the other hand, is a member of a very large family, which includes (among others) the subfamily of the Latin verb *uīuō* 'to live,' hence of *uīta* 'life,' etc. (see Boisacq 1938). Going back to *biós*: if the etymon relating it to the bow string—i.e., to a *pars* of that *totum* which is the weapon—is accepted, *biós* in itself embodies a rhetorical relationship of the synecdochic type.

5. Just one point for now: while I sympathize with the effort to collocate the method of linguistic description within a broader epistemological framework, I cannot help noting that the frameworks usually proposed for tagmemic descriptions (whether they represent a simplifying positivistic approach, as in Pike, or a summary kind of theology—as in Longacre 1976 and also in other works by Pike) are too crude. And yet, there is in them a search for a humanistic perspective, devoid of the usual frigidity, which makes of such frameworks a welcome addition to linguistic description and shows an alternative to the shallow kind of logical games which, too often, are the only

general frame for analyses in the transformational—generative perspective.

6. All these notations, with the exception of the last quoted one, are in Longacre 1976; who, however, in his useful description of "combinations of predications," gives a phenomenology which is still too narrow for the field to which it addresses itself. In such a field, which lies at the boundaries between "emic" and "etic" descriptions, it is impossible to be exhaustive; yet, just because of its lying in this border area, the grid which covers it should be as fine as possible. From this point of view, the basic limitation of Longacre's analysis is the same which plagues most linguistic descriptions: the lack of an integration with the phenomenology elaborated by rhetoric.

To confine myself to the present case: rhetorical analysis would make the descriptions of predicate combinations more delicate, and thus more useful for textual analysis. Linguistic phenomenologies have a way of looking sophisticated "on paper," so to speak—that is, if measured against the few, generally banal, *exempla ficta* of sentences chosen to illustrate them; but they quickly reveal a considerable lack of refinement and intellectual interest when they are brought to bear on real texts. The integration with rhetoric is probably the best way to avoid this embarassing contrast.

But this lack is not felt only in this particular area. For instance: the neglect of rhetorical figures can lead to unfair and linguistically insensitive evaluations of the grammaticality of certain sentences. "We cannot permute the sentence *He started the fire, then sat there for an hour enjoying its warmth* to **He sat there for an hour enjoying the warmth of the fire and then lighted it*, i.e., there is a linearity in the deep structure notion of succession. Here at least deep structures are ordered" (Longacre 1976:117). But not even this haven—at first sight, so safe—should be left to the idea of deep structure ordering; because the sentence type marked with an asterisk is, instead, possible, and it is attested in several texts: it is a realization of the figure of Hysteron Proteron (for which see Valesio 1975a).

7. For this case analysis I combined—as noted—Pike and Pike 1975 (cf. there, for the four-cell tagmeme and the case labels Identive and Referentive, which however are not defined), and Longacre 1976. The latter offers (on pp. 40ff.) the most detailed case typology I know of and, unlike most other writers in this area, he is scholarly enough to recall—indeed, to detail—the achievements of his predecessors. Yet even this very detailed classification is not delicate enough to take care of the Heraclitean example; this is why I had to use other terms, and to expand on the case frame exemplified there on p. 347 (and which is not a part of the list of case frames presented at the beginning of that book).

8. For example. It is interesting that the only illustration for the case category "Differentive" in Pike and Pike 1975 is constituted by two phrases which seem syntactically quaint in English but which exactly parallel our Greek construction:

Scope

There is a door to the house

and

Scope

There is a son to him.

The notion of "Scope" is equivalent to that of "Range" shown above. But if we look more closely, it is precisely this notion of Range (or Scope) which must be made more problematic: even in the case of the door–house example a relationship of Possession emerges as more characterizing of this relationship than one of Range; but this is particularly clear in the son–father sentence. Here the category of Scope or Range is mystifying, because it tends to neutralize the actual complexity of the relationship between father and son into the misleading simplicity of a purely formal relationship. But not even the category of Possession is above obfuscation here: for it goes to the opposite extreme, superimposing a structure of legal ownership and economic accumulation on the biological link (Hegelian shades of master and slave).

Am I saying that one should make of case frames a complete and close system which can automatically account for each single case? No, or at least, this does not seem possible at the present time. But we must strive to make this system as comprehensive and delicate as possible, and at the same time we must be aware that the limitations of the system are not only external, but internal as well. That is: the more delicate our description of semantic relationships, the more acute our awareness that the relationships do not occur in a void, but are inextricably intertwined with various layers of ideological reinterpretations and rationalizations.

9. A last point on the Range noun phrase: in keeping with the general tone of impersonal, objective statement, the definite article here does not identify, singling it out from the general background, a specific individual out of the class of bows, but rather, it labels the individual named as the representative of the whole class. In the first case, the definite article would have been the only trace of subjectivity in this sentence; but, as just noted, this is not the case: the article is, in one terminology (cf. Halliday and Hasan 1973:71) *homophoric*, that is, it identifies the referent irrespectively of any specific situation. Thus the general rhetoric of the sentence—its tone of abstract objectivity—is confirmed.

10. This is the case for the faintly bizarre article by Fraenkel 1938 who, in a certain sense, comes close to rediscovering the wheel by describing what he calls the "geometrical mean" in Heraclitus—which is nothing else but chiasmus. This is a clear proof of the danger of useless reduplication which takes place when the tools of rhetorics are not employed. A troubling statement in that article (in fn. 27), on the other hand, gives a cue as to a possible ideological motivation for this neglect of well-tested descriptive instruments: "It is true that there is much in the style of Heraclitus to remind the reader of the *figurae orationis* as they were taught later by rhetoricians, but in the writing of Heraclitus the subject determines the expression and not the reverse." This is an example of that confusion between rhetoric and rhetorics which still hinders serious analysis of linguistic structures; in particular, this statement is also an illustration of the rhetoric of antirhetoric. Obviously Heraclitus did not have to wait for later rhetoricians in order to employ figures of speech! But, like every writer (like every speaker), Heraclitus is a rhetor. And, no purpose is served here by calling chiasmus by another name.

11. A bibliographic indication is not indispensable in the case of the Italian sentence, which belongs to verbal folklore (although, of course, it would be far from useless to trace its versions and ramifications in written collections

of such minuscule texts, as well as in the field). What I regret is to be unable to quote the specific source of this Johnsonian dictum—which could, therefore, be apocryphal. But this would not detract—on the contrary—from its significance as an item of verbal folklore. (A further confirmation of this folkloric significance: I understand that a variant of this statement appears in the insignia of one among the States of the Union; as was to be expected, that emblematic statement has raised some controversy.)

It should not be passed under silence that, in the Italian idiom, a personification semanticizes (or, hypostatizes) an underlying distinction of grammatical gender (*parola* being feminine, and *fatto* masculine in Italian); while the English personification is, of course, purely semantic, since it does not have a morphological distinction as its basis.

This is interesting not only in itself, but because it shows us that denotative features of grammatical meaning can indeed have connotative implications, like the denotative features of lexical meaning. In Italian, the denotative features [+ MASCULINE] and [− MASCULINE] have a connotation of respectively, 'strong (virile, etc.)' and 'soft (feminine, etc.)', so that the ambiguity of the very words employed—"masculine" and "feminine"—as between grammatical metalanguage and current language faithfully reflects the coexistence of grammatical denotation and its connotation.

Finally, it should not be assumed that the representation of this contrast is confined to the popular register. That the Italian idiom is not unknown to the *langue cultivée* of the literary tradition is proved, for instance, from the following sentence: "non li movendo il fatto, non potevo sperare di far frutto con le parole" ['since the fact did not move them, I could not hope to obtain any result with words']—which is to be read in the opening statement of a letter written (in 1537) by Lorenzo di Pierfrancesco de' Medici, the famous "Lorenzino" (see Lisio 1897 [1957]:152). And, undoubtedly, further research would disclose several other literary implementations, both in Italian and in other languages.

12. 'The cold things become hot, hot becomes cold, humid becomes dry, parched moistens' (Diels–Kranz 1966:126; the text is here cited, as usual, according to Marcovich's edition, on pp. 220–21).

13. The rhetorical structure of this fragment, then, is much more sophisticated than it appears at first glance. Is this compositional refinement sufficient to decide in favor of the attribution to Heraclitus, as against the hypothesis of an imitation? No, if we construe our claim in the terms of that mythology of the author which has limited until now the work of stylistic criticism: sophisticated verbal structures are not the monopoly of Great Authors (the view, hinted at by Sapir among others, of language as a collective work of art is the one which serves as a background to this theory of rhetoric, as part of a more general view of culture and society—in the radically critical and dialectic Marxian tradition). On the other hand, this analysis proves that the text belongs fully to the Heraclitean universe of discourse, that it is worthy to be examined as carefully as the other fragments (thus allowing us to see the situation more clearly than, for instance, in the discussion by Bollack and Wismann 1972, whose reasons for denying the authenticity of the fragment, are, like most statements in that book, left rather nebulous; as for Marcovich 1967, he accepts the fragment without comment).

At any rate, the methodological indication is, once again, what especially matters here: rhetorical analysis is essential in order to clarify problems such as those of authenticity, where vague ideological criteria often play a disproportionate role. Rhetorics as the instrument which demystifies ideology—this, to repeat, is the main theme of the present research.

14. Halliday and Hasan 1973 (235, 238, and passim) point in the right direction, but the distinction is expressed in excessively vague terms; and occasionally, in a contradictory way. For instance: "There are specifically *emphatic* forms of the 'and' relation occurring only in an internal sense, that of 'there is yet another point to be taken in conjunction with the previous one'. This in fact is essentially the meaning that is taken by the 'and' relation when it is a form of internal conjunction" (ibid.:246; the emphasis on "emphatic" is in the original). This reads smoothly—until we realize what is actually being said: namely, that the normal use of the conjunction 'and' is the emphatic one—a statement which would deprive of sense either the lexical items for 'and' in the various languages or the general linguistic notion of "emphasis"! (Actually, the latter development is what tends to take place: we saw above how difficult it is to use the notion of emphasis in a meaningful way.)

15. No, not even this point can be considered trivial. For, studying a language like English we are tempted to see as something natural the link between the syntactic position of the conjunction and its semantic effect: "A conjunctive adjunct normally has first position in a sentence . . . and has as its domain the whole of the sentence in which it occurs: that is to say, its meaning extends over the entire sentence, unless it is repudiated" (Halliday and Hasan 1973:232). The relationship is so straightforward that it is easy to ideologize it into a linguistic universal: what more natural than the fact that the conjunction dominates the whole clause it introduces by taking up its position—like a platoon leader—at the head of the column? But, as we just saw, the situation is much more complex. (As for the divergence between the term "sentence" in the quote and my use of "clause," the distinction should—I think—be carefully respected, and the quoted authors' claim must actually be understood as applying to the clause.)

Languages like Ancient Greek remind us that a generalization such as the one quoted above would be a hasty ideological superimposition: the conjunction does not have to occupy first place in order to dominate the whole clause, including the lexical items which precede it (like the word *érgon* in our sentence). We must go further: this typological divergence also represents two different ways in which the basic structural positions of the conjunction mime (are the icons of) their broader patterns of cohesion. In languages like English, the clause–initial placement of the conjunction is the icon of its semantic domain (noted above). But in languages like Ancient Greek (which, at first sight, look as if they did not display any icon in this area) the position of the conjunction mimes on a smaller scale (within the boundaries of the clause) its interclausal way of cohering: that is, its phoric function, operating simultaneously backward and forward.

16. The necessity of caution and delicate distinction in typological or contrastive analyses of linguistic systems is confirmed, *a contrario*, by the imprudence of a remark like the following: "The fact that *but* contains 'and' is the reason why we cannot say *and but*, although we can say *and yet, and so, and*

then, etc. It also explains why the construction *Although* . . . , *but* . . . , so frequently used by nonnative speakers of English, is wrong; a structure cannot be both hypotactic and coordinate (paractactic) at the same time" (Halliday and Hasan 1973:237).

The last statement betrays a certain stylistic and historical dogmatism. A cursory examination of the tradition of English (and French, etc.) prose would soon show—I believe—that these benighted foreigners have many good "native" accomplices in performing this pretended illogicality: a linguistic structure *can* be both hypotactic and coordinative! (I am thinking here of certain uses of *and* in a clause following an *if* clause which parallel the so-called "*e paraipottatico*" of the Old Italian—and Old Provençal—tradition.) This pronouncement makes us diffident also about other claims. And indeed, the first statement in the above quote is as much an ideological figment as the one just commented. For instance, Standard Literary Arabic (continuing its Classical tradition) allows *wa-lākin(na)*—literally 'and-but'—as a perfectly acceptable variant of *lākin(na)* 'but' (and the persistence of the same stem shows that it would be captious, and *ad hoc*, as far as Arabic is concerned, to oppose the former variant as 'and yet' to the latter translated as 'but').

17. It might be that—as Denniston 1954:162ff. notes—when the additive, or in his terminology "connective," function predominates (a fact which is underscored by the absence of the balancing conjunction *mén* in the preceding clause) "there is no essential difference between *dé* and *kaí*" aside from the syntactic one that the former normally coordinates clauses or sentences while the latter usually links words or phrases. But it is the word "essential" which is crucial here, and ambiguous. There is, I suggest, a semantic distinction between *dé* and *kaí* which, even if it is not considered essential, colors the two lexical items differently and marks their usage in divergent ways.

18. Let me reiterate—lest my occasionally polemic tone be misunderstood—my respect for the tradition. Thus, the description in the old Stephens 1837:111–12 is appropriately delicate: "*Oûn* . . . often expresses the state of mind we are in during enquiry, whilst we are still searching after the truth, and our opinion is as yet undetermined. . . . The following are some of the more usual expressions by which the particles [i.e., *ára*, *mě*, *oûn*] may be rendered in English; *therefore, then, so, accordingly, thereat, in consequence of; as we may conclude or expect, as is likely; in the next place, in due order, in due season; to proceed, now,* etc."

19. "Provided" observe the quoted authors, "'argument' is understood in its everyday rhetorical sense and not in its technical sense in logic (contrasting with 'operator')." The rhetorical sense is indeed the one according to which the concept of argument will be used here.

20. "Much the commonest use of *goûn* is to introduce a statement which is, *pro tanto*, evidence for a preceding statement. This has been well termed "part proof'" (Denniston 1954:448ff.). Another way of putting it is to say that *goûn* "est employée le plus souvent pour affirmer *la réalité d'un point de détail dans un ensemble dont on ne réponde point*; c'est le sens bien connu, le plus souvent traduit par: 'une chose est sure, c'est que'" (Humbert 1954:428, italics in original).

21. Let me note, in passing, that the former of the two indices is not fully consistent: since it announces at the beginning that also the *voces du-*

biae—and the *voces emendatae*—are registered, *oûn* in this fragment would have deserved a place in the index, as a *vox dubia*.

22. Yes, to be sure: glosseme evokes glossematics—which is not the framework here; hence a danger of confusion. But the price to pay for keeping guard against this confusion (being ready to repeat that the concept of glosseme as used in this theory of rhetoric is not meant as an application of glossematic theory) is low if compared with the ensuing advantages. For, we have here an "emic" term which is, both in its form and in its content, in line with the other terms which are at work in this theory: the already established tagmeme and syntagmeme, the ideologeme (which I take up again from a somewhat neglected corner in the Russian formalist panoply of terms), and rheme (which I find necessary to add on my own to the preceding series—for it is here that the core of this rhetorical approach is manifested). Furthermore, the possible confusion is very limited, for—where as the tagmeme (with the syntagmeme) is an essential concept in tagmemic theory, hence it may aptly serve as its symbol—glossematic theory (contrary to what one might expect) does *not* contain a concept of glosseme.

23. "In reported speech, and after verbs of thinking and seeming, *ára* denotes the apprehension of an idea not before envisaged. Usually *ára* conveys either, at the most, actual scepticism, or, at least, the disclaiming of responsibility for the accuracy of the statement. But sometimes the context implies acceptance of the idea, and *ára* merely denotes that its truth has not before been realized"—Denniston 1954:38; for *ára*, cf. Humbert 1954:380–82.

24. We can express this by insisting on the terminology: paronomasia functions by lexical items (or forms), not by lexemes (or terms). I mean by "lexeme" a given form as representative of the whole paradigm of inflectional forms connected to it, so that a lexeme is the form which is normally used to introduce a lemma in the dictionary of the language at issue (although the head-word is, more precisely, part of the lexeme); whereas a lexical item is any form in that paradigm which happens to be actually used in a given textual string. Finally, it may be recalled that both lexeme and lexical item (in the senses just defined) are opposed to glosseme—by which I propose to designate *both* the whole family of variant readings appearing in a certain slot in a text (as explained above) *and* the variant which is chosen as representative of the whole family. An instance from our sentence: *ónoma* is both a lexical item (insofar as it is the form actually appearing in that version of the sentence I choose as representative), a lexeme (since this is the standard form under which the word for 'noun, name' is recorded in a dictionary of Ancient Greek, and it stands for the whole paradigm: genitive *onómatos*, dative *onómati*, etc.), and a glosseme (since it stands for a group of at least two variants in this text: *ónoma* and *oúnoma*).

On the other hand, *oúnoma* is a glosseme, but it is not a lexical item—that is, it is not a lexical item *in this version of the text*—and it is not a lexeme (at least, it is not a lexeme in the standard form of Ancient Greek reflected in the dictionaries and constituting the background of this analysis). And so on for the other cases. (For instance, leaving our test sentence aside: the lexeme of the verb is normally its infinitive form in the modern Indo-European languages, its first person singular present indicative form in Ancient Greek and Classical Latin, its third person singular masculine perfect form in Arabic, etc.)

25. This underscores a problem which is a minor but disturbing stumbling block in the scientific practice of contextualizing texts (one of the basic aspects of rhetorics, in the interpretation I propose). *Context* refers *either* to the *text* as framework of some smaller component (paragraph, sentence, etc.) under analysis (what Eco proposes to call *co-text*), *or* to all that is *not* text, but that surrounds the text and must be analyzed in order fully to understand the text, that is, to what can also be called *intertext*. In what follows, when it is particularly important to mark the distinction, I will use this convention, in order to distinguish the two usages: to write *con-text* when the reference is to the linguistic entity, and *context* in the normal spelling when what is meant is the surrounding semiotic entity.

Once again, the terminological difficulty should not be taken lightly, for it is the symbol of a deeper epistemological problem. In fact, one of the hardest tasks of rhetorics and text linguistics is to determine (with an *empirical* determination, in *concrete* cases) where the linguistic structures end and the non-linguistic structures begin. The opposite meanings of the term "context" serve as the dialectic symbol of this problem.

26. The way in which the notion of "semantic field" is used here warrants some explanation. In the tradition of studies on these topics, semantic field or domain usually designates the structures shared by several lexical items: it is, in other words, the *external* field surrounding several semantic nuclei. See the generic definition of "domain" in Nida 1975:174, as well as more precise definitions such as those by Alinei 1974:54; who distinguishes lexical systems ("the complexes of lemmas which share at least *two* features, one in the same logical-syntactic relation with respect to the other") from lexical domain—"the complex of lemmas which share *one* feature, and in a different relation with respect to the others."

This concept of semantic field is preserved here (it is the concept intuitively at work when I connect 'bow' to 'helmet' and 'shield' on the one hand, 'sword' and 'spear' on the other). But the notion which is being developed in this analysis is a complementary one: namely, the semantic field *internal* to each lexical item, whose figural relations expand, crisscrossing the figural relations internal to one or more other semantic fields (each one associated with another lexical item), and constituting—as we are going to see presently—other figures. But even in this latter sense, the notion of field is more "internal" than the traditional one. What we have, in fact, is a gamut of different degrees in the concept of field, ranging from relatively internal to relatively external; and it is in this sense that I articulate the dimension of field as generally presented in tagmemic theory.

27. See Rossi-Landi 1974:1824ff., with this illustration of the reciprocal actions of utensils leading to the formation of a mechanism: "the archer draws the string of a bow and thereby bends the wood, storing up energy which will later be discharged all at once into the arrow. In the first phase the string acts upon the wood, in the second, the wood upon the arrow through the string. The string so to say belongs to the bow when it is drawn, and belongs to the arrow when it is released. The string is the mediating element. Although they are processed in such a way as to work together, wood, string, and arrow can be useful for something and be considered utensils each on its own account; but the machine 'bow-and-arrows' (one of the most primitive machines) consists of the sum of the *two actions* of drawing and releasing, and

cannot be reduced to one of them alone. Notice that the two actions are similar but certainly not identical; indeed the machine 'bow-and-arrows' benefits precisely from the way they differ. They are moreover separated in time; finally, the man who has accumulated energy by drawing the bow can release it at his discretion, triggering the machine without otherwise intervening in the process."

28. This evokes a peculiarity of Nida's taxonomy with respect to the Hallig–Wartburg one and to that by Bally: while the basic category in the latter two are all lexical, the first-mentioned list mixes categories typically used in lexical description ("Entities" and "Events") with categories which are usually employed for the identification of grammatical features ("Abstracts" and "Relationals").

29. To be sure, one has to make allowance here for the tendency, in the otherwise excellent dictionary just quoted, to string senses one after the other without offering any contextual limitation and specification, thus making the lexical richness of Arabic even more bewildering than it need be.

30. The tragedy, of course, is Sophocles' *Philoctetes*; the characters, respectively, Philoctetes and Neoptolemus; the text should be assigned to the year 409 B.C.—it is thus about a century later than the period in which Heraclitus seems to have reached his full maturity: his "floruit" (usually implying the fortieth year) is put around 500 B.C. The texts of the *Philoctetes* here used are: Cavallin 1875, Jebb and Schickburg 1923, Dain 1960.

31. *Philoctetes* 923–24. Although it does not affect the word we are interested in, let me note that I preserve in translating the first sentence the ambiguity I see in the text: it is not clear whether Philoctetes means for the epithet *tlềmōn* to refer to himself or to Neoptolemus: the word can mean either 'wretched, miserable', or 'reckless' (Paul Mazon's translation in Dain 1960, 'malheureux', leaves no doubt that the first possibility is the one he has in mind; but it does not seem to me that one can be so sure—for instance, when Philoctetes clearly refers to himself later (949) he uses the term *dúsmoros*).

More to the point of this investigation: it seems appropriate to me to translate 'bow and arrows' rather than simply 'bow' in view of the usage of the plural *tà tóksa* in the text, even if the plural (as we saw) refers to the compound structure of the bow at least as much as to the bow plus the objects which feed it. Once again, we have a metonymic configuration.

32. It was represented in 388. As for the texts of these two plays: I consulted Hall and Geldart 1907 and Coulon and Van Daele 1930 for *Ecclesiazusae*; Van Leeuwen 1968 and the quoted Coulon and Van Daele for *Plutos*.

33. The aesthetic nature of the contextualization is missed in Bollack and Wismann 1972:178–81, which ideologically deforms the aesthetic parallel into a simplistic dichotomy: "L'arme de guerre et l'attribut de la paix produisent une nouvelle 'consonance', qui n'est pas 'harmonie', mais désaccord. L'un, l'arc, dit la guerre, l'autre, la lyre, la paix." I just showed that a detailed philological analysis forbids such a univocal link between the lexical item *tókson* (or *biós*) and the connotation of 'war'. And the connection between *lúrē* and the connotative feature 'peace' looks at least equally simplistic.

34. 'As in the case of the bow, the immobile tension of identical contraries generates the differentiated upsurge of movement. Without the curved wooden structure which is controlled by the string, the arrows could not

Notes for Pages 250–256   293

shoot out. Without the constant pressure of the shores, waters would stag-
nate. Since they illustrate in equal manner the logical structure of the shift
from opposition to succession, the bow and the river serve as emblems of the
cosmic process.'

35. Some of the remarks which follow are based on observations of some
colleagues and listeners—among them Carlo Alberto Mastrelli, Ferruccio
Rossi-Landi—none of whom is responsible for the particular developments
presented here.

36. "Every sign, linguistic or nonlinguistic, spoken or written . . . in a
small or large unit, can be *cited*, put between quotation marks; in so doing it
can break with every given context. . . . This does not imply that the mark is
valid outside of a context, but on the contrary that there are only contexts
without any center or absolute anchoring." (Derrida 1977).

Bibliography

Abraham, Werner, and Braunmüller, Kurt. 1971. "Stil, Metaphor, und Pragmatik." *Lingua* 28:1–47.

Adler, Mortimer J. 1927. *Dialectic*. New York: Harcourt, Brace.

Adorno, Francesco, 1961. *I sofisti e Socrate*. Turin: Einaudi.

———. 1969. *Il pensiero greco: Orientamenti bibliografici*. Bari: Laterza.

Adorno, Theodor W. 1963. "Jargon der Eigentlichkeit." *Neue Rundschau* 74:371–385.

———. 1973. *Negative Dialectics*. Translated by E.B. Ashton. New York: Seabury Press.

Adorno, Theodor W.; Popper, Karl R.; Albert, H.; Dahrendorf, R.; Habermas, J.; and Pilot, H. 1972. *Dialettica e positivismo nella sociologia: Dieci interventi nella discussione*. Turin: Einaudi.

Agosti, Stefano. 1974. *Il testo poetico*. Milan: Rizzoli.

Albert, E.M. 1964. "'Rhetoric,' 'logic,' and 'poetics' in Burundi: Cultural patterning of speech behavior." *American Anthropologist* 66, no. 6:35–54.

Alberti, Leon Battista. 1890. *Opera inedita et pauca separatim impressa*. Edited by Girolamo Mancini. Florence: Sansoni.

Alighieri, Dante. 1966–1967. *La commedia seconda l'antica vulgata*. 4 vols. Edited by Giorgio Petrocchi. Milan: Mondadori.

Alinei, Mario. 1974. *La struttura del lessico*. Bologna: Il Mulino.

Althusser, Louis. 1965. *Pour Marx*. Paris: Maspero. Translated by Ben Brewster, *For Marx*, 1970. New York: Vintage Books.

Aly, W. 1929. "Formprobleme der frühen griechischen Prosa." In *Philologus*, suppl. vol. 21, sect. 3. Leipzig: Dietrich.

Anderson, John M. 1971. *The Grammar of Case: Towards a Localistic Theory*. Cambridge: Cambridge University Press.

Anglade, Rene. 1972. "Problèmes et techniques de l'édition des textes modernes: Esquisse d'une typologie des appareils de variantes." *Études Germaniques* 27:45–72.

Apostel, Léo. 1972. *Materialismo dialettico e metodo scientifico*. Turin: Einaudi. Orig. Publ. in French, 1960. *Le Socialisme* 7:4. Brussels.

Aristophanes
Ecclesiazusae.
———. Coulon, Victor, ed. 1930. *L'assemblée des femmes. Oeuvres complètes*, vol. 5. Translated by H. Van Daele. Paris: Les Belles Lettres.
———. Hall, F.W., and Geldart, W.M., eds. 1907. *Aristophanis Comoediae*, vol. 2. Oxford: Clarendon Press.
Plutus.

————. Coulon, Victor, ed. See above.

————. Van Leeuwen, Jan, ed., *Plutus*. Leiden: A.W. Sijthoff.

Aristotle

Opera. Bekker, Immanuel, ed. 1960–1961. Reprinted from 1831–1870 ed. Berlin: W. de Gruyter.

Poetics. Solmsen, Friedrich, ed. 1954. Translated by I. Bywater. New York: Random House.

Rhetoric.

————. Cope, Edward M., ed. 1877. *The Rhetoric of Aristotle with a Commentary*. 3 vols. Cambridge: Cambridge University Press.

————. Ross, W.D., ed. 1969. *Aristotelis: Ars rhetorica*. Oxford: Clarendon Press.

———— Solmsen, Friedrich, ed. 1954. *Rhetoric*. Translated by W.R. Roberts. New York: Random House.

Topics. Brunschwig, Jacques, ed. 1967. *Topiques*. Paris: Les Belles Lettres.

Arnauld, Antoine, and Niccole, Pierre. 1965. *La logique et l'art de penser*. Edited by Pierre Claire and François Girbal. Paris: P.U.F.

Atkins, John W.H. 1943. *English Literary Criticism: The Medieval Phase*. New York: Macmillan.

————. 1951. 2d ed. *English Literary Criticism: The Renascence*. London: Methuen.

————. 1966. *English Literary Criticism: Seventeenth and Eighteenth Centuries*. New York: Barnes & Noble.

Aulitzky. 1922. "Korax." In *Realencyclopedie der Altertumwissenschaft*. 11:1379–1381.

Avalle, D'Arco Silvio, et al., eds. 1973. *Essais de la théorie du texte*. Paris: Galilée.

Bachelard, Gaston. 1936. *La dialectique de la durée*. Paris: Boivin.

Baju, Anatole, ed. 1886–1889. *Le Décadent*. Reprinted 1970–1973. 2 vols. Paris: L'Arche du Livre.

Baker, Sheridan. 1968. *The Complete Stylist*. New York: Crowell.

Baldwin, Charles, S. 1924. *Ancient Rhetoric and Poetic Interpreted from Representative Works*. Reprinted 1959. Gloucester, Mass: Peter Smith.

————. 1928. *Medieval Rhetoric and Poetic (to 1400) Interpreted from Representative Works*. Reprinted 1959. Gloucester, Mass: Peter Smith.

————. 1939. *Renaissance Literary Theory and Practice; Classicism in Rhetoric and Poetic of Italy, France, and England, 1400–1600*. Edited by D.L. Clark. Reprinted 1959. Gloucester, Mass: Peter Smith.

Ballard, D. Lee; Conrad, Robert J.; and Longacre, Robert E. 1971. "The deep and surface grammar of interclausal relations." *Foundations of Language*. 7:70–118. Also in Brend 1974:308–355.

Bally, Charles. 1951. *Traité de stylistique Française*. Genève: Georg & Cie.

Banfi, Antonio, ed. 1953. *La crisi dell'uso dogmatico della ragione*. Rome: Fratelli Bocca.

Banfield, Ann. 1973. "Narrative style and the grammar of direct and indirect speech." *Foundations of Language* 10.

Barker, R.G., ed. 1963. *The Stream of Behaviour*. New York: Appleton-Century-Crofts.

Barthes, Roland, 1964. *Essais Critiques*. Paris: Seuil. Translated by Richard Howard. *Critical Essays*. 1972. Evanston, Ill.: Northwestern University Press.

————. 1966. "L'ancienne rhétorique: Aide-mémoire." *Communications* 16:172–229.

Barwick, K. 1957. *Probleme der stoischen Sprachlehre und Rhetorik.* Berlin: Akademie.

Bateson, Gregory. 1972. *Steps to an Ecology of Mind.* New York: Ballantine.

Baxtin, Mixail. Presumed author of *Marksizm i filosofia jazyka,* 1929. Author given in English edition, Valentin Vološinov, *Marxism and the Philosophy of Language.* Edited and translated by L. Matejka and I.R. Titunik. New York: Seminar Press. Italian translation by N. Cuscito and R. Bruzzese, 1976. *Marxismo e filosofia del linguaggio.* Introduction by A. Porzio. Bari: Dedalo.

Beccaria, Gian Luigi. 1970. "Benvenuto Terracini: Dalla linguistica alla critica." In *Critica e storia letteraria: Studi offerti a Mario Fubini,* vol. 2:780–811. Padua: Liviana Editrice.

————. 1975. *L'autonomia del significante: Figure del ritmo e della sintassi (Dante, Pascoli, D'Annunzio).* Turin: Einaudi.

Bech, G. 1955. "Zum Problem der Inhaltsanalyse." *Studia Neophilologica* 27:108–125.

Becker, Alton L. 1966a. "Item and field: A way into complexity." In Kriedler 1966.

————. 1966b. "A tagmemic approach to paragraph analysis." *College Composition and Communication* 16:237–242.

————. 1967. "Conjoining in a tagmemic grammar of English." *Monograph Series of Language and Linguistics* 20:109121. Edited by F.P. Dineen. Washington, D.C.: Georgetown University Press. Also in Brend 1974:223–233.

Bedier, Joseph. 1903. *Études critiques.* Paris: A. Colin.

————. 1928. "La tradition manuscrite du 'Lai de l'ombre': Réflexions sur l'art d'éditer les anciens textes." *Romania* 54:161–196; 321–356.

————. 1938. "De l'editio princeps de la 'Chanson de Roland' aux éditions les plus récents." *Romania* 64:145–244; 489–521.

Belasco, Simon. 1964. "Tagmemics and transformational grammar in linguistics analysis." *Linguistics* 10:5–15.

Bellert, Irena. 1970. "On a condition for the coherence of texts." *Semiotica* 2:335–363.

Beneš, Eduard. 1968. "On two aspects of functional sentence perspective." *Travaux du Cercle Linguistique de Prague* 3:264–274.

Bense, Max. 1962. *Theorie der Texte.* Berlin: Kiepenheuer and Witsch.

————. 1969. *Einführung in der informationstheoretische Ästhetik: Grundlegung and Anwendung in der Texttheorie.* Reinbeck bei Hamburg: Rowohlt.

Benson, Thomas W. and Prosser, Michael H., eds. 1972. *Readings in Classical Rhetoric.* Bloomington: Indiana University Press.

Bentham, Jeremy.

————, *The Works of Jeremy Bentham.* 1838–1843. 11 vols. Edited by John Bowring. Edinburgh: Tait.

————, *Bentham's Theory of Fiction.* 1932. Edited by C. K. Ogden. London: K. Paul, Trench, Trubner and Co.

————, *Sofismi, politici e altri saggi.* 1947. Edited by Pietro Cespi. Milan: Bompiani.

Benveniste, Émile. 1950. "The nominal sentence." *Bulletin de la Société de Linguistique de Paris* 46:19–36.

————. 1966: 1974. *Problèmes de linguistique générale*. 2 vols. Paris: Gallimard.
————. 1970. "L'appareil formel de l'énonciation." *Langages* 17. Also in Benveniste 1974:79–91, above.
————. *Problems in General Linguistics*. Translated by M. Meek from Benveniste 1966. Coral Gables, Fla.: University of Miami Press.
Bierwisch, Manfred. 1965. "Review of discourse analysis." *Linguistics* 13:61-73.
Bitzer, Lloyd, and Black, Edwin, eds. 1971. *The Prospect of Rhetoric: Report of the National Developmental Project*. Englewood Cliffs, N.J.: Prentice-Hall, Inc.
Blass, Friedrich. 1887–1898. *Die attische Beredsamkeit*. 3 vols. Leipzig: Teubner.
Bobbio, Norberto. 1966. Preface to Italian translation of Perelman-Tyteca, *Trattato dell'argomentazione: La nuova retorica*. Translated by Carla Schick and Maria Mayer, with Elena Barassi. Turin: Einaudi
Bock, Philip K. 1972. "Social structure and language structure." In Brend 1972:441–452.
Boisacq, Emile, 1938. *Dictionnaire étymologique de la langue grecque*. Paris: Klincksieck.
Bolgar, Robert B. 1954. *The Classical Heritage and its Beneficiaries*. Cambridge: Cambridge University Press.
Bolinger, Dwight. 1973. "Truth is a linguistic question." *Language* 49:539–550.
Bollack, Jean, and Wismann, Heinz, eds. 1972. *Héraclite ou la séparation*. Paris: Éditions de Minuit.
Bonebakker, G.A. 1970. "Aspects of the history of literary rhetoric and poetics in Arabic literature." In White 1970:75–95.
Bonheim, Helmut, ed. 1962. *The King Lear Perplex*. San Francisco: Wadsworth.
Booth, Wayne C. 1973. *The Rhetoric of Fiction*. Chicago: University of Chicago Press.
————. 1965. "The revival of rhetoric." *PMLA* 80:8–12. Also in Steinman 1967:1–15.
Bornecque, Henri. 1898. *Quid de structura rhetorica praeceperint grammatici atque rhetores latini*. Paris: Bouillon.
————. 1902. *Les déclamations et les déclamateurs d'après Sénèque le Père*. Lille: Au siège de l'université.
————, ed. See Cicero.
Bourdieu, Pierre. 1972. "Les stratégies matrimoniales dans le système de reproduction." *Annales* 27:1105–1127.
————. 1976. "Le sens pratique." *Actes de la Recherche* 1.
Brandes, Paul D. 1971. *Rhetoric of Revolt*. Englewood Cliffs, N.J.: Prentice-Hall, Inc.
Breck, Theo. 1971. *Brecht und Diderot: Oder über Schwierigkeiten der Rationalität in Deutschland*. Tübingen: Niemeyer.
Brend, Ruth M. 1970. "Tagmemic theory: An annotated bibliography." *Journal of English Literature* 4:7–45.
————. 1972a. "Tagmemic theory: An annotated bibliography. Appendix I." *Journal of English Literature* 6:1–16.
————, ed. 1972b. Kenneth Pike, *Selected Writings*. The Hague: Mouton.
————, ed. 1974. *Advances in Tagmemics*. Amsterdam/London: North Holland.

Breuer, Dieter. 1974. *Einführung in die pragmatische Texttheorie*. Munich, Fink.

Brown, Francis: Driver, G.R.; and Briggs, C.A., eds. 1966. *A Hebrew and English Lexicon of the Old Testament*. Originally publ. 1907. Oxford: Clarendon Press.

Brownstein, Oscar L. 1965. "Plato's *Phaedrus*: Dialectic as the genuine art of speaking." *Quarterly Journal of Speech* 51:392–398.

Brunot, Ferdinand, and Bruneau, C. 1969. *Précis de grammaire historique de la langue française*. Paris: Masson et Cie.

Buccellato, M. 1950. "Per un'interpretazione speculativa della retorica sofistica." *Studi di filosofia greca in onore di Rodolfo Mondolfo*. Bari: Laterza.

———. 1953. *La retorica sofistica negli scritti di Platone*. Rome: Fratelli Bocca.

Buchheit, Vinzenz. 1960. *Untersuchungen zur Theorie des Genus Epideiktikon von Gorgias bis Aristotles*. Munich: Max Hueber.

Büchner, H. 1951. "Das Oxymoron in der griechischen Dichtung." Dissertation. Tübingen.

Burke, Kenneth. 1951. "Othello: An essay to illustrate a method." *Hudson Review* 4:165–203. Reprinted in Burke 1964:152–195.

———. 1964. *Perspectives by Incongruity*. Edited by Stanley E. Hyman. Bloomington: Indiana University Press.

———. 1966. 1st edit., 1941a. *Language as Symbolic Action: Essays on Life, Literature and Method*. Berkeley: University of California Press.

———. 1968. *Collected Poems*, 1915–1967. Berkeley: University of California Press.

———. 1970. 1st ed., 1961. *The Rhetoric of Religion: Studies in Logology*. Berkeley: University of California Press.

———. 1973. 1st ed., 1941b. *The Philosophy of Literary Form: Studies in Symbolic Action*. New York: Vintage.

———. 1974a. 1st ed., 1945. *A Grammar of Motives*. Berkeley: University of California Press.

———. 1974b. 1st ed., 1950. *A Rhetoric of Motives*. Berkeley: University of California Press.

Burnet, John, ed. 1930. 4th ed. *Early Greek Philosophy*. London: Adam & Black.

Bux, E. 1936. "Dall'essere degli Eleati al non-essere dei sofisti." *Archivio di Storia della Filosofia Italiana* 5:191–224.

———. 1941. "Gorgias und Parmenides." *Hermes* 76:363–407.

Calogero, Guido. 1936. "Eraclito." *Giornale Storico della Filosofia Italiana* 17:195–224.

Canter, H.V. 1930. "The Figure *Adunaton* in Greek and Latin poetry." *American Journal of Philology* 51:32–41.

Capizzi, Antonio, ed. 1955. *Protagora: Le testimonianze e i frammenti*. Florence: Sansoni.

———. 1976. *I sofisti*. Florence: La Nuova Italia.

Castiglione, Baldesar. 1964. *Il libro del Cortegiano: Con una scelta delle Opere minori di Baldesar Castiglione*. Edited by Bruno Maier. Turin: UTET.

Certeau, Michel de, and Domenach, Jean-Marie. 1974. *Le Christianisme éclaté*. Paris: Seuil.

Chabrol, Claude, and Marin, Louis. 1974. *Le récit évangélique*. Paris: Aubier Montaigne.

Chaignet, A. E. 1888. *La rhétorique et son histoire*. Paris: E. Bouillon and E. Vieweg.
Chaneles, Sol and Snyder, Jerome, eds. 1972. *That Pestilent Cosmetic Rhetoric*. New York: Grossman.
Charland, Thomas M. 1936. *Artes Praedicandi:Contributions à l'histoire de la rhétorique au Moyen Age*. Paris: J. Vrin.
Chevrier, G. 1966. "Sur l'art de l'argumentation chez quelques romanistes médiévaux au XIIe et au XIIIe siècle." *Archive de Philosophe du Droit*:115–148.
Chomsky, Noam. 1964. "Degree of grammaticalness." In Fodor and Katz 1964.
Christensen, Frances. 1965. "A generative rhetoric of the paragraph." *College Composition and Communication* 16:144–156. Reprinted in Love and Payne. 1969:36–61.
Cicero, Marcus Tullius
———, Bornecque, Henri, ed. 1924. *Partitiones oratoriae, Topica*. Paris: Les Belles Lettres.
———, Caplan, H., ed. 1954. *Rhetoric ad Herennium*. London: Heinemann.
———, Hubbell, H., ed. 1949. *De inventione, De optimo genere oratorum, Topica*. London: Heinemann.
———, Marx, Friedrich, ed. *Incerti Auctoris de ratione dicendi ad C. Herennium*. *M. Tulli Ciceronis Scripta Quae Manserunt Omnia*, vol. 1. Leipzig. Teubner.
———, Tissoni, Gian Galeazzo, ed. 1973. *Qual è il miglior oratore; Le suddivisioni dell'arte oratoria; I topici*. Milan: Mondadori.
Clark, Donald L. 1922. *Rhetoric and Poetry in the Renaissance*. New York: Columbia University Press.
———. 1957. *Rhetoric in Graeco-Roman Education*. New York: Columbia University Press.
Clarke, Martin. 1953. *Rhetoric at Rome: A Historical Survey*. London: Cohen & West. Reprinted 1963.
Colby, Benjamin L. 1970. "The description of narrative structures." In Garvin 1970.
Colletti, Lucio. 1969. *Il marxismo e Hegel*. Bari: Laterza.
Cope, Edward M. 1867. *An Introduction to Aristotle's Rhetoric*. London: Macmillan.
———, ed. See Aristotle.
Corazzini, Francesco, ed. 1854. *Miscellanea di cose inedite o rare*. Florence: T. Barrachi.
Corbato, C. 1958. *Sofisti e politica ad Atene durante la guerra del Peloponneso*. Trieste: Università degli Studi.
Cornforth, M. 1966. "Some questions about laws of dialectics." *The Marxist Quarterly* 16:60–75.
Corradini, C. 1975. *Politica e dialettica*. Pisa: Pacini.
Coultier, J.A. 1964. "The relation of the Apology of Socrates to Gorgias' Defense of Palamedes and Plato's critique of Gorgianic rhetoric." *Harvard Studies in Classical Philology* 68:269–303.
Crane, R.S., ed. 1970. *Critics and Criticism*. 1st ed., 1952. Chicago: University of Chicago Press.
Croce, Benedetto, 1903. "Francesco Patrizio e la critica della retorica antica."

Miscellanea di studi critici edita in onore di Arturo Graf. Also in *Problemi di estetica e contributi alla storia dell'estetica italiana.* 3d ed., 1940. Bari: Laterza.

———. 1907. *Ciò che è vivo e ciò che è morto della filosofia di Hegel.* Bari: Laterza. Retitled *Saggio sullo Hegel.* 1948. Bari: Laterza.

Cromack, Robert E. 1968. "Language systems and discourse structure in Cashinawa." *Hartford Studies in Linguistics* 23. Hartford, Conn.: Hartford Seminary Foundation.

Culler, Jonathan. 1975. *Structuralist Poetics.* Ithaca, N.Y.: Cornell University Press.

Curtius, Ernst H. 1963. *European Literature and the Latin Middle Ages.* Translated by W.R. Trask. New York: Harper and Row.

Dähl, Oesten, ed. 1974. "Topic and comment, contextual boundness and focus." In *Papiere zur Textlinguist,* vol. 6. Hamburg: Buske.

Dal Pra, Mario. 1950. *Lo scetticismo greco.* Milan: Bocca.

———. 1965. *La dialettica in Marx.* Bari: Laterza.

Daneš, F. 1964. "A three-level approach to syntax." *Travaux Linguistiques de Prague* 1:225–240.

D'Annunzio, Gabriele. 1968. *Il Fuoco* (1898). In *Prose di romanzi II.* Milan: Mondadori.

Davidson, Hugh. 1965. *Audience, Words, and Art: Studies in Seventeenth Century French Prose.* Columbus: Ohio State University Press.

Davitz, J.L. 1964. *The Communication of Emotional Meaning.* New York: McGraw-Hill.

DeCorte, M. 1955. "Parmenide et la sophistique." In *Autour d'Aristote: Recueil d'études de philosophe ancienne et médiévale offert à M. A. Mansion:* 47–58. Louvain: Publications universitaires de Louvain.

De Lacy, Phillip. 1958. "*Ou màllon* and the antecedents of ancient Skepticism." Phronesis 3,59–71.

De Lacy, Phillip, and De Lacy, Estelle, eds. 1941. *Philodemus: On Methods of Inference: A Study in Ancient Empiricism. Philological Monographs* 10. Philadelphia: American Philological Association.

Deleuze, Gilles, and Guattari, Felix. 1976. *Rhizome: Introduction.* Paris: Éditions de Minuit.

Della Volpe, Galvano. 1959. *Poetica del Cinquecento.* Bari: Laterza.

———. 1964. *Chiave della dialettica storica.* Rome: Samona e Savelli.

Demetz, Peter, ed. 1965. *Brecht: A Collection of Critical Essays.* Englewood Cliffs, N.J.: Prentice-Hall, Inc.

Denniston, J.D. 1954. 2d ed. *The Greek Particles.* Oxford: Clarendon Press.

Derrida, Jacques. 1967. *De la grammatologie.* Paris: Éditions de Minuit. Translated by G. Spivak, 1976, *On Grammatology.* Baltimore, Md.: Johns Hopkins University Press.

———. 1975. "Le facteur de la vérité." *Poétique* 21:96–147.

———. 1977. "Signature event content." *Glyph* 1:172–197.

Devoto, Giacomo. 1951. *I fondamenti della storia linguistica.* Florence: Sansoni.

Diderot, Denis. 1967. *Le neveu de Rameau.* Edited by Antoine Adam. Paris: Garnier Flammarion.

Diels, H. 1884. "Gorgias und Empedokles." *Berliner Sitzungberichte der Preussischen Akademie der Wissenschaften:*343–368.

Diels, H., and Kranz, W., eds. 1966. *Die Fragmente der Vorsokratiker*. Zurich: Weidmann. From the 4th ed. of 1922.

Dixon, Peter. 1971. *Rhetoric*. London: Methuen & Co.

Dockhorn, Klaus. 1949. "Die Rhetorik als Quelle des vorromantischen Irrationalismus in der Literatur und Geistesgeschichte." *Akademie der Wissenschaften (Göttingen), Nachrichten*:109–150.

———. 1968. *Die Rhetorik bei den Römern, ein historischer Abriss*. Gottingen: Vandenhoeck und Ruprecht.

Doležel, Lubomir. 1972. "Vers la stylistique structurale." In *Introduction à la stylistique du français*. Ed. Joseph Sumpf. Paris: Larousse.

Donnelly, John. 1953. "Incest, ingratitude and insanity: Aspects of the psychopathology of King Lear." *Psychoanalytic Review* 40:149–155.

Dover, K.J. 1960. *Greek Word Order*. Cambridge: Cambridge University Press.

Dressler, Wolfgang. 1972. *Einführung in die Textlinguistik*. Tübingen: Niemeyer.

Dubois, J., and Sumpf, J., eds. 1969. "L'analyse du discours." *Langages* 13.

Dubois, J., et al., the "μ" group. 1970. *Rhétorique générale*. Paris: Larousse.

Dundes, Alan. 1962. "From etic to emic units in the structural study of folktales." *Journal of American Folklore* 75:95–105.

Dupréel, E. 1948. *Les sophistes: Protagoras, Gorgias, Prodicus, Hippias*. Neuchâtel: Éditions du Griffon.

Dürr, A. 1938. *Zum Problem der Hegelischen Dialektik und ihre Formen*. Berlin: Verlag für Staatswissenschaften und Geschichte.

Dutoit, E. 1936. *Le thème de l'adynaton dans la poésie antique*. Paris: Les Belles Lettres.

Eco, Umberto. 1976. *A Theory of Semiotics*. Bloomington: Indiana University Press.

Edinger, Edward F. 1973. *Ego and Archetype*. Baltimore, Md.: Pelican.

Elthen, P. 1960. "Les Sophistes et Platon." *Arguments*, vol. 4, no. 20:6–13.

Elwert, W. Th. 1954. "La dittologia sinonimica nella poesia lirica romanza delle origini e nella scuola poetica siciliana." *Bollettino del Centro degli Studi Filologici e Linguistici Siciliani* 2:152–177.

Engels, Friedrich. 1972. (1878). *Herr Eugen Dühring's Revolution in Science (Anti-Dühring)*, (1848). Translated by Emile Burns. Edited by C.P. Dutt. New York: International Publishers.

———. 1941 (1888). *Ludwig Feuerbach and the Outcome of Classical German Philosophy*. Edited by C.P. Dutt. New York: International Publishers.

———. 1935 (1882). *Socialism: Utopian and Scientific*. Translated by E. Aveling, 1892. New York: International Publishers.

———. 1960. *Dialectics of Nature*. Edited by C.B. Dutt and J.B.S. Haldane. New York: International Publishers.

Enkvist, Nils E. 1974. "Style and types of context." *Reports on Text Linguistics* 1:29–75. Åbo: Åbo Akademi Forskninginstitut.

Ervin-Tripp, S.M. 1964. "An analysis of the interaction of language, topic, and listener." In Gumperz et al., 1964:86–102, and Fishman, 1970:192–211.

Faulhaber, Charles. 1972. "Latin rhetorical theory in thirteenth and fourteenth century Castile." *University of California Publications in Modern Philology* 103.

Faye, Jean Pierre. 1973. *Langages totalitaires*. Paris: Hermann.
Fillmore, Charles J. 1968*a*. "The case for case." *Universals in Linguistics*:1–90. Edited by Emmon Bach and Robert T. Harms. New York: Holt, Rinehart, and Winston.
———. 1968*b*. "Lexical entries for verbs." *Foundations of Language* 4:373–393.
Findlay, J.W. 1959. "Dialectic." *Encyclopedia Britannica*, vol. 7.
Firbas, Jan. 1964. "On defining the theme in functional sentence analysis." *Travaux du Cercle Linguistique de Prague*.
First, Elsa. 1970. "Family Therapy." *New York Review of Books*. February 20:8–15.
Fischer, J.L. 1960. "Sequence and structure in folktales." In Wallace 1960:442–446.
Fishman, J.A. 1965. "Who speaks what language to whom and when?" *La linguistique* 2:67–88.
Florescu, Vasile. 1970. "Rhetoric and its rehabilitation in contemporary philosophy." *Philosophy and Rhetoric*, vol. 3:193–224.
———. 1971. *La retorica nel suo sviluppo storico*. Bologna: Il Mulino.
Fodor, J.A., and Katz, J.J., eds. 1964. *The Structure of Language*. Englewood Cliffs, N.J.: Prentice-Hall, Inc.
Fougeyrollas, P. 1964. *Contradiction et totalité*. Paris: Éditions de Minuit.
Foulquié, P. 1966. 6th ed. *La dialectique*. Paris: P.U.F.
Fourny, P. de. 1953. "Histoire et eloquence d'après Cicéron." *Études Classiques*, vol. 21:156–166.
Fraenkel, H. 1938. "A thought pattern in Heraclitus." *American Journal of Philology*, vol. 59:309–337. Also in *Wege und Formen frühgriechischen Denkens*. 1960. Edited by F. Tietze. Munich: Beck.
France, Peter. 1972. *Rhetoric and Truth: Descartes to Diderot*. Oxford: Clarendon Press.
Franchini, R. 1961. *Le origini della dialettica*. Naples: Giannini.
Frank, Armin P., and Frank, Mechthild. 1966. "A checklist of the writings of Kenneth Burke." In Rueckert 1969:495–512.
Freud, Sigmund. 1966–1974. "The theme of the three caskets," 1913. *Complete Psychological Works*, vol. 12:289–301. 24 vols. London: Hogarth Press.
Fries, C. 1940. "L'origine de la rhétorique antique." *Revue de Philologie* 14:43–50.
Fucilla, J.G. 1936. "Petrarchism and the modern vogue of the figure *adunaton*." *Zeitschrift für Romanische Philologie* 56:671–681.
Funaioli, G. 1946. "La retorica in Grecia e a Roma." *Studi di letteratura antica*. Bologna: Zanichelli.
Fussell, Paul. 1965. *The Rhetorical World of Augustan Humanism: Ethics and Imagery from Swift to Burke*. Oxford: Clarendon Press.
Gadamer, Hans-Georg. 1975. *Truth and Method*. Edited by Garrett Barden. New York: Seabury Press. Originally published in 1960. *Wahrheit und Methode*. Tübingen: J.C.B. Mohr.
Gainsford, T., ed. 1962 (1848). *Etymologicon Magnum*. Oxford: Oxford University Press.
Gallo, Ernest. 1971. *The Poetria Nova and Its Sources in Early Rhetorical Doctrine*. The Hague: Mouton.

———. 1974. "Matthew of Vendome: Introductory treatise on the art of poetry." *Proceedings of the American Philosophical Society* 118:51–92.

Gardin, Jean-Claude. 1974. *Les analyses du discours*. Neuchâtel: Delachaux et Niestle.

Garvin, Paul L., and Spolsky, Bernard, eds. 1966. *Computation in Linguistics*. Bloomington: Indiana University Press.

———, ed. 1970. *Cognition: A Multiple View*. New York: Spartan.

Gelli, Giovan Batista. *Dialoghi: I capricci del bottaio; La Circe; Ragionamento sulla lingua*. 1967. Edited by Robert Tissoni. Bari: Laterza.

Gentile, Giovanni. 1913. *La riforma della dialettica*. Reprint 1954. Florence: Sansoni.

Georges, Robert A. 1970. "Structures in folktales: A generative-transformational approach." *The Couch* 2:4–17.

Gerbner, George, et al. 1969. *The Analysis of Communication Content*. New York: Wiley.

Gesenius and Kautzsch, E. 1963 (1910). *Gesenius' Hebrew Grammar Edited and Enlarged by E. Kautzsch*. Edited by A.E. Cowley. Oxford: Clarendon Press.

Giannantoni, G. 1958. "Dell'uso e del significato di dialettica in Italia." *Rassegna di Filosofia* 7:2.

Gigon, Olaf. 1936. "Gorgias 'Ueber das Nichtsein'," *Hermes* 71:186–213.

Gipper, Helmut. 1963. *Bausteine zur Sprachinhaltforschung* Düsseldorf: Pädagogischer Verlag Schwann.

Gleason, H.A. 1968. "Contrastive analysis in discourse structure." *Monograph Series on Languages and Linguistics* 21:36–63. Washington, D.C.: Georgetown University Press. Also in Makkai and Lockwood 1973:39–63.

Gleitmann, Lila. 1965. "Coordinating conjunctions in English." *Language* 51:260–293. Also in Reibel and Schane 1969:80–112.

Glorieux, P. 1925 and 1935. "La littérature quodlibetique de 1260 à 1320." *Le Saulchoir, Bibliothèque Thomiste*, vols. 5 and 21.

Goedeckemeyer, A. 1905. *Die Geschichte des griechischen Skeptizismus*. Leipzig: Dietrich.

Goffman, Erving. 1971. *Relations in Public*. New York: Basic Books.

Golden, H.H. 1969. "Giulio Bertoni and the aesthetic factor in linguistics." *Studies in Honor of Samuel Montefiore Waxman*:99–112. Boston, Mass.: Boston University Press.

Goldmann, Lucien. 1959. *Recherches dialectiques*. Paris: Gallimard.

———. 1971. "La dialectique aujourd'hui." *L'homme et la société*, no. 19:193–206.

Goldschmidt, V. 1947. *Le paradigme dans la dialectique platonicienne*. Paris: P.U.F.

Gomperz, H. 1912. *Sophistik und Rhetorik*. Tübingen: Niemeyer.

Gonseth, Ferdinand. 1939. *Nouvelles recherches sur la structure dialectique des mathématiques*. Paris: Hermann.

Gorgias of Leontini.
    Frammenti. 1959. Edited by C. Moreschini. Turin: Boringhieri.
    Helena. 1927. Edited by Otto Immisch. Berlin: de Gruyter.

Goth, Joachim. 1970. *Nietzsche und die Rhetorik*. Tübingen: Niemeyer.

Gottesman, Ronald, and Bennett, Scott, eds. 1970. *Art and Error: Modern Textual Editing*. Bloomington: Indiana University Press.

Grabmann, M. 1940. "Die Sophismaliteratur des 12. und 13. Jahrhunderts." *Beiträge zur Geschichte der Philosophie des Mittelatters*, vol. 36, no. 1.

Gramsci, Antonio. 1975. *Quaderni del carcere*. Edited by Valentino Gerretano. Turin: Einaudi.

Greg, Walter W., ed. 1940. *The Variants in the First Quarto of 'King Lear': A Bibliographical and Critical Inquiry*. Oxford: Oxford University Press.

Greimas, A.J. 1973. *Essais de la théorie du texte*. Paris: Editions Galilée.

Grevisse, Maurice. 1959. 7th ed. *Le bon usage: Grammaire française avec des remarques sur la langue française d'aujourd'hui*. Paris: J. Duculot/P. Genthner.

Griffin, Leland M. 1969. "A dramatistic theory of the rhetoric of movements." In Rueckert 1969:456–478.

Grize, Jean-Blaise, ed. 1974. "Recherches sur le discours e l'argumentation." *Cahiers Vilfredo Pareto* 32.

Gudschinsky, Sarah C. 1959. "Discourse analysis of a text." *International Journal of American Linguistics*. 25:139–146.

Guicciardini, Francesco. 1610. *La historia d'Italia, di M. Francesco Guicciardini Gentil'huomo fiorentino, Divisa in Venti Libri, Riscontrata con tutti gli altri historici, & Auttori, che dell'istesse cose habbiano scritto per Tommaso Porcacchi da Castiglione Arretino*. Venice: Appresso Nicolo Polo & Francesco Rampazetto.

————. *Opere*. 1953. Edited by Vittorio de Caprariis. Milan: Ricciardi.

Guiraud, Charles. 1962. *La phrase nominale en grec d'Homère à Euripide*. Paris: Klincksieck.

Gumperz, J.J. and Hymes, Dell, eds. 1964. "The ethnography of communication." *American Anthropologist*. 66:suppl. 5.

Gurvitch, G. 1962. *Dialectique et sociologie*. Paris: Flammarion.

Guthrie, W.K.C. 1969. *The Fifth-Century Enlightenment*, vol. 3 of *A History of Greek Philosophy*. Cambridge: Cambridge University Press.

Guy, Henri. 1910. "L'école des rhétoriqueurs." In *Histoire de la poésie française au XVIe siècle*, vol. 1, of 2. Paris: H. Champion.

Haberman, Frederick W., and Cleary, J.W., eds. 1964. *Rhetoric and Public: A Bibliography, 1947–1961*. Madison: University of Wisconsin Press.

Haldane, J.B.S. 1939. *Marxist Philosophy and the Sciences*. New York: Random House.

Hale, Austin. 1973. "Clause, paragraph and discourse in Languages of Nepal." *Publications in Linguistics and Related Fields* 40. Norman, Okla.: Summer Institute of Linguistics.

Hall, Robert A., Jr. 1963. *Idealism in Romance Linguistics*. Ithaca, N.Y.: Cornell University Press.

Halliday, Michael A.K. 1967–1968. "Notes on transitivity and theme in English." *Journal of Linguistics* 3:37–81,199–244; 4:179–215.

————. 1970. "Language structure and language function." In Lyons 1970:140–165.

Halliday, Michael, and Hasan, Ruqaiya. 1973. *Cohesion in Spoken and Written English*. London: Longmans.

Hallig, Rudolf, and von Wartburg, Walther. 1952. *Begriffsystem als Grundlage für die Lexikographie: Versuch eines Ordnungsschemas*, part 4 of *Abhandlungen der deutschen Akademie der Wissenschaften zu Berlin, Klasse für Sprachen, Literatur und Kunst*. Berlin: Akademie.

Harris, Zellig S. 1952a. "Discourse analysis." *Language* 28:1–30.

————. 1952. "Discourse analysis: A sample text." *Language* 28:474–494.

————. 1963. *Discourse Analysis Reprints*, vol. 2 of *Papers on Formal Linguistics*. The Hague: Mouton.

Hartman, Peter. 1968. "Textlinguistik als neue linguistische Teildisziplin." *Replik* 1:27.

Harweg, Roland. 1968. "Textanfänge in geschriebener und gesprochener sprache." *Orbis* 17:343–388.

Haskins, Charles. 1929. "The early artes dictandi in Italy." *Studies in Mediaeval Culture*:170–192. Oxford: Clarendon Press.

Hatcher, A.G. 1956a. "Theme and underlying question." *Word*: suppl. 12.

————. 1956b. "Syntax and the sentence." *Word* 12:234–250. Also in House-holder 1972:51–62.

Hausenblas, Karel. 1964. "On the characteristics and classification of dis courses." *Travaux du Cercle Linguistique de Prague* 1·67–83.

Havemann, Robert. 1965. 4th ed. *Dialettica senza dogma: Marxismo e science naturali*. Turin: Einaudi.

Hayden, D. 1957. "Notes on Aristotelian dialectic in theological method." *The Thomist*, vol. 20, no. 4:383–418.

Heidegger, Martin. 1962. *Being and Time*. Translated by J. Macquarrie and E. Robinson. New York: Harper & Row From *Sein und Zeit*, 1929. Tübingen: Niemeyer.

————. 1975a. *Poetry, Language, Thought*. Translated by Albert Hofstadter. New York: Harper & Row.

————. 1975b. *Early Greek Thinking*. Translated by David F. Krell and Frank A. Capuzzi. New York: Harper & Row.

Heilmann, Luigi, ed. 1974. *Proceedings of the Eleventh International Congress of Linguistics*. 2 vols. Bologna: Il Mulino.

Heiss, R. 1959. *Wesen und Formen der Dialektik*. Berlin: Kiepenheuer und Witsch.

Hendricks, William O. 1973. "Linguistic Contributions to Literary Science." *Poetics* 7:86–102.

Heraclitus.

————. *Greek Text with a Short Commentary. Editio maior*. 1967. Edited by Miroslav Marcovich. Merida, Venezuela: Los Andes University Press.

————. *Testimonianze e imitazioni*. 1972. Translated by Rodolfo Mondolfo and Leonardo Taran. Florence: La Nuova Italia.

Heydenreich, L.H. 1954. "Dialektik." In *Reallexicon zum deutschen Kunstgeschichte*, vol. 3. Edited by Otto Schmitt. Stuttgart: J.B. Metzler.

Hinks, D.A.G. 1940. "Tisias and Corax and the invention of Rhetoric." *Classical Quarterly* 34:61–69.

Hippocrates.

Collected Works. Opera ediderunt I. L. Heiberg, et al. 1927. Berlin: Teubner.

Hockett, Charles F. 1958. *A Course in Modern Linguistics*. New York: Macmillan.

Holsti, Ole Rudolf. 1968. "Content analysis." In *Handbook of Social Psychology*, vol. 2:596–692. Edited by Gardner Lindzey and E. Aronson. Reading, Mass.: Addison-Wesley.

Horkheimer, Max, and Adorno, Theodor W. 1972 (1947). *Dialectic of Enlight-

enment. Translated by John Cumming. New York: Herder and Herder.

Householder, Fred Walter, ed. 1972. *Syntactic Theory 1: Structuralist*. Harmondsworth, Middlesex: Penguin.

Hovland, Carl I., Janis, Irving L., and Kelley, Harold H. 1953. *Communication and Persuasion: Psychological Studies of Opinion Change*. New Haven, Conn.: Yale University Press.

Hovland, Carl, et al. 1957. *The Order of Presentation in Persuasion*. New Haven, Conn.: Yale University Press.

Howell, Wilbur S. 1956. *Logic and Rhetoric in England, 1500–1700*. Princeton, N.J.: Princeton University Press.

———. 1971. *Eighteenth-Century British Logic and Rhetoric*. Princeton, N.J.: Princeton University Press.

———. 1975. *Poetics, Rhetoric and Logic: Studies in the Basic Disciplines of Criticism*. Ithaca, N.Y.: Cornell University Press.

Howes, Raymond F., ed. 1961. *Historical Studies of Rhetoric and Rhetoricians*. Ithaca, N.Y.: Cornell University Press.

Humbert, Jean. 1954. *Syntaxe grecque*. Revised and augmented from 1944 ed. Paris: Klincksieck.

Husserl, Edmund. 1965. *Phenomenology and the Crisis of Philosophy*. Translated by Quentin Lauer. New York: Harper and Row.

———. 1972. *Ideas: General Introduction to Pure Phenomenology*. Translated by W.R. Boyce Gibson. New York: Collier.

Iordan, Iorgu, and Orr, John. 1970. *An Introduction to Romance Linguistics, its Schools and Scholars*. Reprinted from 1937 ed. Oxford: Blackwell.

Jackendoff, Ray S. 1972. *Semantic Interpretation in Generative Grammar*. Cambridge, Mass.: MIT Press.

Jacobs, Roderick A., and Rosenbaum, Peter S., eds. 1970. *Readings in English Transformational Grammar*. Waltham, Mass.: Ginn.

Jacobson, S.N. 1966. "A modifiable routine for connecting related sentences of English text." In Garvin and Spolsky 1966:284–311.

Jaeger, Werner W. 1934. *Paideia: die Formung des griechischen Menschen*. Berlin-Leipzig: de Gruyter. Translated by Gilbert Highet. 1939. *Paideia: The Ideals of Greek Culture*. 2 vols. New York: Oxford University Press.

———. 1937. *Humanistische Reden und Vorträge*. Berlin-Leipzig: de Gruyter.

Jaffa, Henry. 1957. "The limits of politics: An interpretation of *King Lear*, Act I, scene I." *American Political Science Review* 51:401–427.

Jaffe, Samuel P. 1974. "Nicolaus Dybinus' *Declaracio oracionis de beata Dorotea*: Studies and documents in the history of late medieval rhetoric." *Beiträge zur Literatur d. 15, bis 18. Jahrhunderts*, vol. 5. Wiesbaden: Steiner.

Jakobson, Roman. 1957. "Shifters, verbal categories, and the Russian verb." Reprinted 1971 in *Word and Language, Selected Writings II*. The Hague: Mouton.

———. 1973. *Questions de poétique*. Paris: Seuil.

Jakobson, Roman, and Valesio, Paolo. 1966. "Vocabulorum constructio in Dante's sonnet 'se vedi li occhi miei'." *Studi Danteschi* 43:7–33.

Janet, Paul. 1848. *Essai sur la dialectique de Platon*. Paris: Joubert.

———. 1861. *Essai sur dialectique dans Platon et dans Hegel*. Paris: Ladrange.

Jespersen, Otto. 1965. *A Modern English Grammar on Historical Principles*. 7 vols. 7th ed. Edited by Niels Haislund. Copenhagen: Rinar Munksgaard.

Jones, Daniel, ed. *Everyman's English Pronouncing Dictionary*. 12th ed., revised and enlarged. London: J.M. Dent and Gus, Ltd.

Jordan, Zbnigniew A. 1963. *Philosophy and Ideology: The Development of Philosophy and Marxism-Lenninism in Poland since the Second World War*. Dortrecht, Holland: Reidel.

Jung, Carl G. 1959. *The Archetypes and the Collective Unconscious. Collected Works of Carl G. Jung*. vol. 9. Translated by R.F.C. Hull. Princeton, N.J.: Princeton University Press.

———. 1970a. *Psychology and Alchemy. Collected Works of Carl G. Jung*, vol. 12. Translated by R.F.C. Hull. Princeton, N.J.: Princeton University Press.

———. 1970b. *The Development of Personality: Papers on Child Psychology, Education, and Related Subjects. Collected Works of Carl G. Jung*, vol. 17. Translated by R.F.C. Hull. Princeton, N.J.: Princeton University Press.

———. 1971. *Psychological Types. Collected Works of Carl G. Jung*, vol. 6. Translated by R.F.C. Hull. Princeton, N J · Princeton University Press.

Kallmeyer, W.; Klein, W.; Meyer-Heimann, R.; Netzer, K.; and Seibert, II.J., eds. 1974. *Lektürekolleg zur Textlinguistik*. 2 vols. Frankfurt am Main: Athenäum Fischer.

Karcevskij, Serge. 1937. "Phrase et proposition." In *Mélanges de linguistique et de philologie offerts à Jacques van Ginneken*: 59–66. Edited by Georges Matoré and Jeanne Cadiot-Cueillcron. Paris. Klincksieck

Keane, Patrick. 1975. "On truth and lie in Nietzsche." *Salmagundi* 29:67–94.

Kelsen, H. 1969. "La filosofia di Aristotele e la politica greco-macedone." *Studi urbinati*. new series 1:59–134.

Kennedy, George. 1963. "The Art of Persuasion in Greece." In *A History of Rhetoric*, vol. 1. Princeton, N.J.: Princeton University Press.

Kenyon, John Samuel, and Knott, Thomas Albert, eds. 1953. *A Pronouncing Dictionary of American English*. Springfield, Mass.: G.C. Merriam Co.

Kermode, Frank, ed. 1970. *Shakespeare: King Lear: A Casebook*. London: Macmillan.

Kesting, Marianne. 1970. "Brecht und Diderot oder: Das 'paradis artificiel' der Aufklärung." *Euphorion* 64:414–422.

Kiefer, Ferenc, and Ruwet, Nicholas, eds. 1973. *Generative Grammar in Europe*. Dordrecht, Holland: Reidel.

Kierkegaard, Søren. 1974. *The Sickness Unto Death: A Christian Psychological Exposition for Edification and Awakening*. Edited by Walter Lowrie. Princeton, N.J.: Princeton University Press.

Kinneavy, James. 1971. *A Theory of Discourse: The Aims of Discourse*. Englewood Cliffs, N.J.: Prentice-Hall.

Klammer, Thomas P. 1971. "The Structure of Dialogue Paragraphs in Written English Dramatic and Narrative Discourse." Ph.D. dissertation, University of Michigan.

Koch, Walter, ed. 1969. *Von Morphem zum Textem/From Morpheme to Texteme*. Hildesheim: Olms.

———. 1973. *Das Textem: Gesammelte Aufsätze zur Semantik der Texts*. Hildesheim: Olms.

Koen, F. 1967. "Psycho-rhetorical structures: the paragraph." *Studies in Language and Language Behavior* 5:495–504.

Koen, F.; Becker, Alton L.; and Young, R. 1969. "The Psychological reality of the paragraph." *Studies in Language and Language Behavior* 6:482–498.

Korsch, K. 1966. *Marxismo e filosofia*. Milan: Sugar.

Kreidler, Carol, ed. 1966. *On Teaching English to Speakers of Other Languages*. Champaign: National Council of Teachers of English.

Kristeller, Paul O. 1961. *Renaissance Thought: The Classic, Scholastic and Humanistic Strains*. New York: Harper and Row.

Kummer, W. 1972. "Outlines of a model for a grammar of discourse." *Poetics* 3.

Kuno, Susumo. 1975. "Three perspectives in the functional approach to syntax. In *Papers from the Para-Session on Functionalism*. Edited by R.E. Grossman, L. Gasmessam, and J. Vance. Chicago: Chicago Linguistic Society.

Kuroda, S.Y. 1973. "Where epistomology, style and grammar meet." In *A Festschrift for Morris Halle*:377–391. Edited by Stephen R. Anderson and Paul Kiparsky. New York: Holt, Rinehart and Winston, Inc.

Labor, William, and Waletzky, Joshua. 1967. "Narrative analysis: Oral versions of personal experience." In *Essays on the Verbal and Visual Arts*:12–44. Edited by June Helm MacNeish. Seattle: University of Washington Press.

Lamb, Sydney M. 1966. *Outline of Stratificational Grammar*. Edited by Leonard E. Newell. Washington, D.C.: Georgetown University Press.

Lana, Italo. 1950. *Protagora*. 2 vols. Turin: Universita di Torino, Pubblicazioni della Facolta di Lettere e Filosofia.

Landino, Cristoforo. 1853. "Orazione." In *Miscellanea di cose inedite o rare*:125–135. Edited by Francesco Corazzini. Florence: T. Baracchi.

Lang, Berel, and Williams, Forrest, eds. 1972. *Marxism and Art: Writings in Aesthetics and Criticism*. New York: McKay.

Lang, Ewald. 1974. "Über einige Schwierigkeiten beim Postulieren einer Textgrammatik." In *Generative Grammar in Europe*:284–314. Edited by F. Kiefer and Nicolas Ruwet. Dordrecht, Holland: Reidel.

Lanham, Richard A., ed. 1968. *A Handlist of Rhetorical Terms: A Guide for Students of English Literature*. Berkeley: University of California Press.

Larsen, Helen. 1974. "Some grammatical features of legendary narrative in Ancash Quechua." In *Advances in Tagmemics*:419–440. Edited by Ruth M. Brend. Amsterdam: North Holland.

Lasbax, Emile. 1925–1927. *Cahiers de synthèse dialectique*. Paris: Vrin.

Lasswell, Harold D.; Lerner, D.; and de Sola Pool, Ithiel. 1952. *The Comparative Study of Symbols*. Hoover Institute Studies C: Symbols, no. 1. Stanford, Ca.: Stanford University Press.

Laufer, Roger. 1972. *Introduction à la textologie: Vérification, établissement, édition des textes*. Paris: Larousse.

Lausberg, Heinrich. 1960. *Handbuch der literarischen Rhetorik; eine Grundlegung der Literaturwissenschaft*. Munich: M. Heubner.

Leech, Geoffrey. 1969. *Towards a Semantic Description of English*. Bloomington: Indiana University Press.

———. 1974. *Semantics*. Harmondsworth, Middlesex: Penguin.

Leeman, Anton D. 1963. *Orationis ratio: The Stylistic Theories and Practice of the Roman Orators, Historians and Philosophers*. Amsterdam: A.M. Hakkert.

Lefebvre, Henri. 1947. *À la lumière du marxisme dialectique: I. Logique formale, logique dialectique*. Paris: Éditions Sociales.

———. 1970. *Dialectical Materialism.* Translated by John Sturrock. London: Jonathan Cape.

Leon, Pierre R., et al. 1971. *Problèmes de l'analyse textuelle/Problems of Textual Analysis.* Paris: Didier.

Levi, A. 1966. *Storia della sofistica.* Naples.

Liebert, Arthur. 1929. *Geist und Welt der Dialektik. I. Grundlegung der Dialektik.* Berlin: Metzner.

Liebrucks, Bruno. 1949. *Platons Entwicklung zur Dialektik: Untersuchungen zum Problem des Eleatismus.* Frankfurt am Main: V. Klosterman.

Lindzey, Gardner, and Aronson, E., eds. 1968. *Handbook of Social Psychology.* Reading, Mass.: Addison-Wesley.

Lisio, Giuseppe, ed. 1957. *Orazioni scelte del secolo XVI. Ridotte a buona lezione e commentate.* 1897. Reprint. Florence: Sansoni.

Loenen, D. 1941. *Protagoras and the Greek Community.* Amsterdam: North Holland.

Longacre, Robert E. 1958. "Items in context: their bearing on translation theory." *Language* 34:482–491.

———. 1969. "Prolegomena to lexical structure." *Linguistics* 5:5–24.

———. 1965. "Some fundamental insights of tagmemics." *Language* 41:65–76.

———. 1974. "Narrative versus other discourse genres." In *Advances in Tagmemics*:357–376. Edited by Ruth M. Brend. Amsterdam: North Holland.

———. 1976. *An Anatomy of Speech Notions.* Lisse, Holland: Peter de Ridder Press.

———, ed. 1970. *Discourse, Paragraph, and Sentence Structure in Selected Philippine Languages.* 3 vols. Santa Ana, Calif.: The Summer Institute of Linguistics.

Loos, Eugene A. 1963. "Capanahua Narration Structure." *Texas Studies in Literature and Language*, suppl. vol. 4:697–742.

Lotman, Juri M. 1972. *La struttura del testo poetico.* Milan: Mursia.

Lotman, Juri M., and Pjatigorskij, A.M. 1969. "Le texte et la fonction." *Semiotica* 1:205–217.

Love, Glen A., and Payne, Michael, eds. 1969. *Contemporary Essays on Style: Rhetoric, Linguistics and Criticism.* Glenview, Ill.: Scott, Foresman and Co.

Luporini, Cesare. 1974. *Dialettica e materialismo.* Rome: Editori Ruiniti.

Lyons, John, ed. 1970. *New Horizons in Linguistics.* Hammondsworth, Middlesex: Penguin.

Maccoll, N. 1869. *The Greek Skeptics from Pyrrho to Sextus.* London: Macmillan.

Macherey, Pierre. 1966. *Pour une théorie de la production littéraire.* Paris: Maspero. Translated by Geoffrey Wall, 1978. *A Theory of Literary Production*, Boston: Routledge and Kegan Paul.

Machiavelli, Niccolò.
Opere. 1963. Edited by Mario Bonfantini. Milan: Ricciardi.

MacNeish, June Helm, ed. 1967. *Essays on the Verbal and Visual Arts.* Seattle: University of Washington Press.

Maddalena, Antonio. 1940. *Sulla cosmologia ionica da Talete a Eraclito, Studi.* Padua: Cedam.

Makkai, Adam, and Lockwood, David G., eds. 1973. *Readings in Stratificational Linguistics.* University, Ala.: University of Alabama Press.

Malkiel, Yakov. 1959. "Studies in irreversible binomials." *Lingua* 8.113–160. Now in 1970, *Essays on Linguistic Themes*:311–355. Oxford: Blackwell.

Man, Paul de. 1971. *Blindness and Insight: Essays in the Rhetoric of Contemporary Criticism*. New York: Oxford University Press.

———. 1975. "The timid god: A Reading of Rousseau's *Profession de foi du vicaire savoyard*." *Georgia Review* 29:533–558.

Marache, René. 1952. *La critique littéraire de langue latine et le développement du goût archaïsant au IIe siècle de notre ère*. Rennes: Plihon.

Marck, Siegfried. 1929–1931. *Die Dialektik in der Philosophie der Gegenwart*. 2 vols. Tübingen: Mohr.

Marcuse, Herbert. 1964. *One Dimensional Man*. Boston: Beacon Press.

Marin, Louis. 1975. *La critique du discours: Sur la 'Logique de Port Royal' et les 'Pensées' de Pascal*. Paris: Éditions de Minuit.

Marino, L. 1968. "A. Müller: Dialettica e controrivoluzione." *Rivista di filosofia* 59.

Marrou, Henri Irénée. 1964. *A History of Education in Antiquity*. Translated by G. Lamb. New York: New American Library.

Martens, Gunter, and Zeller, Hans, eds. 1971. *Texte und Varianten: Probleme ihrer Edition und Interpretation*. Munich: C.H. Beck.

Martin, Harold C., and Ohmann, Richard M. 1963. *The Logic and Rhetoric of Exposition*. New York: Holt, Rinehart and Winston, Inc.

Marx, Karl. 1964. *Economic and Philosophic Manuscripts of 1844*. Translated by Martin Milligan, Introduction by D.J. Struik. New York: International Publishers.

———. 1973. *The Poverty of Philosophy* (1847). Translated by H. Quelch, introduction by Friedrich Engels. New York: International Publishers.

———. 1972. *The Essential Writings*. Edited by Frederic L. Bender. New York: Harper and Row.

Marx, Karl, and Engels, Friedrich. 1956–1968. *Werke*. 39 vols. Berlin: Dietz.

———. 1968. *The German Ideology* (1845–1846). Edited by S. Rayzanskaya. Moscow: Progress.

———. 1975. *The Holy Family, or Critique of Critical Criticism* (1845). 2d ed. Translated by Richard Dixon and Clemens Dutt. New York: International Publishers.

Massolo, Arturo. 1967. *Logica hegeliana e filosofia contemporanea*. Florence: C.E. Giunti, Bemporad Marzocco.

Matejka, Ladislav, and Pomorska, Krystyna, eds. 1971. *Readings in Russian Poetics: Formalist and Structuralist Views*. Cambridge, Mass.: M.I.T. Press.

Mathesius, Vilém. 1936. "On some problems of the systematic analysis of grammar." *Travaux du Cercle Linguistique de Prague* 6:95–107.

Mathieu, G. 1925. *Les idées politiques d'Isocrate*. Paris: Les Belles Lettres.

Mattei, Rodolfo de. 1963. *Il pensiero politico di Scipione Ammirato; con discorsi inediti*. Milan: Giuffrè.

McCall, Marsh H., Jr. 1969. *Ancient Rhetorical Theories of Simile and Comparison*. Cambridge, Mass.: Harvard University Press.

McKeon, Richard. 1942. "Rhetoric in the Middle Ages." *Speculum* 17:1–32.

———. 1946. "Poetry and Philosophy in the twelfth century: The Renaissance of rhetoric." *Modern Philology* 43:217–234.

———. 1954. "Dialectic and Political thought and action." *Ethics* 65.1–33.

Melčuk, I.A., and Zolkovskij, A.K. 1970. "Towards a functioning 'meaning-text' model of language." *Linguistics* 57:10–47.

Meleuc, S. 1969. "Structure de la maxime." *Langages* 13:69–99.

Menapace-Brisca, L. 1952. "La Retorica di Francesco Patrizio o del platonico antiaristotelismo." *Aevum* 26:434–461.

Merker, Nicolao. 1971. *Dialettica e storia*. Messina: La Libra.

Merleau-Ponty, Maurice. 1955. *Les aventures de la dialectique*. Paris: Gallimard.

———. 1956. "L'existence et la dialectique." In *Les philosophes célèbres*, pp. 288–291. Paris: Mazenod.

Mey, Jacob Louis, ed. 1975. *Pragmalinguistics: Theory and Practice*. Lisse, Holland: Peter de Ridder Press.

Michel, Alain, 1960. *Rhétorique et philosophie chez Cicéron: Essai sur les fondements philosophiques de l'art de persuader*. 1st ed. Paris: P.U.F.

———. 1962. *Le 'Dialogue des orateurs' de Tacite et la philosophie de Cicéron*. Paris: Klincksieck.

Michelet, Karl L., and Haring, G.L. 1888. *Historisch-Kritische Darstellung der dialektischen Methode Hegels*. Leipzig: Duncker and Humblot.

Miller, Joseph M.; Prosser, Michael H.; and Benson, Thomas W., eds. 1973. *Readings in Medieval Rhetoric*. Bloomington: Indiana University Press.

Montaigne, Michel de.

———. 1603. *The Essays of Montaigne Done into English by John Florio*. Facsimile 1967. New York: AMS Press, Inc.

———. 1931. *Montaigne's Essays*. Edited by J.I.M. Stewart. Translated by John Florio, 1603. 2 vols. London: Nonesuch Press.

———. 1962. *Essais*. Edited by Maurice Rat. 2 vols. Paris: Garnier.

Möntmann, W. 1955. "Die Figur der Synonimie in der altfranzösischen Litteratur." Ph.D. Dissertation, Universität Münster.

Morpurgo-Tagliabue, Guido. 1968. *Linguistica e stilistica di Aristotele*. Rome: Edizioni dell'Ateneo.

Mortier, Roland, 1958–1959. "Diderot sous la prisme de la critique marxiste." *University of North Carolina Studies in Comparative Literature*, nos. 23–24, vol. 2:679–691. Edited by Werner P. Friedrich. Chapel Hill, N.C.: University of North Carolina Press.

Mukařovský, Jan. 1970. *Function, Norm and Esthetic Value as Social Facts*. Translated by Mark E. Suino. Ann Arbor: Department of Slavic Languages and Literature, University of Michigan.

Munteano, B. 1959. "Humanisme et rhétorique; la survie littéraire des rhéteurs anciens." *Revue de l'histoire littéraire de la France* 58:145–156.

Müri, Walter, 1944. "Das Wort 'Dialektik' bei Plato." *Museum Helveticum* 1:152–168.

Murphy, James J. 1974. *Rhetoric in the Middle Ages: A History of Rhetorical Theory from St. Augustine to the Renaissance*. Berkeley: University of California Press.

Murphy, James J., ed. 1971. *Medieval Rhetoric: A Select Bibliography*. Toronto: University of Toronto Press.

Nadeau, Ray. 1959. "Classical systems of stases in Greek: Hermagoras to Hermogenes." *Greek, Roman, and Byzantine Studies* 2:51–71.

Navarre, Octave. *Essai sur la rhétorique grecque avant Aristote*. Paris: Hachette.

Nida, Eugene Albert. 1975. *Componential Analysis of Meaning: An Introduction to Semantic Structures*. The Hague: Mouton.

Nietzsche, Friedrich. 1975. *The Portable Nietzsche*. Edited by Walter Kaufmann. New York: Viking.

Novack, George Edward. 1973. *An Introduction to the Logic of Marxism*. 5th ed. New York: Pathfinder Press.

Ohmann, Richard. 1971. "Speech acts and the definition of literature." *Philosophy and Rhetoric* 4.

Oliver, Robert T. 1971. *Communication and Culture in Ancient India and China*. Syracuse, N.Y.: Syracuse University Press.

Ong, Walter J. 1958. *Ramus: Method and the Decay of Dialogue*. Cambridge, Mass.: Harvard University Press.

———. 1971. *Rhetoric, Romance, and Technology: Studies in the Interaction of Expression and Culture*. Ithaca, N.Y.: Cornell University Press.

Oomen, Ursula. 1971. "Systemtheorie der Texte." *Folia Linguistica* 5:12–34.

Orwell, George. 1950. "Politics and the English language." In *Shooting an Elephant and Other Essays*:84–101. London: Martin Secker and Warburg Ltd. Now in Wermuth 1964:98–108.

Owen, Gwyllym Ellis Lane, ed. 1963. *Aristotle on Dialectic: The 'Topics'*. Proceedings of the Third Symposium Aristotelicum. Oxford: Clarendon Press.

Palek, Bohumil. 1968. "Cross-reference: A study from hyper-syntax." *Acta Universitatis Carolinae Philologia Monographa* 221.

Palmer, Richard E. 1969. *Hermeneutics: Interpretation Theory in Schleiermacher, Dilthey, Heidegger, and Gadamer*. Evanston, Ill.: Northwestern University Press.

Parret, Herman. 1971. *Language and Discourse*. The Hague: Mouton.

Pascal, Blaise. 1904–1914. *Oeuvres complètes*. Edited by Leon Brunschvieg, P. Boutroux, and F. Gazier. 14 vols. Paris: Hachette.

———. [18—]. *Les provinciales*. Edited by Francois de Nuifchateau. Paris: Garnier.

———. 1962. *Les provinciales: Écrits des curés de Paris*. 2 vols. Edited by Jean Steinmann. Paris: Colin.

Pater, W.A. de. 1965. "Les topiques d'Aristote et la dialectique platonicienne." *Études Thomistiques 10*. Frieburg: Editions St. Paul.

Patrick, Mary Mills. 1929. *The Greek Sceptics*, New York: Columbia University Press.

Peirce, Charles Sanders. 1931–1958. *Collected Papers of Charles Sanders Peirce*. Edited by C. Hartshorne and P. Weiss. Cambridge, Mass.: Harvard University Press.

———. 1956. *The Philosophy of Peirce; Selected Writings*. Edited by Justus Buchler. New York: Dover.

———. 1958. *Selected Writings: Values in a Universe of Change*. Edited by Philip P. Wiener. Reprinted 1966. New York: Dover.

Perelman, Chaïm. 1970. "The New Rhetoric: A Theory of Practical Reason." In *The Great Ideas Today*. Chicago: Encyclopaedia Brittanica.

Perelman, Chaïm, and Olbrechts-Tyteca, Lucie. 1952. *Rhétorique et philosophie*. Paris: P.U.F.

———. 1958a. "Classicisme et Romanticisme dans l'argumentation." *Revue Internationale de Philosophie* 12:47–57.

———. 1970. 1st ed. 1958b. *La nouvelle rhétorique: Traité de l'argumentation.* Paris: P.U.F. English translation, *The New Rhetoric: A Treatise on Argumentation.* 1969. Trans. J. Wilkinson and P. Weaver. Notre Dame, Ind.: University of Notre Dame Press. For Italian translation, see Bobbio, 1966.

Petöfi, Janos S. 1971. *Transformationsgrammatik und eine ko-textuelle Texttheorie: Grundfragen und Konzeption.* Frankfurt am Main: Athenäum.

Petöfi, Janos S., and Franck, Dorothea. 1973. *Präsuppositionen in Philosophie und Linguistik/Presuppositions in Philosophy and Linguistics.* Linguistische Forschungen 7. Frankfurt am Main: Athenäum.

Petöfi, Janos S., and Rieser, Hannes, eds. 1973. *Studies in Text Grammar.* Dordrecht, Holland: Reidel.

———. 1974. *Probleme der modelltheoretischen Interpretation von Texten.* Hamburg: Buske.

Pfeiffer, Rudolf. 1968. *History of Classical Scholarship from the Beginnings to the end of the Hellenistic Age.* Oxford: Clarendon Press.

Pike, Evelyn G. 1974. *Coordination and its Implications for Roots and Stems of Sentence and Clause.* Lisse, Holland: Peter de Ridder Press.

Pike, Kenneth L. 1944. "Analysis of a Mixteco text." *International Journal of American Linguistics* 10:111–138.

———. 1959. "Language as particle, wave, and field." *The Texas Quarterly* 2:37–54.

———. 1964a. "Beyond the sentence." *College Composition and Communication* 15:129–135.

———. 1964b. "*Dramatis personae* in reference to a tagmeme matrix." *Oceanic Linguistics, Supplement.*

———. 1964c. "Discourse analysis and tagmeme matrices." *Oceanic Linguistics* 3:5–25. Also in Brend 1974:283–305.

———. 1966. "A Guide to publications related to tagmemic theory." In *Current Trends in Linguistics 3: Theoretical Foundations:* 365–394. Edited by Thomas A. Sebeok. The Hague: Mouton.

———. 1967a. *Language in Relation to a Unified Theory of the Structure of Human Behavior.* 2d rev. ed. The Hague: Mouton.

———. 1967b. "Grammar as wave." *Monograph Series on Language and Linguistics* 20. Edited by E.L. Blansitt. Also in Brend 1974:231–241.

———. 1974. "Recent developments in tagmemics." In *Proceedings of the Eleventh International Congress of Linguistics.* Edited by L. Heilmann. Bologna: Il Mulino.

Pike, Kenneth, and Lowe, Ivan. 1969. "Pronominal reference in English conversation and discourse. . . . A group theoretical treatment." *Folia Linguistica* 3:68–106.

Pike, Kenneth L., and Pike, Evelyn G. 1972. "Seven substitution exercises for studying the structure of discourse." *Linguistics* 94:43–52.

———. 1975. *Grammatical Analysis.* Huntington Beach, Calif.: Summer Institute of Linguistics.

Pinborg, Jan. 1962. "Das Sprachdenken der Stoa und Augustus Dialektik." *Classica et Mediaevalia* 23:148–177.

———. 1967. *Die Entwicklung der Sprachtheorie im Mittelalter. Beiträge zur Ges-*

314 BIBLIOGRAPHY

chichte der Philosophie und Theologie des Mittelalters: Texte und Untersuchungen, vol. 42 bk. 2:345–352. Münster, Westfalen: Aschendorff.

Plan, Pierre Paul. 1904. *Bibliographie rabelaisienne: Les editions de Rabelais de 1532 a 1711*. Reprint, 1970. New York: Burt Franklin.

Plato.
> *Dialogues*. 1964. 4 vols. Edited by Benjamin Jowett. Oxford: Clarendon Press.
> *Gorgias*. 1959. Rev. ed. by E.R. Dodds. Oxford: Clarendon Press.
> *Phaedrus*. 1933. Vol. 4, part 3 of *Oeuvres complètes*. Edited by Leon Robin. Paris: Les Belles Lettres.

Platt, J.T. 1971. *Grammatical Form and Grammatical Meaning: A Tagmemic View of Fillmore's Deep Structure Case Concepts*. Amsterdam: North Holland.

Plebe, Armando. 1968. *Breve storia della retorica antica*. Bari: Laterza.

Plutarch.
> *Plutarchi Cheronensis Moralia*. 1888–1896. Edited by Gregorios Bernardakes. 8 vols. Leipzig: Teubner.

Poliziano, Angelo. 1954. *Stanze cominciate per la giostra di Giuliano de' Medici*. Edited by Vincenzo Pernicone. Turin: Loescher-Chiantore.

Popkin, Richard H. 1964. *The History of Scepticism from Erasmus to Descartes*. Rev. ed. New York: Humanities Press.

Popper, Karl R. 1961. *The Poverty of Historicism*. 2d ed. London: Routledge and Kegan Paul.

——. 1968. "What is dialectic?" (1937) In *Conjectures and Refutations*:312–335. New York: Harper and Row.

Powlison, Paul S. 1965. "A paragraph analysis of a Yagua-folktale." *International Journal of American Linguistics* 31:109–118.

Preminger, Alex S., ed. 1965. *Encyclopedia of Poetry and Poetics*. Princeton, N.J.: Princeton University Press.

Prenant, Marcel. 1948. *Biologie et marxisme*. Paris: Éditions d'Hier et Aujourd'hui.

Prestipino, Giuseppe. 1972. "Momenti e 'modelli' della dialettica marxista." *Critica marxista* 6:7–23.

Preti, Giulio. 1953. "Dialettica deterministica e probabilismo nel pensiero medioevale." In Banfi 1953.

——. 1968. *Retorica e logica*. Turin: Einaudi.

Propp, Vladimir. 1958. 1st ed. 1928. *Morphology of the Folktale*. Translated by Laurence Scott. Edited by S. Pirkova-Jacobson. Bloomington: Indiana University.

Quine, Willard. 1964. *From a Logical Point of View*. Cambridge, Mass.: Harvard University Press.

Quintilianus, Marcus Fabius.
> *Instituto Oratoria*. 1922. Edited by H.E. Butler. 4 vols. London: Heinemann.
> ——. 1970. Edited by M. Winterbottom. 2 vols. Oxford: Clarendon Press.

Rabelais, Francois. 1552. [LE//*QUART LI-*//VR] E DES FAICTS//& dictz Heroïques du//bon Pantagruel.//Compose par M. Francoys Rabe-//lais Docteur en Medicine.//Auec vne briefue declaration d' [aucunes di-//] ctions plus obscures contenues [en]//ce dict liure.//A LYON,//CHEZ BAL-

TASAR ALEMAN.// 1552.//Auec priuilege du Roy. [See Plan 1904 [1970], note 81].

Ramnoux, C. 1968. "Nouvelle réhabilitation des Sophistes." *Revue de métaphysique et de morale* 73:1–15.

Raphael, Max. 1934. *Erkenntnistheorie der Konkreten Dialektik.* Paris: Excelsior.

Rastier, Francoise. 1972. "La grammaire et la rhétorique latine: Une bibliographie." *Documents de travail et pré-publications* 17. Urbino: Centro Internazionale di Semiotica e di Linguistica.

Reibel, David, and Schane, Sanford, eds. 1969. *Modern Studies in English.* Englewood Cliffs, N.J.: Prentice-Hall, Inc.

Reich, K. 1907–1908, 1908–1909. *Der Einfluss der griechischen Poesie auf Gorgias den Begründer der attischen Kunstprosa.* Munich: Straub.

Reid, Aileen A.; Bishop, Ruth; Button, Ella M.; and Longacre, Robert. 1968. "Totonac. From clause to discourse." *Publications in Linguistics and Related Fields* 17. Norman, Okla.: Summer Institute of Linguistics.

Reid, Ronald F. 1960. "Books: Some suggested readings on the history of ancient rhetorical style." *Central States Speech Journal* 11:116–122.

Richards, I.A. 1936. *The Philosophy of Rhetoric.* London: Oxford University Press, Italian translation 1967, Milan: Feltrinelli.

Ricoeur, Paul. 1975. *La métaphore vive.* Paris: Seuil.

Riley, Matilda W., and Stoll, Clarice. 1968. "Content analysis." *International Encyclopedia of the Social Sciences.* New York: Macmillan.

Robin, Leon. 1944. *Pyrrhon et le scepticisme grec.* Paris: P.U.F.

Robinson, Richard 1953. *Plato's Earlier Dialectic.* 2d ed. Oxford: Clarendon Press.

Robinson, W.P. 1972. *Language and Social Behavior.* Harmondsworth, Middlesex: Penguin.

Rodgers, P. 1966. "A discourse-centered rhetoric of the paragraph." *College Composition and Communication* 17:2–11.

Rodier, G. 1926. "Sur l'évolution de la dialectique de Platon." In *Études de philosophie grecque.* Paris: Vrin.

Ross, John. 1970. "On declarative sentences." In *Readings in English Transformational Grammar*:222–272. Edited by Roderick A. Jacobs and Peter S. Rosenbaum. Waltham, Mass.: Ginn.

Rossi, Mario. 1960–1963. *Marx e la dialettica hegeliana.* 2 vols. Rome: Editori Riuniti.

Rossi, Paolo. 1953. "La celebrazione della retorica e la polemica antimetafisica nel *De Principiis* di Mario Nizolio." In Banfi 1953.

Rossi-Landi, Ferruccio. 1974a. "Linguistics and Economics." In *Current Trends in Linguistics 12: Linguistics and Adjacent Arts and Sciences*:1787–2026. Edited by T.A. Sebeok. The Hague: Mouton.

———. 1974b. "Signs and bodies." Paper given at the First Congress of the International Association of Semiotic Studies, Milan.

Rostagni, Augusto. 1955. "Un nuovo capitolo nella storia della retorica e della sofistica." *Scritti minori I: Aesthetica*:1–59. Turin: Bottega D'Erasmo. (From *Studi Italiani di Filologia Classica,* 1922, new series 2.)

Rousseau, Jean-Jacques.
Lettre à d'Alembert.
1758. *Jean Jacques Rousseau citoyen de Genève a M. D'Alembert sur son*

article 'Genève' dans le VIIe volume de l'Encyclopédie et particulièrement sur le projet d'établir un théatre de comédie en cette ville. Amsterdam: Chez Marc Michel Rey.

————. 1967. *Lettre à d'Alembert.* Edited by Michel Launay. Paris: Garnier-Flammarion.

————. 1960. *Letter to d'Alembert on the Theatre.* Translated by A. Bloom. Glencoe, Ill.: Free Press.

————. 1964. *Les réveries du promeneur solitaire.* Edited by Jacques Voisine. Paris: Garnier-Flammarion.

Rueckert, William H., ed. 1969. *Critical Responses to Kenneth Burke, 1924–1966.* Minneapolis: University of Minnesota Press.

Ruhl, Charles. 1973. "Prerequisites for a linguistic description of coherence." *Language Sciences* 25:15–18.

Sabbadini, R. 1891. "Due questioni storico-critiche su Quintiliano." *Rivista di Filologia Classica* 20:307–322.

Sachs, J.S. 1967. "Recognition memory for syntactic and semantic aspects of connected discourse." *Perception and Psychoanalysis* 2:437–442.

Sadock, Jerold M. 1970. "Super-hypersentences." *Papers in Linguistics* 1:1–15.

Saintsbury, George. 1905. *A History of Criticism and Literary Taste in Europe.* 3 vols. New York: Dodd, Mead and Co.

Salvucci, P. 1963. *Dialettica e immaginazione in Fichte.* Urbino: Argalia.

Sandor, P. 1947. *Histoire de la dialectique.* Paris: Nagel.

Sannazaro, Jacopo. 1952. *Opere.* Edited by Enrico Carrara. Reprint 1967, Turin: UTET.

Santini, P. 1968. "Terminologia retorica e critica del *Dialogus de oratoribus.*" *Atti e memorie dell'Academia Toscana* 3.

Sartre, Jean Paul. 1958. Introduction to *Portrait of a Man Unknown* by Nathalie Sarraute. Translated by Maria Jolas. New York: Braziller.

————. 1960. *Critique de la raison dialectique (précédé de: Question de méthode), vol. 1: Théorie des ensembles pratiques.* Paris: Gallimard.

Savonarola, Gerolamo. 1969. *Prediche sopra i Salmi.* Edited by Vincenzo Romano. Rome: Angelo Belardetti.

Scaglione, Aldo. 1972. *The Classical Theory of Composition.* Chapel Hill, N.C.: University of North Carolina Press.

Schegloff, E.A. 1968. "Sequencing in conversational openings." *American Anthropologist* 70:1075–1095.

Schmidt, Siegfried J. 1970. *Text, Bedeutung, Ästhetik.* Munich: Bayerische Schulbuch Verlag.

————. 1973. *Texttheorie: Probleme einer Linguistik der sprachlichen Kommunikation.* Munich: Fink.

Schneyer, Johann Baptist. 1969–1978. *Repertorium der Lateinischen Sermones des Mittelalters für die Zeit von 11501350.* 8 vols. Münster: Aschendorff.

Schwartz, Joseph, and Rycenga, John A., eds. 1965. *The Province of Rhetoric.* New York: Ronald Press Co.

Searle, John R. 1969. *Speech Acts: An Essay in the Philosophy of Language.* New York: Cambridge University Press.

Segal, C.P. 1962. "Gorgias and the psychology of the Logos." *Harvard Studies in Classical Philology* 66:99–155.

Segre, Cesare. 1974. *Le strutture del tempo.* Turin: Einaudi.

Seigel, Jerrold E. 1968. *Rhetoric and Philosophy in Renaissance Humanism: The Union of Eloquence and Wisdom, Petrarch to Valla*. Princeton, N.J.: Princeton University Press.

Serial, Richard H. "Serial bibliographies for Medieval Studies." *Publications of the Center for Medieval and Renaissance Studies* no. 3, Berkeley, Calif.

Sesmat, A. 1955. *Dialectique: Hamelin et la philosophie chrétienne*. Paris: Bloud and Gay.

Sève, Lucien. 1971. "Sur la dialectique." In *Lénine et la pratique scientifique*. Paris: Cern.

Shakespeare, William.
    Complete Works.
    ———. 1906. *The Complete Works Reprinted from the First Folio*. 13 vols. Edited by Charlotte Porter and Helen Clark. Introduction by J. C. Collins. London: Harrap.
    ———. 1955. *Mr. William Shakespeare's Comedies, Histories, & Tragedies*. Edited by Helge Kökeritz. New Haven, Conn.: Yale University Press.
    Hamlet.
    ———. Furness, Horace H., ed. 1965. 2 vols. Reprinted from the 1877 edition. New York: American Scholar Publications, Inc.
    King Lear.
    ———. Furness, Horace H. and Marder, Louis, eds. 1965. Reprint of the 1880 edition. New York: American Scholar Publications, Inc.
    ———. Muir, Kenneth, ed. 1966. Reprint of the 1901 edition. London: Methuen and Co., Ltd.
    ———. Quinn, Edward, ed. 1970. New York: Crowell.
    ———. Vietor, Wilhelm, ed. 1886. *King Lear: Parallel Texts of the First Quarto and the First Folio with Collations of the Later Quartos and Folios*. Marburg: Elwert/Whittakker.

Sichirollo, Livio. 1973. *La dialettica*. Milan: ISEDI.

Sicking, S.M.J. 1964. "Gorgias und die Philosophen." *Mnemosyne* 17:225–247.

Sider, Robert D. 1971. *Ancient Rhetoric and the Art of Tertullian*. London: Oxford University Press.

Simone, Raffaele, ed. 1969. *Grammatica e logica di Port-Royal*. Rome: Astrolabio/Ubaldini.

Slama-Cazacu, Tatiana. 1961. *Language et contexte*. The Hague: Mouton.

Smith, Carlota S. 1971. "Sentences in discourses." *Journal of Linguistics* 7:213–235.

Söter, Istvan. 1937. *La doctrine stylistique des rhétoriques du XVIIe siècle*. Budapest: Eggenburger.

Sokel, Walter H. 1965. "Brecht's split character and his sense of the tragic." In Demetz 1965:127–137.

Solmsen, Friedrich. 1931. *Antiphonstudien: Untersuchungen zur Entstehung der attischen Gerichtrede*. Berlin: Weidmann.

    ———. 1941. "The Aristotelian tradition in ancient rhetoric." *American Journal of Philosophy* 62:35–50,169–190.

    ———, ed. See Aristotle. *Rhetoric*.

Sophocles.
    Philoctetes.
    ———. 1875. Edited by Charles Cavallin. Lund: C.W.K. Gleerup.

———. 1923. Translated by Richard C. Jebb and E.G. Schuckburgh. Cambridge: Cambridge University Press.

———. 1960. Edited by Alphonse Dain. *Oeuvres complètes*, vol. 3. Paris: Les Belles Lettres.

Soskin, W.F., and John, V. 1963. "The study of spontaneous talk." In Barker 1963.

Sprang-Hanssen, Hening. 1956. "The study of gaps between repetitions." In *For Roman Jakobson*:492–502. The Hague: Mouton.

Stalnaker, Robert C. 1970. "Pragmatics." *Synthèse* 22:272–289. Italian translation in Andrea Bonomi. 1973. *La struttura logica del linguaggio*:511–530. Milan: Bompiani.

Steiner, George. 1975. *After Babel*. New York: Oxford University Press.

Steinmann, Martin, Jr. 1966. "Rhetorical research." *College English* 27:278285. Reprinted in Steinmann 1967:1632.

———, ed. 1967. *New Rhetorics*. New York: Scribner's.

Stempel, Wolf-dieter. 1964. *Untersuchungen zur Satzverknüpfung im Altfranzösischen*. Braunschweig: Westermann.

———, ed. 1971. *Beiträge zur Textlinguistik*. Munich: Fink.

Stenzel, Julius. 1972. *Studien zur Entwicklung der platonischen Dialektik von Socrates zu Aristoteles*. Original ed. 1917. Darmstadt: Wissenschaftliche Buchgesellschaft.

Stephanus, Henricus. [Henri Estienne, 1528–1598]. 1572. *Thesauròs tês hellēnikês glôssēs/Thesaurus grecae linguae*. 8 vols. Paris: A. Firmin Didot. Reprinted 1831–1865.

Stephens, Edward. 1837. *A Treatise on the Greek Expletive Particles*. Oxford: D.A. Talboys.

Stockwell, R.P.; Schachter, P.; and Hall-Partee, Barbara. 1973. *The Major Syntactic Structures of English*. New York: Holt, Rinehart and Winston.

Stough, Charlotte L. 1969. *Greek Scepticism: A Study in Epistemology*. Berkeley: University of California Press.

Struever, Nancy S. 1970. *The Language of History in the Renaissance: Rhetoric and Historical Consciousness in Florentine Humanism*. Princeton, N.J.: Princeton University Press.

Sumpf, Joseph, ed. 1971. *Introduction à la stylistique du français*. Paris: Larousse.

Süss, Wilhelm. 1910. *Ethos: Studien zur älterengriechischen Rhetorik*. Leipzig: Teubner.

Svoboda, Ales. 1968. "The hierarchy of communicative units and fields as illustrated by English attributive constructions." *Brno Studies in English* 7:49–101.

Sykutris, J. 1927. "Zu Gorgias' 'Palamedes'." *Philologische Wochenschrift* 47:859–862.

Tabeo, F. 1960. *Retorica e poetica fra Medioevo e Rinascimento*. Bari: Adriatica.

Taber, Charles R. 1966. "The structure of Sango narrative." *Hartford Studies in Linguistics* 17. 2 vols. Hartford, Conn.: Hartford Seminary Foundation.

Tatham, Cambell. 1973. "High-attitude hermeneutics." *Diacritics* 2:22–31.

Thiele, G. 1901. "Ionisch-attische Studien: I. Gorgias." *Hermes* 36:218–253.

Thirwall, Connop. 1833. "On the irony of Sophocles." *The Philological Museum* 2:483–537. Cambridge: Deightons.

Thompson, L.S. 1968. *A Bibliography of American Doctoral Dissertations in Classical Studies and Related Fields*. Hamden, Conn.: Shoe String Press.

Thurot, Ch. 1860. *Études sur Aristotle: Politique, dialectique, rhétorique*. Paris: Durand.

Timpanaro, Sebastiano. 1970. *Sul materialismo*. Pisa: Nistri-Lischi.

Topisch, Ernst. 1964. "Entfremdung und Ideologie: Zur Entmythologisierung des Marxismus." *Hamburger Jahrbuch für Wirtschaft und Gesellschaftpolitik* 9.

Trail, Ronald L. 1973. "Patterns in clause, sentence and discourse in selected languages of India and Nepal." *Publications in Linguistics and Related Fields* 41. Norman, Okla.: Summer Institute of Linguistics.

Traina, Alfonso. 1977. *Forma e suono*. Rome: Edizioni dell'Ateneo e Bizzani.

Trier, Jost. 1931. *Der deutsche Wortschatz im Sinnbezirk des Verstandes: Die Geschichte eines sprachlichen Feldes*. Heidelberg. Winter.

Trilling, Lionel. 1972. *Sincerity and Authenticity*. Cambridge, Mass.: Harvard University Press.

Trimpi, Wesley. 1971. "The ancient hypotheses of fiction: An essay on the origins of literary theory." *Traditio* 27:1–78.

———, 1974. "The quality of fiction: The rhetorical transmission of literary theory." *Traditio* 30:1–118.

Tzetzes, Joannes. 1812. *Exegesis in Homeri Iliadem*. Edited by Godofredus Hermannus. Leipzig: I.A.G. Weigelii.

Untersteiner, Mario. 1950. "Le origine sociali della sofistita." *Studi di filosofia in onore di Rodolfo Mondolfo*:121–180. Edited by V.E. Alfieri and M. Untersteiner. Bari: Laterza. Now in Untersteiner 1967:235–309.

———. 1967. *I sofisti*. 2d rev. ed. Milan: Lampugnani Nigri Editore.

———, ed. 1949–1962. *I sofisti: Testimonianze e frammenti*. 4 vols. Florence: La Nuova Italia.

Vachek, Josef, ed. 1964. *A Prague School Reader in Linguistics*. Bloomington: Indiana University Press.

Vaihinger, Hans. 1903. "Beiträge zum Verständnis der Analitik und Dialektik in der Kritik der reinen Vernunft." *Kant-Studien*. Berlin: Von Reuther und Reichart.

Valentini, F. 1966. *La controriforma della dialettica*. Rome: Editori Riumiti.

Valesio, Paolo. 1968. *Strutture dell'alliterazione: Grammatica, retorica e folklore verbale*. Bologna: Zanichelli.

———. 1969a. "Esquisse pour une étude des personnifications." *Lingua e Stile* 4:1–21.

———.1969b. "Icons and patterns in the structure of language." *Actes du Dixième Congrès International des Linguistes* 1:383–388. Bucharest: Éditions de l'Académie de la République Socialiste de Roumanie.

———. 1969c. "Vocabulorum constructio." *Studi Danteschi* 45:167–177.

———. 1974a. "The art of syntax and its history." *Lingua e Stile* 9:1–30.

———. 1974b. "Paronamasia and the articulation of grammatical rules." *Proceedings of the Eleventh International Congress of Linguistics* 2:1005–1015.

———. 1975a. "Hýsteron Próteron and the structure of discourse." *Diachronic Studies in Romance Linguistics*:208–233. Edited by M. Saltarelli and D. Wanner. The Hague: Mouton.

———. 1975b. "Into a theory of metaphor." *Georgetown University Working Papers in Languages and Linguistics* 11:30–59.

————. 1976a. *Between Italian and French: The Fine Semantics of Active Versus Passive*. Lisse, Holland: Peter de Ridder Press.

————. 1976b. "The virtues of traducement: Sketch of a theory of translation." *Semiotica* 18:1–96.

————. 1977. "The lion and the ass: The case for D'Annunzio's novels." *Yale Italian Studies* 1:67–82.

Vallese, Giulio. 1962. "Retorica medioevale e retorica umanistica." *Studi da Dante ad Erasmo di letteratura umanistica*:39–75. Naples: Scalabrini.

Van Dijk, Teun A. 1972. *Some Aspects of Text Grammars: A Study in the Theoretical Linguistics and Poetics*. The Hague: Mouton.

Vasoli, Cesare. 1968. *La dialettica e la rettorica dell'umanesimo: 'Invenzione' e 'Metodo' nella cultura del XV e XVI secolo*. Milan: Feltrinelli.

Veron, Eliseo. 1971. "Ideology and social sciences: A communicational approach." *Semiotica* 1:59–76.

Verra, Valerio. 1963. *Dialettica e filosofia in Plotino*. Trieste: Università degli studi, Facoltà di Magistero, Pubblicazioni 2.

Verschueren, Jef. 1976. *Speech Act Theory: A Provisional Bibliography with a Terminological Guide*. Bloomington: Indiana University Linguistic Club.

Vetter, Harold J. 1969. *Language Behavior and Psychopathology*. Chicago: Rand McNally.

Viano, C.A. 1958. "La dialettica stoica." *Studi sulla dialettica*:63–111. Turin: Taylor.

Vickers, Brian. 1970. *Classical Rhetoric in English Poetry*. New York: Macmillan.

Vitali, Renzo. 1971. *Gorgia: Retorica e filosofia*. Urbino: Argalia.

Volkmann, Richard E. 1963. Reprint of 2d ed. 1885. *Die Rhetorik der Griechen und Römer in systematischer Übersicht*. Hildesheim: Olms.

————. 1901. "Rhetorik der Griechen und Römer." *Handbuch der Klassischen Altertumwissenschaft*, vol. 2, part 3:1–61. Edited by Iwan von Müller. Munich: Bech.

Vollgraff, Carl W. 1952. *L'oraison funèbre de Gorgias*. Leiden: E. J. Brill.

Vološinov, Valentin. See Baxtin.

Wallace, Anthony F.C., ed. 1960. *Men and Cultures; Selected Papers*. Philadelphia: University of Pennsylvania Press.

Wallace, Karl R. 1943. *Francis Bacon on Communication and Rhetoric*. Chapel Hill, N.C.: University of North Carolina Press.

Waterhouse, Viola G. 1974. *The History and Development of Tagmemics*. The Hague: Mouton.

Webster, T.B.L. 1956. *Art and Literature in Fourth Century Athens*. London: Athlone Press.

Wehr, Hans, ed. 1971. *A Dictionary of Modern Written Arabic*. Edited by J. Milton Cowan. Ithaca, N.Y.: Cornell University Press.

Weil, Eric. 1970. *Essais et conférences*. 2 vols. Paris: Plon.

Wein, Hermann. 1957. *Realdialektik: Von hegelscher Dialektik zu dialektischer Anthropologie*. Munich: Oldenbourg.

Weinberg, Bernard. 1961. *A History of Literary Criticism in the Italian Renaissance*. Chicago: University of Chicago Press.

Weinrich, Harald. 1972. "Die Textpartitur als heuristische Methode." *Der Deutschunterricht*, vol. 24, part 4:3–60.

Wellek, Rene. 1955. *A History of Modern Criticism: 1750–1950, I: The Later Eighteenth Century*. New Haven, Conn.: Yale University Press.

Wermuth, Paul C., ed. 1964. *Modern Essays on Writing and Style.* New York: Holt, Rinehart and Winston, Inc.

West, Dorothy. 1973. *Wojokeso: Sentence, Paragraph, and Discourse Analysis.* Edited by Robert E. Longacre. Canberra: Department of Linguistics, Research School of Pacific Studies, Australian National University.

White, Lynn, ed. 1970. *Viator: Medieval and Renaissance Studies.* Berkeley: University of California Press.

Whitehall, H. 1964. "Modification and shift of emphasis." In Wermuth 1964.

Wilcox, John T. 1974. *Truth and Value in Nietzsche: A Study of His Metaethics and Epistemology.* Ann Arbor: University of Michigan Press.

Wilcox, Stanley, 1942. "The scope of early rhetorical instruction." *Harvard Studies in Classical Philology* 53:121–155.

Wiley, W.L. 1948. "Who named them Rhétoriqueurs?" *Medieval Studies in Honor of Jeremiah Denis Matthias Ford.*335–352. Edited by U.T. Holmes, Jr. and A.J. Denomy. Cambridge, Mass.: Harvard University Press.

Wilpert, P. 1956–1957. "Aristoteles und die Dialektik." *Kant-Studien* 48:247–257.

Wimsatt, William K., and Brooks, Cleanth. 1957. *Literary Criticism: A Short History.* New York: Knopf.

Winkler, Christian. 1931. *Elemente der Rede: Die Geschichte ihrer Theorie in Deutschland von 1750 bis 1850.* Halle: Niemeyer.

Wise, Mary Ruth. 1974. "Social roles, plot roles and focal roles in a Nomatsiguenga Campa myth." In Brend 1974:389–418.

Wolin, Sheldon S. 1975. "Looking for reality." *New York Review of Books,* vol. 22, no. 1:15–20.

Wundt, Max. 1903. *De Herodoti elocutione cum sophistarum comparata.* Leipzig: Teubner.

Young, Richard E.; Becker, A.L.; and Pike, Kenneth. 1970. *Rhetoric: Discovery and Change.* New York: Harcourt, Brace and World, Inc.